The Post-War Years

RED DIRT BASEBALL

Small Town Professional Baseball in Oklahoma 1946-1961

Peter G. Pierce

OKLAHOMA HALL *of* FAME

OKLAHOMA HERITAGE ASSOCIATION PUBLISHING

OKLAHOMA HALL *of* FAME

2015 OFFICERS AND DIRECTORS

Copyright 2015 by Oklahoma Heritage Association Publishing, a publication of the
Oklahoma Hall of Fame.

All rights reserved. No part of this book may be reproduced or utilized in any form or by any means,
electronic or mechanical, including photocopying and recording, by any information storage and
retrieval system, without permission of the publisher.

ISBN 978-1-938923-26-5
Library of Congress Catalog Number 2015955015

Book & Cover Designed by Skip McKinstry

CONTENTS

INTRODUCTION

As told in the first volume of this series, *Red Dirt Baseball — The First Decades* (2013) baseball has a long pedigree in Oklahoma. Towns like Durant, Guthrie, El Reno, and Sapulpa competed in now forgotten leagues that spanned Oklahoma and adjacent states. The First World War saw lower level minor league baseball disappear across the nation as resources were turned to defeating the Kaiser. With Peace, Prohibition, and, as candidate Warren G. Harding termed it, a "Return to Normalcy," — rolling the clock back to 1917 and before, leagues returned like the Western Association, Texas-Oklahoma League, and Oklahoma State League populated with small boom towns like Pawhuska, Bristow, Drumright, Cushing, and Henryetta. With poor economic conditions and drought hitting Oklahoma before the collapse of the stock market in October 1929, minor league baseball all but vanished after 1927 with only Muskogee, Oklahoma City, and Tulsa regularly fielding teams. The vacuum was filled by dozens of town sandlot and company teams. Oklahoma may fairly be characterized as the center of the semi-pro baseball world with Duncan's Halliburton Cementers leading the way with State and National championships.

From the end of the 1942 season through 1945, every professional league with ball clubs in Oklahoma suspended play. The gap was filled by military teams such as the Enid AAF Enid Airs and the Norman Naval Air Station Skyjackets. The people on the Home Front had worked hard, made and saved a lot of money, and had no place to spend it before V-J Day in August 1945. The pent up consumption demand along with millions of veterans returning, including thousands of professional ball players, saw a resurgence in Organized Baseball such as had never been seen nor experienced since.

Like all of the United States following World War II, Oklahoma embraced professional baseball in towns and cities both large and small. This volume focuses on the dozen seasons of the fifteen small cities in Oklahoma that enjoyed Class C and Class D baseball between 1946 and 1957 in three different leagues. After those had vanished following the 1957 season, small town professional baseball experienced one last hurrah in 1961 as Ardmore joined the Class AA Texas League for a short season.

ACKNOWLEDGMENTS

As I related in the Preface to my first book, *Baseball in the Cross Timbers: The Story of the Sooner State League* published in 2009, writing about the history and sociology of minor league baseball in Oklahoma resulted indirectly from Hurricane Katrina in the fall of 2005. I had begun the fall semester at the University of Oklahoma teaching a small seminar on Values and Virtues. A week into the term, the storm hit New Orleans displacing my daughter's family who took over my home in Norman for seven weeks. Assisting them became a full time job necessitating the cancellation of the class. When they returned to Louisiana, I had a good deal of time on my hands. Encouraged by my dear Laurie Williams of Ardmore whose grandmother, Carol Daube Sutton, had been an investor in one of that city's Sooner State League clubs, and with my copy of the 1999 work *Glory Days of Summer* by Bob Burke, Kenny Franks, and Royse Parr in hand, I began researching the towns and cities that hosted franchises in that league. The work took me around the state and into north Texas. Three years later, I had produced a manuscript. I asked my friend, Ardmore attorney Gary Farabough, to review it. He in turn introduced me to Oklahoma's most prolific author, Bob Burke, over breakfast in 2008. Bob, who was a co-author of *Glory Days of Summer*, went through my product and introduced me to his publisher, Oklahoma Heritage Association Publishing, and the one who would become my guide and editor, Gini Moore Campbell. All of them enabled and encouraged me to proceed with a project that in hindsight was grander than I had envisioned culminating in *Baseball in the Cross Timbers*. . With their support, I produced two books on baseball in my adopted town of Ardmore in 2011: *Territorians to Boomers* and *Indians, Cardinals and Rosebuds*. The first chapter in a proposed book on baseball in the Chickasaw Nation expanded to book length with the generous assistance of former Ada players Bobby King and Charlie Hopkins. That became *Eight Seasons of the Herefords: Red Dirt Baseball in Ada* issued in 2013. With those detours, I returned to a project I had envisioned since finishing *Baseball in the Cross Timbers*.

Outside of the stories of Oklahoma City and Tulsa baseball, there was no history of professional baseball in Oklahoma's other towns and cities. I embarked on a voyage to tell that story in a series titled *Red Dirt Baseball*. The first effort resulted in chronologically the first book, *Red Dirt Baseball: The First Decades*, covering the first appearance of professional baseball in the Territorial days in 1904 and ending in 1919. This book, *Red Dirt Baseball: The Post-War Years*, is chronologically the third but second to go to print. The middle volume, *Red Dirt Baseball: Boom and Bust* covering 1920-1942 is in the works. The impetus to complete this history has been the Oklahoma Humanities Council's hosting of the Smithsonian Museum's "Home Town Teams:

How Sports Shape America" between March and December 2015.

The materials that appear in the following pages are based in part on research from my earlier books respecting cities that hosted Sooner State League teams and I repeat my acknowledgements from those. I also have relied on the 1999 overview of Oklahoma minor league baseball in *Glory Days of Summer*. The depth and breadth of that book is remarkable, particularly as the internet databases I've enjoyed did not exist in the last decade of the past century when that book was researched and written.

For the towns in northeast Oklahoma that were members of the Kansas-Oklahoma-Missouri League —Miami, Bartlesville, Ponca City, and Blackwell—I have relied heavily on the extraordinary work of John G. Hall of Columbia, Missouri whose two books, *Majoring in the Minors* (Oklahoma Bylines: Stillwater 1996) and *The KOM League Remembered* (Arcadia: Charleston SC 2004) are definitive, as well as his weekly e-mail, the *KOM Flash Report*. He has generously shared his collection of photographs of K-O-M teams and players in those works. Ardmore attorney Derril McGuire, who carried bats for the Ardmore Cardinals, provided a treasure trove of photos including negatives from the only Major League exhibition ever played in Ardmore. High school pitching phenom Ed Carnett, who began his professional career in 1935 for his hometown Ponca City Angels of the Western Association, shared memories, a round of golf, and his scrapbooks with me. Much of the post-1952 chapter on Ponca City would have been impossible without him. As stated Bob King, second baseman for Ada in 1948 and 1949 and later West Coast scout for the Astros, and his team mate, catcher Charlie Hopkins, as well as the 1952 and 1953 Ada batboy, the late Bill Thrash who spent his career at the Oklahoma Educational Television Authority, shared their scrapbooks and memories. Canadian crooner Kim Ervin, who performed with Frank Sinatra after a season at shortstop for Pauls Valley in 1952 as Irving Kimberg, also shared his photos and reminiscences. Dr. John Kimbrel gave an interview about the last season of the Sooner State League and provided the only extant photos of the 1957 Shawnee club.

Finally, my appreciation to University of Oklahoma President David Boren, Deans Paul Bell and Kelly Damphouse of the College of Arts and Sciences, and the Department of History for indulging my dream of teaching baseball as a worthy subject of American history at the university level. They have let me teach a junior level course on the History of Baseball since 2008. A good deal of the material in the *Red Dirt Baseball* series was researched and written for the lectures and graphic presentations to the students.

X

THE LEAGUES

WESTERN ASSOCIATION
1934-1954

The Western Association was formed in 1905 when the "large" cities of the Missouri Valley League added the two largest towns in the Oklahoma Territory to form a new Class C loop. By 1910, seven of the eight members were in Oklahoma. Dropping a classification in 1911, the league folded to be revived in 1914 for four seasons until World War I cancelled most minor league baseball in 1918. (see *Red Dirt Baseball-The First Decades*).

Revived and operating as a Class D and then C loop between 1920 and 1932, the league like so many others in the low minors suspended in 1933 during the heart of the Great Depression. Under the leadership of Tom Fairweather, who also took the helm of the Class B Three-I League in 1937, the Western Association was resurrected in 1934 and continued to play—with the exception of the War hiatus from 1943 through 1945—for the next twenty years. With a league population of between 150,000 and 250,000 the Western Association maintained its Class C status. When he retired at age seventy after an awful 1949 season, Fairweather had served forty-two seasons in Organized Baseball. The league's directors refused his resignation but when he persisted, they settled on his right-hand man in the Three-I and incumbent secretary of the Association, Howard Goetz from his office in Des Moines, to become a one-man show holding all three offices of the league.

Between 1934 and 1949 Muskogee, under the leadership of Joe Magoto, was the sole Oklahoma member of the loop. When the New York Giants gave up on Ft. Smith, they moved their Association farm club to Enid for 1950. Disenchanted, the next season the Class C farm was back in Ft. Smith after a sale brokered by Magoto. Enid remained in the league with a different franchise as an independent for 1951 before folding.

Goetz turned over the reins to retired veteran National League umpire George Barr in September 1952 for the final two seasons of the Association's existence. As president of the K-O-M League, Barr had presided over its demise following the 1952 campaign.

For its 1954 finale, the Western Association expanded to eight teams with independent Ponca City and Cubs' affiliate Blackwell joining Muskogee as the Oklahoma contingent. The smallest city, Blackwell, won the last pennant, one that would never be awarded.

Despite its success on the field, Blackwell surrendered its franchise in December, 1954 fearing inability to compete in Class C after the Cubs moved their working agreement to Ponca City. St. Joseph, Missouri withdrew when the Philadelphia Athletics set up shop in that town's figurative backyard, Kansas City. Salina and Independence Kansas were unable to secure working agreements. The Cardinals pulled their support from Joplin. The era of independent lower level minor league teams was fast approaching the end. Over a half century of play ended on January 19, 1955 when president Barr announced the Western Association was no more. Only Muskogee had found a new baseball home for 1955 in the Sooner State League.

KANSAS-OKLAHOMA-MISSOURI LEAGUE
1946-1952

George Barr tried unsuccessfully to save lower level minor league baseball. During his tenure as president, he witnessed the failure of the K-O-M League (1953), Western Association (1955), and Sooner State League (1958). (Lg-1))

O f the thirty-four Class D minor leagues hosting teams in well over two hundred small towns across the nation that were born, thrived, withered, and died between 1946 and 1960, none has been more carefully and fully documented than the Kansas-Oklahoma-Missouri League, the "K-O-M. " For over two decades, former Carthage Cubs batboy John G. Hall of Columbia, Missouri has compiled the names, records, and stories of nearly every player who appeared in the K-O-M and memorializes them in his periodic K-O-M Flash Report e-mails and two books, *Majoring in the Minors* and *The K-O-M League Remembered.*

There would have been no K-O-M League without Carthage, Missouri publisher E. L. Dale's leadership and dedication. (Lg-2)

The child of Carthage, Missouri newspaper publisher E. L. Dale, the K-O-M's debut season was in 1946 with a tightly drawn six-team circuit in the Tri-State Mining District. Kansas was represented by the Chanute Owls, Iola Cubs, and Pittsburg Browns. The Carthage Cardinals were Missouri's entry. Oklahoma's Miami Blues and Bartlesville Oilers rounded out the field. Only Chanute finishing . 001 ahead of Miami operated as an independent without a working agreement with a Major League organization in the regular season race; the Blues were a Brooklyn Farm. The playoff final series was a 3-3 tie between Iola and Chanute.

For 1947, the K-O-M added two franchises that would dominate the league, the Ponca City Dodgers, who became Brooklyn's affiliate, and the Independence (KS) Yankees. They were also-runs that season but the future was theirs.

Miami replaced Chanute as Topeka's affiliate as

the Chanute Athletics operated as an independent. Miami won the regular season crown and the play-off pennant vanquishing runner-up Iola.

The line-up for 1948 remained the same with Iola, playing as the "Indians," becoming an independent and Chanute embracing its only working agreement with the New York Giants; all other seasons Chanute was an independent. Pittsburgh purchased the Bartlesville franchise and renamed their prospects the "Pirates. " Boyd Bartley's Ponca City club was the class of the 1948 K-O-M, besting the little Yankees by two games. The Dodgers ran out of steam in the play-offs as the Independence club took the pennant.

Chanute reverted to independent status as the Athletics in 1949 as the Chicago Cubs replaced the Cardinals as the parent team of Carthage. Iola officially became a Cleveland affiliate. The season race was tight with Independence besting Bartlesville by a single game. The two Oklahoma teams that finished in the first division, Ponca City and Bartlesville, were eliminated in the early round of the play-offs. Independence, with a rookie named Mickey Mantle, seized the pennant in a sweep of Iola.

The Korean War began in June of 1950 and the player drain caused by conscription would plague the K-O-M through its remaining years. Iola, Chanute, and Miami, now called the Eagles, completed

K-O-M president Barr with his umpiring crew in 1952. (Lg-3)

the 1950 season as independents with the rest of the clubs retaining their Major League affiliations. Ponca City ran away with the regular season race and then thumped runner-up Bartlesville in four games in the first all-Oklahoma play-off final.

The K-O-M shrank to six teams for 1951 as the operations in Chanute and Independence folded. Oklahoma ball clubs finished as the top three in the regular season race as Ponca City, with manager Bartley in the Army, finished seven games ahead of Bartlesville and seventeen in front of independent Miami. Miami survived the first round only to be swept by the Cubs' farm hands from Carthage.

The same officers who had run the league from the beginning, E. L. Dale as president, Earl Sifers of Iola as vice-president, and A. H. Moorman of Carthage were re-elected at the post-season meeting in November 1951. Chanute and Independence were wanting back into the K-O-M while Coffeyville (KS) and Blackwell (OK) were seeking admission.

Things were looking bright for 1952. It appeared that the same six-team configuration from 1951 would be in place for the following season. In March, the Chicago Cubs dealt a fatal financial blow to the Carthage franchise when it reneged on a $6,000 commitment and the Browns moved their Class D club from Pittsburg to Independence. To round out the last edition of the K-O-M, the Cubs set up shop in Blackwell. The league now had four Oklahoma teams and two, Iola and Independence, from Kansas for a 126-game campaign. Miami secured a working agreement from the Philadelphia Phillies leaving Iola as the sole independent. Charter member Bartlesville failed in July and finished the season in Pittsburg. Remarkably, the K-O-M attendance was up by 103,500 over 1951 with Ponca City and Blackwell setting the pace.

Independent Iola took the last regular season crown by eleven games over Miami and Ponca City behind Joe Vilk's twenty-six wins and with the leading scorer and hitter in the line up. In the first round of the play-offs, the Dodgers eliminated Iola as Miami vanquished Pittsburg *neé* Bartlesville. In an abbreviated finale, Miami bested Ponca City for a pennant that would never be flown.

With his city out of the league, E. L. Dale resigned and was succeeded by former National League umpire George Barr who would head the circuit *in extremis*. The first impediment to a 1953 season was the inability of Pittsburg to secure a new working agreement despite Barr's public complaint to the Major Leagues and the attractiveness of the Kansas city's facilities. In January, 1953 Enid declined the offer to relocate the Pittsburg club there. With only five teams ready to play—Pittsburg, Iola, Independence, Ponca City, and Blackwell—the fate of the K-O-M hinged on what would become of Miami after the Phillies pulled out. On February 24, 1953 Earl Sifers in president Barr's absence announced that due to Miami's inability to obtain a working agreement and the failure of a financial campaign to support play in 1953 as an independent, the K-O-M would suspend in 1953. Blackwell and Ponca City were spurned by the Sooner State League. Rejecting an invitation from the Western Association, Ponca City held out hope for a revival of the K-O-M with Nevada in Missouri and El Dorado and Ft. Scott in Kansas joining the mix in 1954. Barr kept the lights on. On October 4, six cities, Ponca City, Blackwell, Miami, Bartlesville, Pittsburg, and Independence, met with Barr about reorganizing the loop. Without working agreements, none of the former members were willing to commit any resources to pursue a continuation of Organized Baseball in the Tri-State. The Western Association adopted Ponca City and Blackwell for what would prove to be its last campaign. The K-O-M was dead and professional baseball in that part of the country was gone forever.

Jack Mealey ran the Sooner State League from 1947 through 1951. (Lg-5)

CITIES OF THE SOONER
STATE LEAGUE 1947-1957

Cities of the Sooner State League (Lg-4)

SOONER STATE LEAGUE 1947-1957

The only aspect of the Sooner State League that consistently ran without a deficit and imposed some order was the League Office itself. The operation of the league and the interaction among the players, managers, umpires, and owners was as much of a show as that on the field. During its formative years and at its end, the Sooner State League was dominated by its presidents. In the thirteen years of its legal existence, 1946-1959, the Sooner State League had four presidents. The first three presided over the league's formation and operation during eleven seasons of play. The fourth shepherded it to its end.

Holdenville's Jack Mealey found himself as president of the new Sooner State League when his true desire was to operate a team in Shawnee; that was why he attended the organizational meetings in 1946.

He launched the league in August, 1946 and presided until ousted by the owners for a more compliant chief at the November, 1951 meeting. Mealey was a journeyman catcher who began his twenty-year professional career in 1922 at Okmulgee of the Western Association and ended with Muskogee of the same league. The Chicago White Sox purchased him from the Dallas Steers in 1928 and he attended spring training in 1929. He was sent back down to the Steers. He was named to the 1930 Western League All Star team as a catcher with the Wichita Aviators hitting .279 with six home runs. That performance earned him an invitation to spring training with the Pittsburgh Pirates. He never stepped on to the field in a regular season Major League game. His highest classification of play was AAA in the Pacific Coast League with the 1931 San Francisco Seals in their first year at Seals Stadium, the year before Joe DiMaggio joined the team. He then toiled for San Antonio, Galveston, Dallas, and Tulsa of the Texas League. He managed Galveston in the early part of the 1936 season and Muskogee in 1940-1942. In 1939 he caught for Enid's national champion Champlin Refiners and, following the War, managed the Fairview semi-pro team in 1946.

An oil man and rancher from near Holdenville, his relationship with the owners was stormy from the outset. As league president, he hired and fired the umpires. He was constantly on the defensive about the poor officiating, once threatening to suspend the season if the clubs didn't stop harassing the arbiters. At the annual meeting in November following the 1951 season, the owners replaced him with one of their own, Ada Herefords organizer and first field manager, Ucal Clanton.

Mealey was involved in a three-car accident northwest of Seminole on March 3, 1952, in which his wife was fatally injured. The next year, in May, 1953, Mealey achieved his wish of running the Shawnee franchise when he was named business manager of the Hawks. He held that position until the team was sold in February, 1954. He returned to his ranch near Holdenville where he died on August 17, 1971, at age seventy-seven.

Ucal "Uke" Clanton, former Ada co-owner and manager, was elected following the coup that ousted Jack Mealey at the November, 1951 annual meeting; he survived four seasons. With Mealey and Dr. A. R. Sugg, Clanton had framed the strategy for forming the League over coffee in May, 1946. He was selected as the publicity man. To drum up interest, he put out the word that a number of Oklahoma towns had been represented at the May meeting. Upon receiving calls from parties in several of the cities he mentioned, he feigned lack of recall as to who had been present from each town, but invited the caller to a meeting on July 28.

He was a sound baseball man who guided the league during the period of transformation from one dominated by locally-owned and operated independent clubs that signed and developed players for sale to higher classifications to a circuit that served as a largely rookie league for players supplied and paid by Major League organizations. In the season before his tenure began, the player caps were set at three veterans, six limited service players, and six rookies. For 1952, the number of veterans was cut back to two and rookies increased to seven. For the 1954 season, a roster limit of fifteen was retained but only one veteran—usually a playing manager—was permitted while the team had to include at least seven rookies.

Clanton was accused of vacillating in his decisions, and his successor, George Barr, observed that as his weakness. Clanton survived Waco Turner's ouster attempt in 1954 when the oilman promoted

Ucal Clanton (left) had been in baseball since 1916. He led the Sooner State League from 1952 until George Barr replaced him in 1955. (Lg-6)

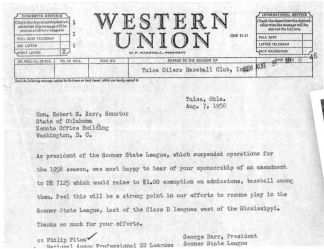

Left: Barr lobbied for Class D baseball. (Lg-7)

Below: Barr was always an umpire first. Part of the uniform from his Florida umpire's school. (Lg-8)

Lawton's Cy Stewart as league president. With a tough, experienced former league president available, the owners retired Clanton in the fall of 1955.

Tulsan George Barr, the third president, succeeded Ucal Clanton following the October 31, 1955, annual meeting and took the league nearly to its end. He presided over the last two seasons of league play as well as a year's effort to revive the last Class D league west of the Mississippi River. He had experience. He presided over the demise of the K-O-M League in 1953 and the Western Association in 1955. After the owners of the remaining franchises announced in October, 1958, that a league comprised of Ardmore, Muskogee, Paris, Ponca City, Seminole and Shawnee would operate in 1959, he submitted his resignation.

Barr was first and foremost an umpire. His career began in 1924 in the Western Association. He served in the National League from 1931 to 1949, and officiated in four World Series and two All Star games. As the plate umpire, he nearly called because of darkness the September 28, 1938 game between Chicago and Pittsburgh when the Cubs' Gabby Hartnett hit the famous walk-off "homer in the gloaming" at lightless Wrigley Field to propel his team to the National League pennant. Barr

Bob Reynolds' short tenure was an exercise in futility considering the turmoil in the National Association. (Lg-9)

owned and operated the first school for umpires and trained Japanese umpires for the U. S. occupation forces. Barr was decisive and forceful. He was the right man in the position. The league never went into the red during his administration. He could not, however, reverse the decline in attendance, a national phenomenon brought on by home television and residential air-conditioning. He died at age eighty-two in the Veterans' Home in Sulphur, Oklahoma, on July 27, 1974.

Bob Reynolds, a friend of Cleveland Indian Hall of Famer Bob Feller from their the Navy days, joined Oklahoma City Indians' owner Jimmie Humphries as business manager of the Texas League club from 1949 until the franchise moved to Corpus Christi in February, 1958. He became president of the league in November, 1958, following Barr's withdrawal. It was a difficult time in baseball. The Minor Leagues were embroiled in turmoil over reclassification of the high minors that would lead to the truncation of Classes B, C, and D into a single Class A in 1963.

As the Sooner State League did not play in 1958, nor pay dues to the governing body of minor league baseball, the National Association, it would have to be officially sanctioned for 1959. Commissioner George Trautman gave the league's teams until February 15, 1959, to secure Major League working agreements. The Paris club signed up with the Phillies and the Cardinals were willing to provide players to Ardmore, but the other teams had no success. On February 12, 1959, President Reynolds announced that that the Sooner State League's revival plan had failed. With the exception of the Texas League Oilers in Tulsa, when the 1959 season began Oklahoma was without any professional baseball. Reynolds remained in Oklahoma City and worked for the Urban Renewal Authority until his death at age fifty-six.

Once the League was up and running, the relationship between Mealey and the owners became contentious. A central issue involved the poor quality of officiating. Mealey ordered umpires to give over-argumentative players ten seconds to return to position or face ejection. After several instances when umpires were in physical danger from fans, he warned owners of fines unless better protection for umpires was provided. Another complaint was the length of games. To cut down on delays by managers, he adopted a rule that a pitcher had to be removed on the third trip to the mound in an inning. Another contention was that he favored Ada and McAlester over other clubs.

It was customary in lower division minor leagues and semi-pro parks throughout the country to pass cash to players who had made outstanding plays, hit home runs, or saved a game. The Sooner State League was no exception. On August 10, 1947 Mealey asked that fans refrain from taking collections or passing cash through the fences to players. He was without exception ignored.

The League had great plans for a little Dixie Series in 1947 between the winners of the K-O-M League playoffs and the Sooner State League champion. It was stillborn when the K-O-M officials decided such a series would be too expensive and unduly prolong the season for the players who, after all, were only paid in the $100-$200 per month range and many of whom attended college on the G. I. Bill. The league was able to carry through with its plan for an All Star game. On July 8, 1947, before 3,000 Lawton fans the hometown Giants beat the Stars 4-3 after seven scoreless innings. The $2,500 netted went to the League treasury.

At the October 27, 1947, league annual meeting the fifteen player limit was retained but the salary cap was raised to the Class D limit of $2,250 per month. The league finished the season with $2,000 in the bank. The owners voted to expand the league to eight or ten and invited Durant, Okmulgee, Wewoka, Shawnee, Chickasha, and Pauls Valley to apply. The Durant group quickly obtained pledges for $20,000. In December, 1947, Chickasha, Durant, Pauls Valley, and Shawnee were awarded franchises. President Mealey stepped down to organize and run the Shawnee franchise. Paul Crowl assumed the league President's duties *ad interim*.

The winter meeting was held in McAlester on January 13, 1948. As the Shawnee franchise could not reach agreement with the owner of the local sports stadium for a lease, Jack Mealey was re-elected as president, and Crowl and Dr. Sugg re-elected as first and second vice-presidents. As a result of his perceived highhandedness with the owners and managers, the owners created a Board of Control to review Mealey's decisions. Seminole's Cy Fenolio, Dr. Sugg, and Crowl were appointed to that committee. The roster limit was raised to sixteen. At the meeting Dr. Sugg moved that any league member that had failed to pay dues forfeit its franchise. He withdrew it after president Mealey stated that he was agreeable but that the only delinquent club was Ada. A 140-game schedule incorporating Chickasha and Pauls Valley as new members was adopted. Eddie Miller of Oklahoma City was appointed statistician. An East (McAlester, Pauls Valley, Seminole, Ada) versus West (Ardmore, Chickasha, Duncan, Lawton) format for a mid-season All Star game was approved but never acted on. A team could bring twenty players from spring training but had to cut five of them within fifteen days after season began. August 17 was set as last day to add players.

At the annual owners' meeting on October 11, 1948, Mealey reported that 1948 attendance was 319,518 and that the League finished the season with $2,000 in the bank. The first change of ownership was completed when the owners approved the sale of the Ada club from Ucal Clanton and Dr. Sugg to Bob Cason. Duncan owner Otto Utt made a claim that Mealey was guilty of favoritism. When Mealey produced a letter to other owners defending Utt, the Duncan cowboy backed down. The winter meeting was set for January 9, 1949, in Seminole. The owners gave Mealey a $500 raise to $1,900. Addressing the owners, Grayle Howlett of the Tulsa Oilers warned that raising the salary cap to $2,250 would spell the end of the Sooner State League. The season began April 26. The largest crowd of the season was 2,400 at McAlester.

The next annual meeting was at Lawton on November 29, 1949. Mealey was retained as president while Paul Crowl remained first vice-president and Ada owner Bob Cason became second vice-president. A proposal to raise the salary cap to $2,600, the Class D limit, was voted down. The owners directed Mealey to attend at least three games at each city during the season. He was to go unannounced both to teams and umpires.

At the January, 1950 winter meeting, Art Willingham's purchase of the Ardmore franchise was approved. A 140-game schedule was adopted. Since 1947, the League had contracted with Worth to manufacture baseballs for official league use. It was an inferior ball and considered "dead" by the players. The

Leadership of the Sooner State League 1948: (L-R) Dr. A. R. Sugg of Ada, Jack Mealey, and Paul Crowl of McAlester. (Lg-10)

9

Worth ball did not come to within 2% of the quality of Major League balls (Reach and Spalding) as mandated by the National Association and had to be abandoned. Sooner Staters had hit 399 home runs in 1949 using the Worth ball. In 1950, they would blast 710 with the new Rawlings ball.

At the annual meeting in Ada on November 19, 1950, the incumbent officers were re-elected. Shawnee was formally admitted. Eddie Miller was re-appointed as statistician and Hugh German, sports writer for the McAlester *News-Capital*, was appointed as the league's

The League changed presidents at the November 18, 1951, annual meeting when Ucal Clanton unseated Jack Mealey. Paul Crowl was again elected first vice-president and Otto Elliott of Chickasha second vice-president. *Ada Evening News* sports writer Charles Rhodes was named publicity director and Eddie Miller was reappointed official league statistician. Ardmore owner Art Willingham announced that he would move the Indians franchise unless the people of Ardmore voted to build a replacement for Tribe Park. The Seminole operation was in financial trouble;

The Worth baseball was the least expensive and deadest ball available to professional leagues. Used in both the K-O-M and Sooner State Leagues, it was banned for not coming within tolerance limits for performance. (Lg-11)

The Sooner State League switched to a livelier ball made by Rawlings. (Lg-12)

publicity manager. A 140-game schedule running from April 29 to September 3, 1951, was adopted. Season openers were to be McAlester at Ada, Ardmore at Pauls Valley, Chickasha at Lawton, and Seminole at Shawnee. At the January 14, 1951, winter meeting in Ada, the schedule structure was changed so that no team would have more than two consecutive series either at home or on the road. A series would consist of two or three games, home for two series, on the road for two. The $2,250 monthly salary cap was retained. Paul Crowl of McAlester, Bob Cason of Ada, and Arthur Willingham of Ardmore were appointed as the audit committee. The league contracted with Rawlings with the price of balls going up to $30.00 per dozen from $22.50 in 1950, $16.50 in 1948, and $14.75 in 1947.

owner Fred McDuff would either sell or walk away and turn the franchise back to the league. The owners approved Chet Fowler's sale of the Shawnee franchise to an investor group led by attorney Irwin Owen. The Chickasha ownership group surprised everyone by announcing that the club was on the brink of insolvency with debts exceeding the $2,000 cash on hand. A sale to Del Rio, Texas attorney A. C. Gonzalez's private minor league organization was approved.

The winter meeting in January of 1952 was eventful. Art Willingham was given permission to move his Ardmore team to Sherman, Texas, the first league location outside of the Sooner State. Fred McDuff had thrown in the towel and let the league have back the Ironmen franchise. Gainesville, Texas, was knocking at the door wanting a Sooner State League franchise and made a play for the Seminole club. A special committee of the owners, however, had approved the shift of that organization to Ardmore. The sale of the Chickasha franchise to A. C. Gonzalez was confirmed yet Otto Elliott remained as league second vice-president. The $2,250 salary cap was retained. A 140-game season beginning April 19 and ending September 6 was adopted. Rawlings balls were 5¢ less expensive.

After the 1952 season, the owners set the president's salary at $2,500. President Clanton reported that the League finished play with $2,062. 72 on hand. There was a fight led by Ardmore president W. C. Peden over team composition. Ardmore and McAlester pressed for increasing the number of veterans by one to three and reducing rookies from seven to six. Leo Tripp, appearing for the Pauls Valley interests, opposed that but did move for a 124-game schedule. Both items failed. Sherman owner Art Willingham, Ardmore president Peden, and the new president of the Ada club, Lawrence Sanford, were elected to the Board of Control. Sanford and Tripp were appointed to audit the league's books. Dick King, Gonzalez's baseball czar, announced that his boss definitely would not operate in Chickasha in 1953 and was contemplating a move to Gainesville, Texas. The League created the Governor' Cup to be awarded to the winner of the post-season Shaughnessy Playoff.

The owners gave Gonzalez until February 3, 1953, to make up his mind whether to move or sell the Chickasha franchise. No schedule could be drawn until the location of his franchise was fixed. Gonzalez departed the scene when he sold the club to a former league umpire, Ernest Shadid, who moved the team to Gainesville. The transfer was approved on February 8 and a 140-game season from April 21 to September 7 was adopted, but not until after Eddie Miller and Paul Crowl walked out over whether a 126- or 140-game schedule had been commissioned in the fall 1952 meeting.

Following the 1953 season, the league treasury was $1,000 in the red but by the time of the annual meeting on November 20, had $1,234. 33 on deposit. Some owners claimed that Ardmore had broken league rules in 1953 by paying too much meal money ($2. 25 instead of the league maximum of $1. 75). Bill Hamilton, Ardmore business manager and former city editor for *The Daily Ardmorite,* admitted the mistake but advised that it was corrected during the second week of the season. There was no complaint about the pay for performance bonus plan the Ardmore president Waco Turner's wife had adopted. President Clanton was re-elected. Cy Stewart of Lawton became first vice-president by winning a coin toss with Paul Crowl. Waco Turner succeeded Lawrence Sanford as second vice-president.

At the February 7, 1954, winter meeting Art Willingham was allowed to move his Sherman-Denison team yet again, this time to return baseball to Seminole. A new statistician was appointed, Ed Williams of Shawnee. A 140-game campaign from April 20 to September 5 with no double headers was adopted.

As early as the 1954 playoffs, Waco Turner was backing Lawton's Cy Stewart to replace Clanton. That battle would be deferred for a year. At the November 14, 1954, annual meeting, the League announced it would operate in 1955 but composition was problematic as Pauls Valley, McAlester, and Seminole lacked working agreements. Clanton was re-elected with Cy Stewart succeeding Paul Crowl as first vice-president and E. L. Bradshaw, who had bailed out the Gainesville franchise, succeeding Turner as second vice-president. The 75¢ ticket cap was removed.

At the winter meeting on January 16, 1955, Turner and Stewart were insistent that the only course for the league to take was to move the Ada or Pauls Valley franchise to Duncan. Lawton objected to the admission of Paris, Texas, due to the 235 mile distance, and Shawnee vetoed Vernon, Texas, for the same reason. Nonetheless, Paris was admitted. Turner and Stewart were elected to the revived overseer of the president, the Board of Control. When a special meeting was held on February 16, 1955, Turner, Crowl, and Don Smith of Paris, were appointed to recommend changes to the league's constitution. A particular sore point was the provision that the winner of the playoff was league champion and entitled to the pennant; in nearly all other leagues the regular season winner got the pennant. After the failure of the Western Association, orphaned Muskogee with its owner Joe Magoto came into the league as the eighth member. For the first time, there were no independent teams in the Sooner State League.

The long knives were out for President Clanton. At the October 30, 1955, post-season meeting, George Barr, retired National League umpire and past president of both the K-O-M League, which folded in 1953, and Western Association, that shut down in early 1955, was appointed president of the last Class D league west of the Mississippi River. Waco Turner, Paul Crowl, and Don Smith of Paris became the Oversight Committee with less power than the old Board of Control.

When the winter meeting was held in McAlester in January 9, 1956, over a strong minority vote and president Barr's recommendation, a 140-game schedule beginning April 24, and ending on Labor Day, September 3, was approved. The minority pressed for a 126-game schedule beginning on May 1. It took seven ballots. The first six were 4-4 ties 140 versus 126. For the first time, seven double headers were scheduled. The Class D maximum salary limit of $2,600 was adopted. A. P. Shuman of Ardmore and Dave Sutton of Ponca City replaced Waco Turner and Don Smith on the oversight committee.

Barr was re-elected president and J. J. Magoto of Muskogee became first vice-president at the fall 1956 annual meeting. The fans would pick the All Stars

who were to play the team in first place on July 4. The league finished the 1956 season with money in the bank. Greenville, Texas, was awarded the franchise of charter member McAlester. A 126-game schedule running from May 1 until September 3 was adopted. The idea for the truncated season was to avoid the wet weather and many rainouts experienced the past several seasons during April and early May.

The League finished profitably in 1957. At the fall 1957 annual meeting, the league dropped the Greenville franchise for failure to pay dues. President George Barr began a search for an eighth team. Milwaukee announced that it would not renew its working agreement with Lawton for 1958 unless "bleak, weather beaten" Memorial Park was refurbished or replaced.

Vernon, Texas and Ada were awarded franchises replacing Greenville and Lawton at the February 2, 1958 winter meeting in Muskogee. The board deferred deciding whether to play in 1958 or postpone to 1959. A week later, first vice-president Joe Magoto of Muskogee, presiding while Barr was running his umpiring school, announced that the Sooner State League would suspend operations. Vernon, Ada, and Seminole had been unable to obtain working agreements. Vernon Chapman of the Shawnee team said a plan to proceed with a four-team league was abandoned because Seminole and Ada didn't have working agreements, although Shawnee and Ardmore did.

On June 2, 1958, representatives of teams met in Ada to revive the Sooner State League. The meeting announced that the league would operate in 1959 with Paris, Vernon, Ponca City, Muskogee, Ardmore, and Shawnee-Seminole. Blackwell, a member of the Western Association in 1954, also expressed interest in joining.

The former owners of Sooner State League teams met on October 18, 1958, in Shawnee and announced that the league would resume play in 1959. The teams would be from Ardmore, Muskogee, Paris, Ponca City, Seminole, and Shawnee. Ft. Smith, Arkansas and Blackwell were possible additions. Working agreements were thought to be assured for at least six. George Barr announced his resignation effective November 16, 1958. Former business manager of the Oklahoma City Indians, Bob Reynolds, was elected league president. Ed Williams drew up a 120-game schedule that was adopted for 1959 with six teams to play from May 4 to August 31.

At the December, 1958, meeting of the National Association, the issue of realignment of the higher minors threw the meeting into such turmoil that President Trautman and the executive committee decided that no applications for recognition of new leagues would be accepted until the realignment issue was resolved. Since it had not fielded teams in 1958 nor paid Association dues, the Sooner State League was no longer a recognized member of Organized Baseball.

At the January 9, 1959 winter meeting, new league President Bob Reynolds set another meeting for February 1. To operate in 1959, the Sooner State League would have to be sanctioned by the National Association. President Trautman gave the six teams until February 15 to have working agreements committed. Because there were only five Class D leagues left —Midwest, Sophomore, New York-Penn, Alabama-Florida, and Florida State— there was feeling among the owners that the Sooner State League was needed to handle rookie development.

Vernon Chapman of Shawnee, A. P. Shuman and A. C. Smith of Ardmore, and Carl Jackson from Seminole attended the February 1 meeting along with scouts Hugh Alexander from the Dodgers, Buster Chatham of Pittsburgh, Hap Morse of the Phillies, and Fred Hawn and Sheldon Bender of the Cardinals. Club representatives James Gill of Paris, Dave Sutton of Ponca City, and Joe Magoto of Muskogee attended

the meeting by proxy. Paris with Philadelphia and Ardmore with St. Louis had firm commitments for working agreements. The other teams needed like arrangements. The league owners were optimistic that Seminole, Ponca City, Shawnee, and Muskogee would secure Major League tie-ups since the league had shown its intention to operate in 1959.

The last meeting of the Sooner State League on February 1, 1959: (L-R) A. P. Shuman of Ardmore, Vernon Chapman of Shawnee, A. C. Smith of Ardmore, and Carl Jackson of Seminole. Eleven days later Bob Reynolds announced that revival efforts had failed. (Lg-13)

It was not to be. On February 12, 1959, Reynolds announced the Sooner State League's revival plan had failed. With it, over a half-century's tradition of disappeared.

The Sooner State League's final season coincided with celebrating fifty years of statehood during the Oklahoma Semi-Centennial Exposition with its "Arrows to Atoms" theme. Small town professional baseball in Oklahoma was relegated to the days of Arrows. Baseball enjoyed privately on color television in an air-conditioned home would be the Atoms.

THE CITIES

ADA
SOONER STATE LEAGUE 1947-1957

The St. Louis Browns between 1947 and 1953 had the lowest attendance in the American League each year, frequently hundreds of thousands less than their Sportsmen's Park tenant, the National League Cardinals. During this period they finished sixth once, seventh three times, and last the other four seasons, twice losing one hundred or more games. The only thing that improved when the Brownies became the Baltimore Orioles in 1954 was attendance; they still lost one hundred games. During these years, the Browns had an established minor league system, many scouts, and regularly a stable full of rookies and limited service players with potential. Unfortunately, few of those prospects were sent to Ada, the bottom rung of the organization's ladder.

Bill Upton, who was released after three weeks and spent most of the 1948 season at Ardmore, was the sole Hereford ever to suit up inside a Major League club house and only then that of the Philadelphia Athletics as they were on their way out

Bill Upton was a St. Louis Browns rookie assigned to Ada for 1948. After a couple of weeks he was released and signed with Ardmore. He was the only Hereford who ever appeared in a Major League game at the beginning of the 1954 season with the last edition of the Philadelphia Athletics. (Ada-1)

SEASON	ATTENDANCE	RECORD	FINISH	AFFILIATION	PLAYOFF FIRST ROUND	PLAYOFF FINALS
1947	41,872	86-51	Second	St. Louis (AL)	Lost to McAlester 2-3	
1948	27,050	63-76	Fifth	St. Louis		
1949	33,525	69-70	Fourth	St. Louis	Lost to Pauls Valley 2-3	
1950	31,981	96-41	First	St. Louis	Lost to Ardmore 2-3	
1951	12,779	54-86	Fifth	St. Louis		
1952	38,387	57-82	Seventh	St. Louis		
1953	36,128	84-54	Third	St. Louis	Beat Shawnee 3-1	Lost to McAlester 1-4
1954	28,482	64-76	Sixth	Baltimore		

Aerial photo of Ada in 1947. (Ada-2)

of town. It was not until after the Ada franchise moved to Paris that the better players began to pass through. The Ada club, which had a full working agreement, was allowed to sign its own players and often did. Only the 1947 club with record attendance turned a small profit. The 1950 pennant winner only broke even. In every other season, the team lost between $5,000 and $14,000.

When the Sooner State League was organized, Ada was the only town in the league that had a facility that might be suitable as the home for a professional baseball team. The Ada firefighters put on a rodeo in the middle of the Great Depression as a fundraiser. Held at the old Ada ball park on West Main, it was more successful than they could have imagined. A 150-feet long concrete and steel grandstand for a rodeo arena was built in 1938 by the Works Progress Administration on the northeast corner of 18th and Broadway across from the Armory, also a WPA project. Ada's semi-pro team, the Independents, made a contribution in the form of lighting from the old park. In 1940, a roof was placed over the stands. An additional 125 feet of grandstand was added in 1942 to increase capacity to 2,500. By the end of World War II, the Ada Rodeo was second in size only to Cheyenne, Wyoming's Frontier Days among outdoor rodeos. Ada was the capital of Hereford Heaven and to

show that a large statute of a Hereford was placed at the Pontotoc County Fairgrounds near the rodeo arena. Bleachers were added every year to bring total capacity to 12,000.

After a season of Sooner State League play, the *Ada Evening News* opined on May 27, 1948 "[y]ou can't mix rodeo performance and baseball games on the same field." That, however, is exactly where the Ada Herefords played home games during their eight seasons. The rodeo grounds forced an awkward configuration. The field was completely bare dirt. As 1948 catcher Charlie Hopkins observed in an interview, "[a] rabbit would have to pack a lunch to walk across the field."

From home plate to the left field fence was 428 feet. The right field fence was a short 275 feet away while center field was a mere twenty feet further than the right field line. The grandstand ran parallel to the first base line with home plate at the northeast end. There were bull chutes in center field and bleachers beyond the right field fence and along the left field line. The fence from center field to the left field foul pole ran parallel to 18th Street. The lighting was notoriously poor. The sports editor of

Hereford Park was superimposed on the dirt surface of the Ada rodeo grounds. The grandstand extended 275 feet down the first base line. The outfield dimensions were dictated by the placement of the rodeo's bleachers. Although 12,000 fans could be seated, the Herefords rarely, if ever, filled even the grandstand. (Ada-3)

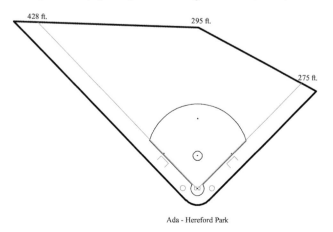

Ada - Hereford Park

the *Seminole Producer* commented "[w]hy elderly men and long term married couples pay admission price to go out there and sit in the dark is beyond me. " Hereford Park was to be a bane as long as the team played there. For ten days in early August, the Herefords had to become a road team as the annual Ada Rodeo was going on. Baseball home games were then played in nearby Sulphur. After the Herefords moved to Paris, American Legion and sandlot teams occupied Hereford Park. The Agri-Plex, a modern indoor arena, stands where Hereford Park was located.

1947

Veteran baseball man Ucal "Uke" Clanton and civic booster Dr. Albert R. Sugg formed the Ada Baseball Club, Inc. on March 10, 1947, six months after the initial meeting in McAlester where the Sooner State League was formed. The company was capitalized with $10,000. Sugg, a prominent physician, and Clanton, a longtime baseball man who had an active career in Oklahoma's semi-pro scene as manager of the Ada Independents as well as an independent insurance agent, were the principal owners. Harrell Allen served as secretary-treasurer. Edwin Free, who would organize the Chickasha franchise in 1948, handled the financial and operating matters until midway through the 1947 season when George Morrison took over the front office. Clanton, the 1916 University of Oklahoma letterman who had appeared in one game for the 1922 Cleveland Indians, guided the team on the field. The Herefords' trainer was Ms. Gussie Pfeifer, Dr. Sugg's nurse. An office was set up at 106 ½ E. Main Street. The highest attendance in Ada's eight-year professional history was achieved in its initial season when 41,872 went through the turnstiles at Hereford Park.

Since Chattanooga Lookouts owner Joe Engel,

the "Barnum of the Bushes," began contests involving fans, players, and owners during the Depression, minor league clubs had put on entertaining but silly diversions. Early in the season, the Ada fans were treated to a foot race to first base between Dr. Sugg and owner-manager Otto Utt of the visiting Duncan Cementers. With Utt having to get past a man standing in the baseline and Dr. Sugg running backward, Utt won when Dr. Sugg fell and shattered his elbow. Dr. Sugg's injury notwithstanding, 1947 would be the Herefords' best season.

Despite the contestants committing eleven errors, the Herefords got off to the right start on April 29, 1947, when they beat Ardmore 14-13 on Ray Kolafa's pinch hit double in the bottom of the ninth. Ardmore catcher Dick Patterson earned the distinction of being the first player in Sooner State League history to be ejected from a game when he was tossed in the bottom of the second inning. After three weeks of play, outfielder Paul Richardville was hitting . 400 and veteran hurler Joe Isaacs was

Forrest Smith was a pitcher before developing a sore arm and collecting the nickname "Woody." He was an outstanding third baseman in the International League winning several Silver Gloves with the Miami Marlins and as a successful minor league manager. (Ada-4)

17

leading the league with a 3-0 record. Ada was in second place behind pacesetter Lawton and would remain there the rest of the season. On June 24, Charlie Mize tossed the league's first ever no-hitter, a seven-inning affair, zeroing out McAlester 1-0.

The mid-season All-Star team that played the pacesetting Lawton Giants included six Herefords: manager Ucal Clanton, Paul Deters, Richardville, Bob Koepka, Jack Wilson, and Forest Smith; only Richardville and Smith would be named to the post-season team.

At mid-season, except for pitchers and catchers, only two Herefords were playing at the same position where they had begun the season.

Henry Kane went on a hitting tear the last two weeks of the season and received cash from the fans through the fence nearly equal to his salary. Previously in the August 1 game against Lawton at Hereford Park, he was cheated out of a home run by an umpire's call. He hit a shot to center but neither the umpires nor most players from each dugout could find the ball. Finally, a boy scrambled atop the bull chutes discovering a ball. Kane was awarded a double.

Paul Richardville was Ada's first hitting star. He later made Ada his home. (Ada-5)

In hitting, Richardville led the league with eleven home runs and 111 RBIs. Forest "Woody" Smith, who would go on to five Silver Glove awards with the International League's Miami Marlins, was tops with twenty-three wins and a 2.00 ERA. Bill Donaghey sent 244 batters to the dugout with bat in hand. Averaging nightly attendance of 598, the club made a profit. In a game marred by nine Ada errors, the Herefords turned the first triple play in league history on August 25 against Duncan. Against fourth-place McAlester in the first round of the playoffs, Ada ended its season losing three of five to the Rockets who went on to take the League's first post-season championship over Ardmore.

1948

Uke Clanton was back at the helm in 1948 starting from scratch. Like the 1947 team, fifteen players and equipment traveled in two station wagons, one driven by Clanton and the other by one of the players. A combination of Browns' farmhands and Clanton's local free agents could only muster sixty-three wins against seventy-six losses for fifth place in 1948. Without 1947's league-leading pitching, the fans stayed away with only 27,050 paying customers cheering "The Cat" Clanton's last team.

The season began with Ada's Orville Makintubbee squaring off against Ardmore's rookie phenom, Tom Kruta of Oklahoma City, at the Indians' Tribe Park. Makintubee scattered eleven hits but five Ardmore errors allowed eight Ada tallys for a four-run victory. Ardmore returned the favor the following evening jumping on Charlie Mize for twelve hits that, combined with Mel Knopp's four errors, allowed fourteen Indians' runs while the Herefords

Charlie Hopkins toiled in the St. Louis Browns' organization before trying managing for Kansas City's farmhands at Seminole in 1955. (Ada-6)

plated but a solo score; Mize quit baseball after that. The Adans dropped the next five contests before Charles Hopkins' first round tripper of the season at the Duncan Bowl gave Bob Yount his first win. The excitement came with the Herefords on defense as they turned a pair of triple plays. The first occurred on May 30 in a 7-3 win at Ardmore. The Ardmore batter lined deep to left fielder Arnold Spence who threw a strike to catcher Hopkins doubling up the runner coming from third. Hopkins then threw out the Ardmore runner on second base with a perfect peg to shortstop Dennis Rackley who applied the tag. The other was performed before the home fans on June 21 in a 4-2 loss to McAlester. With the bases loaded with Rockets, first baseman Earl Bossenberry fielded a grounder then threw to the plate for the force out. Catcher Hopkins fired the ball to Bobby King who was covering first to retired the batter. King then threw back to Hopkins to nail the McAlester baserunner trying to score.

It was not a case of sabotage when the Herefords treated the visiting Chickasha Chiefs to a steak feed on July 1 that put 1947 Hereford Bob Stautzenbach in the hospital with food poisoning. Orville Makintubee, whom the Hereford's had earlier released before he signed with the Chiefs, gained some revenge against his former team mates that evening as he tamped down the Herefords for his seventh win since being shown the door.

Harry Vice's nine inning no-hitter against Lawton on July 13 was emblematic of the 1948 season. Three errors in the fifth inning, including one by Vice himself handling Lawton pitcher Bob Gidding's bunt, allowed an unearned Giants' run to score giving them the win 1-0. There were few high points. One, however, was immediately before the June 21 game when Ada shortstop Dennis Rackley —a converted softball pitcher and team clown— of Chandler, Oklahoma, married lovely Betty Mattheyer at home plate.

The Dennis Rackley-Betty Mattheyer wedding was a big social event in Ada. (Ada-7)

The 1948 Herefords had an average age of 20.5 years. Twenty-seven prospects wore Herefords flannels that season. (Ada-8)

The 1948 Herefords even found a way to lose a doubleheader despite the fact that they outscored their opponent in each game. Chickasha protested an August 22 game, which the Chiefs won, because Ada had signed 1947 regular, Ray Kolafa, after the August 17 deadline. As a result, the Herefords forfeited an August 20 sweep of a doubleheader from Pauls Valley. The Ada nine limped to a 63-76 fifth-place finish. The cussing that umpire Tex Burnett directed to Rackley, Vice, Seminole manager Hugh Willingham, and the fans on September 2, as Ada lost to the Oilers 16-12, just added insult to the injury of a second division season.

The 1948 edition led the league with 958 runs scored and seventy-one home runs but its batters also made 848 strike outs and left 1,286 on base. With two triple plays and the top figures in put outs and assists it is initially surprising that the club was only in the middle of the pack in fielding but 368 errors explains the .936 percentage; forty-six passed balls exacerbated the glove problem. Pitching was the weak spot. Virl Loman's 3.72 ERA was the team's best. No Hereford led the league in any category nor were any selected for inclusion on the All-Star team.

While 1948 began with money in the bank, the attendance drop of nearly 15,000, which translated to an operating loss of approximately $9,750, nearly wiped out both the initial paid-in capital plus the club's surplus profit from 1947. For Sugg, the Herefords had ceased to be a hobby and became work. For Clanton, the team could not afford the luxury of a non-playing manager. It was time to sell.

From a player's standpoint, however, things were not so bad. Ada fans were among the league's most enthusiastic and generous when it came to the low minor league custom of passing cash through the fences and backstops directly to players who had outstanding plays or hit home runs. Ada did not need an appreciation night. Every game was potentially an appreciation event.

On September 5, 1948, the day after the season ended, Robert W. Cason, Jr., a local Ford dealer and American Legion ball sponsor, announced that he was buying Sugg's and Clanton's stock to become controlling shareholder of Ada Baseball Club, Inc. He kept George Morrison, also a shareholder, in the front office. E. W. Kemp, who had been a minority shareholder with Sugg and Clanton, retained his investment.

1949

Under new ownership and new field leadership in the form of Bill Kreuger, the expectations for 1949 were upbeat. Sophomores Earl Bossenberry and Bobby King along with rubber-armed reliever and semi-pro veteran Virl Loman returned from 1948.

Two future stars of the champion 1950 Hereford team would be picked up on the bounce from the White Sox's Seminole club. Bill Milligan, who had been a regular in fifty-four Oiler games, and rookie Steve Molinari, who had appeared in nine contests in Seminole flannels, would light up league

Bobby King toiled two seasons at Ada and then went on to a playing and managerial career in high leagues. He was the Houston Astros' head West coast scout for over a quarter century. (Ada-9)

pitching in 1950 like a pinball machine. But neither Milligan nor Molinari had a particularly sterling season in 1949. While tying a league record with McAlester for playing 143 games in a 140-game season, Herefords carried their bats back to the dugout 987 times, more frequently than any other club, and the team batting average was last at . 230. The . 935 fielding average was in the middle of the Sooner State League pack Gardner, Grass and Loman all had respectable ERAs under 3. 50 but the Herefords' batters just did not score enough runs.

A month into the season, no Hereford was hitting over . 285. Rookie outfielder Fred Boiko set the all-time Sooner State League record for most hits in an inning: a home run and two singles in a 24-3 romp over Lawton. The seventeen Ada runs scored in the seventh inning of that game also set a record. Bill Milligan's twenty-third home run in the season finale on September 4 gave Ada a win over Ardmore and put him in a tie with future New York Giants shortstop Daryl Spencer of Pauls Valley for the most four baggers in a season, a record that would stand until July 10 of the next season. In a close semi-final series, the first-place Pauls Valley Raiders sent the Adans to their off-season homes three games to two.

Cason's 1949 Hereford's sported new uniforms and under Bill Krueger's leadership won a playoff berth. (Ada-10)

1950

The next year, also under Krueger, Cason accompanied the Herefords to the Browns' minor league spring training camp in Pine Bluff, Arkansas. They returned with the best Ada team that ever took the field, winning a franchise record ninety-six games. The 1950 Herefords had strong hitting and solid pitching to take the regular season pennant before 31,981 but lost the championship to McAlester in the playoffs. To shore up the franchise financially, several investors signed "limited liability notes" that could be advanced on by a lender at Cason's request to fund the ball club should operating revenues be insufficient. Fortunately for the signers, Cason announced that the Herefords would have a fair season if they drew above 500 for the last home stand. The team broke even in 1950 and no money was borrowed.

Bill Kreuger, at age twenty-seven, assembled a club that led the league in most hitting categories. With 188 home runs, including a number over Hereford Park's short right- and center-field fences, they surpassed the league record by eighty-four. With one thousand RBIs on the season and seven starters hitting over . 310, the Herefords won ninety-six and lost only forty-one to finish five and one-half games ahead of second-place McAlester. The team batting average was . 300. Fielding was again middling: . 931 with 354 errors. In June, coming off a sixteen-game winning streak with seventy team home runs and Milligan hitting . 400, second sacker Ron Jackson at . 425, and Molinari at . 367, the Herefords attracted national attention in a story in *The Sporting News* on June 14, 1950, "Browns Blasting Farm Team Rocking Sooner Loop with Blasts." It was not all beauty, however. Before the streak began, Ada and Pauls Valley combined

Bill Krueger led the Herefords in 1949 and 1950. He departed the Herefords when his unit was called up for the Korean War. (Ada-11)

1950 Ada Sluggers L-R: Bill Milligan (.332 37 HR), Steve Molinari (.360 39 HR),Fred Boiko (.329 24 HR), Bill Krueger (.349 21 HR) (Ada-12)

on May 4 for one of the sloppiest examples ever of impersonating professional baseball teams. The two nines combined for fourteen balks that scored seven runs, eighteen walks, thirty hits, thirty-nine runs, five batters hit, two wild pitches, and ten errors. Somehow Ada managed to win by a football score of 22-17. Milligan ended the season with thirty-seven homers as Molinari set the all-time Sooner State League record with thirty-nine plus a league best162 RBIs. Don Davenport added thirty-two round trippers, Fred Boiko twenty-four, and manager Krueger twenty-one.

The 1950 Herefords had sound pitching. Bill Donaghey, a twenty-two game winner in 1947, was back to lead the league in wins and percentage, twenty-six wins against five losses and . 839. Workhorse Glass chipped in another twenty wins. In his only season in Organized Ball, Bill Starr lost only one in eleven decisions but had a huge 7. 86 ERA. The playoff jinx continued. This year Ardmore sent Ada home early winning three of five. Five Adans made the All Star team: Don Davenport at first, manager Bill Kreuger at third, Steve Molinari outfield, Bill Milligan utility, and Bill Donaghey on the mound.

The bottom line in the front office was not nearly as stunning as the team's performance on the field. As owner Cason explained in August, nightly paid attendance of 600 was the breakeven point. At that time the club was $8,000 in the red and averaging only 334 paid admissions. Then fans responded but only enough to raise the average figure to 457. They showed their appreciation for the players on the last night of the season passing the hat to raise $1,126. 03 to be divided among the seventeen players on the roster and disabled list.

There were super fans that the team recognized in 1950. Mrs. Ruby Emerich of Ada had watched every Ada game, home and road, from 1947 through 1950. For that she was recognized

Ford dealer Bob Cason bought the Herefords after the 1948 season and underwrote the effort through the disastrous 1951 campaign. (Ada-13)

A short-time Hereford after being released by Ponca City of the K-O-M, John Lazar was killed in action in Korea. (Ada-14)

by the team with an autographed baseball. During the off-season, the Herefords made a contribution to community life. Barnstorming Stars led by the Yankees' Super Chief Allie Reynolds played an Ada team organized by McAlester manager and catcher Vern Hoscheit on October 15, 1950.

1951

At the height of the military draft for the Korean conflict, lower classification players became increasingly scarce. A pitcher who appeared briefly on the 1950 team after his release from Ponca City of the K-O-M League, John Lazar, was killed in action on September 7, 1951.

Stan Galle of Milwaukee appeared briefly for the Washington Senators in 1942. He coached the Spring Hill College nine from 1958 through 1982. The College's baseball field —in used continuously since 1882— was named after him. (Ada-15)

Stan Galle, a good teacher, left scouting to take over the short-handed Herefords. The 1951 season got off to an inauspicious start with McAlester routing the Herefords at home 14-1. The Herefords stumbled their way to only one win in the next six games. On May 12, Ada and McAlester pitchers served up thirty-four walks, a Sooner State League record, in the Rockets' 24-18 triumph. Short on pitchers, Jim Harper went the distance against Ardmore on May 23, giving up twenty-one hits and allowing eleven walks in chalking up one of his nineteen losses by a 20-9 tally. At June 14, the Adans were in the cellar, having won only thirteen of fifty-three outings. By the Fourth of July they had climbed to seventh place at twenty-four victories against fifty defeats only because Seminole had gone into a tail spin losing fourteen of sixteen games.

The Herefords ended McAlester star Dee Sanders' season string of seventy-five and one-third consecutive innings without a walk in the second inning of the nightcap on July 4 when Merle Barth drew a pass. Sanders went on to his thirteenth win by a score of 11-2. On July 9, Ada set the league record for most errors in a game with nine in losing to McAlester. Three weeks later, the club had won just six of twenty-one to remain in seventh. On August 8, Detroit rookie Joe Carolan, sent down on July 19 by K-O-M member Pittsburg (KS) belted the team's only grand slam of 1951 against Sem-

inole. An August Hereford rally combined with Chickasha and Lawton fading lifted Ada to fifth place where they finished the season forty-six and one-half games out of first. The April through July slump injured the Ada club's bottom line irreparably with an average attendance of 183, far below the 600 needed to pay the bills.

Leading the league in batters striking out with 1,116, the 1951 Herefords managed a team batting average of only .248, sixth in the league. Playing 141 games at second base, Galle led the team in hitting at .317. Shortstop Jack Ray, a Pontotoc County player, was the only other Hereford to hit above .300. While leading the Sooner State League with 142 double plays, the fielding was not very good in other areas. The team fielding average was .930 with 388 errors or 2.75 per game. The catchers allowed fifty-four passed balls; Dick Sobeck had twenty-one in forty games behind the plate but redeemed himself in the outfield with a .977 fielding percentage. Pitching was the weakest point. In 1,200 innings, Ada hurlers gave up 1,391 hits, 1,150 runs —only 843 of them earned— and 904 walks. The staff committed twenty-three balks and unleashed eighty-one wild pitches. The combined ERA, not surprisingly, was worst in the league at 6. 33.

The 1951 season was a disappointment both on the field and in the stands. The fifth-place club had the worst record in Herefords history. Having proved that they would not support a loser, the Ada team under the guidance of first-year manager Stan Galle played before only 12,779, just a few more than capacity of Hereford Park for one game. In the eleven years of the Sooner State League, only Duncan's hapless 1947 Cementers with 8,220 viewers had a worse gate.

Cason could not sell enough cars to support his baseball adventure and the other investors were unwilling to risk more money. When a group was being formed to purchase the assets of the Ada club in 1952, the Herefords' business manager, George

Morrison, related to a meeting of potential investors that the cost of running a Sooner State League team would be in the $35,000 range including:

Wages for the manager and players	$ 16,000
Salary for the business manager	$ 1,800
Road expenses	$ 5,000
League dues	$ 2,250
Uniforms	$ 1,500
Bats and balls	$ 2,000
Park maintenance	$ 1,000
Utilities	$ 2,000
Taxes and insurance	$ 500
Telephone, telegraph, office	$ 1,000

He said that the club needed 60,000 paid attendance to break even. The revenues from other sources were simply too little to sustain the operation. The Browns paid $1,500 under the working agreement, concessions netted $2,500 for a season, program advertising brought in $1,400, all the box seats went for $1,800, while season ticket sales never totaled more than $500. This was typical of most Sooner State League teams.

1952

The franchise was sold to Ada Baseball Association, Inc. headed by oilman Lawrence Sanford, Jr. and auto dealer Guy Thrash. With an infusion of cash and enthusiasm, and nearly nightly promotions, the 1952 Herefords were looking for a turnaround. W. A. Delaney and Erwin Hovis served as vice president and secretary-treasurer, respectively, while Foster McSwain, George McRobert, Roy Lawler, and Luther Edge rounded out the board of directors. With initial capitalization of $25,000 and over one hundred shareholders, the new ownership was optimistic.

St. Louis, now under the ownership of Bill Veeck, assigned thirty year-old coach Bill Enos, who had managed the Browns' Pittsburg (KS) K-O-M League team in 1951, to lead the 1952 Herefords. Over 2,200 fans showed up for the opening day win over McAlester and the Herefords responded by finishing the first week of the season tied for first place.

By the second week, they had dropped to third. A winning streak brought their record to fourteen

1952 saw new ownership and field management. L-R Manager Lou Brower, Directors Luther Edge, Guy Thrash, Lawrence Sanford, Promotions Manager Monte Bell. (Ada-16)

Bill Enos played and managed through 1954 in the Browns'-Orioles' minor league organization. From 1955 on he was a major league scout in New England. Enos with his trademark cigar was inducted into Cape Cod Baseball League Hall of Fame in 2001. (Ada-17)

and five and into second place, one-half game behind Pauls Valley. Charlie Rabe joined the team as a highly recruited rookie but lasted only three weeks before receiving his release because he was wild. A few days later, Cincinnati's Lawton farm club signed him and he proceeded to toss eighteen consecutive perfect innings for the little Reds. After June 5, the Herefords collapsed losing nineteen of twenty-four games falling to seventh. On July 13, the Herefords set a league record using seven pitchers in a ten-inning 19-10 loss to Shawnee. The slump continued as the team won only twelve of forty-six contests from June 5 to July 17. On July 10, south central Oklahoma suffered monsoon-like rains. When the sun came out, the all-dirt field at Hereford Park was covered with several hundred gallons of gasoline and burned; even that did not dry the infield sufficiently for play.

The Browns won the contest to ink Waxahachie, Texas phenom Charlie Rabe in 1952. After three weeks hurling with poor control, buyers' remorse set in and he became a free agent. Lawton picked him up on the bounce and was rewarded with eighteen consecutive perfect innings. He spent parts of 1957 and 1958 with the Cincinnati Reds. (Ada-18)

1952 edition of the Herefords finished in seventh with a 57-82 record under three managers. L-R: Top row: Odel Hightower, Dick Sobeck, Don Dielman, Bob Barron, Neil Thode, Moose Arnone, Ron Slawski, Jim England. Front row: Doc McCarn, James Cumbie, Mike Goffredo, Jack Nichols, Lou Medina, Boots Bowers, interim manager Verl Loman. (Ada-19)

There was friction between the management and Enos who was on the Browns' payroll. By the beginning of August with the Herefords mired in seventh place, exacerbated by financial hemorrhaging, the simmering conflict between Sanford's and Enos' personalities spilled over. On August 5, with the Herefords still in seventh with forty-seven wins against sixty-two defeats, Enos, despite being well-liked by the players, was fired at Sanford's insistence and returned to the front office in St. Louis as a scout and minor league instructor. At that point, Sanford on behalf of ownership made public the team's desperate condition: it was $8,000 in debt with only twelve home dates left.

The Herefords set a record with seven home runs against Chickasha on August 16, to impress new manager and part-time pitcher Virl Loman. Loman stayed until August 22, when he went back to pumping gas and nineteen-year old Jim England, who had played for Enos in 1951, finished the season at the helm in seventh place twenty-nine and one-half games behind McAlester. Batting .273 as a team, third best in the league, mediocre fielding and poor pitching doomed the 1952 Herefords from the outset. England set a league record with 612 at bats. He and Dick Sobeck hit .324 and .348, respectively. Only rookie pitcher Harry Byfuss with eight wins against five losses and a 4.63 ERA had a winning record; he was sold to the Senators' organization. The lowest ERA on the team was Charles Kreeger's 4.32. The other starters allowed far too many opponents to cross the plate: Neil Thode ERA 5.15, Endoro Arnone ERA 5.39, Fred Schak ERA 6.20, Joe McCormack ERA 6.40, and Jack Nichols, the leader with eighteen wild pitches, ERA 8.64.

While final attendance was up to 548 per date, considerably better than 1951's 183, 16,000 more than 1951, it still was not enough to pay the bills. Whether baseball would return in 1953 was problematic.

The Sanford group promoted the Herefords producing the best program to appear in the Sooner State League. (Ada-20)

1953

The Herefords' board of directors had three critical issues as preparations for the 1953 season began. The first was hiring a manager who could get along with Lawrence Sanford and was acceptable to the St. Louis Browns' minor league management. The second was whether to accept African-American players on assignment from the Browns. The third was how to promote ticket sales, the life blood of minor league franchises.

The dean of Sooner State League managers, Lou Brower, was lured away from the Giants' Pauls Valley farm club soon after the November 16, 1952

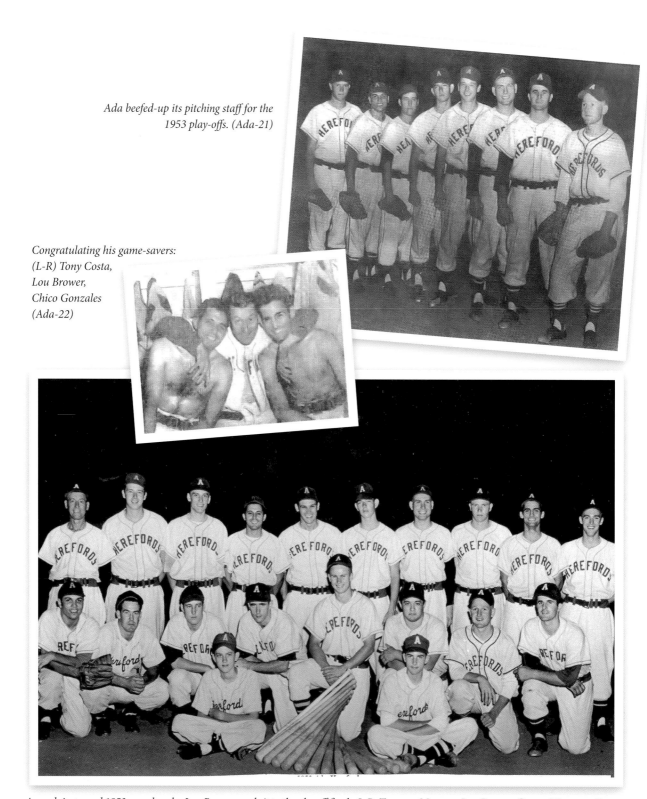

Ada beefed-up its pitching staff for the 1953 play-offs. (Ada-21)

Congratulating his game-savers: (L-R) Tony Costa, Lou Brower, Chico Gonzales (Ada-22)

A much improved 1953 squad under Lou Brower made it to the playoff finals. L-R: Top row: Manager Lou Brower, George Werrman, Ron Slawski, Toni Costa, Bob Norden, Lloyd Bohn, Neil Thode, J.L. Rhodes, Chico Gonzales, Jim Miller. Front row: Pablo Labrador, Doc McCarn, Ron Coburn, Don McGregor, Bob Bonebrake, George Blash, Buddy Yount, Ross Sergo. Batboys Bill Thrash and Bob Cornell. (Ada-23)

annual owners' meeting. Browns farm director, James McLaughlin, informed the Herefords that there were a number of outstanding African-American prospects available. The Sooner State League was no longer segregated as Arthur Willingham had broken the color line the previous season at Sherman when Napoleon Daniels took the mound for the Twins; but his operation was an independent. It was the Browns' practice to send those players out in pairs "because they can be together, live together and in general be happier with an organization." From the 1952 team photo (p.210) it appears that O'dell Hightower, a local free agent, would have the distinction of being the only black Hereford. Like every prior Ada team, the 1953 edition was all-white.

Cline Fowler was hired as business manager. Regarding promoting the team, management took a page from the 1952 K-O-M League team in Independence (KS). A one-day sale of ten admissions for $4. 95 would be the solution. On March 3, the Ada Baseball Association set up a booth at Main and Broadway and began selling cards that, like a meal ticket, could be punched for each admission. An individual could attend ten separate games or a group of ten could go in on one card. Some eight hundred cards were sold.

Following spring training at the Browns' minor league camp at Thomasville, Georgia, Brower brought his team to Ada. The 1953 edition had five returnees from 1952: right fielder James Cumbie, outfielder Larry Burford, catcher Mike Goffredo, relief catcher Doc McCarn, pitcher Neil Thode, and shortstop Ron Slawski. Outfielder Tony Costa and first baseman Bob Norden as military veterans had "national service" status and did not count against the fifteen player limit. Infielder Chico Gonzalez was the other limited service player. The rest were rookies: catcher-outfielder George Blash, shortstop Canadian Don McGregor and hurlers J. L. Rhodes,

Earl Higgins, Bill Williams, Bob Albert, George Werrmann, and Reg Pitre.

The Herefords dropped the April 21, 1953 season opener at McAlester 4-3 with Ada taking the second before returning to Hereford Park. The scheduled April 23 home opener hosting McAlester was rained out. The following day's twin bill before 1,500 saw Ron Slawski's grand slam propel the Herefords to an 8-4 win for Reg Pitre's first victory. Rocket pitcher Ron Saatzer won the nightcap for himself with the second grand slam of the day. After dropping a pair to the Sherman-Denison Twins and Shawnee Hawks at home, Ada vanquished the Dodgers' farmhands from Shawnee 16-7 behind Norden and Slawski's round-trippers in a game that saw twenty-eight hits and nine errors. Rookie J. L. Rhodes had five hitless innings before a four-run sixth to drop the following night's decision. The wins continued. Catcher Mike Goffredo preserved J. L. Rhodes' two-hit shutout on May 14 against Lawton by tagging Lawton catcher Harold Ridley after his team mates carried him off the field to the dugout in celebration of the Reds' first homer of the season; their enthusiasm prevented him from touching home plate. Ridley was credited with a triple. The Herefords took the second game on James Cumbie's RBI to give Werrmann another win. When Sherman-Denison came to play the next evening, a television was set up in Hereford Park so that the fans would not miss the heavyweight fight between Rocky Marciano and Jersey Joe Walcott.

When McAlester returned to town, Tony Costa's grand slam and Chico Gonzalez's walk off double moved the Herefords into first place with a 13-12 victory. On June 18, the Adans were in first place two games ahead of Ardmore and still there a month later. A slump over the next fortnight found the Herefords in fourth but only one and one-half games out of second. With eighteen days remaining in the season, third place looked like a lock with

Ada leading McAlester by four games. On August 8, they had blasted Sherman-Denison 20-5 also with seven home runs including three in the first inning by Don McGregor, Ron Slawski, and George Blash.

Unofficial final tallies showed Ada in a second place tie with Shawnee; post-season adjustments would drop the Herefords to third, one and one-half game behind the Hawks. Ada eliminated Shawnee in four games and then fell to nemesis McAlester four games to one in Ada's only appearance in the playoff finals. At . 270, the 1953 Herefords led the league in team batting, and were tops with 1,997 total bases, and 147 home runs. Ada pitchers posted the league's best with 996 strike outs. Fielding was weak once more but pitching improved markedly. It all added up to a third place finish and Ada's last trip to the playoffs. Bob Norden and Ron Slawski tied for the league lead in home runs with thirty-one apiece. Rhodes led all Sooner State League pitchers with twenty-one wins. The staff posted a group ERA of 4. 18 with Reggie Pitre leading the team at 2. 63 in 106 innings. The highest ERA on the staff was only 4. 46 by Lloyd Bohn.

1954

The Browns became the Baltimore Orioles soon after the end of the 1953 season. The relocation was a surprise to no one. Seller Bill Veeck had been trying to move the St. Louis American League franchise since the day he bought the team. The move did not change the relationship with Ada. The working agreement was to remain in force for the 1954 season. Poor advance sales of advertising and season tickets were a harbinger of problems to come in 1954. Sanford tried to obtain $3,000 in limited liability notes, essentially partial guaranties, from investors and civic leaders to finance the season but with little success.

With sophomore staff ace J. L. Rhodes and . 364 hitting veteran Doc McCarn returning for his third season at Ada, manager Brower hoped to match the performance of his 1953 Herefords with the rookies and limited service players sent from the Orioles' minor league camp. With the exception of Rhodes and Russell Gramlow, released after his only decision, all the pitchers were rookies: James Wolcott,

Russ McDonald after striking out thirteen Pauls Valley Raiders. (Ada-26)

J. L. Rhodes of Pierce, Oklahoma starred for thee Herefords in 1953 and 1954. (Ada-24)

Early season stars: (L-R) Ed Budnick, Ron Barbian, J. L. Rhodes. (Ada-25)

Jan Christensen, Roman Schultheis, and Rich Tait; Russ McDonald and Rueben Saager had seen limited action in under forty-five innings in 1953 to maintain rookie status. First sacker Ron Barbian, who had been in the Philadelphia Athletics' organization in 1953, and Harold Norton, released after eight games, were the only limited service players. Catchers Ed Budnick and Ralph Vulpitta, infielders Jack Whereatte, Ken Hinton, and John Densmore and outfielders Bruce Lane and Rich Lubinski were rookies. None of the 1954 Herefords were veterans.

Left hander Rhodes got Lou Brower's second season at the helm off to a good start with an 8-0 six-hit shutout over McAlester. Nearly ten percent of the season's attendance, 2,674, showed up in the season-opening win. After that, average game attendance was only 300-350. Play was sporadic, though, due to weather. Ada had six rainouts in the first month of the season. Ada exploited doormat Pauls Valley. In one contest Rich Lubinski's three-run homer provided the difference in the Herefords' 14-11 win. In another, Russ McDonald sent thirteen Raiders to the dugout with bats in hand. The Herefords nearly pulled off a win against Shawnee on May 6, despite George Green holding them to one hit, when they scored five runs on seven walks and five errors; Shawnee held on to win 6-5.

On May 22, the Herefords extracted some revenge by tattooing Hawk hurler Walt Callahan for eleven hits and taking thirteen walks in route to a 15-1 blowout. Two days later, on May 24, John DeSousa gave up a league record-tying five triples to Shawnee dropping a 12-7 decision. At that point, the Adans were tied with Lawton for sixth place having won fourteen of thirty-one starts, just one game out of fifth. A month later they were playing . 500 ball and clinging to fourth place with McAlester one-half game behind. Ada had the distinction of allowing McAlester's Rod Kanehl five hits in five trips on July 4, for his thirty-second

Slugger Walt Massefski joined the Herefords on the bounce from the Cubs' farm team in Gainesville. He was a star the next season at the Ada franchise's new home in Paris, Texas. (Ada-27)

consecutive game with a hit to set the Sooner State League record.

Before July 31, Sanford had made the three prior $1,750 semi-monthly payrolls out of his own pocket. He was unwilling to do so a fourth time. The players went unpaid. Baltimore terminated its working agreement with Ada and released most of its players under contract. Unable to get anyone to pay the $10,000 asking price for the Herefords, on that same day, Ada Baseball Association, Inc. surrendered its franchise to the Sooner State League and the remaining players became league property. From the opening day roster of the Herefords, outfielders Lubinski, Vulpitta and Hinton, first baseman Barbian, Adan Doc McCarn, and Rhodes remained. Others included utility man Massefski, who had been picked up in May after being released by the Cubs' Gainesville club, rookie second baseman James Samford, infielder Allan Bailey acquired from Seminole, third sacker Harlie Page sent down from York of the Piedmont League, pitchers John DeSousa and Don Cartwright on loan from the Orioles' Americus, Georgia farm club, and hurler Dale Kingma returned from Aberdeen of the Northern League. Fern Smathers fresh from class at Southeastern Oklahoma State College secured the first string catcher's position at mid-season hitting at a torrid . 429 pace before dropping to . 323 at season end. Another late signee, Darrell Newhouse, joined the pitchers for sixteen games.

For two days, the League itself operated the team as the Ada "Sooner States." Meanwhile, with a $1,750 subsidy from the League's treasury to cover the missed payroll, Charles Mayfield, owner of an Ada oilfield cementing firm, took over the franchise operations as Ada Athletic Association, Inc., and changed the team's name to "Cementers." He kept Cline Fowler in the front office. He fired Lou Brower and hired an Ada service station operator Jerry Densmore, not to be confused with rookie third baseman John Densmore, to assume field command. In his only prior foray into professional baseball, manager Densmore had hit . 197 in seventeen games for the 1950 Herefords. He was not able to lift the new Cementers to the first division nor did attendance pick up.

The pickup Cementers won eighteen of forty-four under new management. Ada went out of Organized Baseball with a whimper losing its last game to McAlester 8-4 to finish twenty-eight games off the pace. The sixth-place team drew 28,482 for the season.

The Herefords' team batting average of . 285 was topped only by the . 300 of the 1950 champions. The 1954 edition was the most iron-gloved of a franchise with a history of poor fielding. With thirty-nine passed balls and 432 errors, the Adans fielded . 922. The pitchers were seventh in the league with a collective ERA of 5. 53 and leader in gopher balls with 176. Rhodes again was the ace at

Denison, Texas native Fern Smathers reached the top of the Orioles' farm system then traded himself to DuPont Co. where he worked in Baton Rouge until retiring. (Ada-29)

3.82 ERA supporting a winning 18-13 record. The sole All Star who wore a Hereford uniform was Walt Massefski, also the Herefords' leading hitter at . 363 with seventeen home runs. Rich Lubinski had the most home runs with twenty-eight. Rhodes, who had thirty-nine wins against nineteen losses after his second season, again was the top hurler on the staff even though serving up thirty-two homers.

Mayfield claimed that the problem with the Ada team all along had been the hook up with the Browns/Orioles. He had created bad blood and it was a certainty Ada would not be in the Orioles'1955 farm system. Despite his best efforts following the season, Mayfield was unable to obtain a working agreement with any other team at the Major League Winter Meeting. The Orioles, and with them the Major Leagues, had blacklisted Ada in general and Charles Mayfield in particular. The franchise was turned back on December 26, 1954. The only baseball played in 1955 and since has been sandlot on the dirt lot.

Rich Lubinski survived the transition from Herefords to Cementers at season end. He led the team in home runs with twenty-eight. (Ada-28)

ARDMORE INDIANS 1947-1952
ARDMORE CARDINALS 1953-1957
ARDMORE ROSEBUDS 1961
SOONER STATE LEAGUE 1947-1957
TEXAS LEAGUE
MAY 27-SEPTEMBER 1, 1961

Tribe Park in 1953 after improvements and additions made by Waco Turner. The original plant by Dutch Prather was much smaller and primitive. (Ar-1)

SEASON	ATTENDANCE	RECORD	FINISH	AFFILIATION	PLAYOFF FIRST ROUND	PLAYOFF FINALS
1947	27,943	72-67	4th	Cleveland	Beat Lawton 3-2	Lost to McAlester 1-4
1948	37,944	60-78	6th	Cleveland		
1949	43,348	57-81	7th	Sherman-Denison	(Big State League)	
1950	44,454	75-65	4th		Beat Ada 3-2	Lost to McAlester 2-4
1951	40,742	99-40	1st		Beat Pauls Valley 3-0	Lost to McAlester 2-4
1952	24,362	49-91	8th			
1953	43,000	91-46	1st	St. Louis (NL)	Lost to McAlester 1-3	
1954	31,090	72-67	4th	St. Louis	Beat Shawnee 3-2	Lost to Lawton 0-4
1955	33,731	65-75	5th	St. Louis		
1956	47,110	83-56	1st	St. Louis	Beat Paris 3-2	Lost to Seminole 3-4
1957	36,301	74-52	2nd	St. Louis	Beat Muskogee 3-0	Beat Paris 4-0
1961	35,925	57-83	6th	Baltimore		

During the more than two decades that followed the demise of the 1926 Boomers of the Western Association, Ardmore had to settle for amateur and semi-pro baseball. Strong American Legion teams were fielded and businesses sponsored teams of employees as well as youth ball clubs.

When Ardmore received one of the charter Sooner State League franchises, a place to play had to be found. WPA-built Walker Field was owned by the Ardmore public schools and was unsuitable for baseball. The new baseball entrepreneurs turned to minor league veteran Murl "Dutch" Prather for help.

Tribe Park was hurriedly thrown up immediately before the 1947 season under the supervision of Prather. The $10,000 structure was located on the old Phillips show grounds, a place where circus big tops and tent revivals had been held at the then north end of Washington Street at Boundary (now Monroe).

Ardmore in 1946 looking east. Ardmore grew to 25,000 during World War II with defense industry and the Army Air Force gunnery school where bomber crews were trained. (Ar-2)

The ground was leased through the end of the 1954 season by Industrial Ardmore, Inc., a private corporation. Industrial Ardmore, Inc. in turn owned the ball park and leased it to the non-profit group that held the franchise. It originally seated approximately 1,200 in an uncovered grandstand. The expense of a roof was cost-prohibitive.

When Art Willingham acquired the franchise in 1950; he also leased Tribe Park and had a sublease on the ground. After two seasons, he announced that he would move the club if the city did not build a new ball park. At the annual Sooner State League meeting in November, 1951, Willingham summarized the facility: the lighting is mediocre, the playing field is fair, and the stands are deplorable. Falling seventy-one votes shy of the sixty percent majority threshold needed to incur

Fans climbed the poles during the over-capacity contest between the Chicago Cubs and St. Louis Browns on April 6, 1953. (Ar-3)

Following a heavy spring rain, the infield was soaked with gasoline and burned to make it playable for the first and only Major League game played in Ardmore. (Ar-4)

public debt, Ardmore voters turned down a December, 1951, $75,000 bond issue for a new baseball facility. Willingham was good to his word: the Indians moved to Sherman.

Ardmore interests were able to persuade a league committee to relocate the distressed Seminole franchise by promising that a new stadium would be built by the start of the 1953 season. That did not happen. However, when Waco Turner succeeded W.C. Peden as president of the ball club in the fall of 1952, he accelerated planned improvements to Tribe Park to put the facility in condition for an April 6, 1953, exhibition game between the St. Louis Browns and the Chicago Cubs. He doubled the capacity by adding new boxes at field level, extended the grandstand, added bleachers on both ends, built concrete dugouts, quadrupled the size of the press box, and built two new clubhouses for the players. He moved his crews from the golf course at Dornick Hills Country Club to put the playing surface in its best condition ever. When an inch of rain fell the evening before the exhibition, Turner had a tank truck driven to the field. A drilling crew soaked the infield dirt with dozens of barrels of gasoline and then lit it. The infield was baked dry for the Major Leaguers. For 1954, Tribe Park was renamed to reflect the new tenants, Cardinal Park.

Talk of a new ball park came with each season. A one-year extension of the ground lease was obtained for the 1955 season. At that point the Ardmore School Board, which had become the landowner, made the ball club's decision for it when the Board decided to build Will Rogers Elementary School on the site of Tribe Park.

In early 1956, Cardinal Park was constructed by the Community Youth Foundation, a local non-profit that operated the public swimming pool, on land at the east end of Main Street selected by A.P. Shuman and purchased and donated by Turner, Ward Merrrick, and Leon Daube. The press box,

Cardinal Park opened in 1956 and was home to the Cardinals for two seasons then in an expanded model for the Rosebuds in 1961. (Ar-5)

With the grandstand and bleachers removed, Cardinal Park hosts a few sandlot games. The oil derrick stanchions remain. (Ar-6)

clubhouses and lighting were moved to the new facility as the demolition of Tribe Park proceeded into early 1956. The stanchions for the lights were replaced by oil derricks. It was, like Tribe Park, roofless. The fences were short: 310 feet to left, 371 feet to center and 320 feet down the right field line. With the capacity expanded to 2,800, it was the home of the Ardmore Rosebuds of the Texas League from June 4, 1961, until the season's end. Since then the stands have been removed and replaced with a few bleachers. A few junior high school games are played there today.

1947

Talk of a rookie league in southern Oklahoma had begun before the outbreak of the War. It resumed in 1946 under the impetus of Ucal Clanton and Dr. A. R. Sugg of Ada and Paul Crowl of McAlester. Ardmore was invited to send a representative to an organizational meeting of a Class D league to be known as the Sooner State League. Oil man and Ardmore booster Waco Turner, who had won and lost fortunes, attended the September 4, 1946, affair at the Aldridge Hotel in McAlester. As the dust settled, a six-team circuit emerged with franchises in Ada, McAlester, Seminole, Okmulgee and Shawnee; Lawton and Duncan soon replaced the latter two. Turner came away with the sixth charter franchise which he turned over to a community trust, the Ardmore Athletic Association. Its sole purpose was to provide for perpetuation of baseball in Ardmore. The trustees were William Steele, who led the local Jaycees and served as president, V.E. "Hoot" Gibson, treasurer, Frank Richie, Earl Milam, Ernest L. Massad, Judge John C. Caldwell, and McMillan

Dutch Prather of Stratford, Oklahoma managed Ardmore for part of 1947 and in 1949. He also managed and played for Pauls Valley (1948), Chickasha (1948), Duncan (1950), and Seminole (1951). He opened an umpiring school with Ucal Clanton in 1956. In the interim, he farmed and umpired in the West Texas-New Mexico and Evangeline Leagues. (Ar-7)

Lambert. At a November, 1946, League meeting, Richie, Caldwell, Steele, and Dutch Prather represented the Ardmore group.

Prather was a veteran of twenty seasons in the minors when he came to Ardmore. A native of Stratford, Oklahoma, he had risen to the top level of the minors in 1937 as the regular first baseman for Sacramento in the Pacific Coast League. Most of his seasons, however, were played in Classes C, B, and A. He began managing in 1941 at Pampa in the West Texas-New Mexico League and was coming off a stint in 1946 as the playing manager of the Tyler Trojans of the newly formed East Texas League. He was hired by the trustees of the Association to get the franchise ready to play ball when the 1947 season opened. He first served the club as business manager, securing a working agreement with Cleveland of the American League through the Indians' Class A-1 Texas League affiliate in Oklahoma City who supplied old uniforms and a few players for Ardmore's use. Prather wore his third hat as talent scout and manager of the fledgling little Indians. Earlier Ardmore teams had sported names such as Territorians, Blues, Giants, Ardmoreites, Peps, Producers, Snappers, and Boomers. The new team was named the Indians due to the affiliation with Cleveland.

The League required that a fifteen-member team have at least seven rookies with the rest being veterans and limited service players. When spring tryouts and drills were concluded, Prather was the only veteran in uniform. The rest were raw rookies or players with one or two seasons under their belts. During the season, pitchers Oscar Kuver and Al Blacha, both picked up from Lawton, Roy Burrell, previously released by Seminole, and Mark Pike, later sold to Seminole, were the only players who had played a season in Organized Baseball. As *The Sporting News* observed in its June 24, 1947, issue, manager Dutch Prather was signing every player who could not make another team. But in the Sooner State League that was the situation with most of the other five clubs. The limited working agreement with Cleveland gave the Ardmore club much autonomy but little help on the field. What players Cleveland did send were sifted through the screen of Jimmy Humphries' Oklahoma City Indians of the Texas League.

Eighteen position players and eight pitchers rotated through the Ardmore clubhouse. The line-up stabilized by the end of May. Colonel Stephens caught. Popular Bill Hughes was the regular first sacker, being relieved occasionally by Prather. Morris Card held down second base while Harold "Red" Sollars covered shortstop. Jim Hayman, signed on the bounce from Duncan, played third. Robert Andrlik, Homer Smotherman, and Noel Philly roamed the outfield.

Tribe Park was a mess. High grass in the outfield and infield was such that a ball could be lost or a hard grounder stopped, center field and right field were uphill from the infield while the left field was tilted down. There was deep sand in the infield making it prone to creating erratic bounces contributing to errors. The lighting was bad. Visiting managers from the third base dugout could barely see their right fielders. Sensitive to criticism by Ada columnist Charley Rhodes, Mike Hill of *The Daily Ardmoreite* wrote on June 15, 1947: "Tribe park was built in a hurry by a group of livewire businessmen when use of other parks was denied and the men did a fine job of getting it ready for the season to open." The criticism was valid though.

During the 1947 season, because of post-War shortages it was several weeks before a switch for the lights was obtained. Until then, an electrician had to scurry up the light poles to turn the lights off and on before and after each game. Clay was needed in the batter's box and mound. A fix would have to wait until 1948. When it came, new dugouts, a larger press box, and forty feet of additional stands were added. Before the 1948 season, Ardmore Athletic Association spent $3,000 on new concessions.

The Association financed the team's start up by selling up to three trust certificates per person for $100 each; $60 would go to upkeep of the team and $40 for season admission. Season tickets were $40 for sixty-eight games. Hoot Gibson, Ardmore Athletic Association treasurer, reported that after the first nineteen games of the season 7,819 adults and 654 children had attended. Revenue was approximately $5,000. Expenditures totaled $5,127.25. Those were comprised of salaries $3,700, lights and ball park rental $855, public address system $195, eleven dozen balls $162.25, and bats $225. Players were paid between $75 and $125 per month. The team saved the expense of a bus by traveling in private cars and taxis. That proved to be an object lesson in being penny-wise and pound-foolish.

Ragged as the play was, four Ardmore Indians appeared in the July 9, 1947, All-Star game against first-place Lawton: Prather, Card, Philley, and Kuver. Prather was ripping opposing pitchers at a .428 clip at mid-season. He had even won a couple of games using the rule book. On June 5, trailing by a run Ardmore was awarded a forfeit against Ada because there were eighteen Herefords in uniform. President Mealey later sustained Prather's protest of an 8-4 loss also at the hands of Ada on August 9. Catcher Mike Koepka had been taken out of the game but several innings later appeared as the Hereford's third base coach. Final score: Ardmore nine, Ada zero.

Ardmore's fans, like most others in the league, tipped players for home runs and outstanding performances. With the poor officiating, they backed their players. Noel Philley was fined $30, about one week's pay, as a result of an argument with an umpire. The fans passed the hat and raised $28. While it was against league rules for a team to pay a player's fine, there was nothing in the book about fans picking up the tab. Indians catcher Dick Patterson won the distinction of being the first player to be ejected from a Sooner State League game when he was sent to the showers in the second inning of the season opener against Ada. In beating Seminole 28-2 on June 12, the Indians' twenty-five hits and twenty-eight runs set a then-record for the league. The Indians ran wild against Duncan on June 26, stealing fifteen bases on former team mate Howard Dunn and former McAlester Rocket George Abbott. Robert Andrlik had five of those swipes. Prather could also bend the rules. He talked Duncan's Otto Utt into moving a home series against the Indians to Ardmore so Prather could attend the Oklahoma Jaycees convention being held there.

Attendance for the opening season was 27,943, fourth in the six team circuit, far above Duncan's 8,220 but considerably below Ada's 43,657. Ardmore Athletic Association lost about $2,000 in its first year of operation.

1948

Prather departed for the greener pasture of Pauls Valley to assume command of that city's new entry for the 1948 season taking with him the battery of Oscar Kuver and Colonel Stephens. The Ardmore nine struggled through 1948 with a sixth-place team and two managers.

Don Smith, who spent 1947 at Oklahoma City, was selected to try his hand at assembling and managing a team. The day before the season was to open, he had spent the morning in Marietta, Oklahoma, picking up a supply of bats and took receipt of a shipment of uniforms from Oklahoma City. After a four-hour workout, he opened the boxes to find that the ragged uniforms sent were in worse condition than the ones his players were wearing. He learned that the former owner of the Marshall, Texas, club had thirty-five sets of flannels. After running down the Indians' business manager who was in Hugo, Oklahoma, looking at a bus, he received the go ahead to buy them. Smith and Cleveland scout Hugh Alexander then drove the 140

miles to Paris, Texas, secured the uniforms and made it back to Ardmore at 2 p.m. on game day. With Mrs. Smith and a couple of tailors ripping off "M's" and sewing red on navy "A's", manager Smith made it to Tribe Park where he distributed jerseys and trousers then conducted pre-game drills. Sleepless for thirty-six hours, Smith took his place in right field. His two errors contributed to the 8-4 loss to Ada.

Four Indians had returned from the 1947 squad. Smith and Jim Cooke, who would succeed him on July 14, were the only veterans among the twelve position players and nine pitchers who wore the Indians' "A." Limited service players Bob Hutchinson and Lew Pilkington, who was injured in an exhibition game, were the only others who had appeared in a professional game. They assisted thirteen rookies to a sixth-place finish. This was a middle of the pack team hitting .260 and fielding .936 with weak pitching. Indicative of the pitching was Vern Glaser who was 3-3 in seven appearances. He gave up forty-six runs on fifty-one hits along with thirty-one walks in forty innings. He only hit four batters and uncorked but a single wild pitch.

The lighting system at Tribe Park always had been temperamental. Before one of the frequent power failures in 1948, Seminole had runners on second and third. When lights came back on, the bases were loaded. The umpires did not notice until the screaming Ardmore fans pointed to Oilers' manager Hugh Willingham on first base. The umpires chased him to the dugout.

The rule book table was turned on June 9, when Duncan manager Jess Welch got the Indians' acting manager ousted from the dugout. With Don Smith away at a funeral, Cleveland scout Red Alexander was substituting. Because he was not on the Ardmore roster, he was made to sit in the stands. Ardmore's 8-7 and 11-10 sweep of the Cementers on August 8 turned into a pair of 9-0 forfeit losses when Duncan manager Otto Utt protested that shortstop Jerry Whalen and pitcher Ken Johnson were not on the Indians' roster.

Smith at .303 and Cooke with a .285 average were the top hitters while the rest of the position players finished in the low- to mid .200s. The team managed only twenty-five home runs. Two pitchers had winning records: rookie Ernest Trujillo at 16-11 and carryover Charlie Githens at 5-1. Seventeen-year old Trujillo struck out nineteen Adans and walked only one on April 30, giving up two hits for a 5-3 win. Every Ada batter excepting two was a strike out victim. First baseman Bill Hughes, who hit .222 in 1947, tried pitching with some success. In his first start on May 2, he batted-in the tying and winning runs to nip McAlester 6-5 on twelve hits. He went 4-2 in 1948. A bright spot in an otherwise bleak season happened on the last day. The Indians ruined rookie pitching phenom, Buddy Yount's, perfect season by handing McAlester a loss in the finale. Despite the poor showing on the field, attendance was up by 10,000 to 37,944. Cleveland dropped Ardmore from its farm system because it had been informed

the Indians would not operate in 1949. The arrangement with Cleveland through Oklahoma City was never satisfactory and player aid was negligible.

What the Indians lacked under the ownership of the Athletic Association was a good working agreement, a bus, and a professional business manager. The club spent $4,700 on commercial buses and taxis getting to games. Cleveland stuck them with return train fare for players brought to Ardmore for spring training who were later released. At the end of the 1948 season, Ardmore Athletic Association had a $5,500.04 deficit and no way to pay it. On October, 24, 1948 the trust gave Prather, who had been fired at Pauls Valley and finished the season playing for Chickasha, a ten-day option to buy the franchise, equipment and contracts for $3,500. Industrial Ardmore, Inc., the business entity that had the ground lease and that owned Tribe Park, gave him a forty-day option to buy the facility for $10,724. Prather called a public meeting for October 26; fifty-eight showed up. Prather was unable to close the deal by himself.

The sixth place Ardmore Indians. The 1948 Indians in their "new" jerseys. The batboys are wearing the 1947 hand-me-downs. Manager Jimmie Cooke is on the far right, top row. Bill Upton, who appeared for the Philadelphia A's in 1954, is third from right on the top row. Other members are Hobart Campbell, Bill Creech, Bill Hughes, Marco Guglielmo, Bob Rose, Red Sollars, Pinky Patton, Barrett Sparks, Ernie Trujillo, Jerry Whalen, Vernon Brown, Denny Mitchell. The corrugated metal fence in the background indicates the picture was taken on the south, first base side of Tribe Park. (Ar-8)

1949

Out of that meeting a committee chaired by Ted Alderson was formed to acquire Prather's options. Members were Lloyd Roberts, Albert York, Bob Barnett, J. B. McCullough, Will Abram and Prather. John Judd of the First National Bank & Trust Company of Ardmore chaired a finance committee and bank trust officer Louis Bastin acted as secretary-treasurer. The committee raised $2,125 in cash at the meeting. It was resolved that Ardmore Baseball Club, Inc. be formed to acquire the franchise and lease. The company would offer one thousand shares at $25 each sold through Messrs. Judd and Bastin. Hugh A. Pruitt, a wholesale produce merchant, pledged $2,000. Other wealthy Ardmoreites there chipped in $3,000 more. They immediately asked the Ardmore City Commission for a bond election to build a new ball park. The articles of incorporation were filed and on November 29, an organizational meeting was held. Officers and directors were elected by those who had bought shares. Barnett, McCullough, and Roberts were elected to the board of directors as were Eddie Lotz and restaurateur Louis Priddy who would serve as president. Johnny Ferris was hired in March, 1949, as business manager. The board approved a working agreement with the Class B Sherman-Denison Twins of the Big State League, which in turn was affiliated with the Washington Senators.

Ardmore's Dutch Prather, unemployed as a manager since leaving Pauls Valley in the cellar, landed the job as the 1949 field general. The change of ownership meant that baseball would be played in 1949 but without a Major League affiliation. With Bill Hughes the only returning player from 1948, Prather was starting from scratch. During his attempt to buy the team, he had negotiated favorably with the Washington Senators whose main scout, Joe Cambria, kept a pipeline of roughly thirty-five

Cuban Lindbergh Chappoten managed to get on Prather's bad side and was sold to Duncan where he thrived through the 1950 move to Shawnee. Over-stocked with veterans, in 1952 he was traded to Texarkana for twenty sets of uniforms. (Ar-9)

Harold "Red" Sollars came to Ardmore in 1947 where he married a local girl. He worked in his father-in-law's plumbing business while earning a teaching certificate. He taught and coached at Ardmore High School as well as owning a sporting goods store. He moved his five daughters to Arizona in 1966 where all became teachers. (Ar-10)

The 135 pound stringbean from Caimguey, Cuba, Armin Somonte was 53-35 in three seasons at Ardmore and the only Sooner State League pitcher to hurl two no-hitters. (Ar-11)

Cuban players coming to Sherman-Denison. Lower classification teams were needed to absorb the overflow. Close to Sherman, Ardmore was a natural ally. Nine of the 1949 Indians were products of the Cambria system; their average age was nineteen and one-half. Prather remarked in spring training "It's bad enough to have to teach these boys baseball. But I've got to teach 'em English, too." Rookie Joe Nodar from Havana, the only one to speak any English, served as translator when the Dutchman could not make himself understood.

Lefty Armin Somonte and right-hander Lindy Chappoten were the aces of the pitching staff. Chappoten was 7-2 at Ardmore until released on July 14, while Somonte had thirteen each of wins and losses. Before the season, Prather had boasted that this pitching staff was the best in all Class D; the hurlers proved him wrong. The 1949 Indians were, relative to the rest of the league, an above-average hitting team at .254 and middle of the pack as far as pitching was concerned. They were not the most bobbling collection of fielders Ardmore ever put on a diamond but they were close. They committed 409 errors in 138 games for a .925 fielding percentage but managed two triple plays.

First baseman and pitcher Bill Hughes, was a fan favorite. When his daughter was born, the fans took a collection for a layette and hospital expenses. One time their support went too far. When umpire Jerry Pooler called him out at first base, Hughes, as the potential tying run, protested vociferously and got the boot. After the game, which Chickasha won 15-12, Ardmore fans milled around Pooler, threatening him physically. The visiting Chiefs surrounded him and escorted him to their bus. President Mealey fined the Ardmore team $150 for failing to provide adequate police protection and suspended Hughes for three games.

Prather could not make the team gel even after Red Sollars was sent down from Burlington. About all the Dutchman accomplished beyond thirty-eight RBIs was getting the Indians a second chance to win a game that had been lost to Seminole 5-4. Once again, a player who had left the game reappeared in a coaching box. A replay of the last half-inning of the game three weeks later did not change the result.

The only bright spot was rookie Armin Somonte's 6-0 seven-inning no-hitter against Pauls Valley on June 13. With the team in seventh place the Dutchman was fired on July 25 after the Indians had lost fourteen of their last seventeen games. Rookie Tom McVay, a July 15 graduate of Southeastern State College, was named interim manager. After two days, Duncan's former manager Jim Skidgel replaced him. Skidgel had managed Duncan from June 1 until July 12, between Ed Marleau and Hosea Pfeifer. After Duncan owner Otto Utt gave him the pink slip, he played fourteen games in the outfield for Ada. When Prather was fired, Skidgel solicited the Ardmore job and was allowed to switch to his third team of the season. The change didn't help. The Indians crawled across the line in seventh place.

As part of Prather's separation, the club bought his stock and elected three new directors in hope of improving the franchise's financial stability. Pruitt, shoe seller Raymond Hill, and appliance dealer Dewey Wood joined the five incumbents.

As an independent in 1949, the Ardmore team drew 43,348 who witnessed a 57-81 seventh-place finish. The management of Ardmore Baseball Club, Inc. announced in October of 1949 that the franchise would not operate in 1950 because of an operating deficit of over $5,000 comprised mainly of delinquent federal taxes. A drive to procure guarantors and new money to retire the accumulated debt secured pledges of over $8,000. A shareholders' meeting was held on November 17. Pruitt was present and presented a slate of directors to replace the incumbent board. Oilmen Ward Merrick and Leon Daube, Pruitt, Chevrolet dealer Claud Arnold, Hill, dairyman Ray Colvert, Gene Woerz and Floyd Allen of Ringling were nominated and elected by acclamation. That board never met. Apparently Pruitt had not gotten those gentlemen's consent to be nominated. Several of those elected declined to serve. None of the pledges were honored. The franchise had been turned back to the league.

Pitcher Mitch Chetkovich (left), owner Art Willingham and new manager Bennie Warren during pre-season drills. The Hardy Murphy Coliseum is in the background. Warren and Chetkovich were the only veterans in Ardmore's 1950 spring camp. Among his other tasks, Willingham drove the team bus. (Ar-12)

1950

As 1950 began, Ardmore Baseball Club owned equipment and uniforms, a bus, twelve player contracts, and Tribe Park on land leased by Industrial Ardmore, Inc. Industrial Ardmore had a mortgage on all of Ardmore Baseball Club's property to secure payment of the $8,000 owed on the Park. Arnold (not to be confused with 1950 University of Oklahoma quarterback Claude Arnold), the local Chevrolet dealer, speaking for the controlling interest of Ardmore Baseball Club announced that the property was for sale and that the assets would be offered to the highest bidder. The corporation had 397 shares outstanding. Proxies from 227 were collected authorizing a sale conditioned on keeping the team in Ardmore.

Arthur Willingham, of Sherman, Texas, who founded the first post-War Sherman-Denison team in 1946, made a no-cash offer to take out the owners by assuming the debt the Indians had accumulated. With nothing else on the table, on January 14, 1950, he became the new owner of the club by assuming $5,379 of team debt in a transaction that eliminated dissenting minority shares. Ardmore Baseball Club executed a deed in lieu of foreclosure to Industrial Ardmore that had the effect of extin-

Opening night 1950. Monty Stratton (in business suit), a friend of new team owner Art Willingham, threw out the first pitch of the 1950 season in Ardmore. Accompanying him to his right is Queen Nancy Dulaney and her attendants. Player escorts left to right are Stan York, Ernie Klein, and Joe Nodar. (Ar-13)

guishing the liens. Industrial Ardmore then leased Tribe Park to Willingham for $500 per month, he assumed the ground lease for $400, and agreed to pay insurance of $500. The transaction closed February 1, 1950. He named his son, Bob N. Willingham, to become the business manager and set up shop in the office of Willingham Drilling Company, 30 ½ N. Washington. Young Willingham did not last through spring training. Glenn Snyder, veteran of the Tulsa Oilers, Nashville Vols, and a 1946 player for Sherman, was named as playing business manager. He managed to hit .349 in 129 games and set the league record for doubles with fifty-eight.

Willingham, who held his own tryouts in Cuba, called the shots in the office while retired Major Leaguer Bennie Warren, who had settled in Oklahoma City, was signed to manage the 1950 edition of the Indians. Six Indians were back from 1949 including Cubans Ernesto Klein, Joe Nodar and Armin Somonte. In all, six of his players were Cuban. Many of the rest had prior ties to Willingham from his ownership of East Texas League and Big State League teams. Veteran pitcher Mitch Chetkovich, who had a cup of coffee with the Phillies in 1945, was 12-7 on the mound and led the throwers in batting at .323. A novel experiment at the end

Armin Somonte was a winner on Player Appreciation Night in 1950. Somonte is third from left. Others are L-R Bennie Warren, Justice of the Peace and announcer Puny sparger, Somonte, Joe Nodar, Jack Wilson, Marv Hochendorff, Ernesto Klein, and Maurice Bridge. (Ar-14)

of the season paid off. A double header on Labor Day was split with a morning game and an evening game. Both were well attended. The Ardmore independent went 75-65 in 1950 for a first-place finish before 44,454 fans, the highest attendance in Ardmore baseball history. Warren guided the Indians past Ada's talent-packed Herefords in the first round of the playoffs before losing the finals to McAlester's Rockets who were staffed by several future New York Yankees. Warren was named manager of the All Star team. Nodar led the team in batting with .349, Warren at .303 stroked twenty-one home runs, and John Wilson drove in 118 runs including nineteen home runs.

1951

With the Korean Conflict putting men in uniform, Ardmore had "draft insurance" in its connection with the Cambria Cuba pipeline and owner Willingham's connections on the island. A dozen Cubans were under contract when spring training began; nine of them made the team. Six were back from 1950. In terms of talent, this was the best team Ardmore fielded since the 1923 Snappers and 1925 Boomers of the Western Association.

Each Cuban player had a very good 1951 season. With them and the rest of the club, the Ardmore nine dominated the Sooner State. The team averaged 9.2 runs per game. The Indians led the league in seven categories —a .300 average, 1,289 runs, 1,475 hits, 2,115 total bases, 291 doubles, 1,107 walks and 1,073 RBIs. With 768, they struck out fewer times than any other club. At .950, the 1951 Indians had the best gloves of any Ardmore team. The pitching staff led with 1,062 strike outs, 104 complete games, and gave up only 600 walks, the league's fewest. The ERA was fourth at 4.24, and runs-per-game average was 5.3 but the batters gave the pitchers an average margin of nearly four runs.

Armin Somonte, All Star left hander, was 24-11 with a 2.82 ERA, a league record 341 strike outs and five shut outs to his credit including his second no-hitter, a 18-0 thrashing of Lawton on August 8. Harold Warren, Bennie's nephew, was 22-5 completing twenty-five games and giving up only 3.51 earned runs per nine innings. All Star outfielder Joe Nodar hit .328 while Havana native and fellow Cuban Ernesto Klein hit .301. Bennie Warren's .354 with twenty-two home runs plus his .991 average behind the plate with no passed balls in 101 games landed him a spot on the All Star team. Rookie second sacker Manuel Temes earned an All Star spot by tying for the league lead with 195 hits and 155 RBIs and averaging .340 at the plate. The Indians won the regular season pennant going away with a 99-40 record and a winning percentage of .712. After eliminating Pauls Valley in a three game sweep, the Indians could not shake the McAlester hex losing the finals to the fourth -place Rockets four games to two. Four Indians were named to the All Star team: Warren as catcher and Cubans at second

base, center field, and on the mound. Attendance, however, slipped to 40,742.

In 1951, the Ardmore business community sold $1,475 worth of ticket books, the fans raised $1,650 for the players' fund, and Waco Turner handed out $1,800 in cash performance bonuses to players. Success on the field and at the gate did not overcome the glaring defect in the franchise: Tribe Park. When Art Willingham acquired the franchise in 1950, he also leased Tribe Park and had a sublease on the ground. After two seasons, Willingham cited the strain of commuting between Sherman and Ardmore as a reason to sell the team. He delivered an ultimatum to the citizens of Ardmore: provide a new ball park or Ardmore would lose its team. When the voters turned down a $75,000 bond issue by seventy-one votes of 2,100 cast—Oklahoma requires a sixty percent vote—in the December, 1951 election, the fate of Ardmore baseball, at least in the current incarnation, was sealed. At the January, 1952 League meeting, Willingham was granted approval to move his franchise to his hometown.

With seven Cubans, the 1951 Ardmore Indians won the regular season setting a league record for wins. L-R Top row: Orel Dryden, Jack Rose, Lloyd Stout, Darrell Pierce, Glen Groomes, Ernesto Klein, Craig Whitstone, Glenn Snyder, manager Bennie Warren, owner Arthur Willingham, announcer Puny Sparger, Maurice Bridge. Front row: Harold Warren, Jack Fuller, Osmaro Blanco, Joe Nodar, Hector Bonet, Armin Somonte, Manuel Caldaso, Manuel Temes. (Ar-15)

Sherman, Texas, had become an open territory when Arturo Gonzalez moved his Class B Twins to Paris after the 1951 season. Ardmore was without professional baseball.

1952

Ardmore was not the only Sooner State League city to have a franchise in jeopardy. On January 14, 1952, Fred "the Ironman" McDuff surrendered his Seminole franchise back to the league after a touted sale to a local buyer fell through and valiant efforts of local baseball man Hugh Willingham came to naught. McDuff had saved baseball in Seminole in August, 1950 but as an independent could not assemble the talent nor the support to sustain "McDuff's Seminole Ironmen" beyond 1951. Duncan, without baseball since Otto Utt moved his Uttman to Shawnee at the end of the 1950 season, and Gainesville and Paris, Texas, each of whom had lost their Big State League clubs, as well as Ardmore —two weeks after Art Willingham moved the Indians —were bidding for the right to join or re-join the league. A trio of Ardmore business and professional men, Marietta jeweler W. C. Peden, attorney Lester Cooke, and American Legion executive and machine shop operator A. P. "Pink" Shuman, appeared before a committee of league owners in Sherman. Based on their promise to build a $75,000 ball park before the 1953 season, Ardmore landed the franchise by four votes to three. The league approved the move on January 27, 1952. The worst team in Seminole's history was about to become the worst Ardmore ever fielded.

The new Ardmore Indians started with less than McDuff did. None of the 1951 Ironmen appeared on the Ardmore roster; the most talented of those had signed with Shawnee. In fact, the only player from the 1951 Indians to play at Tribe Park in 1952 was Havana's Ernesto Klein whom

Ernesto Klein Wallerstein was a child of Hungarian Jewish immigrants to Havana. A product of the Joe Cambria system, he appeared for Ardmore between 1948 and 1952 where he played third base. An injury in early 1953 ended his playing career. (Ar-16)

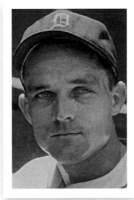

Jackie Sullivan had a cup of coffee with Detroit in 1944. He quit as Ardmore's 1952 manager a few weeks into the season when the club refused to break league rules and pay a $25 fine he incurred for baiting an umpire. He returned to the West Texas-New Mexico League. (Ar-17)

independent Vernon, Texas, returned after forty-six games. Five-year old Tribe Park was run down and deserved all the criticism the past tenant, Art Willingham, heaped on it. The Cuban connection was cut off with the new Sherman Twins assuming Ardmore's place in the Cambria queue.

Carl "Jackie" Sullivan, a hot-tempered second baseman who consistently hit over .300 in Class D, was hired to assemble a club as a non-playing manager. Of the thirty-one who appeared for the 1952 Indians, ten were rookies who never got through the season or were discards from another Class D team. For five more, Ardmore was where their careers ended. Only one player, rookie Glen Crable with a 13-14 record and 4.39 ERA, made it to the AAA level. Only three of the 1952 Indians were in Organized Baseball in 1956.

The 1952 season was plagued from the start. Joe Nodar had run a tryout camp in Havana and sent the Indians seven players. Sullivan scouted all over north Texas and picked the best he could find from a tryout camp at Farmersville. The Cubans

Waco Turner made and lost fortunes. His Daisy Bradford No. 3 well in the East Texas field with hundreds of surrounding acres sealed his success. He saved baseball in Ardmore following a disastrous 1952 season. (Ar-18)

and the rookie cowboys with veterans Sullivan and Royce Mills formed the 1952 Indians. Twenty-two pitchers appeared in fewer than twenty-seven innings. Fourteen position players saw action in fewer than ten games. The team went from first in 1951 to last in every category in 1952. The club's .245 batting average complimented having the fewest hits, runs, total bases, triples, RBIs and the most strike outs. With 430 errors, the 1952 team's .923 fielding average bested the ball-bobbling 1950 Indians for the worst.

Sullivan was fined $25 for arguing with an umpire on April 30. He quit as manager in a pique May 2 when the team would not break league rules and pay it. Veteran pitcher Mills, who came over from Lubbock with Sullivan, served in the dugout for three days until Hugh Willingham could trade his deputy sheriff's uniform for Ardmore flannels. He gave up on July 8. In his third season, limited service pitcher Clyde Baldwin took over for a week then went on the disabled list. Pitcher Julian Morgan, who had been in Organized Ball since 1938, became the fifth field leader on July 13.

On the field, Charlie Rabe of Lawton had Ardmore's number. He threw eighteen consecutive hitless, scoreless innings against them on June 20 and June 24. The first nine innings were in relief. The second was a 2-0 gem. Bennie Warren, now at the helm of Sherman, gave his old club a remembrance on August 31, when he hit a grand slam out of Tribe Park.

The fans responded by staying away. Attendance dropped to 24,362 from 40,742 the previous year. W.C. Peden, president of the club, announced that the team was for sale after finishing the 1952 season $5,000 in the red. The Ardmore Chamber of Commerce launched a campaign to raise $20,000.

The franchise lacked the cash for train or even bus tickets home for the 1952 Indians who finished the season. In a post-season exhibition to raise travel expenses for the players, Ardmore traveled to Blackwell where the Indians won the "Booby Bowl" 5-4 in eleven innings against the Blackwell Broncos, fifth-place finisher in the K-O-M League's final season.

1953

Peden called a public meeting for November 13, 1952, to decide the fate of baseball in Ardmore. Oil millionaire Waco Turner came to the rescue bringing an entrepreneur's energy and acumen and, of most immediate need, money. He became president of Ardmore Baseball Association and immediately began a search for a working agreement. He hired *The Daily Ardmoreite* city editor Bill Hamilton to serve as business manager; he become Turner's sports captain. Quickly Ardmore became the seventh Class D team in the St. Louis Cardinals' farm system and with that a stream of good players flowed south. The word at the Cardinals' Albany, Georgia, spring camp was that a player wanted to be on Waco's team. Turner's wife, Opie, set up a lucrative bonus system. Bennie Warren, who led the 1951 Indians to the best Ardmore record ever and the playoff finals, was hired away from the Willingham organization. The team began the season as the Indians. After Waco Turner jawboned the St. Louis front office for new uniforms identical to the National League club the Indians became Cardinals. The 1953 team responded with one of the best records in Ardmore baseball history and the among the highest attendances.

When Waco Turner succeeded W.C. Peden as president of the ball club in the fall of 1952, he accelerated planned improvements to Tribe Park to put the facility in condition for an April 6, 1953, exhibition game between the St. Louis Browns and the Chicago Cubs who were returning together from spring training in California. He doubled the ca-

pacity by adding new boxes at field level, extended the grandstand, added bleachers on both ends, built concrete dugouts, quadrupled the size of the press box, and built two new clubhouses for the players. Turner moved his crews from the golf course at Dornick Hills Country Club to put the playing surface in its best condition ever. When an inch of rain fell the evening before the exhibition, Turner had a tank truck driven to the field. A drilling crew soaked the infield dirt with dozens of barrels of gasoline and then lit it. The infield was baked dry for the Major Leaguers.

Bennie Warren of Oklahoma City played for the Phillies and Giants between 1938 and 1947 with a detour to Norman, Oklahoma to play for the Navy's Skyjackets. He managed Ardmore in 1950 and 1951 and again in 1953 and part of 1954. He followed Art Willingham to Sherman for 1952. After Ardmore released him, he took the helm of Pauls Valley for the balance of the 1954 season. (Ar-19)

Ageless Satchel Paige played his last Major League season with the 1953 St. Louis Browns. When the charter train carrying the Browns and Cubs pulled into Ardmore, all the players were escorted to the Hotel Ardmore for a luncheon and a little pre-game glad-handing. All, that is, except Satchel Paige, the only African-American on either squad. Jim Crow was the law and custom in Oklahoma and Ardmore was no exception. Paige was escorted east from the train station by the Ardmore Colored Chamber of Commerce, which had purchased five hundred tickets for the game, for his rest before starting the afternoon contest.

Two of the hapless 1952 Indians appeared for the 1953 Cardinals, light hitting Bob Folkert, who retired after the season, and Glen Crable who was at 13-14 the best hurler of 1952; he was 17-13 in 1953. Tom Anderson, who played semi-pro ball for Marietta, Oklahoma, in 1952, came back to Ardmore with the club from spring training in Albany, Georgia, but was released the day before the season began; Ardmore had a surplus of outfielders. Anderson remained as the team's bus driver and trainer for five seasons. Future Major Leaguers Jackie Brandt, Bob Blaylock, and Marty Kutyna toiled for the Cardinals' 1953 farm club. At .270

An early season photo of the 1953 Ardmore club. Waco Turner (standing right) and his wife Otie (top left) outfitted them in new flannels with the name "Indians." (Ar-20)

they tied with Ada for the highest team average and outscored opponents 1,004 to 763. Al Viotta's .385 batting average was good enough only for second place in the league competition behind McAlester's Russ Snyder's Silver Bat winning .432, the best in all the minors. The pitching staff's collective 4.38 ERA was balanced but not outstanding. Fielding at .939 was good enough for fifth. In the most important category, however, at 91-46 the Indians finished the campaign six games up on Shawnee. A competitive pennant race that Ardmore won put attendance up by nearly 20,000 over 1952.

Jim Farmer tied the league record for walks on May 27 with twenty-one; coupled with ten Shawnee hits, he dropped the decision 22-4. Blaylock, a seventeen-year old who joined the club in June fresh from Muldrow, Oklahoma, High School, recovered from being hit in the face by a line drive off the bat of Sherman-Denison's Van Anthony on July 9, to

Turner twisted the parent Cardinals' wings to dress his rookies in the same togs as the St. Louis club. Those would be worn through 1957. (Ar-21)

finish the season 9-1 with a 3.48 ERA. Outfielder Al Viotta exacted some revenge near the end of the season when he sent Anthony to the hospital for facial stitches while stealing home. Ardmore won a protest of the July 31 game McAlester had won on the field when rookie catcher Don Saatzer conferred with Rockets' manager Bill Cope who was sitting in the box seats because of an indefinite suspension he had earned for shoving an umpire the previous game. On August 5, rookie Roy "Peanuts" Moore treated the home town fans to a no-hitter against Sherman-Denison. He pitched around five errors but lost the shutout when he gave up seven walks to let three Twins cross the plate in the ninth inning for a 7-3 Indians victory.

Rookie Jackie Brandt, who received a $150 signing bonus and $200 per month, was hitting .342 at mid-season earning a place on the All Star team along with manager Warren and Viotta, who led the league in runs and RBIs. McAlester extended its playoff *gris gris* against Ardmore, eliminating the Cardinals in the first round.

1954

Bennie Warren was back at the helm as the 1954 season began. Things got off to a rough start on the field. Nature rained out five games. Manager Warren and pitcher Peanuts Moore were ejected for arguing on May 3; Moore with a sore arm was soon released and finished his career with Pauls Valley. The home team won 6-5. In the same game, umpire Leo Hanning cleared the Ardmore bench in the seventh inning for heckling. Late May was particularly rough. Bucking league rules, Waco Turner ordered that ticket price be dropped a third to 50¢ after attendance lagged. With the Cardinals in seventh place and not yet having won twenty games, the parent Cardinals fired Warren on June 15, and brought in Frank Mancuso.

All Star and future Major Leaguer Gene Green hit five of his thirty-four home runs against Shawnee on July 15 and July 16 driving in seven runs. By August 5, the Cardinals had only climbed to sixth place at 50-57. A week later they had passed Ada for fifth at 55-59. By season end, the 72-67 Cardi-

Frank Mancuso caught for the American League champion St. Louis Browns. After replacing Bennie Warren, he led the Cardinals through the 1955 campaign. He served over thirty years on the Houston, Texas city council before finally hanging up his spikes. (Ar-22)

Mancuso's 1954 club finished fourth and eliminated first-place Shawnee in the opening round of the play-offs. Hall of Famer Travis Jackson's Lawton Braves swept the little Redbirds in the finals. Gene Green (top row second from left) spent all or part of seven seasons in the Major Leagues. (Ar-23)

nals had edged out the 72-68 Gainesville Owls by one-half game for fourth place. President Clanton ordered that Lawton and Ardmore play a rained out game since the Owls had played one more game. National Association president George Trautman overruled Clanton and declared Ardmore was the sole occupant of fourth and in the playoff. His rationale was that game must be made up only if there were a tie for fourth place. In the first playoff round, the Cardinals whipped Shawnee, regular season winner by ten and one-half games, but were swept in the finals by Lawton in the little Braves' first year working with Milwaukee.

A team batting average of .285 along with leading the league with 2,337 total bases and 191 home runs were only good enough to place third in hitting during the 1954 season. Shawnee ran

away with the pennant. The Ardmore bats were good enough to make up for the shabby fielding —.932 with 354 errors— and second division 5.37 ERA pitching. The pitching staff led the league only in balks. As 1954 attendance tumbled to 31,090, club president Waco Turner announced the team's demise. As close acquaintances of Turner repeated, baseball would be a big hit in Ardmore or Waco would not be in the game long; he has no use for a lemon. The board of directors voted to close down the franchise as of October 1. Turner returned the working agreement for the 1955 season and cancelled the planned exhibition between St. Louis and the Chicago White Sox on April 5, 1955.

Tom Anderson of Marietta nearly made the 1953 club. Waco Turner offered him job security with the ball club where he remained as trainer and driver through 1957. (Ar-24)

1955

Something happened in the next two weeks; perhaps Turner called on St. Louis owner Augustus Busch. In any event, the working agreement was revived and the Ardmore Cardinals were good to go for 1955. The cancellation of the exhibition stood.

Frank Mancuso was re-hired. St. Louis, however, sent down a second division club. Fifth in the final standings, the Cardinals' .241 was sixth in batting despite 115 home runs, seventh in pitching with a team 4.57 ERA, and barely third in fielding at .943. Mike O'Conner set a then-league record for strike outs in a nine-inning game: twenty-one on July 1 against Ponca City. By identical scores of 2-1, the Cardinals swept Shawnee on May 25. Idabel, Oklahoma, native Charlie Purtle got his twentieth win August 19, despite giving up fourteen hits, 9-7 over Ponca City. He had been deprived of a no-hitter earlier in the season when McAlester stroked a single in the top of the ninth inning. Roger Cook threw a one-hitter against McAlester on August 26, winning 6-0. With Seminole leading 5-3, an eighth-inning Mancuso rhubarb with plate umpire Leo Hanning resulted in forfeiture on September 1. The Cardinals lost big in the last game of the season 28-5. Bob Dennis, Lawton third baseman, had seven hits, eighteen total bases and twelve RBIs on the way to setting three all-time league records.

Only 33,731 Ardmoreites passed through the gates at Boundary and Washington Street in 1955. Perhaps the poor attendance was a sign of bad karma resulting from a fan stealing Paris catcher Rob Sternper's glove and $25 from the visitor's dugout on May 6. Maybe it was the fifth-place finish thirty and one-half games out. Whatever it was, Waco Turner walked away. New management led by A.P. "Pink" Shuman, who was promptly elected to the league's board of control, re-signed with St. Louis.

Talk of a new ball park came with each season. A one-year extension of the ground lease was obtained for the 1955 season. After that campaign, the Ardmore School Board, which had become the landowner, made the ball club's decision about looking for a new home field for the Cardinals when they decided to build Will Rogers Elementary School on the site of Tribe Park.

The fifth-place 1955 Cardinals were the last to play at Washington and Boundary. None ever saw the inside of a Major League club house. (Ar-25)

1956

Waco Turner had expended a huge amount of energy and treasure to take Dornick Hills Country Club from a bankrupt, poorly maintained links to the host of a regular stop on the PGA tour. A turf fight on the country club's board and his expulsion as both president and a member caused him to figuratively kick the dust of Ardmore off his boots. He had begun building his own country club, Burneyville golf resort, in late 1955.

Occupied with golf, he relinquished the presidency of the ball club to Shuman in December, 1955. Austin Smith, Felix Simmons, and Earle Garrison joined him as officers. C. P. Sebastian was hired as business manager and would remain in that role through the 1961 season of the Rosebuds. The next month the Community Youth Foundation

broke ground for the new ball park on property at the east end of Main Street Shuman had located and Turner, Leon Daube, and Ward Merrick had purchased. Oklahoma Governor Raymond Gary and league president George Barr were in attendance to celebrate the new ball park when the Cardinals and Lawton played the first game there on April 24, 1956. The Braves ruined Ardmore's debut at home blanking the Redbirds 5-0 on four hits.

The parent Cardinals reached into the lower levels of its farm system for the last manager of the Ardmore club, J.C. Dunn. At age thirty, he had been a successful teacher of the game as well as a hard hitting Class D first baseman. Having attained the AAA level, a serious injury ended his hope of reaching the Show.

Dunn's 1956 charges got off to a slow start, languishing in the second division the first month of the season. Mental lapses plagued the young

J. C. Dunn led the Cardinals including a first-place finish in 1956 and sweep of the play-offs in 1957. He had a last hurrah at the end of the 1961 season with the Rosebuds. Dunn survived gunshot wounds from a Ponca city hotel porter in a much-reported 1957 incident. He taught shop and coached baseball at Ardmore High School until murdered in October, 1973. The crime remains unsolved. (Ar-26)

The 1956 edition won the regular season crown before dropping the play-off final to the "Miracle" Seminole Oilers. L-R Top row: Jim Henric, John Bartek, Walt Matthews, Gene Oliver, manager J. C. Dunn, Larry Riggs, Phil Jantze, Jim Turk, Dick Wodka. Fornt row: Ron Voyles, Ron Ott, Pete Aviotti, Bob Stangel, Vince Kipela, Curt Jantze, Jim Bradley, Tom Fassler. Batboys: Ray Filippi (L) John Saunders (R). A taller Saunders would also serve as the batboy for the Ardmore Rosebuds in 1961. (Ar-27)

players. Jim Bradley, who was a rookie at McAlester in 1952, lost a home run on June 8, when he failed to touch home plate. Gene Oliver, who would begin a ten-year Major League career in 1959, knocked one out of Cardinal Park on June 20, with a man on first. That man was manager Dunn who was holding to see whether the ball would clear the fence. Oliver was supremely confident and ran past Dunn. Dunn was still on first while Oliver was called out and credited with a single. Then the Redbirds charged, led by Bobby Stangel's fifteen-game hitting streak and thirty-seven stolen bases and Dick Wodka's ten wins, to take over first place by mid-season They never looked back to finish three and one-half games ahead of Lawton with an 83-56 record. Regular season attendance jumped to 47, 110, 56,052 counting the playoffs.

Dunn hit for the cycle on August 6, driving in seven runs while Oliver had a home run, double, and two singles and six RBIs to crush second-place Lawton 22-5. At Appreciation Night on September 1, the fans presented Dunn with $1,000 and the team reciprocated with Gene Oliver hitting his thirty-ninth home run, tying a league record, and John Bartek becoming the only twenty-game winner in the league as they clinched the pennant with a 5-3 win over Lawton. It was like the good old days of Bennie Warren's Indians.

Ardmore led the league in most hitting categories —runs, hits, total bases, doubles, home runs, and RBIs— despite a .273 team average, middling most years but the best in a well-balanced League in 1956. It was a good fielding team with a .9427 average and errors per game down to a manageable 2.2. The Cardinals should attribute their regular season finish by three and one-half games over Lawton to their regular season dominance over McAlester with wins in sixteen of nineteen contests.

Three of the top ten Sooner State hitters were members of the Cardinals. Phil Jantze hit .343, Dunn .336, and Oliver .334. Pitchers John Bartek

finished 21-6, Wodka 15-9, Turk 15-9, and Vince "the Finn" Kipela 14-9. The staff ERA was 4.39. Aviotti, Jantze, Oliver, and Bartek were named to the All Star team. Vince Kipela led the league with 276 strike outs and set a league fielding record with no errors in 231 innings, a perfect 1.000.

The Cardinals edged a strong fourth-place Paris team to reach the 1956 finals against Seminole. Burl Storie's light-hitting but hard throwing Oilers —the team's batting average was .248, ERA was 4.23— came from last place in July to finish third. They were not to be denied. They put away Ardmore 16-5 in the seventh game of the final series on September 16, to win the only championship for that franchise and the second flag for the city of Seminole.

Dunn and club president A. P. Shuman before the Cardinals opened on the road at Lawton. (Ar-28)

1957

J.C. Dunn was back at the helm for the shortened 126-game 1957 season. Teams were allowed sixteen members with two veterans, up to six limited service players, and at least eight rookies. The season had been shortened to avoid the rain that had plagued the early weeks of the prior two seasons. On May 1, three of four openers, including the game at Ardmore, were rained out.

The Cardinals jumped into second place on May 9, when they snapped newcomer Greenville's six-game opening winning streak, and then went on to win five in a row before Shawnee's Hawks knocked the Cardinals from the air 7-4 on May 12. On May 15, St. Louis native and starter Tom Fassler drove in five runs with a triple and a single before being relieved in the sixth. Reliever John McFadden added two singles and two RBIs to save Fassler's first win 14-2 over Lawton. Four errors and nine hits in the fourth inning gave Shawnee a 15-4 win over the Cardinals on May 19. Left hander Don Mitchell threw eighteen scoreless innings before Seminole tagged him for four runs on May 21; he managed to hold on for an 11-4 win putting Ardmore in first place. In his next start on May 27, he dropped a twelve-inning match to Muskogee. The next day, Fassler gave up four runs in the first inning. Dunn sent Bill Dikeman to warm up. Dunn went to the mound a couple of times to make more time for his reliever to get loose. The umpire accused him of delaying the game. Dunn characteristically disagreed. The result was a 9-0 loss to Muskogee on a forfeit and a tumble to second behind the little Giants.

Ardmore's mastery over Yankee farm teams came to an end on June 20, when the Greenville Majors hit past the Cardinals 6-1. McAlester had dropped thirty-six straight in Tribe Park and Cardinal Park since 1953. The Majors had lost the first two there in 1957. After that Ardmore caught fire. Winning five of six from second-place Muskogee in a July 17-21 series and scoring sixty-six runs, the Cardinals went to 54-26, ten games ahead of the pack. The Giants trailed 44-36, a half-game ahead of Paris at 43-36. Losing five straight to Greenville, Ardmore's lead was cut to one and one-half game over Paris before rallying to go seven and one-half games up on August 6.

Two nights later, manager Dunn was shot twice by an angry hotel porter who was gunning for cen-ter fielder Coy Smith. The night before, Ardmore had lost to the Ponca City Cubs on future Hall of Famer Billy Williams' walk off single. Returning to the hotel in Ponca City, several of the players procured through the elevator operator-porter the services of a couple of ladies of the night. There was a dispute over terms of payment and the Ardmore players, out-numbering the porter, beat and kicked him. Outfielder and All Star Coy Smith was the ring leader. The porter promised them that "I'll get you." The next evening during the second inning, Dunn was returning to the Cardinals' dugout after scoring. The porter fired several shots intended for Smith, who set out running when he saw the as-sailant, but hit Dunn. With bullets in his left breast and upper right leg, Dunn went to the hospital and everyone else to the showers; the game was contin-ued the next evening.

With veteran scout and manager Mike Ryba as interim leader, the Redbirds lost seventeen of their last thirty games including those after Dunn's return on August 22. Ardmore lost five of eight to Lawton with the August 28 loss foreclosing a first-place finish. Paris edged them by one-half game for the regular season crown.

In the first playoff round, Dunn had two dou-bles and a single to pace his Cardinals to a 10-4 win over Muskogee. On Appreciation Night at Ardmore, he had four hits including a home run for a come-from-behind 10-9 win. The sweep was completed with a 5-4 victory at Muskogee.

Paris, the winner over Shawnee, faced Ardmore in the finals. In the first match at Paris, J. C. Dunn broke open the game in the ninth inning with a three-run blast, followed by Jim McKnight's solo homer for an 8-3 win. The Cards won game two 10-5 on Dunn's three RBIs and McFadden's relief. Back in Cardinal Park, the home team clipped the Orioles 10-8 with McKnight's five RBIs and Dunn's home run. On September 10, Norman Frye, 11-7 during the season, handcuffed Paris on four hits to win 6-1. The championship clincher was Frye's last professional game, the last Ardmore Cardinals game, and the last Sooner State League game.

Statistically the 1957 Ardmore Cardinals team did not look like a champion. While 718 runs and one hundred stolen bases led the league, the team hit only .265. The power that had carried the team in past years was absent in 1957; only eighty-one balls cleared the short league fences. Jim McKnight led the league by batting .341 and driving in 112 runs. The best-fielding Ardmore team since 1951, its .94504 average was only sixth. The pitching staff failed to lead the league in any category and finished barely third with a 4.11 ERA. Keller, 15-6, was the only hurler to finish in the league's top ten with a 3.20 ERA.

The owners agreed to suspend Sooner State League play in 1958 with hope of reconfiguring. As the Minor Leagues consolidated and farm systems shrank, the last Class D league west of the Mississippi quietly disbanded in February, 1959. The baseball organization in Ardmore remained alive with Tom Anderson succeeding C. P. Sebastian as business manager in January, 1958, and Pink Shuman remaining as president. In 1961, their tenacity was rewarded.

1961

Oil and ranching millionaire Tom O'Connor, Jr., tired after three seasons of losing money, sold the Class AA Texas League Victoria, Texas, ballclub to Derrest Williams after the 1960 season. Williams, who had played semi-pro ball and owned and managed at Texas City, had been the general manager of the "Rosebuds." The team was so named because Victoria was known as the "Rose City" on account of the rose garden in Riverside Park (where the ballpark was located), and the Victoria teams in the early part of the century had borne that moniker.

Closing the transfer of the Rosebuds. Top: C. P. Sebastian, Derrest Williams, Ardmore City Manager. Seated: A. P. Shuman. (Ar-13)

Williams scrambled to secure a working agreement after Detroit moved its AA farm elsewhere. On April 4 he told the Victoria 'Buds Boosters that Ardmore interests had offered $100,000 for him to move the team. Williams said he demurred because he wanted to keep the team in Victoria even though season ticket sales were $20,000 under 1960. The first five weeks of the 1961 season saw attendance at Riverside Park plummet to unsustainable lows. In twenty-four home dates at Victoria, the Rosebuds drew 12,969. Without the 1,664 at the season opener and 1,392 at the swansong on May 26, attendance averaged 314, poor for even a Class D team. Williams, losing $500 per night, obtained permission to quickly move the team to Ardmore, Oklahoma. The 1961 Rosebuds left Victoria for good after winning a 10-3 contest over Tulsa on May 26. The next day the move to Ardmore became official while on a road trip to Tulsa.

On May 27, the Ardmore Baseball Association, which had owned the Class D Cardinals in the Sooner State League, opened for business as operator of the Ardmore Rosebuds. A. P. "Pink" Shuman remained president of the group. Jack Caro, who had begun the season on the Rosebud's roster, followed the franchise to Ardmore as business manager; Williams, who retained ownership of the franchise, remained in Victoria with his beer distributorships. Offices were set up in the lobby of the Hotel Ardmore. Ardmore's population at 21,000 was 50,000 smaller than Victoria.

Except for the 1952 season, Ardmore's Sooner State League teams had drawn between 31,000 and 47,000. Attendance between Victoria (12,969) and Ardmore (35, 925) would be 48,894. To prove that Ardmore could support a higher class of baseball, Shuman had arranged for the Houston Buffaloes to

George Staller managed the Rosebuds. He had appeared briefly with the Athletics during the War years. (Ar-30)

play the Tulsa Oilers in a 1958 regular season game. The contest drew an overflow 3,100 Ardmoreites to Cardinal Park. While by far the smallest city in the Texas League, 1961 Ardmore attendance numbers beat the last place drawing team, Jimmy Humphries' Rio Grande Valley Giants who relocated to the now-open city of Victoria in June.

Ardmore was not a strange place, however, for five players who had spent time in the Sooner State League. Both Dennis Loudenback and Al Owen appeared for the 1956 Ponca City Cubs. Jim "Rube" Melton played his rookie year, 1949, at Pauls Valley where he was an All Star with a 23-8 record. Pitcher Marshall Renfroe spent the 1956 and 1957 seasons as a Yankees' farmhand at McAlester and Greenville. The 1956 and 1957 Ardmore Cardinals' player-manager, J.C. Dunn, following serving the same role at Dothan of the Alabama-Florida League from 1958 through 1960, had his second look at pitching above the Class B level. Coming in for the last four games of the season after Mickey McGuire was called up to Rochester of the International League, he hung up his spikes after batting .188 with no home runs or RBIs in sixteen at bats.

The Ardmore Rosebuds made their first home appearance at expanded 2,800-seat Cardinal Park on Sunday, June 4. Under threatening skies, 1,441 watched the Austin Senators top the Rosebuds 5-3 with the wildness of former Senator Mike Marinko accounting for the margin of victory

All was not copacetic, however. Referring to fan complaints about the club preventing bleacher fans who paid 75¢ for a seat moving to the $1.25 grandstand *gratis* and the policy of making fans return foul balls hit into the stands, *The Daily Ardmoreite* sports editor Doyle May wrote "We never thought we'd see the day when Ardmore fans would use such petty excuses to stay away from a game." It was fairly easy to move around Cardinal Park since the bleacher area was nearly indistinguishable from the general admission seats in the grandstand. Only restricted admittance to the box seats was enforced. As to foul balls, nearly every ball that did not land in fair territory landed outside of the park. There were always a dozen or so youths —mostly from the neighborhood— standing in the west parking lot ready to chase fouls and earn a free pass upon return of the errant ball.

The year 1961 saw the Rosebuds affiliated with Baltimore of the American League. The Orioles were unique in 1961 by having working agreements with two Class AA teams, a limited one with Victoria and a full one with the Little Rocker Travelers of the Southern Association. With a long tradition, better facilities, and better travel connections, Little Rock was the favored farm club.

George Staller, who played for fifteen years including twenty-one games with the Athletics in 1943, managed the club. The eighteen team members who came over from Victoria were catchers Jim Carver and Ken Worley, first basemen Clint McCord and Bob Nelson, second baseman Dennis Loudenback, third baseman Charlie Strange, shortstop Mickey McGuire, utility man Al Owen, left fielder Al Nagel, center fielder Bill Parsons, right fielder Jim Fridley, and pitchers Alex Castro, George Gaffney, Don McLeod, Buster Narum, Merlin Nippert, Marshall Renfroe, and John Stokoe.

Following the move, Art Burnett came over from Tulsa and stayed for twenty-nine games before he was sent down to Greenville S.C. in the Sally League and then to finish the season for Monterrey of the Mexican League. Joining the Ardmore squad on June 14 from Little Rock were Pete Ward and bonus baby pitcher John Papa; Worley and three-year Rosebud veteran Parsons were released to make room for the new arrivals. Roger Kudron of the Travelers joined them three weeks later. Bill "Turkey" Thompson came in a trade that sent Jim Fridley to Mobile of the Southern Association

on June 22. Atoka's Billy Joe Dasher, a University of Tulsa student, was acquired from Topeka and reported on June 7; he was released on July 1, re-signed August 10, and then sold to Birmingham three days later. Bob Nelson was sent down to Stockton to make room for pitcher Mike Marinko on loan from Austin. Sooner State League veteran Jim "Rube" Melton of Pauls Valley signed as a free agent for a four-game look-see; he did not stick. Veteran Dick Ewin appeared in twenty-three games hitting .196 before the Rosebuds released him. San Antonio sent 1960 Texas League home run champion Duke Ducote on June 22, just one week after he was demoted from AAA Houston. Catcher Frank Zupo was sent down from Rochester on July 20. In August, the Milwaukee Braves reassigned their farm hands John Stokoe to Eau Claire, Wisconsin, of the

Frank Zupo was a bonus baby in whom the Orioles had a large investment and hope that he would succeed All-Star catcher Gus Triandos. He never made it as a Big League hitter. He finished pro ball as a Kansas City A's property with Dallas of the Pacific Coast League. (Ar-31)

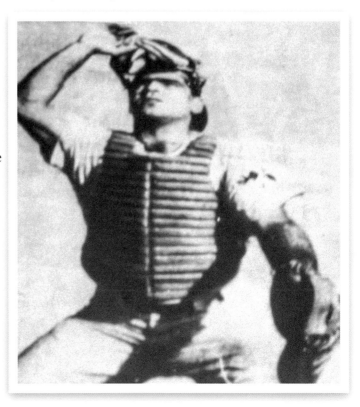

Al Nagel hit four home runs in the Ardmore Rosebud's first series on the road at Amarillo. After part time play in Vancouver in 1962, he retired from the game. (Ar-32)

Pete Ward had the most success season among the Rosebuds. He followed nine major League seasons with eight as a minor league manager. (Ar-33)

Northern League and Marinko to Macon, Georgia, of the Southern Association, leaving the Rosebuds short-handed.

Four members of the squad had some limited Major League experience: Jim Fridley with Cleveland in 1952, Baltimore in 1954, and Cincinnati in 1958, Bob Nelson with Baltimore 1955 through 1957, Frank Zupo with Baltimore parts of 1958 and 1959, and Marshall Renfroe, a brief stay with San Francisco in 1959. Six more were to spend time in the Majors following their sojourn in Ardmore: Mickey Mc-Guire at Baltimore in 1962 and 1967, Pete Ward with Baltimore during part of 1962, Chicago White Sox 1963 through 1969, and New York Yankees in 1970, John Miller with Baltimore during 1962 and 1963 and again in 1965 through 1967, Buster Narum with Baltimore in 1963 and Washington 1964 through 1967, Merlin Nippert of Mangum, Oklahoma briefly with Boston in 1962, and John Papa, Baltimore for parts of 1961 and 1962.

Despite those past and future Big Leaguers, the 1961 Rosebuds must fairly be called a weak team. One reason was staffing. It was the Orioles' second string AA farm club, obliged only to provide a manager and at least five players. In a six team league, they were fifth in batting at .242, fifth in fielding at .962, and last in pitching. The team ERA of 4.39 was nearly a full earned run higher than fifth-place Rio Grande Valley/Victoria. The mound staff pitched the fewest innings, 1,195, and gave up the most hits, 1,248, most runs, 719, most earned runs, 583, most walks, 611, and hit the most batsmen, forty-three. The club produced only eight shut outs. Kudron gave up twenty-two home runs followed by Renfroe with seventeen. The only positive was that no one committed a balk. Bonus baby John Papa fielded 1.000 but had a win-loss percentage of .000 and allowed 17.37 runners per nine innings. George Gaffney had the only winning percentage, allowed the fewest runners per nine innings with

7.74 but fielded a semi-pro .852. On his way out of Organized Baseball, Renfroe unloaded thirteen wild pitches and led the team with ninety-five walks and fourteen losses. Narum had a staff-best 115 strikeouts. The ace among the pitchers was Alex Castro who posted a record of 10-11, completed ten of sixteen games started, struck out 111, walked only forty-four, and posted a 3.27 ERA although he allowed 11.46 runners per game.

The other problem with the team was the revolving door. Twenty-one position players and twelve pitchers appeared for the Ardmore version of the Rosebuds. Of the twenty on the April 16, opening roster at Victoria, eight finished the season at Ardmore. Two of the most effective pitchers, Don McLeod and Merlin Nippert, were on loan from the Braves' and Red Sox' organizations, respectively. Mike Marinko and John Stokoe were also Braves' property. The team's sole All Star, Charlie Strange, was borrowed from the Giants' organizations, as was pitcher Marshall Renfroe.

Ward led the team with an average of .307 and also had the highest on-base percentage at .374. Al Nagel's twenty home runs helped him to a .433 slugging percentage and a tie with Dennis Loudenback for most home runs and RBIs. Strange led the team with 543 at bats, sixty-seven runs, 152 hits, 211 total bases, and five triples. These statistics are misleading, however, as Strange's on-base percentage was only .273 and slugging percentage .388. The team was lead-footed. The Rosebuds stole only thirteen bases all season; with six, Pete Ward had nearly half.

There were a couple of busts. Art Burnett who had led the Texas League in 1960 with 111 runs managed only eleven in one hundred at bats before he was moved on. Slugger Duke Ducote had lost his mojo hitting only .195 with three home runs before being released in August. For seven players Duke Ductoe (.195), J.C. Dunn (.188),

Dick Ewin (.196), Dennis Loudenback (.267), Clint McCord (.285), George Gaffney (8-7, 3.61), and Jim Melton (0-0) Ardmore was the last professional team they would play for.

While bleak for the most part, there were some exciting times and stellar performances.

- On May 29, Al Nagel hit four home runs in a single game, a feat not seen in the Texas League since 1903.

- The Texas League played an interlocking schedule with the Mexican League in a union called the Pan-American Association with two All Star games and a post-season championship series that replaced the old Dixie Series with the Southern Association. The Ardmore club left on June 30 for an eighteen day road trip south of the border. It began inauspiciously when Mexican customs officials refused to let pitchers Alex Castro, a Cuban, and Don McLeod, a Canadian, enter without an American re-entry visa. Things were held up until the United States consulate issued the necessary documents.

- In the ninth inning of the July 11, inter-league game at Monterrey with the Rosebuds leading, the local fans began throwing objects and firecrackers at the Ardmore outfielders. This spread to the rest of the stands. When umpire Hank Stein could not get the crowd to halt the barrage, he forfeited the game to Ardmore. As the team was leaving the stadium, some four thousand angry fans stoned the bus, breaking four windows but causing no injuries. Mexican League President Eduaro Orvanaños formally apologized to Texas League prexy Dick Butler while the owner of the Sultans did likewise to Ardmore's owner.

- The Ardmore fans were not content to forgive and forget. The Mexico City Red Devils ducked stones thrown at the team bus by the locals on July 26.

- Behind Don McLeod's three-hitter, the Rosebuds won the third game of a triple header at Mexico City on July 9. Due to rain outs, two inter-league games between San Antonio and the Mexico City Red Devils were made up followed by the scheduled match between the Mexico City Tigers and the Rosebuds. Ardmore played the first game of another triple header on July 15, losing to the Red Devils. The next day, McLeod threw a one-hitter at Mexican League leader Veracruz.

- Relief catcher Jim Carver hit the Rosebuds' first and only grand slam at Cardinal Park on July 27, against Poza Rica.

Jim Carver hit the Rosebuds' only grand slam a home against Poza Rica before a few hundred fans including the author. The Orioles' organization had a surplus of catchers. Carver was demoted to Charlotte for 1962 and received his release early in that season. (Ar-34)

- The Ardmore nine was 16-8 against Mexican League competition. The best series record Ardmore had against a Texas League team was 10-13 versus fifth-place Rio Grande Valley/Victoria.

- The Rosebuds' longest win streak, six games, ended on July 23 with a loss to the Monterrey Sultans.

- The dugouts emptied in a battle royal after pitcher Marshall Renfroe, frustrated by successive Tulsa homers, decked future Cardinal Mike Shannon at Texas League Park on August 21, en route to a 4-0 loss on Paul Toth's near no-hitter.

- A. P. "Pink" Shuman, long time American Legion baseball leader, an officer of the Sooner State League Cardinals, and Ardmore club president, became ill in July and resigned. He was honored before 1,384 at Cardinal Park on August 10.

The only Texas League All Star among the Rosebuds, Charlie Strange was on loan from the Giants' system. (Ar-35)

Needing to focus on his interests in the Corpus Christi-Victoria area, Derrest Williams advised the League on July 30 that he wished to sell the franchise. By August 10, due to injuries and trades, Ardmore was reduced to a sixteen man roster from the normal twenty-one. That same day Rosebuds'

batboy, John Saunders, took ten stitches in the fore-
head following being struck by a broken bat. The
Rosebuds finished the season with a 57-83 record in
sixth place thirty-three games behind the champion
Amarillo Gold Sox. The Rosebuds ended the season
with thirteen loses to only three wins the last two
weeks of August. The team was just going through
the motions. The Rosebuds lost their last game
played in Ardmore to Victoria 20-3 on August 30.
They finished the season, fittingly, in Victoria on
September 1 with a 2-1 loss despite Buster Narum
limiting the Giants to four hits; two, unfortunately,
were home runs.

The two complaints about Ardmore were
Cardinal Park — too small and the field poorly
maintained— and its small population. The owners of Tulsa and San Antonio wanted larger cities
in the league. Albuquerque and El Paso were both
open. Despite reports in *The Sporting News* that
Waco and Opie Turner were again coming to the
rescue of baseball in Ardmore, they could not
come to terms with Williams. Ardmore Baseball
Association quickly raised $10,000 for work on the
playing surface. But the fix was in. On October 12,
the Rosebuds were sold to Duke City Baseball, Inc.
and became the Albuquerque Dukes. A bitter Doyle
May later wrote a column "Ardmore Never had a
Chance." That was a matter of fact.

Ardmore, the smallest city to have AA Texas
League baseball, has been without professional
baseball since. And with the departure of the Rosebuds, Minor League baseball outside Oklahoma
City and Tulsa passed from Oklahoma. It is not
without irony that small town Organized Baseball
in Oklahoma ended with a last place team in the
same league and same town where it began in 1904.

*The Rosebuds had two versions of their scorecards. The one on the
bottom was used in the June 4 opener. The top one was used during
the late July home stand against Mexican League teams appearing
under the Pan-American Association agreement. (Ar-36)*

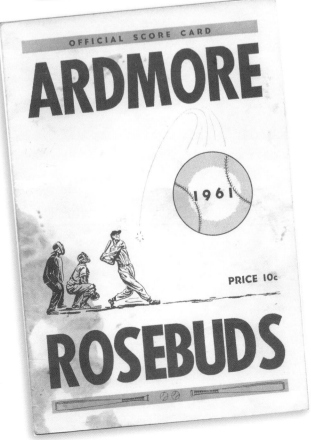

BARTLESVILLE OILERS
1946 AND 1947
BARTLESVILLE PIRATES
1948 – JULY 6, 1952
KANSAS-OKLAHOMA-MISSOURI LEAGUE

SEASON	ATTENDANCE	RECORD	FINISH	AFFILIATION	PLAYOFF FIRST ROUND	PLAYOFF FINALS
1946	46,822	47-73	Sixth	Pittsburgh		
1947	64,074	68-56	Fourth	Pittsburgh	Lost to Miami 1-3	
1948	64,090	71-52	Third	Pittsburgh	Lost to Independence 2-3	
1949	51,000	71-55	Second	Pittsburgh	Lost to Iola 1-3	
1950	56,250	73-48	Second	Pittsburgh	Beat Carthage 3-1	Lost to Ponca City 1-3
1951	34,296	77-45	Second	Pittsburgh	Lost to Carthage 2-3	
1952	34,276	59-65	Fourth	Pittsburgh	Moved to Pittsburg, KS July 7	

Peter B. Mitchell of Tacoma, Washington and owner of the ball club in that city, purchased the Bartlesville franchise in the Western Association in December, 1937 promising to run it as an independent and granting the city the right to keep the club if he decided to sell. After a 61-78 last place finish in 1938 with poor attendance, he decided to look for a better opportunity. The Western Association owners were eager to shed the two smallest members of the league, both Oklahoma company towns, for larger markets. On January 8, 1939, the Bartlesville Chiefs became the Topeka Owls while the Ponca City Angels traded their wings for a halo, becoming the St. Joseph, Missouri, Saints.

Municipal Athletic Field, built in 1932 and a first class minor league facility, had stood vacant since Mitchell folded his figurative tent. It hosted some exhibitions, semi-pro games, and the local American Legion team and even became the spring training home of Casey Stengel's Kansas City Blues in 1945. But it was not home to a real professional ball club.

1946

That changed on March 31, 1946 when Bartlesville was granted the last franchise in the newly organized Kansas-Oklahoma-Missouri League, one of thirteen new Class D circuits that popped up like mushroom after the War. Headquartered in Carthage, Missouri where league president E. L. Dale ran the local newspaper, it was a compact loop with Iola, nearby Chanute, and Pittsburg, Kansas on the north, Carthage, Missouri on the east, Miami, Oklahoma on the south and Bartlesville on the west. The ball club's organizers led by H. W. Trippett had to move quickly with the season opening only two months away. Municipal Athletic Field with its fourteen feet high, symmetrical outfield fence—340 feet from home plate in every direction in fair territory—had to be leased and put into shape. To assemble a team, they turned to Buffalo, Kansas native Claude Willoughby who threw for the Phillies from 1925 through 1930 then finished his tour of the Show with Pittsburgh in 1931. Courted by both

Municipal Athletic Field was home to the Bartlesville K-O-M teams. It was unique in that the distance to the fence in all fair territory was 340 feet. Completely remodeled in 1998, the facility near downtown is called Doegnes Stadium. (Bv-1,2)

Claude Willoughby led the first edition of the Oilers to a dismal 47-73 finish in sixth place. (Bv-3)

Brooklyn and the New York Giants, Willoughby cast his lot with his old club, the Pirates, for a working agreement. As the home of the first producing oil well in Oklahoma as well as Phillips Petroleum Company, the team naturally would be called the "Oilers."

The first edition Oilers were essentially a rookie club. Four veterans appeared all season. Two were position players. Thomas Hawk, a third baseman and shortstop, saw limited service in twenty-seven games batting .267. The other veteran was light-hitting Ed Suveda who held down shortstop in seventy-six games. His fielding, .858, was nearly as poor as his hitting, .112.

Erby Carroll at age twenty-seven was the old man on the team who threw ninety-nine innings in fourteen games with a 3.55 ERA and a 5-7 record. Robert Horsman, 25, was the other senior hurler with 202 innings in forty-two games for a 8-15 record and 4.32 ERA. Jack Bumgarner of Norman, brother of the late actor James Garner, was the only limited service player on the roster, having played a full 1945 season. As a pitcher, he was 9-12 in thirty-five games posting the team-best ERA of

1946 Bartlesville Oilers. (Bv-4)

2.83 in 178 innings. He also played some outfield in thirty-seven games.

The rest of the pitchers were rookies. No one had a winning percentage. Ike Henderson was closest at 9-10 in 160 innings. Wayne Grose was 11-15 with a respectable 2.92 ERA and the workhorse of the staff throwing 231 innings. Jeff Peckham posted a 3-6 record in ninety-six innings. The rest of the pitchers, James Mann, Fred Schneider, George Alves, Richard Blasi, Warren Dent, and William Ward had one win and four losses among them.

William Glenn appeared in 120 games behind the plate and in the outfield batting .271 and leading the club in triples (8) and home runs (7). Jerry Cross held down first base much of the season before departing for Miami. Regular second baseman John Jordan led the Oilers with 463 at-bats, thirty-two doubles, sixty-four RBIs and a .307 average at the plate; he finished the season with Chanute. Third base was a revolving door with light-hitting (.180) Leonard Stanford beginning the season, replaced by Hawk and Wes Nettles before he took refuge at Miami. Suveda was a bust at shortstop and was relieved of duty when William Waggener came over from Pittsburg and added his .222 bat to the Oiler cause. The manager's son, Keith Willoughby roamed the outfield in 110 games batting .281 without power. Joining him were part-time catcher Carl Del Grande who hit .293 in eighty-seven games after spending the first six weeks of the season at Muskogee, Howard Weeks, a .255 hitter, Glenn from time to time, Oscar Engel, and Fred Pralle, .303 in eighteen games.

With the weakest batting team in the K-O-M, it is no surprise that the Oilers finished sixth in a six-team league. Remarkably, Bumgarner was selected for the post-season All Star team as a utility player. Bartlesville did finish out of the cellar in the attendance category. With a population of about 17,000, the Oilers had 46,822 paid admissions.

Most of the 1946 Oilers were out of Organized Baseball by 1948. None ever saw the inside of a Major League locker room. The greatest complaint among rookies was that managers didn't give much instruction and the veterans and limited service player didn't give much help. There was a glut of players after the War so the Major Leagues didn't need to expend many resources in development. It was still the time of "catch and release."

A new crop would appear in 1947.

1947

Claude Willoughby went back to his farm never to manage again. At the helm for the K-O-M's second season in Bartlesville was retired Oklahoma City Indians pitcher Ed Marleau. Bartlesville hosted spring training for the little Pirates as well as sister Class C farm teams Keokuk and Fargo. Returning to the Oilers from 1946 were Carl Del Grande, Ike Henderson, Robert Horsman, Bill Waggener and Keith Willoughby. The team's average age was

twenty-one with five under twenty. Over the 1947 season, ten limited service players, two veterans, and thirteen rookies donned Oilers flannels. Two, rookies Bill Pierro and R. T. "Dixie" Upright, would have a cup of coffee in the Major Leagues. Pierro was first spending July 15 through September 19, 1950 with the last place Pittsburgh Pirates; his 10.55 ERA in twenty-nine innings sealed his place outside of Organized Baseball. Upright had twelve seasons in the minors, mainly in the Southern Association, with a lifetime average of .306. He spent three weeks at the beginning of the 1953 season with the final edition of the St. Louis Browns batting .250 in eight trips to the plate.

The pitching was much stronger in 1947. Rookie Carroll Dial of Altus led the staff with 233 innings in thirty-eight games posting a 22-5 record and team top 3.32 ERA. He was followed by 12-5 veteran Ed Willshaw with a 3.63 ERA. On August 24, Willshaw turned in the first Bartlesville no-hitter as be blanked Iola 8-0 after retiring two pinch-hitters on outfield flies to end the contest.

Ed Marleau, former pitcher for the Oklahoma City Indians, guided Bartlesville during the 1947 and 1948 seasons to winning records and play-off appearances. He was unsuccessful in his 1949 attempt to turn around Otto's Utt's 1949 Duncan Uttmen. (Bv-5)

Bill Pierro was the first Bartlesville alumnus to reach Forbes Field —briefly at the end of the 1950 season. (Bv-6)

1947 Bartlesville Oilers. L-R Ed Willshaw, Ralph Liebendorfer, Nick Najjar, Lou Tond, Ken Galbraith, Dixie Upchurch, Carroll Dial, Ed Marleau, Al Solenberger, Elmo Maxwell, Lou Godla, Jim Fink, Bill Pierro, Wayne Caves, Jess Nelms, Bill Waggoner, Charles Stock. (Bv-7)

1947's Dixie Upright spent most of his playing days in the Southern Association. He had eight at-bats with the 1953 St. Louis Browns. (Bv-8)

Limited service hurlers Nick Najjar, on the bounce from Iola, — 7-8 and 4.00 ERA— and Ike Henderson returned from 1946 —10-10 and 4.50 in 174 innings— joined with veteran Robert Horsman, also from 1946 before departing for Chanute —3-4, 4.02 ERA. The other two rookie pitchers were Pierro — 8-9 and 4.30 ERA— and Ralph Liebendorfer — 4-8 and 4.74 ERA— before shipping out with Maxwell to Tallahassee. In a rare tie, on May 23 Liebendorfer fanned seventeen Ponca Cityans and walked fourteen before the game was called for rain in the tenth inning. Off season, Pierro played for the best basketball team in the land, Bartlesville's AAU Phillips 66ers.

Marleau juggled his line-up with only a couple of players holding down a single position for more than one hundred games. Behind the plate and at first base, the fielding was above par for Class D. Elmo Maxwell (67 games) before a transfer to Tallahassee, Del Grande (47 games), and Cluster Blankenship, a limited service player acquired from Miami, (12) guarded home. During late July, Del Grande asked for home leave. When he became incommunicado, the manager worried. He apparently had jumped contract and was playing the last month of the season at a cooler Fargo in the Class C Northern League. Tulsa rookie Wayne Caves was at first base for eighty-three games aided by fellow rookies Upright (25 games), Bill Christman (11 games), and George Grennan (10 games). Tony Smeraglia started the season at second base but his

.870 glove earned a release on May 27; he landed with Otto Utt's abysmal Duncan Cementers in the Sooner State League. Lou Golda was sent down from Keokuk of the Central Association and did a competent job for 108 games. The left side of the infield was the Achilles heel. Jim Fink (89 games) fielded at .886. He had replaced Charles Stock who gloved .870 in twenty-nine appearances. Shortstop was worse. Bill Waggener fielded a miserable .805 before Fink replaced him with a weak but better .830 performance. In the outfield, Al Solenberger was in all 125 games. His partner most frequently was Upright for eighty-one games. Limited service players Ken Galbraith (58 games), Jesse Nelms (18 games) and Willoughby (24 games) joined rookies Stock (35 games), Bob Hyatt (12 games), pitcher Dial (13 games), and John Arceneaux (10 games) filling the outfield.

The Oilers led the K-O-M in batting with a .279 team effort that produced 1,261 hits. Loren Packard of Miami edged out Upright for the batting crown by .0004 percentage point. Between June 24 and July 15, Bartlesville won thirteen games against three defeats to move into third place. With a 68-56 record seven and one-half games behind Miami and a fourth place finish, the Oilers were to make their first of five appearances in the post-season play offs. Squaring off against the tough Miami Owls, Marleau's charges were vanquished in four games. Three were named to the post-season All Star team: Dial, Solenberger, and Upright. A fourth Oiler, Carl Del Grande, had joined them on the mid-term roster selected by the managers and writers that faced off against Miami on July 9. Solenberger set the all time K-O-M record for at-bats with 530. And the local fans had come out in droves leading the K-O-M attendance with 64,074, five thousand more than the closest rival. The Bartlesville Oilers were actually a money-making operation.

1948

The Bartlesville franchise had done so well at the cash register, that the Pittsburgh front office bought the team lock, stock, and barrel. The first thing done was to rename the ball club the "Pirates." Henceforward, the Class D farmhands would don hand-me-down flannels and even wear the Pirates' gold "P" on their black caps. There was a good chemistry in the clubhouse, so the new owner retained Ed Marleau at the helm. For 1948, he welcomed back Caves, Godla, Najjar, Nelms, Pierro, and Stock to spring training at home. Six more limited service players came through the Municipal Athletic Field clubhouse. Only Godla had played for pay before the previous season. Seventeen rookies would take the field at some point in 1948.

The 1948 season was notable as the year of the dead ball. The K-O-M had helped vote down a motion to mandate uniformity of baseball manufacturing standards and, after 1946 and 1947 with the Wilson ball converted to the less expensive Worth baseball. Unfortunately, it was of inferior quality and was easily beaten out of shape. It was a good year for pitchers. As a league, the K-O-M batted only .226 in 1948. The top home run producer had only thirteen. Pierro had 300 strikeouts.

Four pitchers carried the team accounting for forty-four of the little Pirates' seventy-one wins. Pierro was the ace of the pitchers winning seventeen against eight losses in 130 innings in thirty-one games with a 2.15 ERA. He also had six shut outs for a K-O-M league record. Rookie Dave Elliott matched his ERA, threw fewer innings, appeared in two more games, and had a 12-7 record. Nick Najjar posted a 12-5 record with a 2.49 ERA in only one hundred innings in nineteen games. Rookie Norm Carpenter was 5-8 with a 2.68 ERA and was the only other hurler to throw over one hundred innings. Arriving from Carthage by way

of the Cardinals' Albany (GA) farm, limited service thrower Ken Maxwell had three each of decisions in thirteen games but a relatively high 4.42 ERA. The high point among the mound staff was Pierro's one-hit 4-2 victory over Miami on June 9. Only Owls' manager Art Priebe put wood on the ball.

The trend at Bartlesville was becoming development of talent. Everyone in the organization was Black and Gold striving for Forbes Field. Limited service Charles Stock was the jack of all trades catching thirty-six games, playing hot corner in twenty-four, and cruising the outfield in eleven more. Rookie Ray Birch was the regular catcher. At first base rookie Sal Catalano was the regular backed up

1948 Bartlesvile Pirates. Back row L-R: Rufus Bedford (business manager), Tex Howard, Sonny Catalano, Pete Maropis, Gary Hegedorn, Norm Carpenter, Ed Marleau. Middle row L-R: Ray Birch, Calvin Frazer, Lou Godla, Rolf Moeller, Leroy Sanders, Don Gaines, Charles Stock. Front row L-R: Al Solenberger, Nick Najjar, Dave Elliott, Lou Tond, Jonny Girrens, Bill Pierro. (Bv-9)

by Caves. Golda once again had a lock on second base excluding Art Dercole who was shuttled off to Iola. Rookie Don Haines had seventy-eight games at third and thirty-five at shortstop while Calvin Frazer had the same numbers at shortstop and third base before being promoted to Fargo of the Northern League. In the outfield Solenberger again appeared in most games as did rookie LeRoy Sanders. Usually, rookie Pete Marpois joined them but Willis Carruth, Bill Jarrett, and Jesse Nelms, who also caught, could be found guarding the pasture.

Al Solenberger. (Bv-10)

Solenberger led the K-O-M with 134 hits and Godla scored the most runs with eighty-three. Pierro's 300 strike outs averaged 11.4 per game and set the K-O-M record that was tied in 1952 by Jim Owens of Miami. Solenberger repeated as an All Star as did Pierro. Newcomer Haines and Najjar joined them. At 71-52 when the season ended, Bartlesville made its second playoff appearance. The Pirates again lost in the first round to the Yankees' club from Independence (KS) three games to two. The fan kept coming, 64,090 of them. It looked like the Pirates made a good investment.

1949 Bartlesville Pirates. Top row L-R: Leroy Mehan, Bill Paine, Dean Jongewaard, Bob Pinard, Jerry Dahms, Bob Wheeler. Middle row L-R: Trusten Scotten, Rolf Moeller, Cal Frazer, Dick Drury, Ed Wolfe, Kyle Bower. Front row L-R: Ed McLish, Bill Herring, Ted Gullic, Stan Miller, Harry Neighbors, Rufus Bedford (business manager). (Bv-12)

1949

Marleau, who also owned a beer joint near Texas League Park in Oklahoma City, took summer work in 1949 with Otto Utt's Duncan Uttmen of the Sooner State League. Believing he had a free hand to form and develop a winning independent, he soon ran afoul of the irascible Utt and was unemployed one month into the season. He retired to his bar for good.

Ted Gullic would run the little Pirates for three seasons. An outfielder and third baseman, he broke into baseball in 1928 and divided his time between that season and 1930 with Muskogee and Tulsa. He was called up to the St. Louis Browns for 1930 where he was a regular. With the exception of 1933 when he was back in St. Louis, he spent his summers between 1931 and 1942 with the Milwaukee Brewers of the American Association. Too old to

Ted Gullic managed the Bartlesville teams to three straight second place finishes between 1949 and 1951. He had spent a dozen seasons with the Milwaukee Brewers of the American Association. (Bv-11)

68

be drafted, Gullic was with the Portland Beavers in the Pacific Coast League from 1943 through 1948, taking 1947 off. Bartlesville was his first managerial job and he was good at it. He suffered through 1952 with the Pirates hapless operation in Class B Waco resulting in a 29-118 season, one of the worst in minor league history. He hung up his spikes after leading the Yankees' Boise prospects in 1953.

Pittsburgh sent him a very young roster. Only ten of the twenty-eight who came through could buy a 3.2 Oklahoma beer. Eight were teenagers. Frazer, Haines, and Maropis returned from 1948 for more seasoning. Gullic juggled his players. Eleven were around for fewer than thirty games. Only Frazer, Tristan Scotten, Dick Drury, and Harold Neighbors, who joined the team from high school on June 17, saw action in more than ninety.

Behind the plate were William Herring, Gerald Dahms, who came to the club on July 19, Tom Chandler and late comer from the Pirates' Tallahassee farm, Hugh Bradshaw. Chandler, Udo Jansen, Dean Jongewaard, who joined the club at mid-season, and Sal Catalano all saw duty at first. Stan Miller and Scotten covered second base. Haines was at third base in more than half the games relieved by Neil Huff and Scotten. Frazer settled at shortstop from the first day of the season. Drury and Neighbors were regularly patrolling the outfield but Scotten saw action there in sixty-two games while Maropis, Reimold before being shipped off to Duncan, Ben Perry, Chandler, Robert Pinard, and Alex Stewart who left for Chanute after eleven games, were occasional visitors.

Gullic worked his pitchers hard. All but Kyle Bowers (7-1 2.08 ERA 52 innings), who appeared from high school on June 28, and short time (six days) Major Leaguer Ed Wolfe (9-4 4.60 ERA 94 innings), who was promoted to Modesto, threw over one hundred innings. Ed McLish (16-7 3.79 ERA), brother of the Major Leaguer with the longest

name, Calvin Coolidge Julius Caesar Tuskahoma McLish, was the workhorse with 197 innings to his credit. He was followed by Robert Wheeler (10-9 4.20 ERA 163 innings), Rolf Moller (8-7 3.88 ERA), William Paine (7-4 3.93 ERA 135 innings), and Robert Pinard (6-9 4.06 ERA 113 innings).

The Pirates finished the season in second place at 71-55, a single game behind frontrunner Independence who had a rookie shortstop named Mickey Mantle. Facing off against the third place Iola Indians, the Bartlesville curse again worked its bad *gris gris* with the Pirates eliminated three games to one. The little Pirates led the K-O-M in hitting in most categories: .266 average, 832 runs, 1,141 hits, 191 doubles, 786 free bases, 737 RBIs and 1,159 left on base. Dick Drury won the batting crown with a .317 average. Surprisingly, Harry Neighbors was the only Pirate selected for the All Star squad. The team and their play was the good news. A decline in attendance to 51,000 was the bad.

Bv-13 *Ed Wolfe was promoted to Modesto mid-season and appeared briefly with the parent Pirates. (Bv-13)*

Harry Neighbors was an All Star and the most popular 1949 Pirate. He led the 1950 K-O-M in RBIs and was second in home runs. (Bv-14)

1950

Pittsburgh ran a shell game with players making it difficult for a manager to field a consistent line up. Only twenty three players appeared for Bartlesville in 1950. Four were shipped off to

Pittsburgh outfitted its farm system in shorts for 1950. Their top club, the Hollywood Stars, is shown here. The experiment didn't last long. (Bv-15)

The shorts trend was brief in Bartlesville. Gullic had his club back in regular baseball trousers after a week of raspberries. (Bv-16)

Greenville, Alabama to fill gaps there. To cover the left side of the infield, Gullic had to call the Class B Waco Pirates for reinforcements. A couple of releases decimated the outfield. It could have been a very bad campaign but Gullic pulled a figurative rabbit from his hat and molded his rookies and limited service players into a second place team that finally overcame the first round playoff jinx. He had Dahms, Elliott, sent down from Waco, and Wolfe, back from Modesto, from 1949. The rest of the faces were a new mix of rookies and sophomores, the theoretical composition of a Class D ball club.

Ed Wolfe was back from Class C and Gullic worked him for a full season. He averaged eight innings in each of his twenty-five appearances with success: his ERA was 2.98 and he was the winning pitcher in fifteen of his twenty-three decisions. The best performer, however, was Dave Elliott who had sat out 1949 after a good rookie season at Bartlesville in 1948. Down from an uneventful start at Waco, he was 9-6 in

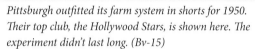

twenty outings with a K-O-M best 2.04 ERA. His string of thirty-four scoreless innings came to an end on May 24 when Elliott's team mates committed six error to let Ponca City plate six runs; Elliott still prevailed 11-6. The rest of the mound staff were rookies. Fresh from high school, Tom Gera too had an ERA under 3.00 (2.78) winning five of seven decisions in eight starts. Ron Kline, who would go on to throw in the Major Leagues for seventeen seasons, got off to an above average start in twelve outings, eight as a starter. His season record was 5-2 with a 3.81 in a short season. Dave Cochran, another rookie had the same record as Kline but with a better 3.19 ERA. James Mehan (11-8 4.38 ERA) and Charles Sauvain (10-6 3.28 ERA) rounded out the staff.

Bob Graham spent most of 1950 behind the Pirate's plate. He was backed up by Gerald Dahms when he wasn't roaming the outfield. Rookies John Phillips and Harold White shared first base duties. Dean Miller was the primary second baseman. Sol Campagna and Don Hedrick competed for third base until both were transferred to the Pirates' farm in Greenville (AL). To fill the gap, Gullic had to call

Ron Kline was Bartlesville's most successful product with seventeen seasons in the Major Leagues. (Bv-17)

1950 Bartlesville Pirates.
Top row L-R: Don Hinchberger,
Chuck Sauvain, Dean Miller,
John Gilbert, Ed Wolfe, Tom Gera.
Next row L-R: Don Labbruzo
(business manager), Sal Campagna,
Segal Drummond, Hal White,
Leroy Mehan, Don Cochran.
Next row LR: JJim Williams,
Harold Blaylock, E. C. Leslie,
Bob Bonaparte.
Front row L-R: Ron Kline,
Jerry Dahms, Bobby
Joe Graham, bat boy,
Ted Gullic, Harry Neighbors.
(Bv-18)

Sug Haines back from Waco to finish the campaign. Leslie was the regular shortstop but played the keystone in forty-six games. His substitute was Segal Drummond who was called up at the end of the season for bench duty with New Orleans; he was in over his head at Class AA. Haines also made ten appearances at shortstop. Neighbors was a fixture in the outfield and Donald Hinchberger, down from Waco then up to Hutchinson (KS) of the Western Association, played two-thirds of the games beside him. The other position was a revolving door with James Williams and James Ryan, two of the quartet sent to Greenville, Dahms, Milton Lindberg, and popular Rudy Ortiz filling the gaps. Lindberg was released and found work with Ardmore of the Sooner State League. Ortiz landed a spot with Duncan of the same league as it moved on to Shawnee.

In team batting behind regular season champion Ponca City, the Pirates' .251was good for second place. Bartlesville also led the K-O-M with 732 runs, 181 doubles, 73 home runs, and 620 RBIs. The little Pirates struck out the fewest times but were a lead-footed bunch with only fifty-five swipes, by far the fewest in the league. As a team, they were the top glovemen with a .949 fielding average.

The fans were back for 1950, 56,250 of them. In the playoffs for the third time, the Pirates vanquished the Cubs' prospects from Carthage in the first round. Facing off against Ponca City in the finals, the Dodgers' rookies under Boyd Bartley bested Gullic's crew three games to one.

1951

Gullic's spring camp had many new faces and a few old ones. Al Solenberger, an All Star in 1948 and 1949, now had veteran status after spending the 1950 season in the California League. Ron Kline, a member of the 1949 and 1950 squads, was back for more seasoning. His 1950 second sacker, Ernest Leslie, returned. Another 1948 alumnus, pitcher Louis Tond, who had a 16-7 season for the Oilers, was now a veteran after toiling at Class C Hutchinson (KS) the previous season. Another pitcher, Don Cochran, was back from the 1950 squad.

In terms of winning percentage, the 1951 Pirates were the best team Bartlesville ever fielded. In addition to Kline, Duke University product Brandy Davis spent half of 1952 and the end of 1953 in Forbes Field's bucolic setting.

Speedster Brandy Davis was a graduate of Duke University. He and Ron Kline were promoted to New Orleans of the Class AA Southern Association at the end of the 1951 season. He joined the parent Pirates in 1952. (Bv-19)

Again, Kline was the workhorse who had come into his own. He posted an 18-4 record in 209 innings in twenty-eight appearances with a 2.33 ERA. Close behind was sophomore Don Cochran also with twenty-eight appearance for 192 innings, an 18-6 record and 3.33 ERA. The rest of the pitchers were rookies who all managed to sport winning records. Don Anderson had a 2.75 ERA in 131 innings with wins in nine of his thirteen decisions. John Quinn managed a 7-6 record in 106 innings with 3.99 ERA which, while respectable on many teams, was the highest among Gullic's starting rotation.

Gullic enjoyed some stability among his position player. Early on he released rookies Don Bussan, Calvin Pool, and Richard McKinney who later emerged with Miami. Pitcher Dick Sutter jumped the team on June 15 never to return to

Organized Baseball. Rookies William Phillips and Joe Buckstead rotated at the catching position. Hugh Castiex beat out Harold White and Ed Gigliotti for first base. Once again, Ernie Leslie owned second base. Manny LaCosta ruled the hot corner but with a weak glove (.881) after replacing Segal Drummon's weaker glove (.846). Ernesto Garcia, who would spend eighteen seasons in the Mexican League, played all the games at shortstop. Solenberger was an ironman in the outfield and late arriving Brandy Davis, who missed spring training, was an outfield staple until he was called up to New Orleans with Ron Kline on August 17. A number of others shagged flies including Leo Kedzierski before being called up to Hutchinson then, after his release, finishing the 1951 campaign with independent Enid of the Western Association. Don Paulsen, Drummond, Bill Phillips, and Bussan appear in the official record as having more than ten appearances.

Bartlesville bracketed Ponca City's roaring start. After beating the Dodgers in the season opener, Ponca City reeled off eighteen consecutive wins before coming to Municipal Athletic Field on May 24 where the streak ended. Three weeks into the season, the Pirates were the only team that had tagged the frontrunner. Kline had four shutouts and finally got his no-hitter on June 14 as he vanquished Pittsburg 5-1. After the start, Ponca City took and held the first position all season. The Pirates finished seven games behind despite a .631 winning percentage. In their fourth playoff, Tommy Warren's independent Miami Eagles took the Pirates in four games before falling to Carthage in a three game sweep. The 1951 Pirates must have felt some *shadenfreude* as Ponca City also fell in the first round.

1951 Bartlesville Pirates. Top row L-R: Ted Gullic, Lou Tond, Merlin Jorgenson, Don Cochran, Ron Kline, Dick Sutter, Dan Anderson. Middle row L-R: Bill Phillips, Hugh Casteix, Ernie Leslie, Many LaCosta, Leo Kedzierski, Brandy Davis, Joe Buckstead. Front row L-R: Segal Drummond, John Quinn, bat boy, Ernie Garcia, Al Solenberger. (Bv-20)

Kline, with 208 strikeouts, Leslie, hitting .316 and Davis, who tied teammate Bill Phillips for the home run title, were named to the All Star squad. Solenberger was denied a trifecta despite batting .300 and leading the K-O-M with a .475 on base percentage. Don Cochran, who tied Kline for the most wins in the K-O-M was overlooked. Manny LaCosta hit .354 in 106 games; his absence from the All Stars was conspicuous. Perhaps it was his fielding. Also conspicuous was the absence of fans. Attendance plummeted to 34,296

1952

KOTV of Tulsa began broadcasting in earnest in 1950 and could be received in Bartlesville with an antenna. The station increased its power to 100,000 watts in 1952 easily taking in the Bartlesville market. Attendance dropped between 1950 and 1951 by 21,954 or thirty-nine percent. The little Pirates were getting into the parent club's pocket.

Gullic was promoted to take over the Pirate's pathetic Big State League club at Waco for 1952. The parent Pirates called on experienced minor league manager and pre-War Phillie and Wartime Yankee Hershel Martin to try to make something of the rookies sent to Bartlesville. Martin was a native of Ponca City and had played at Oklahoma A & M. He began his career in Organized Baseball in 1932. He was a National League All Star in 1938. As a playing manager, Martin had never finished lower than second and won two West Texas-New Mexico pennants in four seasons at Albuquerque. He not only managed and played but was president of the Bartlesville operation.

Only Joe Buckstead returned from the 1951 squad. The roster was dominated by teenagers. Even with Martin at age forty-two and veteran Chico Bernal at twenty-six added in, the average age was just over twenty-one. The only stability in the Pirate's

lineup were the Abril twins, Ernest and Manuel, who held down two of the outfield positions season long.

There were few bright spots. Rookie Sterling Davis tagged the Blackwell pitcher for a three-run homer to win the May 9 contest 5-2. Less than a week later, the Pirates went twelve innings with Ponca City before prevailing 9-8 taking up a record three hours and fifty-five minutes. Miami embarrassed the Pirates 20-5 beginning with a first inning grand slam by catcher Ed Sacks. That was more typical. Pitcher Joe Marx was named to the mid-season All Star team.

As John G. Hall remarks in his 1996 definitive work on the K-O-M, *Majoring in the Minors*, the 1952 Pirates "couldn't draw flies." About 550 fans would show up to watch a mediocre assemblage; nothing like the hard-hitting and fast throwing squads to which Bartlesville's people had become accustomed. It was easier and more comfortable to stay home and watch television. As club president, Martin was accountable to the legendarily parsimonious Branch Rickey for the financial performance of the Bartlesville operation. Martin would leave the team in the hands of nineteen year old catcher Ed Hays as he would scout the Tri-State mining district for a suitable and more hospitable home for the operation. Pittsburg (KS) had lost its K-O-M club to Independence (KS) after drawing just over 22,500 for the 1951 season. With that charter member of the K-O-M now an open city, it looked better than the charter city where Pirates called home and hopefully new fans would be more appreciative.

Ponca City native and Oklahoma A & M graduate Hershel Martin took over the Pirates for their last season both as business manager and field manager. Accountable to Branch Rickey in Pittsburgh, he "solved' the financial woes of the franchise by moving the club to Pittsburg, Kansas on July 5. (Bv-21)

With most players in their late teens and early twenties, fraternization with local belles was inevitable.
Nick Najjar on the far right is the one with a mouthful. (Bv-22)

Only 16, 478 had gone through the Bartlesville turnstiles in the two months since the season opened. The Pirates were playing almost .500 ball with a 30-31 record. When the Pirates finished their July 4 road trip, they turned north to Kansas to become the Pittsburg (no final "h") Pirates. Municipal Athletic Field, now a renovated gem of a ball park known as Bill Doneges Memorial Park Stadium, went dark for Organized Baseball.

The new beginning at Pittsburg was inauspicious as Iola shut out the Pirates 4-0 before 1,300 onlookers at Jay Cee Park as the clouds opened in the ninth inning and the game was called. The local citizenry showed a little more interest as 17,789 turned out to see Martin's charges. Two weeks before season end, Martin walked away leaving Hays

in charge, one of the two youngest managers in Organized Baseball —Jim England of Ada's Sooner State League entry was the other— as the Pirates limped to a 59-65 season, the franchise's second losing campaign but still good enough for fourth place. The change of venue had not improved play. In fact, the Pirates were 29-34 at Pittsburg. In a truncated, sudden death post-season, the Phillies' Miami farmhands behind future Major Leaguer Jim Owens put away the Pirates 4-0 then went on to breeze past Ponca City to win a pennant that would never be awarded. When Miami could not secure a working agreement for 1953, it became impossible for the league to carry on. The Kansas-Oklahoma-Missouri League formally disbanded in February, 1953.

BLACKWELL BRONCOS
K-O-M LEAGUE 1952
WESTERN ASSOCIATION 1954

SEASON	ATTENDANCE	RECORD	FINISH	AFFILIATION	PLAYOFF FIRST ROUND	PLAYOFF FINALS
1952	51,000	57-69	5th	Chicago (NL)		
1954	39,637	79-61	4th	Chicago (NL)	Eliminated Topeka 3-0	Beat St. Joseph 4-1

Founded as a town with the opening of the Cherokee Outlet in September 16, 1893, the place had been the home of Col. A. J. Blackwell since he settled there with his Cherokee wife in 1882. Remembered as a raconteur and local despot, he narrowly escaped the hangman's noose for treason against the Cherokee Nation in 1894, fleeing ultimately to Chelsea, I.T., another city he had founded, where he died in 1903.

Blackwell became a rail crossroads in 1899 when the St. Louis and San Francisco Railway's north-south line intersected with the Atchison, Topeka & Santa Fe's east-west line finished the same year. Transportation made the town a regional agricultural trade center. With the discovery of oil and gas in 1901, the town's fortunes grew. By the time Blackwell fielded its first professional baseball team in 1924, it was home to oil companies, a refinery, brick plant, glass manufacturing, and a meat processing plant as well as several grain elevators. The population had grown to over 7,000.

After two seasons in Organized Baseball, Blackwell's Gassers folded along with the Southwestern League at the end of the 1926 season. Through the Depression and after World War II, Blackwell fielded semi-pro teams called the Oilers and was member of a circuit that included Stillwater, Fairfax, Perry, Crescent, and Enid. Under the guidance and field play of OU baseball coach Jack Baer, the Blackwell Boosters reached the National Baseball Congress tournament in 1951.

Blackwell made its first try to join the Kansas-Oklahoma-Missouri League, universally known as the "K-O-M," on November 7, 1948. A Chamber of Commerce group headed by Glenn Brumbaugh had $6,500 in hand and was actively raising pledges to underwrite the 1949 season. That plea and a couple of others fell on deaf ears. The K-O-M was openly planning to expand to eight teams for 1952 and at its owners' February 3, 1952 meeting awarded franchises to Enid and Blackwell. When the Carthage, Missouri franchise failed later that month, and with the Pittsburg, Kansas club approaching insolvency, the owners reversed themselves at a special meeting at Bartlesville on February 17. Because Blackwell had been promised the Pittsburg club, it was at the top of the list. With Carthage's failure, though, the league immediately moved that operation to Blackwell, withdrew the offer to Enid, and moved the Pittsburg operation to Independence, Kansas to operate as a six-term circuit for 1952 with no Missouri member.

Founder of the Dave Morgan Foundation, Blackwell oil millionaire and civic booster Dave Morgan finally had won for his city a place in Organized Baseball. The semi-pros had a professional quality facility, Morgan Field, and a working agreement with the Chicago Cubs. Minor league veteran pitcher Al Reitz, who had managed Carthage in 1951, was tapped to lead the newly named Broncos in what would turn out to be the K-O-M's final 126-game campaign that began April 30 and ended on Labor Day followed by a three-game playoff.

The Cubs sent a typically mediocre crew to Kay County. A set of twins, Kansans Harold and Gerald Cruciani, appeared together briefly for the Broncos. The Bronchos were 4-12 on May 14. Jerry Staab had won all but one of the four victories including a 4-1 drubbing of Independence on May 13. The next night the Broncos lost a heart breaker to Bartlesville when Sterling Davis hit a three-run homer to give the Pirates a 5-2 win. The nineteen-game hitting streak of Ponca City's Clyde Girrens was halted

June 21 at Blackwell. Two nights later Iola manager Floyd Temple's grand slam paved the way for a 14-4 rout on the road. Wild left-hander Andy Vargas, who saw action briefly with the parent Cubs at the ends of the 1950 and 1951 seasons, was sent down by Topeka for further work on control. When he first appeared for Blackwell on July 14, he threw a 5-0 one-hitter at the Independence Browns and would have earned a gem had he covered the base on Jim Murray's slow roller between first and second. Despite Ray Mladovich's grand slam to hand Blackwell a 8-2 loss, on July 24 the Broncos escaped the sixth place berth they had occupied since the season began slipping one-half game over the Browns' Independence farmhands. Another Vargas outing four days later saw him post fifteen strikeouts, thirteen walks, two hit batsmen, and three wild pitches. In spite of him, the Broncos prevailed 11-6 over Ponca City. By August 14, Blackwell had increased its record to 45-60, padding its lead over Independence and moving to within striking distance of the former Bartlesville Pirates who had moved to Pittsburg (KS) on July 7.

While forty-two players wore Broncos flannels in 1952, the line-up was remarkably stable. The club

Shortstop Wayne Benstead traded his glove for a veterinary clinic. (Bl-3)

Mayor Al Porter hosted Blackwell's first pro team since 1926. (Bl-1)

Second sacker Fred Bade came over from Carthage. He played in all 127 games. (Bl-2)

divided catching duties between Dan Priest, Wayne Baker, later dealt to Iola, and his replacement Don Keeter on the bounce from Ponca City. George Beck and Charles Lacoste divided duties at first base. Fred Bade played all 127 games at the keystone while Chet Bonczek handled the hot corner in 119 contests, leading the league in fielding for third basemen.

Wayne Benstead was the regular shortstop with Serapio Mentado providing relief. Tom Paddock, Don Gersey, and Tom Kordas roamed the outfield in most games. Gersey and Paddock were the top batters with .299 and .296 averages, respectively; Dan Priest hit .313 but appeared in only forty-nine games. Joe Adametz, Roy Sorensen, Tom Gudeiran and Harold Sumner formed the core of the pitching staff together appearing in 114 games. Adametz was the staff ace with a 3.20 ERA and 13-9 record.

John Patrick Brosnan, brother of Jim Brosnan who would spend nine seasons with the Cubs, Cardinals, Reds, and White Sox between 1954 and 1963, appeared in eight games for the Broncos before receiving his draft notice. When he left for the Army, his record was two wins against three losses. While he was in basic training, his record improved to three wins. Manager Reitz had protested a game in June for which Brosnan was the pitcher of record. After winning his protest, the game was completed on July 15 from the point of protest. The Broncos prevailed and Brosnan was credit with the win *in absentia*.

The fans selected Don Keeter, Chet Bonczek, and Tom Paddock to join with the other All Stars on July 10 to face pace-setter Ponca City. Before a full house at Conoco Park, the Stars took the Dodgers by a 12-5 score.

The excitement of the season came on August 4. After giving up twelve runs to the Pittsburg (KS) Pirates in the top of the first inning, most of the record Blackwell crowd of 4,000 had long headed home when Tom Kordas crushed a grand slam homer in the sixth inning then hit a solid game-win-

Blackwell embraced its Broncos producing one of the best programs in the K-O-M. (Bl-4)

ning single in the bottom of the tenth to give the home team a 16-15 victory.

Two Broncos were selected for the final K-O-M All Star team selected by the official scorers. Don Gersey, batting .299 with a .418 On Base Percentage, was no surprise. What was surprising was naming Andy Vargas to the squad. He appeared in only eighty-seven innings in thirteen games, compiled a 5-6 record with a 5.79 ERA, and walked 104 while striking out eighty-seven.

While league president George Barr struggled to find working agreements and a sixth team for 1953, the Broncos were, as things turned out, the last K-O-M team to suit up for a game. During the playoffs on September 4, Ardmore, cellar-dweller of the Class D Sooner State League, made the trip up U.S. Highway 177 to Morgan Field. Both clubs

The 1952 Broncos traveled in a new bus. The rambling wreck Carthage used stayed there. (Bl-5)

with empty treasuries, the Ardmore Indians met the Broncos in what was termed the "Booby Bowl" to raise funds to provide transportation home for the players. The Broncos dropped the finale in eleven innings by a tally of four to five.

The K-O-M suspended play never to return on February 24, 1953. Recognizing the handwriting on the wall, Morgan sought membership in the Sooner State League. The parsimonious Sooner State owners rebuffed his overture because of concern over increased travel costs; the league was fairly compact by design with only a couple of trips requiring overnight stays.

The lights at Morgan Field went dark in 1953. The Oklahoma Semi-Pro League had become defunct. The Blackwell Baseball Club, now under the leadership of grocer Jack Rafferty, was kept alive in hope of a reorganized K-O-M or an invitation from another league. A paid attendance of 51,000 for the 1952 edition of the Broncos proved that Blackwell, with about 7,500 residents, would support a professional club even one with a losing record. Neighbor Ponca City announced through its president Ted Parkinson that his city would sit out the 1953 season in hope of a revived K-O-M in 1954. Seven cities, including Blackwell, met on October 4, 1953 with a view toward resurrecting the old league. When it became apparent that working agreements necessary for a Class D league to survive would not be forthcoming, the plan was abandoned.

A month later, George Barr, who had been elected Western Association president a year earlier, announced that Ponca City had been awarded a franchise in that league for 1954. Further, with an intent to expand to eight teams he said that Blackwell and Iola, Kansas, both K-O-M orphans, were being considered to fill out the loop. On January 10, 1954, as the Western Association adopted a 140-game schedule to be played between April 25 and September 6, Blackwell, Ponca City, and Iola, Kansas were admitted. None had working agreements but were hopeful to receive outright or limited agreements with Major League clubs by opening day.

Blackwell proceeded as an independent under the leadership of J. R. Roberts. At a booster banquet on January 18 attended by president Barr, Joe Consoli, veteran of eleven minor league seasons and 1953 manager of independent Fond du Lac in the Wisconsin State League, and business manager A. C. "Swede" Gunderson, who had served in the same role for Albuquerque the previous year, were introduced. Ten thousand dollars were raised in ten minutes. Blackwell under the name "Broncos," was ready to play ball. All that was needed were players.

To assemble a roster, Gunderson scouted among free agents while Consoli held a "free baseball school" at Morgan Field from March 24 to 27. Advertising in *The Sporting News*, over one hundred hopefuls appeared. Forty-four appeared at one time or another on

1952 Blackwell Broncos.
Top row L-R: Hal Summer, Tom Guderian, Tom Kordas, George Beck, Stan Bonczek, Joe Adametz, Roy Sorensen, Don Keeter.
Front row L-R: Walt Vonderheide, Fred Bade, Andy Varga, Don Gersey, Al Reitz, Wayne Benstead, Tom Paddock, Danny Priest. (Bl-6)

the Broncos' roster. Seventeen appeared in fewer than ten games. Veterans Gordon Bragg and Walter Buerger played ninety-one and forty-seven games, respectively, for Blackwell while another journeyman Al Kubski appeared in 134 as both first baseman and, after June 30, manager replacing Consoli. Other signees were Don Mooney and John Williams who followed Consoli from Fond du Lac. Don Richards, Ken Hughes, John Crossley, Dick Tyndall, David Wondra, and Charles Re were early season Broncos picked up as free agents. Pitcher Israel Ten came over with experience in the Longhorn and West Texas-New Mexico Leagues. Larry Good was on loan from the Cubs organization. Stan Arthur came aboard via the U.S. Army after a 1952 rookie season in the PONY League. Other independent hurlers who appeared during the first part of the season were Loren Beckman, Pete Braun, Larry Foley, Bob Isbell, Tom Langston, Larry Larrinaga, John Olstad, Ray Reichelt, Carlee Smith, and Kyle Wright.

The Broncos under Consoli settled into fourth place. Attendance was down relative to 1952. With the ball club in financial *extremis*, on June 18 Dave Morgan again came to the rescue becoming owner, assuming all outstanding debts, inking a full working agreement with the Chicago Cubs, replacing Gunderson with 1952 field manager Al Reitz, and, having been swept by Ponca City despite being in the first division, replacing manager Consoli with first baseman Al Kubski on June 28. With the disbanding of the Cubs' Hickory (NC) farm club, second baseman Pat McCollar, outfielder Frank Pecci, and pitchers Babe Franciscovich, Russ Wingo, Leo Davis, and Marty Garber joined the Broncos. Other Cubs farmhands sent to Blackwell included Bud McClure, Sam Frazier, and Gene Nelson.

Dean Manns beat out John Sweich for regular catching duties. Kubski held down first base all season. Ken Hughes would have been at second all season but for Uncle Sam who drafted him away on June 25. Pete McCotter stepped in with a good performance. Won-

dra became a Cubs' signee and continued at third base as did Good at shortstop. Outfielders Bragg and Richards were dealt to Iola, then being operated by the league, soon after Kubski assumed command. Buerger was dealt to Ponca City. Mooney followed Consoli to Erie (PA). Frank Pecci, Pete Plyler, Elmer Westfall, Dick Jennings, and Paul Beck took over the outfield for the rest of the season. Consoli's last line up had Manns behind the plate, Kubski at first, McCotter at second, Wondra at third, Good at shortstop, Westfall in right, Mooney in center, and Back in left. Kubski's first line up was unchanged save for Bragg replacing Beck. On the mound, Russ Wingo, Leo Davis, Stan Frazier, Martin Garber, Bud McClure, and Gene Nelson joined holdovers Arthur and Ten.

Early on league President George Barr took Buerger to the proverbial woodshed for repeated use of profanity, fining him $25 and warned the next time would cost him $50 and a ten day suspension. On May 30, the Broncos turned a triple play when Shortstop Good took a grounder, flipped to Hughes at second

Al Reitz managed the K-O-M Broncos and returned as business manager for the Cubs-affiliated 1954 Western Association club. (Bl-7)

Frank Pecci came when the Broncos signed a working agreement with the Cubs on June 18. (Bl-8)

Outfielder Pete Plyler was another Chicago farmhand who came with the working agreement. (Bl-9)

Walt Buerger began the season with the Broncos but was released when the infusion of Cubs prospects arrived. He finished the season with Ed Carnett's Ponca City Jets. (Bl-10)

for the force out who relayed to Kubski at first who then nailed the runner coming from third at the plate. On June 7, three eighth inning Blackwell pinch hitters reached base on a single, walk, and error scoring four to take Hutchinson 8-7. Fueled by Buerger's grand slam, The Broncos took his future team mates at Ponca City 13-5 on June 13. By the start of a three game series with Ponca City, the Broncos had moved into fourth place.

Several teams were heading for the rocks. The league took over the Iola franchise and sued to have it placed in receivership in June. At a special meeting in early August, Dave Morgan moved to shorten the season to end August 22. It failed with four of the seven voting teams in opposition. The season finished on September 6 with Kubski knocking out number thirty-seven and Dave Morgan donating the receipts for the day's doubleheader to the Crippled Children's Hospital in Oklahoma City. Paid attendance for the campaign was 39,637, a significant drop from 1952's 51,000.

As a team, the Broncos batted .273, just a point behind pacesetter Topeka. They were best in the Association with 4,687 at-bats, 898 runs, 1,280 hits, 1,950 total bases and 777 RBIs. Wondra led the Western Association with 138 runs while Kubski had 144 RBIs while tying the Association record with 37 home runs. Good, Kubski and Wondra all hit over .300. Israel Ten was the top hurler, working 209 innings while building a 17-6 record with a 4.26 ERA. Arthur was on his heels with an 11-7 season and 4.26 ERA in 167 innings. Frazier had a lower ERA, 4.15, but was the hard luck thrower at 10-13. Davis was 10-2 in fourteen start with a team best 3.33 ERA.

Finishing in fourth place nine games off the pace at 79-61, the Broncos faced off against the first place Topeka Owls and swept the first round in three games. St. Joseph's Yankee farmhands had vanquished the Giants' Muskogee club in five. After dropping the second game to the Saints, Blackwell went on to win the next three contests to capture the pennant for 1954.

Jack Rafferty and Phil McMullen represented Blackwell at the November, 1954 annual league meeting. Blackwell was listed as a "certain entry" for 1955. Things changed over the winter. Morgan reported to the January 9, 1955 Western Association meeting that an advance ticket drive by a booster group led by Jack Raffety had failed to raise enough to guarantee the Broncos' viability for the upcoming season. Additionally, the Cubs had moved their Class C affiliation to Ponca City. With Topeka, Independence, and Salina unable to secure working agreements, the league along with the Broncos folded on February 1.

The loss of professional baseball was not the only disaster to hit Blackwell in 1955 and, in comparison, the demise of the Broncos was minor. On May 25, a F5 tornado struck the town and surrounding area in Kay County taking twenty lives, injuring 280, and devastating the city.

Blackwell following the May 25, 1955 F-5 tornado. (Bl-11)

CHICKASHA CHIEFS
SOONER STATE LEAGUE
1948-1952

SEASON	ATTENDANCE	RECORD	FINISH	AFFILIATION	PLAYOFF FIRST ROUND	PLAYOFF FINALS
1948	35,640	73-63	Fourth		Lost to McAlester 1-3	
1949	59,309	78-61	Third		Lost to Lawton 0-3	
1950	43,759	80-59	Third	Dallas (Tex Lg)	Lost to McAlester 0-3	
1951	21,107	46-94	Sixth	Okla. City (Tex. Lg.)		
1952	27,494	78-62	Third		Lost to Pauls Valley 1-3	

Chickasha hosted briefly one of the four ball clubs in the 1904 Southwestern League. The city's entries in the Western Association and Oklahoma State League in the 1920s brought home pennants. After a quarter century hiatus, Organized Baseball returned when the Grady County seat along with Pauls Valley expanded the Sooner State League to eight teams for the 1948 season. The Chickasha nine finished out of the first division only once and that was in the year of five managers.

In the ten seasons of its life, the franchise that originated in Chickasha in 1948 had three homes: half the years in Chickasha, two and a bit of a third in Gainesville, and the rest in Ponca City. It operated most of its life as an independent and finished as a Chicago Cubs affiliate. This franchise can boast one of the two Hall of Fame member the Sooner State League produced, Billy Williams who played at Ponca City in 1956 and 1957.

1948

The manager of Ada Country Club, Leslie Rottier, organized Chickasha's 1948 entry into the Sooner State League. With Edwin Free, who had been business manager of the Ada team during the first half of the 1947 season, and Gordon Love, a former Adan who had moved to Chickasha, he incorporated Chickasha Baseball Club, Inc. with 2,000 shares at $10 each capitalization. Free and Love were brothers-in-law with ties to the oil business. Love served as president while Free and manager Ray Honeycutt cobbled together a team from local free agents, Honeycutt's 1947 team mates from Henderson, Texas, of the Lone Star League, career D-leaguers, and castaways from Ada, Ardmore, and Pauls Valley (including fired Pauls Valley manager Dutch Prather).

An old softball diamond on the northwest end of the Army's abandoned Borden General Hospital was fenced, graded, sodded, and surrounded by a makeshift grandstand. When finished, the Chiefs were able to abandon the 12th Street Grounds facility used all spring. With standing room, 1,100 could be accommodated. The April 25, 1948, *Chickasha Daily Express* bears quoting, hyperbole notwithstanding: "[o]ut of the low land at the northwest corner of the Borden area has risen one of the best parks in the league. Complete with electric scoreboard, press box, and 120 fifteen hundred-watt lamps, the field is said to be the most modern in the circuit." The wooded setting was attractive but amenities were lacking.

Veteran third baseman for Enid's sandlot teams and World War II era semi-pro champion Enid Airs, spray hitting Ray Honeycutt had spent summers since 1936 in the minors. He took the Chiefs to the playoffs each season of his tenure. It could be said that his 1951 departure to manage his hometown Enid Buffaloes in the Western Association marked the beginning of the end of baseball in Chickasha.

Only twenty-four players passed through the Chiefs' clubhouse in 1948. That team was assembled from fourteen rookies, seven sophomores and three veterans (Manager Honeycutt, Dutch Prather on the bounce from the helm of Pauls Valley, and John Quick in his final season). Brooklynite Vic Stryska, who would be an All Star pitcher, and Fleming Flatt, who didn't make the cut at the end of spring training but saw action for Duncan and Pauls Valley,

Ray Honeycutt came from managing Henderson, Texas in 1947. He led the Chiefs through 1950. He departed to lead his hometown independent Enid Buffaloes in the 1951 Western Association. (Ch-1)

The site of the 1948 ball park on the northwest edge of Borden Park. (Ch-2)

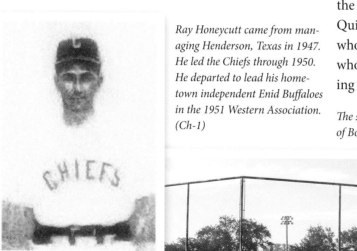

came from Rogers Hornsby's baseball school. Sooner State cast offs included Russ Ritter who was at Lawton and Seminole in 1947, Ada all-state footballer and former Hereford, Orville Makintubee, Bob Stautenback who was an original member of the Ada Herefords, and Charles Githens who toiled for the 1947 Ardmore team. Al Blackaby spent 1947 at Tyler while Chester Hunt was down the road at Henderson with manager Honeycutt. Floyd Geiger, who would manage at Seminole in 1950, was a Ballinger Cat in the 1947 Longhorn League. The official scorers around the League

Russ Ritter had played at Lawton and Seminole in 1947. (Ch-3)

were confused mightily by two Joe Filipiwicz's names on the roster. Both from Brooklyn and both pitchers, the unrelated Joes didn't make the first cut after the season began. Each appeared in six games. Joe E. was 0-1 in fourteen innings yielding fourteen runs on twenty hits and five walks. Joe J. got a win but dropped three in twenty-nine innings with twenty-seven runs on twenty-eight hits and twenty-two free passes.

The Chiefs dropped their franchise opener at Pauls Valley 4-3. Unlike most Sooner State League independents, Chickasha had a stable lineup most of the season with Al Blackaby at catcher, Russ Ritter at first, Frank Smodic at second, Jim Carney at third, Floyd Geiger at short, Homer Thompson in left, Art Punyko in center, and Stautenback in right. Manager Honeycutt led the club in hitting at .338. The surprise was rookie workhorse Vic Stryska. He amassed a 24-14 record pitching three hundred innings.

In a show of goodwill, when the Chiefs played at Ada on July 1, the city held a steak feed for them at the local country club where Chiefs' organizer Rottier managed. Stautenback was hospitalized later for food poisoning. That night Orville Makintubee handcuffed his hosts and former team mates 8-5 for his seventh win since Ada cut him. The next night manager Honeycutt put a battery of twins on the lineup card. John Kaiser pitched and brother Joe caught. John went on in baseball, Joe soon quit.

Vic Stryska set Sooner State League records in his professional debut throwing 300 innings for a 24-14 record. The Brooklyn native signed with the Yankees' organization but never made it to the Show. He led Carta Vieja of Panama to the winter ball Caribbean championship. (Ch-6)

A veteran of the East Texas League, Al Blackaby followed Honeycutt to Chickasha and caught three seasons for the Chiefs. (Ch-4)

Over one hundred fans anteed up to save the Chiefs. This ad appeared before the 1949 season opener. (Ch-5)

83

Finishing fourth by eleven and one-half games over Ada, the Chiefs were only four games out of second. Making their debut in the playoff, the Yankee farm hands from McAlester eliminated the Chiefs in four games. The makeshift 1,100-capacity field on the northwest corner of Borden Park saw 35,640 through the turnstiles. The Chiefs led the League in RBIs (786) and finished second in hitting at .264. They were the best fielding team at .945 with 107 double plays. Rookie Vic Stryska, one of the best pitchers in the league who set six records—most games, most innings pitched, most batters faced, most hits, most starts, and most complete games— didn't receive much help from the rest of the staff. John Kaiser and Patton both posted .500 winning percentages but had 4.57 and 4.58 ERAs. Hunt at 12-10 allowed 5.08 earned runs per nine innings. Help came from pickups Makintubee, released by Ada, and Githens, cut by Ardmore, but their combined twenty-one wins were not enough to capture the regular season crown.

1949

Ed Free resigned in March, 1949. Rottier gathered a new, local investor group that purchased the franchise and team from the original owners. Chickasha Baseball Club dissolved on March 22, 1949, and The Chickasha Chiefs, Inc. was incorporated the next day. Rottier gave up the country club job and moved his home from Ada to become club president and business manager. There were over one hundred investors. The board included Rottier, C. W. Evans who was vice-president, Jack McRae secretary-treasurer, and as directors Otto Elliott, B. B. "Bodie" Benson, Wade Heister, A.C. Walker, Dr. M.R. Williams, and Charles L. Miller. The team christened a new ball park southeast of the 1948 location and directly south of Memorial Stadium, the high school football field. The west wooden grandstand from the 1921 vintage old ball park at the Grand Avenue fairgrounds was moved west to 20th and Iowa. The light towers were re-lo-

The Grady County Commissioners erected a grandstand at the new fairgrounds for the 1921 Western Association club. It was moved to 20th St. and Iowa for the 1949 season. (Ch-8)

Promoting opening night of the 1949 season in Chickasha. (Ch-7)

cated. Bleachers were added at both ends. Sunken concrete dugouts with gravel floors were installed. The ball park lacked club house facilities so the high school football team's locker rooms were used. It had a roof on which was perched a press box. With bleachers, 1,700 could be seated. There the Chiefs played winning baseball there for nearly a season and a half.

In addition to Honeycutt, catcher Blackaby, Geiger, Punyko, Ritter, Thompson, and pitchers Kaiser and Makintubee returned for 1949. The club had an Oklahoma flavor with pitcher Jim Treat from Atwood, and infielders Kelly Wingo from Shawnee, Ivan Wilkerson from Chickasha, and Floyd Geiger from Tulsa. The story, however, was Pete Runnels, a fast third baseman signed out of Lufkin in deep East Texas. Runnels led the league with a .372 batting average and 183 hits on his way to a Major League career with the Senators, Red Sox, and Colt .45s. He was a Sooner State League All Star. In addition, he married at home plate.

Two of the owners persuaded the Oklahoma Pardon & Parole Board to release to their custody McAlester Outlaws star pitcher, Ed Haney, of Dale, Oklahoma, who had served thirty months of a ten year sentence for second degree forgery. Signed on May 3, he went 2-4 with a 4.82 ERA in his only professional season (he was throwing for the Oklahoma State Reformatory at Granite in 1951). Makintubee and rookie Bill Walker each were 15-8 with 2.49 and 3.16 ERAs. Kelly Wingo led in runs with 123 and was the only Chief to play in every game. Walker appeared in twenty-five of the first fifty-two games of the 1949 season starting only one. Twice between the opener and late June, he pitched in four consecutive games. Of the twenty-four games in which he threw relief, Chickasha won fifteen. On May 15, John Wyssman got credit for a win with a pitching performance that saw five hits yielded, two each of walks and strike outs and a league record

Honeycutt found Pete Runnels in the east Texas oil town of Lufkin. After leading the league in batting with a .372 average, the Senators bought his contract. He went on to hit .291 in 1,799 Major League games. He was named to the American League All Star team in 1959, 1960, and 1962. (Ch-10)

John Wyssman set the Sooner State League record with eleven wild pitches in a game. (Ch-9)

eleven wild pitches. Jim Treat, a product of South-eastern State College in Durant, threw six hitless innings before scattering four singles for an 8-2 win over Duncan on June 11. Sometimes it's better to be lucky. The Chiefs shut out Ada 7-0 on May 21 when Hereford Stuart Chestnut committed six errors allowing three runs; Chickasha batsmen also stole seven bases.

The 1949 Chiefs once again were second in team batting (.262) and first in fielding (.950). Continuity and consistency marked the Chickasha lineup. Lou Comparin, Art Punyko, Les Taylor, Homer Thompson and Russ Ritter played the outfield. Ivan Wilkerson played most of the games at first base, Wingo played every game at second and occasionally shortstop, Floyd Geiger held down short-stop, and third base was the domain of All Star Pete Runnels. Al Blackaby was usually behind the plate. This was largely the 1948 lineup. As in 1948, the team's 78-61 record put them in third and earned the club's second trip to the playoffs. Lawton, which would win the playoffs, swept the Chiefs in the first round. Notably, though, a franchise record 59,309 fans watched the Chiefs play. Surprisingly, that figure did not top the league. Pauls Valley drew over 61,000. In any event, the Chickasha Chiefs erased the $8,483 deficit from 1948, spent $5,644 improving city-owned Borden Park Field and had money in the bank. Team management estimated that the Chiefs added $50,000 to the local economy.

1950

Depth of pitching had been the Chiefs' problem in 1948 and 1949. By signing a working agreement with Dick Burnett's AA Texas League Dallas Eagles for the 1950 season, the club hoped to reverse that history. Honeycutt remained as manager but there was significant turnover on the roster. Comparin, Taylor, and Wilkerson were the returning position players; Comparin and Wilkerson were later cut to make the sixteen-player limit on May 25. Dick Anderson at age twenty-four was the sole veteran in camp. Jim Treat, Dick Hobbs, the 1949

1950 Chickasha Chiefs. (Ch-11)

tough luck pitcher, and Makintubee were back. However, during training Makintubee's tuberculosis reappeared, he was hospitalized at the Talihina sanitarium, and never recovered. At the Dallas Eagles' spring training camp at Gladewater, Texas, site of the Eagle's Class C farm club, business manager Rottier remarked that "if [the players assigned to Chickasha] can't do it, we'll get more from Dallas." East Central State College of Ada basketball player and future league umpire, Sam Stuckey, made the club. Ada resident and former Hereford Paul Richardville signed as a veteran after the season began as did A.B. Pearson after the National Association declared him ineligible to play for Pauls Valley. Former St. Louis Browns pitcher Ed W. Cole, at the end of his career, joined the team late in the season and was 10-4 in relief. Bill Hair, a pitcher, was sent down from Class B Gainesville to help out. Only a dozen rookies passed through during the season.

The 1950 season opened well with a home field

win over Pauls Valley 23-4. Shortstop Charlie Watts was four for six including a two-run shot. The 1950 ballclub got off to a good start and after initially occupying the league lead settled into a comfortable third place. The Chiefs again finished third but again lost in the first round of the playoffs to McAlester.

On August 12, 1950, following an eleven inning game with Ada, manager Ray Honeycutt and business manager Les Rottier were leaving the high school locker room around midnight (games began at 8:15 p.m.) when they noticed a blaze. A fire had broken out in the all wooden stands and quickly spread to the roof. Rottier scrambled up to the press box to reach a telephone to call the fire department. He had to jump for his life from the end of the roof sustaining burns to arms and face. The outfield fence and north bleachers escaped harm.

The Chiefs lost the concessions area, mowers, chairs, public address system, and seat cushions among other things, damages totaling over $3,000.

The local paper reported the fire that destroyed the grandstand and other Chiefs' property. Boosters pitched in to have the field ready for play within three days. (Ch-12)

Managers of the two expansion teams, Ray Honeycutt of Chickasha and Red Phillips of Pauls Valley. (Ch-14)

Fire Destroys Borden Park Ball Stands

Fire completely destroyed the baseball grandstand of Borden park around midnight Saturday, just a few minutes after fans attending the Chickasha-Ada baseball game had left.

Manager Ray Honeycutt and President Les Rottier were just leaving the nearby dressing room when Honeycutt spotted the small blaze.

Twenty minutes later the entire stand had burned down. Cause of the blaze was unknown.

The pair rushed to the park, and Rottier broke into the press box to call the fire department.

Before he could leave, the flames had spread to the point of trapping Rottier on the roof of the stands. He ran to one end and jumped off, but not before receiving burns about the face and neck.

The stands and fence were insured for a total of $10,000 according to City Manager John Hamman.

However, most of the fence and the bleacher on the north side was saved.

The diamond was acclaimed by many as the most beautiful in the Sooner State league, providing the best seating.

Ed Cole neé Kisleuskas played for twenty seasons from 1931 through 1951 including stints with the 1938 and 1939 St. Louis Browns. He tossed a perfect game for Jack Mealey's Galveston Texas Leaguers in 1935. He was 10-4 with a 2.48 ERA for Chickasha. (Ch-13)

Two days later a gathering was called by funeral director Jodie Servier to raise replacement funds; 250 attended and passed the hat for $715. On the 16th three hundred fans showed up in the drizzle for Operation Grandstand. In two hours, the debris had been cleared and jumpers for the bleachers from the Chickasha Rodeo Club installed. One hundred men spread sand over areas of the sidelines and infield scorched by the fire and spread gravel over the spectator area. When the Chiefs returned on August 17, they found bleachers in place of the grandstand but a field that was ready for play. The voters approved a $15,000 bond issue. Adding the bond money to $10,000 insurance proceeds, Blair Construction was engaged to construct a new pre-cast concrete and steel facility capable of seating 1,814.

In late July, the *Chickasha Daily Express* editorialized about the financial peril of the ballclub, that gate receipts and net concessions were simply insufficient to pay the operating costs, and that unless the current stock subscription drive were successful, the Chiefs would fold. Attendance for 1950 slumped to 43,759. The Chiefs' only manager, Ray Honeycutt, resigned at season end to take over the Western Association team in his native Enid for 1951. The outlook for the Chiefs was bleak.

1951

For 1951, the league dropped the player limit to fifteen from sixteen but increased the number of veterans from four to six and required that a team have only four rookies. Such a configuration would have been perfect for the 1950 veteran-heavy squad. At the height of the Korean Conflict, however, there was competition for lower classification players. Kelly Wingo, who played every game for Chickasha in 1949 and managed at Seminole and Shawnee in 1950, was selected to lead the 1951 team. A new working agreement with the independent Oklaho-

ma City Indians was in place and the cause of some optimism. Honeycutt promised to send help from his Class C team as he could. The team opened the 1951 season comprised entirely of Oklahomans: four from Chickasha, one from Grady County, and the remainder from within seventy-five miles of Borden Park Field. With conscription for the Korean War at its highest, however, seven Cuban players later joined the Chiefs. One of them, rookie Camilo Pascual, was 0-2 with a 6.16 ERA but Joe Cambria recognized his talent and signed him to a Senators' contract. Pascual went on to an eighteen year Major League career and back-to-back twenty game seasons for the 1962 and 1963 Minnesota Twins.

Perhaps Ray Honeycutt was the glue that held the 1948-1950 teams together. The pre-season optimism was misplaced. Wingo was fired on May 16. He was followed by four successors before the season ended. Wilkerson was manager for five days when Jackson was brought in from Sherman for sixteen games and then Wilkerson was manager again. Chet Bryan, the Norman High School and future Oklahoma State University coach, took over on July 7. Inexplicably, first baseman and interim manager Ivan Wilkerson, outfielders Charles Tuttle, and recently signed 1949 and 1950 Chief Lou Comparin, and pitcher Paul Walker were suspended on July 20 by club ownership and replaced by catcher Manuel Escobido, first baseman Orlando Benitez, and outfielder Leon Damilowski. Bryan jumped ship on August 8. Texan Willie Reyes finished at the helm. There was no continuity in the line-up. Only six position players played in seventy or more of the 140 games. The closest to appearing in all games was Juan Medina with 120.

Wingo and third sacker Willie Reyes, picked up after the season began, were the only veterans. Wilkerson, Stuckey, and Treat were the only players back from 1950. Harley "Doc" Lefevers, the Chickasha High School football coach, was signed to pitch. Del

Gray, and pitcher Herb Cadenhead were limited service players. Twenty-three rookies appeared at one time or another on the Chickasha roster. The team finished with a .329 winning percentage (46-94), tied with Lawton for sixth without field leadership. They tumbled to sixth in team batting at .252, failed to win the fielding crown for the first time with a weak .939 average, and were sixth in pitching with a 5.06 ERA giving up a league high 101 home runs.

Since the old ball park burned nearly a year before, games were played before an ersatz grandstand borrowed from the Chickasha Rodeo Club. The new facility costing $21,600 was dedicated on July 19, 1951 and named Sooner Park because the high school, American Legion team, and others used it beside the Chiefs. The new home didn't help. Only 21,107 watched the confusion during the year of five managers. Today, as Elliott Field it is the home of Chickasha High School's Fighting Chicks and retains the same dimensions: 327 feet to left, 365 feet to center, and 321 feet to right.

Cuban Camilo Pascual had an unimpressive 1951 start with Chickasha but Joe Cambria recognized his raw talent. By 1954, he was with the Washington Senators. He had back-to-back twenty win seasons for the Minnesota Twins. He was a long time scout for the Los Angeles Dodgers. (Ch-16)

Ivan Wilkerson of Oklahoma City played his entire career for Chickasha. He served as interim manager twice in 1951. He quit the game after Chet Bryan became the Chief's fourth manager of 1951. (Ch-18)

Kelly Wingo was a Shawnee high school phenom in 1934 and played in the semi-pro ranks through 1941. He was a regular for Muskogee 1946-1948 before joining Chickasha in 1949. In 1950, he managed Seminole and then the Shawnee club after removal from Duncan. He led Chickasha through May 15 in 1951. He played a month for Dutch Prather's 1951 Seminole Ironmen. After being released, he joined Roy Honeycutt at Enid in the Western Association. He played semi-pro in Shawnee through 1954. (Ch-17)

Willie Reyes had spent three seasons toiling for A. C. Gonzalez at Sherman-Denison. He took over the Chiefs from Chet Bryan on August 14, batting .256 with seven homers and 54 RBIs. (Ch-19)

Funded through insurance and a bond issue, Sooner Park was dedicated on July 19, 1951 and was home of the Chiefs for the remainder of their sojourn in Chickasha. (Ch-15)

Del Rio, Texas attorney Arturo C. Gonzalez got the baseball bug in 1948 and assembled a mini-farm system with teams in Classes B, C, and D. Chickasha was his last acquisition and ended after a single season with the franchise sold to a former umpire who moved the operation to Gainesville, Texas. (Ch-20)

Ray Taylor of Fredrick, Oklahoma, joined Art Willingham's Sherman-Denison club and remained after it was sold to A. C. Gonzalez. He skippered Gonzalez's 1950 and 1951 teams. When Chickasha entered the fold, Taylor was assigned north. As a playing manager, he led the Sooner State League with a .356 batting average. After guiding a Gonzalez team in 1953, he took over the floundering independent Seminole Oilers in 1954 keeping them out of the cellar. (Ch-22)

The 1952 Chiefs were largely Cubans who had played for Taylor in 1951. (Ch-21)

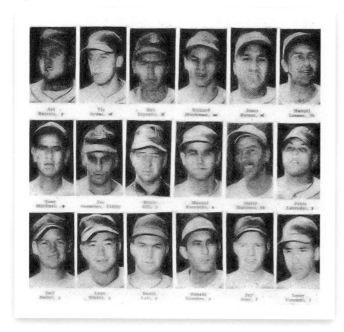

1952

At the fall, 1951, league owners' meeting, Chickasha surprised the group with the announcement that the team had only $2,000 on hand. A month later they announced that the assets of the club were being transferred to Arturo C. Gonzalez of Del Rio, Texas, a baseball hobbyist. Gonzalez had seen Art Willingham pick up the Ardmore franchise in a no-cash assumption transaction and had done the same to acquire his minor league chain.

The Elliott investment group's sale to Arturo C. Gonzalez was approved at the 1951 annual League meeting. The franchise was quickly folded into the Gonzalez operation as its fourth with Decatur of the Mississippi-Ohio Valley League, Sweetwater, Texas, in the Longhorn League, and Paris of the Big State League, three of whom boasted batting champions in 1952. As the price for the team, Gonzalez agreed to assume the club's debts and hold the seller harmless; Chickasha Chiefs, Inc. formally dissolved on April 11, 1952. The former owners of the franchise were glad to walk away from their investment with only experience and Arturo Gonzalez's promise to pay the team's creditors; they didn't want the figurative cheese, they just wanted out of the trap. By the end of the campaign, the individual former shareholders were being bombarded by calls from the 1951 Chief's long unpaid vendors who didn't care about any assumption agreement; they were looking to the old investors to pay up.

Second baseman for Gonzalez's 1951 Big State team at Sherman-Denison, Ray Taylor, was selected to assemble a roster from the chain's stable of players and rookies signed after tryouts. Attorney Gonzalez had found a loophole in the rules of Organized Baseball that permitted him to supply his teams with seasoned players. Time spent playing professionally in Mexico and Cuba did not count toward becoming a veteran. Players with four or five years of seasoning south of the border could be treated as rookies and limited service players. Gonzalez had tapped into the Cambria pipeline of Cuban players early on. Seventeen of the twenty-two who wore the 1952 Chiefs' uniform were Cubans. The seven Anglos included the manager, Ray Taylor, a veteran from Frederick, Oklahoma. Two others, Don Ford and Joe Samalion, were sold to Art Willingham's Sherman Twins. Taylor was to go on to lead the league in batting at .365. The pitching was steady with only one of six allowing more than four earned runs per nine innings. The rotation of Arturo Berreuto, Charles Hinkle, Jesus Zavala, and Reynaldo Ramirez had sixty-one wins. The relievers headed by Miguel Hernandez added fifteen more. Team ERA was 3.50. The hitting was adequate at .249 for Taylor's preferred kind of hit and run small ball. Some-

thing was lost in translation, however, as only 27,494 came to the new Sooner Park to witness the Chiefs' third place finish.

There was one notable strange call during 1952. In the game at McAlester on June 25, pitcher Lou Zavala would up and fell down after tripping on the pitcher's plate. Even though the ball never left his hand, umpire Clayton Varner called a ball. On June 29, the Chief's rallied on Mannie Martinez's grand slam, one of only seventeen Chickasha homers in 1952, to come back from a five run deficit to beat Pauls Valley 10-7. The final professional game played in Chickasha was a 6-0 shutout over the hapless 1952 Ardmore Indians.

Much of the action in 1952 was in the front office and Del Rio. Gonzalez initially hired Kinion Karas from the *Lincoln Journal* as business manager. By May 1, Doyle May, future sports editor of *The Daily Ardmoreite*, took over the front office; Don Dicker from the other Class D team, Deca-

The Chiefs were locked out of Sooner Park as the former owners sued Gonzalez to make good on his indemnity. The Grady County Sheriff allowed the team to have their uniforms and equipment to play the first round play-off at Pauls Valley. (Ch-23)

Sooner Park was renamed Elliott Field in honor of long time baseball supporter Otto Elliott. (Ch-24)

tur, Illinois, succeeded him August 1. Lagging attendance was a problem. As early as June 11, *The Sporting News* reported that Gonzalez was speaking to Duncan officials about moving the Chiefs down U.S. Highway 81. Dick King, Gonzalez's baseball overseer, likewise had expressed concern over attendance early in the season but said the team would stay in Chickasha through the September. Gonzalez confirmed that commitment. Yet then again on August 1, Gonzalez announced that the Chiefs were moving to Seminole the next week and that his new business manager, Don Dicker, was going there to set up a ticket drive for the remaining twenty-four games. The league owners were stunned. Neither President Clanton nor any team owners had approved the move. Nothing happened. The Chiefs stayed put. Seminole was disappointed.

After the last regular season game, all the property of the ballclub was seized by Grady County Sheriff Hack Perrin to provide security for payment of a claim by the former owners on Gonzalez's indemnity. The case was brought by Bodie Benson, owner of a construction company, on behalf of the former directors of Chickasha Chiefs, Inc. who, under Oklahoma law, were personally liable to the club's creditors who were unpaid when the corporation dissolved the previous April. The former owners' claim against attorney Gonzalez was based on his promise to pay those creditors. The case was settled as part of Gonzalez's exit from Chickasha.

With the Chiefs in the playoff semi-finals against Pauls Valley, they were looking at a three game series forfeit. Sheriff Perrin, who had custody of the property, released the bus, road uniforms, and equipment for the Chiefs to play the entire series in Pauls Valley. Everything else in Sooner Park remained under levy. Perrin would not let the club play the third and following games in Chickasha. The Chiefs' were eliminated in four games at the Raiders' home field, losing the finale 9-5 on September 8. Gonzalez was made to honor his debt assumption, leaving a bad taste in his mouth about Chickasha. He put the team on the block. The new grandstand at Sooner Park would never again see professional baseball following the Chiefs' departure to Gainesville.

DUNCAN CEMENTERS
1947-1948

DUNCAN UTTMEN
1949-1950

SOONER STATE LEAGUE

SEASON	ATTENDANCE	RECORD	FINISH	AFFILIATION	PLAYOFF FIRST ROUND	PLAYOFF FINALS
1947	8,220	39-99	Sixth	Topeka, Kansas	(Western League Class A)	
1948	27,066	54-83	Eighth			
1949	36,678	65-74	Fifth	Tyler, Texas	(East Texas League Class C)	
1950*	15,950	51-85	Seventh	Henderson, Texas	(East Texas League Class C)	*moved to Shawnee August 18

The 1938 Halliburton Cementers. (Dn-3)

Duncan was a good baseball town. During the oil boom of the 1920s, Duncan fielded competitive teams in the Oklahoma State League. Following that circuit's demise, Erle Halliburton, whose 1919 patented cementing process became the foundation for an industrial empire, formed his company team, the semi-pro Cementers who played championship ball through 1939.

The story of post-War baseball in Duncan and its demise is centered on the personality of one Otto Utt. Charley Rhodes of the *Ada Evening News* on December 26, 1954 wrote a postscript:

"Baseball in Duncan never had a chance to catch fire due to the penny-pinching operation of Otto Utt who didn't give Duncan anything closely resembling a first division club."

The story of the first four years of the franchise is the story of Otto Utt. Big, stubborn, hot tempered, unsophisticated, and parsimonious, Otto Utt was a decent if ineffective manager, certainly better than his performances as a businessman and diplomat. A native of Pueblo, Colorado and son of a cowboy, at age 25 in 1931 he was playing in his second season of professional baseball while working as a heater in a steel mill in the off-season. He first played at Norton of the Nebraska State League and then Wilkes-Barre of the New York-Pennsylvania League where he hit .342 and .316 respectively.

Claims that he played for the Giants and Browns had only a scintilla of truth: he had spent a few days in spring camp with each. He never saw the inside of a Major League clubhouse.

After 1931 he made his way to Duncan and became a mainstay of the semi-pro Halliburton Oil Cementers. The year 1937 found him in the Ft. Worth Cats' spring camp but he didn't make the cut and returned to the Cementers. He was a member of the 1935-1939 Halliburton teams including the national champions that traveled to Puerto Rico for the world championship tournament in September 1939. After the Halliburton club was disbanded, Utt lost his job, played some sand lot ball with fellow Cementers alumnus Jess Welch for Duncan Merchants in 1941, and then built the Tampico Café at the corner of Highway 81 and Chestnut and the Hit Roller Rink behind his home at 1412 Chestnut; he was repairing the building's roof when Pearl Harbor was attacked. A skilled welder with a shop behind his Chestnut Street house, Utt was much in demand, employing about ten assistants and doing steel work on major buildings in town.

When the Sooner State League's Shawnee franchise became available in 1946, he secured it and, with the support and patronage of Erle P. Halliburton, formed the Duncan Cementers. In his own way, Utt was quite the entrepreneur although he considered

The 1935 Halliburton Cementers squared off against Satchel Paige's Bismark, N.D. semi-pros for the national championship. (Dn-1)

The 1937 edition was the Oklahoma champion. (Dn-2)

himself a poor businessman. With other irons in the fire, he tried unsuccessfully to run the ball club on a shoestring. He dealt in players unsuccessfully and usually under some financial duress. According to Don Webb, visitors' batboy in 1947 and the Duncan home team batboy in 1948 and 1949, Utt sold slugger John Reimold for $100. The teams he managed both finished last in the league. He sold the team to Shawnee interests after the end of the 1950 season.

Otto Utt was one of the most colorful characters to appear in a league the national press had called "zany." He had not been known as an abuser of umpires during his seventeen years in the minors and with Halliburton Oil Company's semi-pro team. His motivation, though, was to entertain the fans and keep them coming to the ball park. In some cities in the Sooner State League, Sunday baseball was illegal. In Duncan it was a matter of free market. Otto Utt observed that "[i]f the preacher can put on a better show than my Cementers, the Sunday night venture won't be a success for most of the fans will be in church." In the Sooner State League, however, he collected frequent ejections. Among the most entertaining was when he once paid a $10 fine by bringing a bag of one thousand pennies to the plate and presented them to the umpire. The league rule was that a player who had been fined could not appear at bat until the fine had been paid.

Umpire Bob Rice ejected Otto Utt, who was neither on the roster nor in uniform, in the seventh inning of the 1948 season opener at Duncan for protesting too much at third base. As he was escorted from the field, he screamed "You can't do that to me. I own the park!"

When the manager owned—or at least rented—the ball park, the umpires were not necessarily in charge of the game. On June 20, 1950, with lights popping at the Duncan Bowl due to high winds and the beginning of a rain storm, Otto Utt asked the

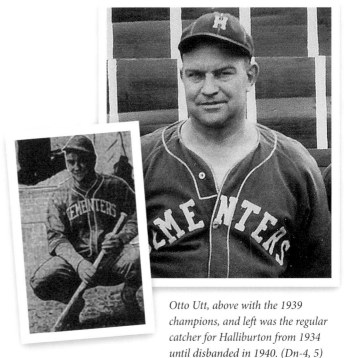

Otto Utt, above with the 1939 champions, and left was the regular catcher for Halliburton from 1934 until disbanded in 1940. (Dn-4, 5)

plate umpire to call the game. When he refused and ordered the game continued, with the Uttmen leading Pauls Valley by four runs after five and one-half innings, Utt unlocked the switch box, turned off the lights, and declared the game over.

Utt again earned an ejection in a game at Ada on July 25, 1950. He refused to leave and, just as the police were about to intervene, ran to center field, hopped the fence into the rodeo bull chutes and explained that he was off the field and out of Hereford Park. There were actually brahma bulls in the enclosure prompting him to quickly return to the field and gladly accept his escort.

After sale of the Uttmen, he returned to Duncan, wound up his several business interests and moved his family to a one thousand acre ranch near Wilson in 1956 trading and raising cattle. Returning to Duncan in 1964, the family home burned to the ground destroying the photographic record of the Cementers and Uttmen. He attended the Halliburton event in 1964 recognizing the company's athletes. He died of a cerebral hemorrhage while working with a horse in Duncan in June, 1966 at age sixty.

1947

Like each of the new Sooner State League franchises, Duncan needed a home field. Utt initially sought to purchase from the Duncan School Board the plot where the first Cementers games were played (without an outfield fence) south of Halliburton Stadium, the high school football field; he was turned down. In January, 1947, he scraped together $1,650 to buy a land-locked ten acre tract. Characteristically jumping the gun, Utt began dirt work before a road had been built to it through Memorial Park. On his own he cut west from Highway 81 north and west of Halliburton Field. After an initial denial, faced with a *fait acompli* the Park Board relented and recommended a 220 yard dirt road extension of Pine Street west across Highway 81. He began pouring concrete for stadium footings but realized his task was impossible and had to stop on March 21.

Utt had exhausted his own capital. The downtown business community, with whom he shared mutual dislike, was persuaded to form a for-profit company, Duncan Improvement Corporation, to contract with Utt to finish the ball park. Utt contributed the land and his sweat equity for a minority in-

terest. Theoretically, the profits from the rental to the baseball franchise would repay the shareholders. The promoters of Duncan Improvement Corporation, a group of Duncan businessmen and civic leaders, had a large vision of Duncan becoming a base for spring training for independent minor league clubs. It had served that role in the 1920s. There was even talk of moving in old Army barracks to house the baseball prospects. Erle Halliburton was one of the organizers. The Duncan Touchdown Club undertook the job of selling subscriptions.

In the prospectus for the stock, it was represented that the company would receive 3¢ on the first 35,000 paid admissions to the new ball park, 7¢ on those between 35,000 and 50,000, and 14¢ on all tickets sold over the first 50,000. They projected attendance of 70,000 had a revenue stream of $4,900. How wrong they were. Duncan Improvement Corporation, the owner and landlord, received a percentage of the baseball franchise's gate in 1947 of $269.70 and $811.98 in 1948. For 1949 and 1950, they took a sure thing. A flat $1,000 per season was charged.

The money to build the Duncan Bowl was finally raised on April 10, and $20,500 was turned over to Utt nineteen days before the season. With bad weather and a late start, Duncan's team would

Rodeo bleachers and chicken wire made up the first home of the Duncan Cementers. There was no outfield fence. (Dn-6)

be homeless for some time. The ball park was not ready when Duncan's first home stand began on May 2. The fact that Duncan had the lowest attendance in Organized Baseball in 1947, only 8,220, is in some part attributable to the fact that Duncan could not host a game until well into the season. Another was access. Today the ball park is on paved Pine Street in the middle of the Duncan High School campus and Memorial Park. In 1947, it was at the end of a 220 yard dusty, dirt trail Otto Utt had cut west from U.S. Highway 81, the old Chisholm Trail. Excessive dust was a problem. Duncan Improvement Corporation and Utt blamed each other and demanded a solution. Finally, after Utt's share of revenue from outfield fence sign sales was deducted from the $500 the company would provide, he agreed to oil the road.

The Duncan Bowl, as it was known during the days of the Sooner State League, was a poured concrete crescent dug into a hill into which aluminum benches were set. It was ahead of its time. All Sports Stadium in Oklahoma City (1962-1998) was a much larger version of the Duncan Bowl. With a capacity of 1,650, the roofless bowl was cozy. The aluminum fence, a donation from Erle Halliburton, was 315 feet away from home plate down the left

field line, 375 feet to dead center, and 320 feet to right. Home plate faced northeast. It lacked dugouts (players sat on benches) until the 1950 season when the League forced Utt to install them. The facility only later had clubhouses; before then players for both sides had to dress at home or in the hotel.

Otto Utt was not invited to the September, 1946, meeting among the original organizers of the Sooner State League but when the effort to place a team in Shawnee failed, he became the franchisee from Duncan. At the November, 1946, meeting, Utt and Cecil Blake represented Duncan interests. Utt operated as a sole proprietor figuratively and often literally out of his hip pocket. He served as business manager each year except 1949, the franchise's best year financially and on the field.

The Duncan clubs were never in the business of developing young players for the Major Leagues; Utt just tried to keep a team on the field, playing a game of catch and release. In fact, the only Utt player to reach the majors was Joe Stanka who had been optioned from the Dodgers' farm club at Ponca City. Owner Utt's teams played small ball, hit and run, on the cheap. Dozens of players were signed. Roughly a third did not last beyond their rookie season. Only a few played more than three years in

Utt's Duncan Bowl design was ahead of its time. It is still in use today. (Dn-7)

Organized Baseball, living a gypsy existence among other Class D and Class C independent, hometown teams. Many players were from southwest Oklahoma or had recently played in West Texas or New Mexico. Duncan never had a working agreement with any Major League team although not initially without suitors. The New York Giants approached Utt in January, 1947, and then turned to Lawton, the regular season champion, after being spurned. Utt was afraid of the baseball draft. He didn't want to be cheated out of a big payday when a prospect he had found was ready to sell upstream for a handsome profit.

With Erle Halliburton's blessing and the company's purchase of red uniforms similar to the Halliburton Oil semi-pros, Utt took the name "Cementers" for his D league team. The season began on April 29 with a road series at Lawton's Memorial Park. After losing the first three as a visiting club, for the scheduled reciprocal series at Duncan the Cementers simply donned their home uniforms and acted as hosts to Lawton at the little Giants' home venue. Duncan dropped all six games. The Duncan Bowl was still unready when a two-game series on May 6 and 7 with Ada had to be played at Hereford Park with the Cementers as the home team. H. M. Nicholson notched the first Cementer win with a two-hitter in Hereford Park.

After that series in Ada and another in Seminole, the Cementers played their first series in Duncan on an unlighted practice field south of Duncan High School's Halliburton Field. Utt rented bleachers from the Chickasha Roundup Club and strung chicken wire to keep the fans from the field and the fouls from the fans. There was no outfield fence. The Cementers, who arrived in town having prevailed in only three of fourteen outings, won all five games played in the sunshine there. The scheduled debut of the Duncan Bowl on May 29 was rained out. The Cementers finally got to play a

game there on June 2, 1947, christening the stadium with an 8-5 win over the league-leading Lawton Giants. Three days later, Ada outfielder Paul Deters hit the first home run in the Duncan Bowl.

The ball park situation was a metaphor for the play on the field. The three 1947 Cementers with prior professional experience were Mike Pruitt, most recently from Halliburton's semi-pro club, Utt, and Pitcher Jim Morris, on option from Topeka. Several players were college boys and recent high school products. H. M. Nicholson, who played in ten games for Duncan and twenty-four for Ardmore, came from Miami, Oklahoma's junior college, Northeastern State. Charles Clark, who hit .068 in sixteen games, had played for Durant's Southeastern Oklahoma State. Clint Clark, who posted no wins in four decisions with a 6.51 ERA in eight starts, and Carl Stewart, who threw without a decision, were signed out of rural Empire High School southwest of Duncan. Pitcher George Reid, 9-14 with a 4.52 ERA, and catcher *neé* fullback Don Williamson from Davis, the leading hitter at .330, were products of Cameron State College of Agriculture, a junior college in nearby Lawton.

The 1947 team committed 535 errors, nearly four per game. No wonder only one Cementer pitcher, Nicholson, had a winning season record, 11-10, with most of his wins coming while he was throwing for Ardmore. Not until June 2 had the Cementers defeated each of the other five teams. The Otto Utt-managed 1947 club finished a distant last winning thirty-nine of 138 contests, a .283 winning percentage fifty-eight games behind first place Lawton. Home attendance was 8,220, the lowest in Organized Baseball. Utt's men had the lowest batting average (.227), and the fewest hits, runs, and RBIs. Yet Utt (forty games .351 average), Donnie Drumm (seventy-seven games .328 average), and Williamson (135 games .306 average) acquitted themselves well. The batters stood too close to the plate —seventy-seven Cementer batters were hit— and struck out more often than the rest of the Sooner State teams. They were the worst fielding club in League history with a .902 team average in spite of setting the all-time league record for assists in a game with twenty-five against Ardmore on May 18. Fred Holdsclaw's 127 innings of 2.98 ERA hurling was more than offset by Fred Malek's eighty-seven innings yielding 8.28 earned runs per nine innings. Remarkably, considering that Utt was scrapping the bottom of the baseball barrel, only thirty-four players donned a Cementers uniform that season.

1948

The 1948 season began with Utt as owner being ejected from the season opener against Lawton. He was heard yelling to the umpire "You can't do that to me, I own the park." Utt had turned the field leadership over to friend and Duncan High School basketball coach, Jess Welch. A former semi-pro Halliburton Cementer who had a few seasons in the low minors, he began with a core of five holdovers from 1947 and two veterans, Utt and Frisco Roberts.

With employees of oil drillers taking up most of the available rooms in town, for spring training Utt had to rent the old armory (now the Stephens County Historical Museum) to house prospects military-style. Five rookies were signed and released during the season. As the school year approached, Welch returned to the classroom and gym on July 21. Utt by default took over and hit .421 in fifteen games. In a notable incident, outfielder Paul Perrin jumped at the crack of the Ada hitter's bat and collided with the wall in Duncan's left field as the ball sailed out of the park. When he didn't get up, the umpires and Duncan team went out to attend to him. The game was delayed fifteen minutes. What actually happened was that he slipped on some sand and managed to get his foot stuck under the metal fence. He couldn't

Jess Welch was an athlete, teacher, coach, and founder of the Duncan Youth Council. (Dn-8)

pull it out without a serious cut from the aluminum flashing on the bottom. A team mate cured him by going around the fence, removing his shoe, and freeing him.

Welch got the Cementers to seventh place before going back to school. Utt took the helm for the rest of the campaign and led the players to the cellar. In July, rumors originating from Utt spread that he had been offered a "substantial amount of money" for the franchise and that Duncan businessmen and Dick Burnett's Dallas Eagles were in contention. His asking price was $15,000.

The Duncan Bowl hosted 27,066 fans who watched a last place team struggle to an improved fifty-four victories in 137 starts, but that was still thirty-six and one-half games off the pace. The 1948 season ended with catcher Don Drumm marrying at home plate and then banging out a triple and two singles to propel Duncan over Lawton by a score of 13-5. Drumm then quit the game having played his entire career as a Cementer. By 1954, with the exception of rookie Frank Golob, all the 1948 Duncan Cementers were out of Organized Baseball. The team hit a respectable .257 but tied for last in the field with .930. The pitching staff had a 4.32 ERA but thanks to errors and passed balls were scored on at the rate of 6.22 runs per nine innings with 15.35 base runners per nine. The team only scored 5.6 runs per game.

1949

Before the October, 1948, League meeting Utt said he was moving to oust President Jack Mealey because "[f]or two years Mealey has been letting a few teams get away with murder." When the confrontation occurred and accusation was made, Mealey offered to read a letter he had written defending Utt. This took the wind out of Utt's sails and the matter was dropped.

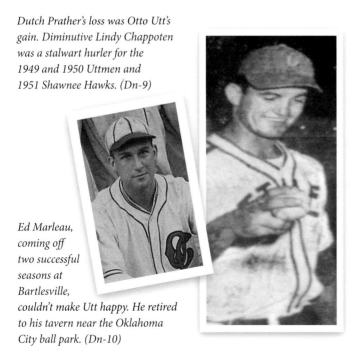

Dutch Prather's loss was Otto Utt's gain. Diminutive Lindy Chappoten was a stalwart hurler for the 1949 and 1950 Uttmen and 1951 Shawnee Hawks. (Dn-9)

Ed Marleau, coming off two successful seasons at Bartlesville, couldn't make Utt happy. He retired to his tavern near the Oklahoma City ball park. (Dn-10)

Utt's patrons at Halliburton Oil Company decided that the Sooner State League team's reputation for rowdiness on and off the field did not reflect well on the company, and declined to buy uniforms for 1949; two consecutive last place finishes may also have figured into the calculus. Shelling out $1,200, Utt bought new flannels with blue lettering and piping and changed the team's name to the" Uttmen." It was not until the *Duncan Banner's* sports writer Tom Constabile complained in print that Utt finally removed the name Cementers from the side of the team bus. The same writer had earlier opined that 1949 was Utt's year to put up or shut up: "[i]f [Utt] doesn't come through, he'll have to call it quits in Duncan." Poor access to the Duncan Bowl and excessive dust depressed attendance.

Ed Marleau, after some success managing the Pirates' operation at Bartlesville, had been lured away from his beer joint near Texas League Park and retirement in Oklahoma City to try to shape up the Duncan nine. Spring training was an *ad hoc* affair. Once again, the aspirants, rookies and veterans, slept in the National Guard armory. Meals were found nearby at Utt's Tampico Cafe, specializing in Mexican food, on Highway 81. The new skipper inherited a veteran pitching staff —Charlie Deal, Frank Golob, and Glen Smith— and later Cuban rookie right hander Lindy Chappoten picked up from Ardmore mid-season. Don Williamson and team captain Frisco Roberts were the foremost of four returning position players. Owner Utt even signed outfielder Ted Crapp of the House of David barnstorming team. The Uttmen made a run for the first division but lack of leadership at the top damaged stability and the small ball Utt demanded didn't score enough runs. Glen Smith, for example, struck out sixteen Seminole batters on August 10, but dropped the decision 2-1.

Marleau lasted only until May 31 before the ever impatient Utt fired him. Journeyman infielder Jim Skidgel, who was to soon land in Ada before becoming the only player to appear for three Sooner State League teams in a season when he took the helm at Ardmore, assumed the lead but clashed with owner Utt about personnel and style of play. Skidgel was popular with the players and stood up for them against the poor officiating endemic in the Sooner State League; the Dean of league managers Lou Brower said in his parting shot in 1954 that it was the worst he'd seen in thirty years in the game. Skidgel was fined $25 for precipitating a shower of soda bottles when he refused to leave the home field following being ejected. When he was fired on July 12, twenty-three year old catcher and former Yankee farm hand with the 1947 McAlester club, Hosea Pfeifer, took the field job. The Duncan fans liked what they saw. Attendance at the Duncan Bowl rocketed to 36,678.

The 1949 Uttmen were the best Duncan team fielded: fourth in the League in batting (.249) having the fewest strikeouts (674) and in an effective tie for fourth in fielding with "only" 352 errors. Utt favorite Glen Smith had eleven wins against fourteen losses in thirty-five games with a 2.98 ERA and Charlie Deal and Lindy Chappoten had winning records. The staff as a whole gave up 833 runs while the Duncan batters scored only 786. Duncan's last best chance for a playoff berth evaporated.

The financial success such as it was in 1949, was largely attributable to Utt acknowledging he was not a businessman and hiring Al Silen of Tulsa as business manager. Utt again announced that he had received "a substantial offer," this time from Vernon, Texas, whose team was moving to Roswell, N.M. in 1950. He openly offered the team for sale for $25,000; there were no takers. There were rumors in 1949 that Otto Utt was maneuvering to move the team to Shawnee and in fact Silen opened negotiations there but was thwarted by the city commission that owned and operated new Memorial Park. From a town with a population of nearly 16,000, 36,678 fans watched

the 1949 Uttmen, who with three managers during that season, finished the highest in team history, fifth, with sixty-five wins against seventy-four losses, four games out of fourth place.

1950

Utt refused purchase offers from a group of several of the Duncan Improvement Corporation shareholders between seasons; he would rather hold out for his price or deprive Duncan of baseball. The 1950 Uttmen opened in Duncan under field management of young catcher Hosea Pfeifer who carried over from the previous season. With Cuban Lindbergh Chappoten and Frank Golob leading the pitching staff, the team had a good chance to escape the second division.

The final edition of the Uttmen began the season with guarded optimism for a first division finish inasmuch as the two star pitchers were back. Williamson, Lance Roberts, who led the 1949 team with a .339 batting average, and Drumm were, how-

1950 *Uttmen hitters (L-R) Bill English, new manager Kelly Wingo, John Reimold. (Dn-11)*

101

ever, gone. The 1950 Uttmen couldn't buy a break. When veteran John Reimold bounced a ball off of the flag pole 385 feet away in center field outside the fence, the umpire called the ball in play. In an economy move to save Pfeifer's $400 per month salary, Utt fired him on July 26. After a short stint as interim manager, Utt picked up unemployed Dutch Prather to lead the field effort.

Seventy-two games into the season, just over half way, the Uttmen were in sixth place having won thirty-one of seventy-two. Utt announced that the team was for sale at a price of $20,000. Everything including player contracts went. Utt stated that he wished to remain in Duncan since it was home but only on his terms and that he expected the team to be back in 1951 unless it sold. The team played its last game in the Duncan Bowl in late July. Attendance in Duncan had fallen to about two hundred per game, 6,600, in thirty-five dates. The Uttmen left Duncan for a road trip in early August, 1950, and didn't return. On August 8, Utt announced that five Duncan home games against Seminole and McAlester between August 13 and 17 had been moved to Shawnee's Memorial Park. Pitcher Bill Heerdt married Virginia Darity

of Duncan before the August 13 game. The Uttmen celebrated with a thirteen to eight win over McAlester. After losing to Seminole the next night, Utt announced the team was not returning to Duncan. Heerdt beat Seminole on six hits 11-5 on August 15. When the Uttmen beat McAlester on August 17, Utt made application to formally move the franchise to Shawnee. Cy Stewart wanted the team to remain in Duncan because of the proximity to his Lawton club. As the vote to move had to be unanimous, he finally relented that afternoon. The move was effective the next day. On August 18, the franchise formally became Shawnee's, Prather was fired, and Shawnee High School hero Kelly Wingo named as manager on August 23. For the season, 15,950 saw the Uttmen in Duncan and Shawnee.

The team hit .246 with Reimold leading the club at .298. Golob managed to win twenty games and Chappoten eleven. The rest of the mound staff, including the twenty-five who saw service in less than ten games each, combined to win only twenty. Without those two starters, the Uttmen had a .259 winning percentage and would have qualified as the worst team in the history of the Sooner State League. As it turned out, the move to Shawnee and a change of ownership was to transform the franchise into a winner.

Relocating the Uttmen was not greeted with unalloyed enthusiasm. McAlester favored the switch since

The heart of the Uttman rotation, Lindy Chappoten, Frank Golob, Bill Heerdt. Golob, of Pueblo, Colorado won twenty games for a 1950 team that won only fifty-one. Golob pitched for the transplanted Uttmen at Shawnee through 1955. (Dn-12)

Donnie Williamson was one of the original Duncan players. He toiled for Utt through 1949. He joined Pauls Valley for the 1951, 1952, and 1953 seasons. (Dn-14)

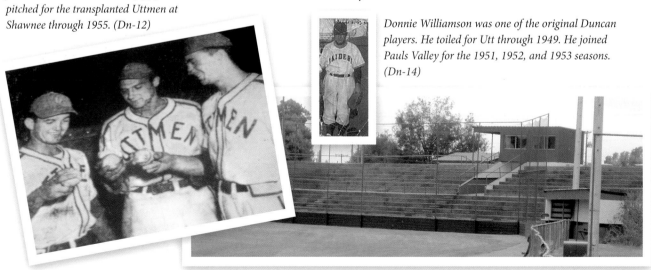

Inside the Duncan Bowl. (Dn-13)

games at Shawnee could be a one day turn around rather than overnight stays as was the case with playing at Duncan. Lawton estimated that with Shawnee in the league it would incur additional expenses of about $700 over a season. Lew Johnson, the sports editor of the *Lawton Constitution* didn't mince words:

> Just how much longer are league officials going to allow Otto Utt to bully his way around the circuit? The rotund baseball 'executive' has soured what used to be one of the top baseball cities in the state on the national pastime, and is now starting on No. 2 — with the unanimous blessing of presidents around the league. I imagine Duncan fans are relieved . . . . They should be. . . .Otto has given them everything but a baseball team since the league was formed in 1947.

Temporarily displaced by the Shawnee Rodeo, the former Uttmen, now the Shawnee Hawks, returned for two games on July 11 and 12, 1951. Eight hundred fans watched each game. Those were the last professional games played in Duncan.

Duncan Improvement Corporation was literally left holding the Bowl. The ball park was rehabilitated during 1952 and 1953 and renamed Sportsman's Park exactly six years after the Cementers played the first game there. In 1961, as part of the company's judicially supervised dissolution, Duncan Improvement Corporation deeded the Duncan Bowl to Independent School District No. 1 of Stephens County. With a better outfield fence moved in from right to center ten feet from the days of the Uttmen and vastly improved lighting, the Duncan Bowl now is the home field of the Duncan High School Demons.

Two stalwarts of the Sooner State League, each with six seasons, began their professional careers at Duncan. Catcher and later first baseman and outfielder Don Williamson played for Duncan 1947-1949 and, after being sold to Tyler, Texas, in the East Texas

League in 1950, returned close to home to Pauls Valley in 1951-1953. Pitcher Frank Golob of Pueblo, Colorado, won forty of seventy-five for bad teams between 1948 and 1950 with thirty-seven complete games in fifty-seven starts. In 1950, he won twenty games for a team that won only fifty-one on the season. He went on to be the most successful pitcher in the league's history.

Otto Utt's cellar dwellers had one player who would appear in a Major League game. Hammon, Oklahoma's Joe Stanka, who was on assignment from the Brooklyn K-O-M team at Ponca City, finished with one win in nine decisions with an 8.72 ERA in his rookie year for the 1950 Uttmen. After a brief appearance with the American League champion 1959 Chicago White Sox, he excelled as one of the first American pitchers in Japan. Duncan produced two All Stars. Former Halliburton Cementer Mike Pruitt, who had pitched for the 1941 Wichita Falls team in his one previous year in professional baseball, was named to the first, mid-season 1947 All Star team; no Duncan player was named to the post-season selection. Frisco Roberts, a semi-pro player from around Okemah, in his last professional season was chosen as the All Star utility infielder in 1949. In the only year the League chose an alternate All Star team, Frank Golob and Truman May were selected.

The 1950 Ponca City club was overstocked with pitchers so the Dodgers optioned Hammon, Oklahoma rookie Joe Stanka to Duncan where he had one wins against eight losses. Stanka was the only Duncan player to reach the Major Leagues. His greatest success came in Japan. (Dn-15)

103

ENID GIANTS
1950
ENID BUFFALOES
1951
WESTERN ASSOCIATION

SEASON	ATTENDANCE	RECORD	FINISH	AFFILIATION	PLAYOFF FIRST ROUND	PLAYOFF FINALS
1950	40,713	71-63	Fourth	New York (NL)	Lost to Hutchinson 1-2	
1951	39,584	45-79	Seventh			

Back-to-back national champion Champlain Refiners. (Ed-1)

Before the War, Eason Oil had won the National Baseball Congress semi-pro world series championship in 1937 and was runner-up in 1938. Champlain's Refiners had copped the same national title in 1940 and 1941.

Enid Army Air Field opened in 1942 and its baseball team, known as the Enid Airs, quickly rose to national prominence. For three consecutive seasons, 1943, 1944, and 1945, the Enid Airs appeared in the finals of the NBC semi-pro world series. Pitcher and outfielder Cot Deal, who played thirteen minor league seasons at the AAA level and made appearances with the Boston Red Sox and St. Louis Cardinals, was the MVP of the tournament in 1944 and 1945. The Enid Airs were loaded with talent including Enid natives Lew Kretlow, a ten season Major League pitcher, and semi-pro star, and minor leaguer Ray Honeycutt. Other minor leaguers who appeared for the Enid Airs were Okemah's Odie Strain, Monty Basgall, Lew Morton, Nick Popovich, and Bill Hankins among others. While they dropped the 1943 final to the Camp Wheeler (GA.) Spokes and 1944 to the Sherman (TX) Flyers, the post-VJ Day tournament in 1945 went the Airs' way behind Deal's pitching as Orlando (FL) Army Air Base was vanquished.

Enid hosted the Oklahoma Semi-Pro Tournament each season between 1946 and 1948. The Airs made their swan song appearance there as airmen were discharged from service. A new semi-pro league had been formed that included the Enid Cardinals, Woodward Boosters, Stillwater Boomers, Clinton Jaycees, Perry Merchants, and the powerful Elk City Elks. While a diversion for college players—Clinton was loaded with OU players while Stillwater was a virtual copy of the Oklahoma A & M Cowboys' squad—the money for some, particularly Elk City, was better than minor league pay. In fact, the 1950 Elk City team

1937 national semi-pro champion Eason Oil. (Ed-2)

1944 runner-up and 1945 champion Enid Airs. (Ed-3)

Perhaps the best semi-pro team ever, the 1950 Elk City Elks won the Oklahoma crown. Home run king with the 1954 Roswell Rockets, Joe Bauman (top, fourth from left) also ran a filling station during the oil boom there. Hurler Dee Sanders (top, third from right) threw 75 1/3 innings without a walk for McAlester in 1951. Manager Dwight "Rip" Collins (front, third from right with trophy) and Bill Stumborg (front, far left) both guided Fred McDuff's 1951 Seminole Ironmen. (Ed-4)

arguably was the best semi-pro ball club ever assembled. Professional baseball in Enid had a hard act to follow after World War II.

1950

The New York Giants had owned and operated the Western Association franchise in Ft. Smith, Arkansas from 1938 through 1949. After twelve seasons of losing money and with the local authorities unable to deliver on stadium improvements, Minor League Director Carl Hubbell determined that the Giants would no longer be the town's baseball "meal ticket" and through his assistant Jack Schwartz announced to the November, 1949 league meeting that the party was over. Enid had every indication of being a strong baseball town hungry for Organized Baseball. The Giants moved their operation to the main city of the Cherokee Strip.

The New York Giants were owned by the Stoneham family since the glory days of John Mc-Graw. Horace Stoneham had inherited the team in 1936 and indeed had an apartment at the top of the centerfield tower in the Polo Grounds. It was time for the scion of the family, twenty-two year old Charles H. "Pete" Stoneham to leave behind the good life of Manhattan and run the family operation in bone dry—Prohibition was still the law in Oklahoma—Enid. The man who lead the Giants' farmhands in Ft. Smith to a second-place 86-54 record before 62,534 fans and landed a place on the league's All Star team, Herb Kollar, was tapped for a reprise.

The 1950 season saw the blossoming of the Joplin shortstop, Mickey Mantle, who led in every batting category. The rest of the league played in his shadow. The Giants with a 71-63 first division finish eighteen games behind Mantle's Joplin Miners did give a credible performance.

Kollar was only twenty-seven but the old man on a team whose average age was 21.9 years. Pitcher Klon Greene was the only returning player from the 1949 Ft. Smith squad. The ball club he brought back to Enid was comprised of limited service (under three seasons in Organized Baseball) players and rookies. Consistent with his mission to develop prospects rather than bring pride to the host city, there was little turnover on the Enid Giants and a remarkably stable regular line up.

Ronald Neff, who had spent the previous two seasons at Class D Oshkosh caught eighty-six games, while rookie Oscar Fernandez largely replaced him in the latter half of the season. Seton Hall product

Bud Kollar was in the Giant's stable managing in their minor league system including at Muskogee in 1953. (Ed-6)

1949 Ft. Smith Giants were uprooted and placed in Enid for 1950. (Ed-5)

Bob Harrison spent his rookie season at Lawton in 1949. He went on to appear briefly with the Baltimore Orioles. (Ed-7)

and rookie Roy O'Neill also saw some time behind the plate. Kollar held down first base in all 134 games, earning a berth on the All Star team. Bob Ludwig who had toiled in the Giants' low minors in 1944, 1948 and 1949 was the regular at second base. Team batting leader at .318 was James Jones who held down the hot corner. Big (6' 2") Al Majewski at shortstop was sent down to Class D Bristol (TN) and replaced for the rest of the season by diminutive (5' 5") Harry Musselman who had three years in the Giants' farm operations. He couldn't take the field, however, because Majewski's uniform swallowed him; a new one had to be sent from New York. Converted pitcher Art Dunham, in his third season, speedster Raymond Johnson, with thirty stolen bases, and Bill Wells, acquired from the Pittsburgh organization, roamed the outfield. They were relieved occasionally late in the season by Randolph Yandoli, called up from Class D Lenoir (NC) with a 15-4 pitching record; he didn't throw for Enid.

The regular pitching rotation accounted for fifty-two of seventy-one wins but only half the losses. Bob Harrison, who was 12-10 the previous season with Lawton, was the workhorse with 215 innings in thirty games but had hard luck in finishing with a 12-16 record. He went on to have a cup of coffee with the Baltimore Orioles. Sophomore John Boback led the Giants in wins with a 17-11 tally in 209 innings of thirty-five games. Holdover Klon Greene was 12-6 while new acquisition Walter Kuras won ten of sixteen. Boback was ERA leader at 3.36, closely followed by Harrison. Leonard Fassler, who had posted a sterling 1.45 ERA at Lawton, was called up in late July and gave up only 3.05 earned running per nine as he went 4-2 in sixty-two innings.

The Giants made the playoffs but were eliminated during the first round by the Pirates' prospects from Hutchinson (KS). Kollar was the only All Star. His .577 slugging percentage was only a single point behind the league's best by Topeka's Butch Nieman.

Well contributed seventeen round trippers to the cause. Jones led the league in triples and doubles and had the most Giants' hits with 154 and at .318, highest batting average. With competition from a good (45-15) Vance Air Force Base team, the Cherokees, it should not have come as a shock to the Giants' front office that attendance barely topped forty thousand, 40,713 to be exact, last in the Western Association. That was attained only because a fan-led movement to keep the Giants began in August to draw one thousand per contest for the remainder of the season.

Dismayed and disappointed with the Oklahoma prairie, young Pete Stoneham gladly returned to the fleshpots of New York and the Giants decamped Enid. Tired of losing money, the Giants got Muskogee owner Joe Magoto to broker a sale of the franchise to a Ft. Smith group for $1,000 and, in appreciation, signed a working agreement with his independent operation for 1951, thus the birth of the Muskogee Giants.

It appeared that Enid was finished in Organized Baseball. A new group, Enid Sports, Inc., was formed led by grocer Abe C. Hathoot. On November 26, 1950 with the Chicago Cubs having pulled the plug on the Springfield (IL) operation, the Western Association owners awarded that franchise to the Enid group. While longing for a working agreement with anyone, the Enid group announced to the meeting that they were prepared to play at the Class C level as an independent. And that is how the 1951 Enid entry would play.

A crowd at the Enid ball park. (Ed-8)

1951

The proprietors of the new Western Association franchise had a ball park, some capital, and enthusiasm. They needed over the winter a name, a schedule, a field general, and a roster. On the first count, "Buffaloes" was chosen. On the second, a truncated 126-game campaign was designed to begin on April 29 and end on Labor Day, September 3. On the third, Ray Honeycutt, a local sandlot infielder who had made it to the top level of the minors with the International League's Jersey City Giants before the War, had guided the Henderson Oilers to an East Texas League pennant and the Chickasha Chiefs of the Sooner State League to three consecutive first division finishes, was the man. More importantly, he had accomplished his success without the aid of a Major League working agreement. Through his minor league network, service with the Enid Airs, a keen ear to the ground, and semi-pro connections, Honeycutt had assembled teams from what the Major Leagues considered discards and made winners of them. He was exactly the man Enid Sports, Inc. needed in the dugout. Always a playing manager, Enid offered him free reign to assemble a line up and guide them from the bench. It appeared that Chickasha's loss was Enid's gain (it certainly sent the Chiefs into a disastrous season).

Model of Buffaloes Field exterior. (Ed-9)

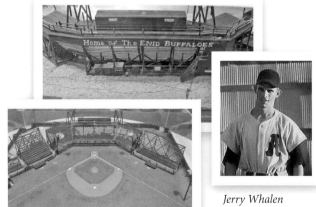

Interior model of Buffaloes Field. (Ed-10)

Jerry Whalen joined Enid after two seasons at Ardmore. (Ed-11)

While *The Sporting News* reported that the Buffaloes had a limited working agreement with Brooklyn, in fact only one had played in the Dodger organization in 1950. Like he did at Chickasha, he mixed rookies, limited service players (those with under three seasons in Organized Ball), semi-pro alumni, and veterans to concoct a squad. With the Korean War rolling at full speed, Honeycutt had an advantage over the Major League organizations. He was able to "draft-proof" his team by selecting players who had fulfilled their military commitments, were deferred or likely to avoid induction until September, or been declared 4-F, physically unfit for military service. The pre-season report in *The Daily Oklahoman* was that Honeycutt's Buffaloes would not have Uncle Sam to fear as much as weak pitching and lack of power.

Veterans were the core. Jack Southwick, with the only winning record among Enid hurlers at 11-9, and who had been a Brooklyn farmhand since 1946, and Bob Mistele, finishing with one win against seven losses, recently a semi-pro who had played several seasons for Oklahoma City and Paris, anchored the pitching staff. Mistele had bested Bob Feller in Navy ball. Merrill McDonald at first base, also a 1946-1949 Dodger property, along with shortstop Odie Strain of Okemah, who spent ten seasons in the Yankees' minors, led the infield. Jack McQuillin, who played before the War and from 1947 through 1950 toiled with some success at Muskogee for the Browns' organization, was an outfield regular.

The other two outfielders were in their third seasons. Jerry Whalen had spent 1948 and 1949 at Ardmore in the Sooner State League. Leo Kedzierski began with Lawton in 1949 then after a good couple of months at Iola in the K-O-M moved up to Topeka to finish 1950. Another Iola alumnus, pitcher Howard Hunt, was to spend his sophomore season with the Buffaloes. Behind the plate, Honeycutt turned to Carl Brewington who had played briefly with the White Sox farm at Seminole in the Sooner State League then caught for the Elk City Elks as they romped to a semi-pro championship in 1949.

Two rookies rounded out the pitching staff: Robert Minter and Clyde Robinson. A Texan, Minter was 4-12 in 140 innings of thirty-three games posting a 6.30 ERA. Tuskahoma product Clyde Robinson had the best ERA on the club at 3.97 while nearly breaking even with a 10-11 record. Two recent Oklahoma A & M graduates wore Enid flannels. Bob Bartlett had signed with the Red Sox after his time with the Cowboys but received his walking papers after batting .100 in eleven games for a Class D affiliate. He didn't do much better at Enid going 5 for 47 at the plate in seventeen games. On the other hand, Frank Kempa of Bartlesville earned the second base spot batting .293 in 116 games. The rookie star, however, was Harry Winston Havenstrite of Enid, a new graduate of Phillips University.

A baseball rookie, Havenstrite was a real veteran. The 1940 census found him as an eighteen year old, married gas station attendant in Enid. Fast forward to 1945: he was a Marine on Iwo Jima watching the flag being raised on Mount Suribachi. The next day he was hit by Japanese fire and evacuated to Pearl Harbor. Later the baseball coach at Oklahoma City's Northeast and then elite Northwest Classen High School, he hit .259 in 110 games for the Buffaloes, mainly at third base and shortstop, while striking a team best twenty-seven home runs with a .484 slugging percentage. He was named as Enid's only All Star as a utility player. His first professional at bat in the season opener on April 29 produced a game-winning home run as Enid topped Joplin 10-8. Thin on pitching, he hurled eighty innings in fifteen games for Enid with a 4.95 ERA winning three and losing the decision in eight contests. He played two more professional seasons at Clovis in the West Texas-New Mexico League before contracting sepsis from a spike injury and heading to the classroom and coaches' lounge at age thirty.

Winston Havenstrite, a Marine veteran of Iwo Jima, was an Enid native who stepped off the Phillips University campus to star for the Buffaloes. An injury at Clovis in 1953 ended his playing days. He went on to a successful career in high school coaching. (Ed-12)

Holding on to sixth until July 18, the Buffaloes finished seventh at 45-79 ahead only of Ft. Smith by a game and a half. Enid had the lowest attendance with 39,564. Kempa and Whalen led in batting with .293 and .292. McQuillin led with 136 hits; only Kempa, Havenstrike, and Whalen had over one hundred. Odie Strain clubbed the only grand-slam of the year on July 26 against cellar-dweller Ft. Smith. The team was lead-footed with only forty-seven thefts for the season. Jack Southwick at 11-9 accounted for nearly a fourth of the Buffaloes' forty-five victories.

The 1951 season had not been happy but Hathoot and company were determined to carry on into 1952. The caprice of the St. Louis Cardinals sealed the fate of professional baseball in Enid. The Cards declined to renew their working agreement with St. Joseph (MO), the Western Association leaving with seven teams, an unworkable number. For the next season, one franchise had to be pulled. Geography dictated that the outlier had to go. On January 20, 1952 the Western Association voted to contract to six clubs with Enid being the figurative odd man out. The league assured Enid it would get the first shot at a franchise if the Western Association expanded. Spokesman Eber Higgins of Enid Sports, Inc. told the public that Enid would press on with construction of a new baseball facility in that hope. Buffaloes Park was soon to be demolished. A lack of a ball park is what prompted Enid to spurn an overture to join the K-O-M for 1953. A new facility would be built but not until 1999 when David Allen Memorial Ball Park opened. Organized Baseball departed the Cherokee Strip in 1952 never to return.

LAWTON GIANTS
1947-1951

LAWTON REDS
1952-1953

LAWTON BRAVES
1954-1957

SOONER STATE LEAGUE

SEASON	ATTENDANCE	RECORD	FINISH	AFFILIATION	PLAYOFF FIRST ROUND	PLAYOFF FINALS
1947	24,248	98-42	First	New York NL	Lost to Ardmore 2-3	
1948	33,861	77-59	Second	New York NL	Lost to Seminole 2-3	
1949	45,501	87-52	Second	New York NL	Beat Chickasha 3-0	Beat Pauls V'y 4-1
1950	31,817	37-101	Eighth	New York NL		
1951	17,252	46-94	Seventh	New York NL		
1952	52,807	63-77	Sixth	Cincinnati		
1953	18,029	47-89	Seventh	Cincinnati		
1954	47,431	81-58	Second	Milwaukee	Beat McAlester 3-2	Beat Ardmore 4-0
1955	45,554	95-44	First	Milwaukee	Beat Paris 3-1	Beat Muskogee 4-2
1956	30,550	80-60	Second	Milwaukee	Lost to Seminole 1-3	
1957	15,605	59-66	Sixth	Milwaukee		

A little known fact is that the Sooner State League was not Lawton's first venture in Organized Baseball. In 1911, Lawton under the name "Medicine Men" had participated in the new Texas-Oklahoma League for a few weeks until it became the victim of poor management and skittish players.

Lawton was easily the strongest and most stable franchise in the Sooner State League. Lawton was the only city in the Sooner State League to host the same franchise for all eleven seasons. It experienced three eras that may be divided two different ways. One way is to categorize by affiliations: New York Giants 1947-1951, Cincinnati Reds 1952-1953, and Milwaukee Braves 1954-1957. The other is performance: Champions I 1947-1949, Losers 1950-1953, and Champions II 1954-1957. The Lawton franchise was stable. It had only two sets of owners, the Lawton Baseball Association, a community non-profit, from 1947 through 1953 and Lawton Braves, Inc. from 1954 through 1957. The team had only four managers, fewer than some Sooner State League members had in a single season: Lou Brower (1947-1950), Ray Baker (1951), Tuck McWilliams

(1952-1953), and Hall of Famer Travis "Stonewall" Jackson (1954-1957). Two Major Leaguers bracketed two minor leaguers. The club had a working agreement each year of its existence. Lawton finished in the second division four times in eleven seasons. In the others, it finished first twice and won the playoffs three times. The only profitable season was 1949. The 1951 season, however, was a disaster on the field and gate. The team had a $35,000 cumulative operating deficit following the campaign. The shareholders, however, voted to ante up more money and keep the franchise alive. The new affiliation with Cincinnati begun in 1952 was not as successful as hoped. Army Capt. Bill Henry, a sportscaster in civilian life, moonlighted and took over the business manager's job for 1953. For the 1954 season, the club's assets were transferred to Lawton Braves, Inc. that held the franchise through 1957. Its owners were Ted Warkenthin, A. W. "Bill" Williams, a druggist, who also held the lease on Memorial Park, and R. T. Currell. L. C. "Cy" Stewart served as president and business manager in 1954 and 1955. Burt Alford held that post the next two years.

Lawton's first venture into professional baseball was the 1911 Medicine Men.
The club folded seven weeks into the Texas-Oklahoma League season. (La-1)

1947

Dick Ward and Hershel Passon had to take a cab to Duncan and then thumb a ride with Otto Utt to the first meeting of the Sooner State League in Ardmore on December 15, 1946. They were awarded the Okmulgee franchise and soon thereafter incorporated the Lawton Baseball Association. Lumber dealer B.A. "Gus" Allen served as president. Bob Leggett was vice president, C.E. Price was secretary-treasurer, and Glen Powers, E.B. Lacy, Ewing Gafford, Julius Johnson, Jack Hanna, Jess Stanley, and Lewis Fouts completed the board of directors. They hired the original promoter, Dick Ward, as business manager. A campaign was launched to sell six hundred shares at $25 each. With each share would come a season pass. The American Legion, Jaycees and Lions Club agreed to sell two hundred each.

Oklahoma City's Lou Brower guided the Lawton Giants for four seasons between 1947 and 1950. He also managed Pauls Valley in 1951 and 1952 then Ada in 1953 and 1954. (La-2)

Ed Albrecht of the 1947 Giants was the first Lawton player in the Majors. He won the St. Louis Browns' last game of 1949 and made the trip north in 1950. After a disappointing start, he languished in the minors through 1953. (La-3)

When baseball returned to Lawton in 1947, the principals of the franchise owner were allowed to build a ball park on land owned by Comanche County in what is now the northwest corner of Ahlschlager Park. All games were played during the day until the Giants hosted Ada on May 13 under the new lights. Home plate was in the northwest corner with the first base line running directly south and the third base line directly east. Until 1952, the fences were 341 feet in left field, 392 feet to center, and 320 down the right field line. There was a tiny, three-person press box. Bleachers were parallel to both baselines. A single row of four seat boxes stood in front of the bleachers.

Lou Brower was lured from retirement in Oklahoma City to lead the 1947 team. The New York Giants signed a full working agreement with the new Lawton club after Otto Utt of Duncan turned down their overture. Winning six of seven exhibitions before the season was a precursor of the season to come. The tenants of the Polo Grounds delivered a team that took the lead on the first day of the 1947 season and never relinquished it. Duncan, incidentally, started and finished in last place as an independent.

Mayor George Hutchins threw a strike for the first pitch at Memorial Park on April 29. The first six games there were played in the afternoon because the lighting was not ready. The Giants swept Ada 3-2 and 5-4 before turning on Duncan for three more. In the May 3 tilt, Russ Ritter, who spent most of the season at Seminole after the Giants released him, hit the first home run at Memorial Park. The season went the Giants' way, at least until the playoff.

As was to be the rule each season in the Sooner State League, good pitching was the key to a pennant. Seven of the eight pitchers who appeared for Lawton finished the season. As a staff the Lawton pitchers has a collective ERA of 2.67, rare for Class D. Rookie Murray Baugh, the only player on the roster from Comanche County, won sixteen games with a 2.37 ERA.

Rookie Joe Galioto led the league in wins with twenty victories against five losses and percentage for those with over 150 innings (.800) and a 2.33 ERA; but he also launched thirteen wild pitches. Another rookie, Dempsey Sterling, threw ninety innings in relief to earn a 9-1 record. Future St. Louis Brown Ed Albrecht posted a 2.69 ERA in ninety-seven innings and an 8-5 record. Veteran Bill Morgan was 11-2 in 107 innings and spun an incredible 1.85 ERA web. Al Blacha, who appeared in thirteen games, was released when Leonard Hurgin, who had the team's only losing percentage, was sent down from Class C Ft. Smith; this was Hurgin's first and last season in Organized Baseball.

With an average of only two errors per game, the Giants led the circuit with a .949 fielding average. Team batting was about equal in the first division of the League. There was virtually no difference between Lawton's .263 batting average compared with McAlester's .266 and Ardmore's .264. The Giants had only two .300 hitters, outfielders Leonard Pasciak at .305 and Howie Weeks, a Bartlesville alumnus, at .304. In the first year of the league, very good pitching and fielding could combine with average hitting to win ninety-eight games and a pennant. Lawton fans showed their appreciation by presenting manager Brower with over $1,000 in cash and merchandise before the season finale on September 3. At mid-season, the Giants dropped a 4-3 contest to the All Stars from the other five teams.

Fourth place Ardmore didn't get the message about Lawton's prowess. The Indians upset the Giants in five games before going on to lose the final series to McAlester. On September 11, the Giants played an exhibition game against Ft. Sill to raise money to send the players home. Everyone on the Lawton roster pitched as the Giants won 6-4. Negro League star Ossie Littleton, doing his time in the Army, went four for four. Post-season All Stars included Marvin Blaylock, a future New York Giant

After two seasons under Brower's tutelage, Marv Blaylock came up to the Polo Grounds at the end of 1950. He landed the full-time first base slot for the Phillies in 1955 and 1956. (La-4)

and Phillie, at first base, Paciak, and Weeks in the outfield, and Ted Drakos as utility man. Lou Brower was manager of the year.

1948

The Giants finished a successful inaugural year on the field but experienced a disaster from a financial viewpoint. With each share of stock, a season pass was issued that had the effect of suppressing the gate. A $14,000 deficit had been accumulated, leaving only $9,000 capital for the next season. With a $15,000 payroll and several thousand more needed to buy equipment, the budget for 1948 was $30,000. Attendance needed to reach 48,000 to break even. With a new coat of paint and improvements throughout, for 1948 the capacity at Memorial Park was expanded to 1,800. Directors Fouts and Pont Ramsey were placed in charge of keeping up the park and playing field. Director Stanley was detailed to coordinate with the Lawton City Council and Comanche County Commissioners to obtain better road access to Memorial Park.

Lawton native Ewing Gafford was a 1941 University of Oklahoma journalism graduate who served as an Army officer during the War. He joined *The Lawton Constitution* after release from the service and was active in launching the Giants with the paper's blessing. He had been the announcer for Lawton High School games and also called the local boxing matches. He was a master salesman and took the club a long way toward meeting the subscription target. Gafford took over the business manager's position from Ward after the 1947 season. In May, 1948, Gafford purchased the Magnolia service sta-

An All-American center for OU, John Rapacz bided his time in Lawton before reporting for the football Giants' training camp. He was an All-Pro center for the Giants in 1949, 1950, and 1951. His last baseball foray was with the 1951 Lawton club where he hit .288 and fielded .987 in twenty-two games. (La-5)

at 77-59 the Giants still managed to end up in second place two and one-half games ahead of Seminole.

Marv Blaylock was back as were Howie Weeks and Marcel Poelker who was killed in Korea on September 25, 1951. Pitcher Dempsey Sterling also returned to contribute seven wins in his final season. Rookie Bob Giddings had a great year going 25-8, averaging only 3.20 earned runs. Rookies Charles Menke (2.99 ERA) and Paul Merritt (4.30 ERA) each won fifteen games. Rookie catcher John Rapacz, All Big Seven center for the University of Oklahoma, caught forty-five games with a fine fielding average of .984 before shoving an umpire and receiving an indefinite suspension. Once again, Lawton was eliminated in the first round of the playoffs, this time by Seminole. Tom Marinos was named to the All Star team as third baseman despite fielding only .863 at that position. Howie Weeks repeated in the outfield and set a then league record by being hit twenty-one times by opposing pitchers. Ron Samford, who would play for the Giants, Tigers and Senators over five seasons, began his career in Lawton. After seventeen games he was promoted to Ft. Smith.

tion on Cache Road near Ft. Sill, home of the Army's field artillery, and wore both hats as long as possible.

During his tenure, the president of minor league baseball, George Trautman and his wife visited Lawton. Gafford saw to it that the city rolled out the red carpet. During the June 22, 1948, game he attended, Trautman inquired "who were the four people who kept running out to the parking lot after every foul ball?" Gafford responded "Club directors." The balls remained the team's property; unlike today, there were no souvenirs.

Brower's second Lawton team had among the best gloves in the league in 1948 but they fell to last in batting with .248 and the superb ERA of 1947 ballooned to 4.16. Finishing thirteen games off the pace,

1949 Sooner State League champions. L-R Top row: Manager Lou Brower, Jim Shindell, Ed Glover, Jim Spencer, Eldon Schrader, Ray Myers, Dick Bornholdt. Middle row: Jim Griffin, Ray Ditto, Bob Harrison, Joe Micchiche, Mike Giovani. Front row: Marvin Webster, Arnie Fritz, Dick Rosak, Tom Stapleton, Vince Speranza. (La-6)

1949 first base All Star Dick Von der Haas. He went to Pauls Valley for 1950 as part of the Giants' purchase of Daryl Spencer. (La-7)

1949

The 1949 team had a profile like the two previous clubs: very good pitching, good fielding and adequate hitting. The crew had a 2.58 ERA, 1,004 strike outs, and allowed opposing batters to hit for a weak .199 average against them. In his only season in professional ball, Jim Spencer led the team with a fine 1.96 ERA as well as contributing twelve wins. All Star Joe Micciche had a low ERA, 2.23, and a 20-6 record. Eric Schrader returning from a 0-6 1948 season turned his game around with a 2.07 ERA and 16-6 record. Sophomore Vince Speranza was 15-8 with a 2.37 ERA. Rookie Bob Harrison, who played for Enid in 1950, rounded out the staff going 12-10 and allowing 2.98 earned runs per nine innings. He tasted a couple of cups of coffee with the Baltimore Orioles in 1955 and 1956. Dick Born-holdt was the only .300 hitter. At .303, he led the team with sixteen home runs and ninety-two RBIs. First baseman Dick Von Der Haas was named to the All Star squad. The Giants swept Chickasha in the first round of the playoffs and then took Pauls Valley in five games. This set of little Giants was the last competitive team Lawton was to see until 1954.

1950

Ray Ditto, Arnold Fritz, Ray Meyer, and Dick Von der Haas found themselves in Pauls Valley for 1950 as a result of the parent Giants' purchase

of Daryl Spencer from the Raiders for $10,000 and them. What New York sent to Lou Brower was a weak hitting, ball bobbling set of position players and one of the worst mound staffs to play in the league, twenty-six of whom appeared in fewer than ten games. They were extraordinary in their ineptitude as the 1950 Lawton club lost 101 game, finished sixty-four games under 500, were fifty-nine games off the pace and fourteen and one-half games behind the seventh place Duncan Uttmen. They were 0-10 on the season until handing McAlester the Rockets' first loss 17-11 on May 7. Near the end of the season on August 30, the Giants combined thirty-four hits, seventeen walks, and eight Ada errors to send the Herefords packing by a 34-16 football score. In his last year in baseball, veteran Jim Ashcraft was the top batter at .279. The only bright spot on the club was the pitching of Leonard Fassler. He threw a one-hitter in his first start to beat McAlester 1-0. Before moving up to Class C Enid, he was 8-5 for the Giants with a 1.46 ERA. Without him the Giants would have been the worst team in league history with a .232 winning percentage.

1950 scorecard. (La-8)

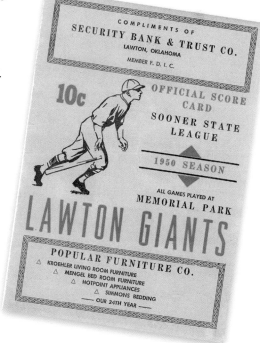

1951

For 1951, Lou Brower was gone and New York farm hand C. Ray Baker took the helm. Baker had guided Muskogee for three seasons between 1946 and 1948. Again, the parent Giants provided a weak crew. Only one played professional ball after 1957 and none ever played in a classification higher than Class A. The pitchers collectively had a 4.96 ERA and were low in the league with 726 strike outs. On May 12 and 13, they gave up fifty-two runs in losses to Ardmore 23-1 and Pauls Valley 29-4. Bill Reynard threw eight and one-third hitless innings before Bruce Swain dropped in a fluke double scoring two runners who had gotten free passes for a 4-2 loss on May 15. The moundsmen lacked a Fassler. Jim Waldrip had the only winning record at 6-5. He also had the low ERA at 4.37. In the hitting department, the last edition of the Giants was last in average (.240), home runs (32), and total bases (1,512). They committed 425 errors and allowed 331 unearned runs.

The 1951 Giants had a Black Cat Night with everyone who brought a black cat receiving free admission. A month later, Lawton had won only

Reds' farmhands (L-R) Vince Downs, John Prokopochak, Ralph Sita. (La-9)

Joe Dembrosky was hit by pitches thirty-two times for a Sooner State League record. (La-10)

two games at home. Fan and later co-owner Bill Williams camped out in a tent atop the visitors' dugout. Armed with a shotgun and equipped with a radio, refrigerator, and meals from local merchants, he spent eight nights there to break the jinx. Lawton beat Chickasha 10-6 on July 16, the first night of the vigil.

Vince Capece was named the most popular player for 1951 and received a watch, gifts from team mates, and cash from fans. Those were the only awards connected with the season. New York moved its Class D working agreement to Pauls Valley for 1952. The Giants era was over and Lawton was half way through the Losing Years.

1952

Hopes were high when the 1952 season began with a new name, new uniforms, new manager and new players. The fences at Memorial Park were shortened in 1952 from 341 to 339 feet in left and from 392 to 366 feet in center. The short right field porch remained at 320. The Lawton Athletic Association had a new product to offer that had to be better than what New York had provided the past two years. But with 1951 attendance at just over 17,000, the franchise was in danger of folding. One more season with attendance under 40,000 would do in the new Reds. Vigorous promotion and a more exciting if not statistically much superior team on the field can be said to have kept baseball alive in Lawton. When the ticket stubs were counted for the 1952 season, over 52,000 Lawtonians passed through the turnstile at Memorial Park.

Spring training and tryout camp for 1952 was held at the Cincinnati minor league campus at Columbia, S.C. New manager and former catcher Tuck McWilliams brought west with him four products of the tryouts: Canadians Vince Downs and Sal Lucchetta, Bob Shomo, and Lawton native Luverne Thompson.

Manager McWilliams wasted no time in earning an ejection. On May 2, after the heave ho he dressed in street clothes took a seat in the stands by the Lawton dugout and conferred with Reds players from time to time. Shawnee manager Lou Fitzgerald protested that McWilliams was managing from the stands under suspension. Two weeks into the season the Reds were stuck in seventh place with an 8-14 record and were still there on June 5 at 17-24. Lawton picked up some pitching strength when Charlie Rabe was signed on June 11; the Browns' coaches at Ada cut him because he was wild. On June 19, the Reds climbed to sixth place where they remained for the balance of the season. On the way to setting the league record for consecutive hitless innings, All Star Rabe hurled a no-hitter at Ardmore on June 24 for a 2-0 win.

Nick Ricco struck out the side in the second, third, and fourth innings and added six more on July 12, versus Ardmore but lost in the ninth 2-1 because his second baseman Jim Dembrosky booted one to allow the winning run. Ralph Sita's single ruined John Wortham's bid for a no- hitter on July 21, as Sherman beat the Reds 5-0. The Lawton nine overcame Mel Tuscher's grand slam to slip past Ardmore 16-13 on August 6.

Injuries plagued the 1952 Reds. In June, pitcher Bob Wood suffered a broken leg when he was hit by a fast ball. On August 11, the Reds found themselves without a catcher. Ray Zari and Ron Heughens were both on the disabled list. John Caddy, who was recuperating from a June 28, ankle break, was activated but refused to report putting manager McWilliams at age forty-three behind the plate. Joe Dembrosky passed Howie Weeks' record of being hit by pitches twenty-one times and went on to get tattooed eleven more times for the second league record the Reds produced.

1953

The 1953 Reds tried the Lawton fans' patience and they responded by staying away. A sixth place team in 1952 drew nearly 53,000 fans. The seventh place 1953 Reds attracted only 18,000. The pitching staff was a tryout camp; ten of nineteen who appeared saw action in less than ten games. As a staff, with fifty-three they had the fewest complete games and most walks (1,110), more than even lowly Gainesville. The collective ERA was a whopping 5.44. The only winner on the staff was Ed Allison at 14-5 with a 3.87 ERA. The team was seventh in fielding at .932. The players at shortstop fielded .864, .857, and .813 accounting for fifty-two of the Reds' 360 errors. The team batted .246 with a weak .350 slugging percentage. Bill Campo (.325) and Bill Schimchak (.312) had batting averages over .300. Doug Davidson batted only .188 but drew 108 walks; when coupled with his eighty-seven hits he had a .336 On Base Percentage.

1952 and 1953 (L-R) manager Tuck McWilliams, with 1953 hopefuls Ray Wallace and Ron Heugens. (La-11)

This team was able to turn a 365 feet blast over the fence into a triple. Bill Ridley, who hit a puny .167, appeared to have hit the first Lawton home run of the season on May 20. As he rounded third, he was enveloped by the entire team and carried back to the dugout. When the umpire gave the Ada catcher a new ball, he stepped on home. Ridley received credit for a triple because he never touched home plate. Catcher Jack Gannon hit one over the fence with the bases loaded on July 3, to beat Pauls Valley 10-9. It was the first grand slam at Memorial Park since 1949. Gene Fedak, who set the league record with twenty-five wild pitches in a season, struck out eleven Owls and scattered four singles on the way to beating hapless Gainesville 11-5 on July 22. The Reds dropped their finale on September 7, to McAlester. While fourteen Lawton batters were walked, only Jack Vandersee got a hit. The Reds were outscored once again.

1954

The Milwaukee Braves brought Lawton into the fold of one of the best farms organizations in 1954. It also brought Hall of Fame shortstop Travis "Stonewall" Jackson to develop the rookies and sophomores sent to Lawton. The name and uniforms changed. Once again, pitching and fielding carried the Lawton entry.

If the 1954 season in the Sooner State League had been a motion picture, the title could have been "Shawnee and the Seven Dwarfs." The Hawks finished ten and one-half games ahead of the second place Braves and led the league in hitting, fielding, and pitching. As a team, Lawton batters surpassed only last place Pauls Valley as they tied Seminole for sixth place with a .260 average. The Braves had a .380 slugging percentage. Veteran Carl Hrovatic earned a place in the All Star team outfield by finishing second in the league in hitting with a .370 average and fielding at .950. Rookie Dan Staniec began his first of three years in Lawton striking out 108 times in 302 at bats and hitting a paltry .132. Three year Brave Ken Aycock did better at .233. The club fielded well in this league at .942. On the mound, All Star Wendell Doss was head and shoulders above the rest of the staff finishing fourth in the league behind three Shawnee hurlers with a 3.00 ERA and a 24-12 record. Bob Gilmore was second on the squad going 13-5 with a 3.34 ERA. There was much movement through the Lawton bullpen. Of the seventeen who threw for the Braves, nine pitched fewer than forty-five innings.

Travis 'Stonewall' Jackson was John McGraw's Hall of Fame shortstop between 1922 and 1936. He won pennants for Lawton in 1954 and 1955. (La-12)

The Braves in action against Gainesville in 1954. (La-14)

Ken Aycock spent 1954-1956 with the Lawton Braves. (La-13)

Short timer Hank Asmussen managed to hit McAlester's Tony Young three times in a game on May 17. At the time, Lawton was in fifth place, slipping to sixth by June 3. Before 1,800 on June 25, the largest crowd of the year, the Braves split a double header exchanging shut outs with Shawnee. In a record one hour and seventeen minutes Lawton ended Frank Golob's seven- game winning streak 2-0. Shawnee took the nine inning second game 7-0. The Braves were by then in fourth place. On the day before reporting for induction into the armed forces, Norris Dorsey won his fourth game in thirteen appearances gaining a split with Shawnee 7-3 on three hits in the nightcap. The Braves had nipped the Hawks 2-1 in the early game for the first sweep against Shawnee since September 1, 1952. Three weeks later, the Braves had taken third and a week later, on July 29, grabbed and held on to second. Hrovatic had five straight hits in the August 5, 8 to 5 victory. Lawton was the only team to win the regular season series against Shawnee eleven games to nine. In the playoffs, Lawton just got by McAlester as upstart Ardmore sidelined Shawnee in five games. The Braves went on to win the playoffs in a four game sweep of the Cardinals. For that Travis Jackson was named All Star manager. The fans were obviously pleased with the turn around as they presented him with a new car at halftime of a Lawton High School football game.

1955

For 1955, Lawton gave Shawnee better than it had gotten in 1954 winning fourteen of twenty on the way to a first place finish with ninety-five wins. That was seventeen and one-half games over the Hawks. The Braves then went on to win the playoffs for a pennant double. The 1955 Braves led the league in all categories. The 1955 mound staff included future six-season Major Leaguer

Ron Piche of the 1955 club made his Major League debut with Milwaukee in 1960. He appeared in 134 major League games over six seasons. (La-16)

Ron Piche. Dale Hendrickson led the staff with an astounding league record 1.26 ERA and a 21-8 tally. As a group, only Jim Miller at a respectable 3.27 ERA was above 3.00 earned runs. In fact, the 1955 Braves allowed only 342 earned runs all season for a team 2.49 ERA. Backing up the pitchers, the position players fielded .950. They hit only .264 but as they outscored their opponents 858 to 507, were on base four of every ten at bats, and had a slugging percentage of .402; batting average wasn't a factor.

Hendrickson was the story. He had his eleventh win of the season by June 28, and had enjoyed streaks of thirty-nine consecutive scoreless innings, sixty innings without an earned run, and three straight shut outs. And in the June 28 game, he batted in both runs to tame Paris 2-1. He struck out 256 batters in 243 innings. He walked only 105. When Ron Piche blanked Seminole 8-0 on July 17, Lawton tied the league record for shutouts Shawnee had established in 1953. In the last game of the season, on September 3, third sacker Bill Dennis raised his average above .300 by going seven for seven with three home runs, a double, and three singles generating eighteen total bases and twelve RBIs. He set league records in all three categories. Additionally, his three homers tied a league record. Lawton had fifty-five at-bats in the route. The Braves had no difficulty in the playoffs

Chuck Hoffses divided his two-year career between Lawton and Class C Eau Claire. (La-16)

1955 Lawton Braves. The 1955 season could have been titled " Lawton and the Seven Dwarfs." The Braves ran away with the regular season then took the playoffs for the pennant. . L-R Top row: Manager Travis Jackson, Henry Aycock, Bill Jackson, Dan Staniek, unidentified, Paul Lockridge, Jerry Miller, Lee Freeman, Billy Dennis, Pete Peterson. Front row: Ron Piche, Charles Hoffses, Gary Anderson, Phil Williams, Joe Pearce, Dale Hendrickson, George DeMeules, Bob Dudley. (La-17)

with Hendrickson winning each of his three starts. The Braves vanquished Paris in four games and then took Muskogee in six for the championship, the second time that a regular season winner won the playoff. Curiously, no All Star team was selected in 1955. Perhaps they would have all been Braves.

1956

The 1955 edition was an impossible act to follow. In 1956 the fences at Memorial Park were changed again: 339 feet to left, 366 to center, and 335 to right. With the strong prevailing south wind, home runs were not cheap even with short power alleys. Yet the 1956 Lawton nine was in the thick of the 1956 pennant race all season finishing three and one-half games behind winner Ardmore with an 80-60 record. This was a relatively strong batting team finishing second with 110 home runs and a .266 average. Rookies Bill Gilmore (.331) and Doug Smith (.310) cracked the .300 mark. Their gloves were tops in the circuit with a collective .944 average. Once again, the Braves led the league in pitching but with a much higher 4.09 ERA. They were stingiest with home runs, yielding only seventy-five four baggers. Don Eason at 2.53, Jim Kuykendall at 2.53, and Hank Hemmerly at 2.97 were the top

hurlers accounting for forty-eight of eighty wins on the season. Four throwers had ERAs above five. George Pearson at 9.79 and giving up sixty-seven homers in forty-eight innings finished at the back of the league pack.

Twins Don and Ron Eason formed the battery combing to beat Muskogee 6-0 on May 5. Don retired the side on three pitches in the seventh inning. Don Eason began the season with twenty-five scoreless innings and no earned runs before Muskogee manager Dick Klaus tattooed him for a home run as he registered his first loss, 2-0, on May 10. In his first game after being sent down from Class C Boise, Ken Hansen on June 28 had two home runs and a sacrifice.

On July 3, Dan Staniec surpassed McAlester Rocket Don Leppert's record of 283 consecutive Sooner State League games by playing his 284th. He went on to play every game in 1956 which with the 140 from 1955 and seventy-five from 1954 put him at 355, a very unusual feat in Class D. Hansen's three consecutive home runs on July 17 and 18 matched Ponca City's Don

Don Staniec played in 355 games for Lawton between 1954 and 1956. (La-18)

Loudenback's feat on July 12 and 13. Manager Travis Jackson had to release his son Bill, a southpaw, who was 4-2 in 1955 and 0-0 in nine games in 1956; he returned to high school teaching and coaching. The Eason battery beat McAlester 8-1 on July 29, for Don's thirteenth win. The Eason twins received their draft notices and reported for induction on August 16. Neither played professional baseball again. On August 26, Ken Aycock had an inside the park home run as Lawton swept Muskogee. The Braves were the comeback Seminole Oilers' first victim in the play-offs losing in four games. Of all the players on the 1956 team, Hemmerly advanced the farthest playing at AA Austin in 1960 through 1962 and then being called up to the Toronto Maple Leafs of the AAA International League.

1957

The team lost $7,500 in 1955, much of it back taxes, and $6,040 in 1956. The three owners were ready at that point to return the franchise. Col. E.C. Williams chaired a January 24, 1957 meeting attended by serious fans Cy Stewart, D.E. Stewart, C.E. Price, Fred Bentley, Gordon Anderson, Mundy Bohl, Francis Lynch, Lydia Lynch, E.R. Aker and business manager Alford. The owners present, Warkenthin and Williams, explained the working agreement arrangement with Milwaukee and outlined the cost of keeping ball in Lawton for 1957. A plan to find "Sixty Samaritans" to each underwrite $100 each for the upcoming season was adopted. The direction taken was to emulate Green Bay's community ownership of the Packers football team. The thinking was that a baseball team may never be profitable but was necessary for a town like Lawton. There was a lot of interest but after all was done, only $525 was ever received.

"Good field, no hit" summarizes the 1957 Braves. At .952, they were the best in the league with their gloves, but with a team batting average of only .237 and a league low 1,344 total bases it is no surprise that they were outscored 541 to 509 for a 59-66 sixth place finish. To win, the Lawton club needed performances like Bobby Knoop and Russ Blankenship gave on August 12 with back-to-back home runs in the second inning and back-to-back doubles in the third to score the three runs needed to beat Greenville. Those were few and far between.

At the start of the season, manager Jackson said that the 1957 pitching staff would be his best. They did not measure up to 1955 but led the league with a 3.63 ERA. Harold DeMars was 7-3 with a 2.19 ERA while Paul Dean, Jr., who left SMU for a baseball career, was the best 4-16 pitcher in baseball with a 2.94 ERA; the batters simply didn't hit when he was pitching. When he was the pitcher of record, the Braves played at a .472 pace; the rest of the time they played .505 ball. He gave up only sixty runs— forty-six earned—in 141

Paul Dean, Jr. had a 2.94 ERA and was the best 4-16 thrower in the game in 1957. (La-19)

innings. Dean won his first outing on May 6, beating Seminole on five hits in a seven inning game 3-1. He got a save on May 26, striking out three and walking the same. By June 9, he had lost his fourth in a row despite yielding no more than three runs in any game and a total of nine for the four. Three of the four were lost in the ninth or tenth inning including a June 9 walk-off home run by Billy Williams of Ponca City. He dropped to 1-7 then threw two consecutive shut outs only to be shelled 9-2 by Shawnee. Bill Holmes, who was to spend the next seven seasons in the Milwaukee farm system, had a 2.97 ERA but a 10-14 record.

Games were lost on mental errors. On June 24, Gary Anderson, acting manager while Jackson was at his son's wedding, handed the umpire an old line-up card Jackson had prepared. As the Braves were rallying in the fourth inning, Paris manager Barney Lutz protested the visitors were batting out of order. That squelched the rally and the Orioles went on to win. Even though the shortened schedule delayed the opener until May 1, the Braves saw fourteen of

Bob Knoop began in the Braves organization in 1957 before being taken by the Angels in 1963 for whom he started from 1963 through 1968. A gifted fielder nicknamed 'Nureyev" for his acrobatics, he was a 1966 All Star and won three Gold Gloves. (La-20)

their first twenty-six games rained out including six at home; that meant back-to-back double headers at season's end. Jackson's team won twenty-seven of their last thirty games in 1957 to leave Ponca City in seventh and come close to ousting Greenville from fifth. Regular catcher Lee Freeman, who added a .288 bat to the cause, spent 112 games behind the plate committing only sixteen errors and allowing only eighteen passed balls for an outstanding .983 fielding percentage. Only two from the 1957 team were in baseball in 1964.

As Bill Holmes was toiling in his last season at Class A Charleston of the Eastern League, Bobby Knoop, who was a Sooner State League All Star, was making his Major League debut with the expansion Los Angeles Angels where he would play five years including starting the 1966 All Star game as the American League's second baseman.

A wooden structure, age and use weighed on Memorial Park to the point that by 1957 the need for a new ball park was obvious. Lawton Jaycees began a drive for a new park in July of 1957, engaged an architect, and made a presentation of a model to the City Council. To be located in Elmer Thomas Park, it would be steel and concrete with a roof and large enough to attract a Big State League franchise

The parent Milwaukee Braves had given the city an ultimatum that unless Memorial Park was rehabilitated with a new field and club house, it would not send its players there. Milwaukee even offered to loan their field superintendent to see that a new infield was properly prepared. The City fathers, however, demurred and private funding could not be arranged. With that hope dashed, Williams and Warkenthin who had personally leased the facility agreed to demolish the ramshackle site of eleven years of baseball in exchange for the salvage. It went down in the spring of 1958. The light towers were moved to Lawton High School. By May of 1958, Memorial Park was no more.

MCALESTER ROCKETS
SOONER STATE LEAGUE 1947-1956

SEASON	ATTENDANCE	RECORD	FINISH	AFFILIATION	PLAYOFF FIRST ROUND	PLAYOFF FINALS
1947	43,657	73-67	Third	New York AL	Beat Ada 3-2	Beat Ardmore 4-1
1948	63,060	91-47	First	New York AL	Beat Chickasha 3-1	Lost to Seminole 4-2
1949	56,733	58-82	Sixth	New York AL		
1950	58,048	92-48	Second	New York AL	Beat Chickasha 3-0	Beat Ardmore 4-2
1951	42,028	91-48	Third	New York AL	Beat Shawnee 3-0	Beat Ardmore 4-2
1952	52,395	87-53	First	New York AL	Beat Shawnee 3-1	Beat Pauls Vly 4-3
1953	40,485	83-56	Fourth	New York AL	Beat Ardmore 3-1	Beat Ada 4-1
1954	53,410	76-64	Third	New York AL	Lost to Lawton 2-3	
1955	47,295	65-75	Sixth	New York AL		
1956	32,302	60-79	Seventh	New York AL		

The McAlester ball club in nearly every category was the premier franchise in the Sooner State League. The Rockets won the playoff championship five of the six times they reached the finals. They finished the regular season in first place twice. They won over ninety games three times. They finished in the first division seven times. The 63,060 attendance in 1948 was highest in the league's eleven seasons. Average annual attendance of 48,941 was over ten thousand more than the closest rival. The Rockets drew over fifty thousand fans in five of ten campaigns. They had over forty thousand paying customers through the turnstiles at Jeff-Lee Athletic Park every season except the last for the poorest performing team in the franchise's history. Even the 32,302 supporters in 1956 surpassed the average annual attendance of seven of the fourteen other cities that hosted teams including charter member Ada. The Rockets declined as a franchise when they ceased to have strong leadership on the field, Paul Crowl in the front office, and a stable full of Yankee prospects.

L-R Irvin Gladstein, Lawton Jones, Paul Crowl, Matt Patterson, M. M. Schene. They served as officers of the McAlester Rockets from 1947 through 1955. Matt Patterson replaced Paul Crowl as president in the rockets' last season in 1956. (Ma-2)

1947

In November, 1946, according to Paul Crowl, the group that would operate the McAlester franchise had $67,000 in the bank, $4,200 for lights, and plans for a 2,827 seat grandstand. The McAlester Athletic Association was incorporated on January 24, 1947, by hardware and sporting goods store owner Paul Crowl, Irvin Gladstein, a wholesale dealer in salvage and plumbing fixtures, and Lawton Jones. Initial capitalization was $10,000. On February 17, the organizational meeting was held with Crowl elected president, grocer Matt Patterson vice-president, and Gladstein secretary-treasurer. Meleo Schene and Jones completed

Jeff-Lee Athletic Park. (Ma-3)

the board of directors. Crowl and Schene were instrumental in forming the Sooner State League. Gladstein, who passed away in 1995 at age eighty-eight, was a super fan. He even wrote a short story "Utility Man" for the Winter 1950 edition of *Popular Sports.* The five were to remain directors through most of the club's existence. Matt Patterson succeeded Crowl when he stepped down in 1955. Dan Boatright was the business manager during the 1947 season and then assisted the paid business managers, Burt Lorince (1948-1954, 1956) and Rogers LaPrelle (1955).

McAlester signed a working agreement with the New York Yankees before the 1947 season. The Yankees were to provide ten players and a manager Bill Neborak, whose most recent experience had been in semi-pro ball in New Jersey. Unlike most other managers, Neborak did not play.

On March 3, the name of the team was announced. Tom Brecheen, father of St. Louis pitcher Harry "The Cat" Brecheen, was the winner, being the first of six to suggest "Rockets." "Bombers" was second. The elder Brecheen was an employee at the Naval Ammunition Supply Depot south of McAlester where ordnance is manufactured to this day.

The McAlester City Council hired Blair Engineering of Tulsa, to erect an athletic park at 4th and Polk in the southwest quadrant of Jeff-Lee Park, site of the high school football field and cinder track and municipal pool and bath house. Looking over the roof of the first base grandstand, the Masonic

Temple and McAlester High school could be seen atop the town's main hill.

The first of the pre-cast concrete and steel grandstands in the Sooner State League, it was aligned southwest to northeast. The playing field covered much of the McAlester High School football field and running track. Home plate was sixty feet and six inches southwest of the pitcher's mound which was below the south goal post. The left field line extended north roughly parallel to the football stadium on the west for 328 feet. The left fielder would take a position along the fifty yard line and face south. The east wooden visitors' football stands were removed for baseball. The center fielder would stand where the east stands had been looking southwest; straight away center was only 358 feet from home plate. The right field line ran west to east roughly parallel to Polk Avenue for 340 feet. The right fielder would have to play in front of or behind the running track (about twenty feet wide) that ran roughly from center field south to a point some 280 feet down the right field line. Though covered with dirt and sodded over, the track was a unique obstacle.

The grandstand was a roofed 275 feet crescent extending from third base near the south end of the bleachers south of the football stadium gradually curving so that behind home plate it turned east and extended to first base. Behind two rows of box seats that were elevated twelve inches above the field were twelve tiers of seats with the first row four feet above the field. The boxes accommodated 132 while the grandstand and bleachers sat another 1,750.

A berm south of the football field on which fans had sat for years was leveled to make way for the east stands. There were bleachers on either end of the grandstand. The high school football stadium along and beyond the left field line was available in case of overflow crowds. In appearance it was much like the Sooner Park in Chickasha built in 1951. The first game played there was an exhibition on April 26, won by the Rockets over the strong, touring St. Joseph (Michigan) Auscos.

After the Rockets' season, the field reverted to football. The outfield fence was taken down, the pitcher's mound leveled, and the dirt covering the cinder track removed. Bleachers for visiting schools could be set up on the east side of the field.

Bill McPhail, Yankee Director of Minor League Operations, joined the dignitaries including president Jack Mealey, Mayor Walter Arnote, and the commander of the Naval Ammunition Depot, Captain John F. Goodwin, for the opening game that the Rockets won 12-7 over homeless Seminole. On June 13, Charlie Nichols lost a no-hitter when Duncan third baseman Jim Hayman's single trickled off an outfielder's glove. He walked three, struck out nine, and faced only thirty batters in the 7-0 win. There was a five minute delay in the June 18, McAlester-Ada game when a rabbit dashed on to the field in the seventh inning. The scared hare raced for the stands but was forced back by screaming fans. Both teams took up the chase. McAlester bat boy Lou Crowl pegged the rabbit with a perfect pitch and the game went on. Three days later, the fleet-footed Rockets stole fourteen bases from Seminole catchers John Houge and George Sojka. Pitcher Norman Rollins set a Sooner State League batting record when he received six consecutive walks from Duncan hurlers on August 1.

Neborack supplemented the New York rookies and limited service players—four had one or two

Bill Neborak played professionally before World War II. The Yankees plucked him from the semi-pro ranks to lead McAlester. He quit on July 4 and was replaced by Dick Korte, a former Yankee farmhand who, in turn, quit the game three days later. Neborak returned and took the Rockets to the pennant. (Ma-4)

Tommy Evans played 1947-1949 and part-time in 1951. He was elected Pittsburg County Treasurer in 1950. He later was athletic director at the Oklahoma State Penitentiary. (Ma-5)

years prior experience—with one veteran, Atoka's George Abbott, who was cut after eight games, and local favorite Tommy Evans. Outfielder Leo Bellar and catcher Chick Ketterman, were released soon after the season opener. Abbott and Milton Ohnimus

though pink slipped reappeared at Duncan. The lineup crystallized quickly. All Star Hosea Pfeifer was behind the plate, Bill Landers was at first, Fred Nachbar at second, A.B. Everett at third, Tommy Evans at shortstop, All Star Russell Hawley in left, Gene Bernett in center, and Charles Fontana in right. Even though finishing third at 73-67, the Rockets led the League in batting including average (.266), hits (1,244), total bases (1,030), doubles (206), stolen bases (289), and stranded the fewest runners (1,076). Hawley led the league in batting at .382 with Everett at .355 and Fontana at .313. The team was second in the field at .939 but would have been much better had All Star third baseman Everett not bobbled seventy-four plays for a .860 glove average. His league record eighty-six stolen bases, however, ameliorated his failings at the hot corner. The pitchers allowed only four fewer runs than the team scored (744 vs. 740). The season-long rotation of Vern Brown, All Star Jesse Childress, Charles Nichols and Norm Rollins combined for forty-nine wins.

In the playoffs, Ada took the Rockets the distance. The fourth game won by the Rockets 18-17 at Ada drew a protest from Ada manager Clanton because a ball that bounced over the head of left fielder Russ Hawley after passing through the infield was declared lost on the basis of Hawley's shrug and indication the ball had passed through the heavy wire fence in left (it had not); the tying run would have scored had play not been stopped. President Mealey disallowed the protest—the first time ever—because Clanton did not go out with an umpire to look for the ball. Back home, the Rockets edged Ada 2-1 on September 9 on the strength of the arm of Al DeMartini. Meanwhile, Ardmore had

1947 McAlester Rockets. L-R Top row: Ray Lobelle, Vernon Brown, Hosea Pfeifer, Charles Nichols, Leslie Bush, Bill Landers, Jerry Schold, Jess Childress, Al Demartini, Bill Neborak. Middle row: Russell Hawley, Tommy Evans, Gene Bernett, Norm Rollins, Fred Hachbar, Charles Fontana, A.E. Everett. Front row: batboys Paul Crowl, Jr. and Lew Crowl. Catcher Bob Newbill not pictured. (Ma-6)

upset Lawton in five games. In the finals, McAlester easily handled the Indians in five games. Charles Nichols was winner of the rain-abbreviated fifth game 2-1 scattering five hits.

Fans and businesses were generous with the players. For driving in the winning runs in a July game, Russell Hawley received $100, close to one month's salary. Fans were always passing cash through the fences when players had big plays. When Tommy Evans had an emergency appendectomy and Hosea Pfeifer and his wife had a daughter, the fans in the stands passed the hat raising $338.55.

Rookie Charles "Buddy" Yount rocked the league in 1948 winning seventeen straight games until Ardmore derailed him in the last game of the season. He developed a sore arm in 1949. He threw for Chickasha in 1950 where he was 13-5. Called up for action in Korea, he played Class C ball in 1952. He joined Ada for their 1953 pennant run. (Ma-8)

1948

The 1948 ball park sported a new electric scoreboard, a new press box, padding on the rails of the grandstand, additional bleachers seating several hundred, new light standards in the left and right field foul areas, and new club houses suitable for a professional baseball venue. The City of McAlester earned a percentage rental of $676.85 for use of the ball park in 1948.

The working agreement with the Yankees was renewed for 1948. Vern Hoscheit was assigned to manage the New York rookies. As Whitey Herzog remembers in his autobiography, *White Rat*, Hoscheit played catcher, drove the bus, dispensed meal money, and did the laundry. Three players other than Hoscheit had prior professional experience. Al Billingsley played in nineteen games for the Yankees' K-O-M club at Independence, Kansas; he would be the All Star second baseman in 1948.

Local boys Tommy Evans and Howie Martin were back from the 1947 champions.

Like 1947, the lineup was set early in the season. Hoscheit and Bob Knoke handled chores behind the plate. The infield featured Cromer Smotherman at first, Billingsley at second, Evans at third from shortstop in 1947, and Bob Dahn at shortstop. Charles Buck, Clarence Darrah, Martin and Dick Neuberger handled the outfield. The pitching staff was balanced with six of seven hurlers winning ten or more games. The story in 1948 was Allen, Oklahoma's Buddy "Red" Yount. By July 24, he was undefeated in ten decisions. He had won seventeen by the last day of the season when he was scheduled to start. Sixth place Ardmore extracted a measure of vengeance for the rest of the league's teams when the Indians ruined his perfect season on the last day. He later dropped a playoff game to Seminole.

The 1948 team was speedy, again leading the league with 269 stolen bases. On their way to a regular season pennant and berth in the playoff finals, the Rockets logged ninety-one wins to finish thirteen games ahead of second place Lawton. They led the league in four hitting categories: a team .283 average, 1,300 hits, 1,829 total bases, and ninety-five triples.

Presenting the 1947 pennant. Center is Paul Crowl. To his right are Matt Patterson and league president Jack Mealey. (Ma-7)

All Star Smotherman won the batting crown with a .347 average. Manager Hoscheit, the All Star catcher, was next on the squad at .335 in 123 games. Billingsley (.313), Buck (.301), Darrah (.305), and Martin (.302) rounded out the +.300 players. The .939 fielding percentage was third; without Evans' fifty-seven errors at third and Buck's twenty-two in the outfield, the Rockets easily would have been the league's top fielders. Three Rocket hurlers boasted ERAs under 3.00: starters Rocky Shaneck (10-5, 2.98) and Buddy Yount (17-1, 2.11) as well as reliever Harold Morris (19-2, 2.86). Tom Hesketh, Bruce Schroeder, and Carl Sellers each won eleven games. Bob Curtis, whose 5.85 ERA was last on the staff, was the only hurler with a losing percentage with five wins against six losses.

Hoscheit did nothing for the team's ERA by his one venture on the mound. In two-thirds of an inning on May 9, he gave up seven runs on seven hits to hand Chickasha a lead the Rockets couldn't overcome. The Rockets did extend the life of a condemned rapist for about thirty minutes. Lewis Grayson was scheduled to be electrocuted at 10:00 p.m. on July 24. Rockets' publicist Hugh German of the *McAlester News-Capital* was assigned to cover both the execution and the ballgame that began at 8:15 p.m. Warden Clarence Buford delayed the State's retribution until German arrived in the witness room. Yount failed to get a decision in his fifteenth start because he was ejected in the tenth inning with the score tied 4-4. Staneck came in for the win over Lawton 5-4 in the eleventh. "Old Sparky," Oklahoma's electric chair, worked as always.

In the playoff, the Rockets made quick work of Chickasha in four games. Down three games to one against Seminole, the Rockets barely got past Oiler manager Willinghams' blooper ball for a 3-2 win to draw within a game of tying the series. On September 18, Buddy Yount faced Harry Olmstead at Seminole's Oilers Park. Don Wescott relieved Olmstead in the seventh while Morey Morris took over from Yount an inning earlier. Wescott gave up a run in the bottom of the seventh that resulted in a 6-5 Oilers victory and the first pennant to fly over Seminole. Nonetheless, grateful Rocket fans presented Hoscheit with a new car after the season.

1949

Most of the 1948 Rockets had been promoted to Yankees' clubs in Class C or Class B. The second McAlester team that Holscheit would lead had several veterans passing through for a few games. Tommy Evans and pitchers Bob Curtis and Clarence Wheeler were the only returnees; neither pitcher played the full season. The positions were not, unlike 1947 and 1948, fixed early on. They could not find a first baseman; six players filled that spot during the season. Don Leppert held down second base and Karl Swenson played more than half the season at third sharing with Evans. Darrell Waska was steady at shortstop. Hoscheit caught 101 games and backup Jack Barna played 21 behind the plate.

A Rocket in 1949 and 1950, Don Leppert appeared for the Orioles at the start and end of the 1955 season. (Ma-9)

Carl Zellar of Alderson, Oklahoma played in the outfield next to another rookie, Whitey Herzog in 1949. He began 1950 in the same outfield until optioned to Miami of the K-O-M where he feasted on that league's pitching. Drafted before the 1951 campaign, he rejoined the Rockets in 1953 hitting .317. He spent the next two seasons with a Yankees' Class C team before retiring. He drowned in a fishing accident in 1963. (Ma-10)

Bobby Tuminello of Baton Rouge was dubbed the "swamp rabbit" as he chaperoned seventeen year old Dorel Herzog in 1949 and 1950. They were reunited at Joplin in 1951. After a disappointing season, he realized his future was elsewhere. He returned to LSU for his degree. A scratch golfer, he irritated manager Hoscheit by taking his clubs on road trips. (Ma-11)

Whitey Herzog (left) and Jack Urban both went on to play in the Majors. Herzog entered the Hall of fame for his managerial and front office skills remarking "Baseball has been very good to me since I quit playing it." Urban played two seasons for the Kansas City Athletics and one for the St. Louis Cardinals. (Ma-12)

1950

The 1950 squad looked and played like the 1948 champs. Hoscheit was back for a third year. Herzog, who got a $50 per month raise to $200, Leppert, Tuminello, Jack Urban, and Carl Zellar came back with him. Howie Martin could not be lured back to the field from his turntable at the local radio station. Only eight pure rookies appeared. There was more stability on the roster. Hoscheit divided catching duties with Tom Self and Ray Burtner. Ed "Arky" Dickson was solid at first base with a Major League .989 fielding average. Leppert owned second base. John Jennings played seventy games at third base and fifty at shortstop while Jerry Morgan saw duty at third in thirty-one games and in forty-eight at shortstop. Herzog, Clint Weaver, and Jack Taylor patrolled the outfield with Self and Zellar helping out. Team hitting was strong at .285. Clint Weaver led the circuit at .378 with thirty-six home runs followed by Jack Taylor at .367, Herzog at .351, and Leppert at .330. Even pitcher Jack Urban who played a little outfield was .319 in 135 at bats. The Rockets fielded a respectable .949. The

Rookie Whitey Herzog had an error-free season in left field while Pat Lyons and Alderson, Oklahoma's Carl Zellar were beside him in most games.

McAlester's first second division team hit a weak .235 with the fewest total bases and only thirty-four home runs. Herzog's .279 batting average was the best of any regular. Fielding was mediocre at .935 with Hoscheit and Herzog leading at their positions. Only Bob Tuminello (6-7, 2.56) and Morey Morris (4-8, 2.61) had ERAs under 3.00. Bob Childs and John Harsey tied for most wins at ten each. The staff gave up 793 runs while their team mates scored only 623. Hoscheit repeating at catcher was the only All Star. The team did have three future Major Leaguers but each would need another year of seasoning at McAlester. Herzog, who received a signing bonus of $1,500, was paid $10 per month more than rookie Mickey Mantle at K-O-M League champion Independence, Kansas.

Mel Wright of the 1950 Rockets played eleven seasons and was a Major League coach and scout for twenty-one more. (Ma-13)

pitching was solid, the best in the League. The starting rotation of Urban (23-5, 2.15), Tom Hesketh (15-6, 2.26), Mel Wright (15-7, 3.02) and Tuminello (17-9, 3.35) accounted for seventy wins. Yet, this team that won ninety-two games finished second to Ada in the standings and batting. To lead the league in 1950 would require a team average over .300 and more than ninety-six wins.

The Rockets didn't realize that they were facing Major League pitching when they played an exhibition against the Penitentiary squad. Inmate hurler Tommy Warren, late of Brooklyn, and future Miami and Seminole manager, was touched for fifteen runs. The Rockets made quick work of Seminole on June 29, for a 2-1 win in a league record one hour and seventeen minutes. With Duncan playing a home game in Lawton on May 5, the Rockets and Uttmen

1950 champion McAlester Rockets. L-R Top row: bat boy, Tom Hesketh, Miles McWilliams, Whitey Herzog, Jack Taylor, Eddie Dickson, Jerry Jennings, Clint Weaver, Mel Wright, Barry Arney. Front row: batboy, Manager Vern Hoscheit, Roger Hanners, Don Leppert, Ray Burtner, Jack Urban, Jerry Morgan, Benny Coomer, Bob Tuminello, batboys. Herzog, Wright, Leppert, and Urban would all appear in the Major Leagues. Carl Zellar has entered the Army when this photo was taken. (Ma-14)

combined for thirty-three walks and ten balks in a sloppy contest McAlester won 20-8. In the playoffs, the Rockets swept Chickasha while Ardmore was eliminating Ada. The Rockets took the first two at McAlester, dropped two and won one at Ardmore, and captured the pennant at Tribe Park. The Rockets dominated the All Star team with Leppert, Weaver, Herzog, Urban, and, for the third time, Hoscheit, selected as the best at their positions.

1951

Never before or after was the disparity between the first division and second division so great as in 1951. The teams finishing first through fourth each won at least ninety games. The fifth place team lost eighty-six. Two tied for sixth with ninety-four losses. McDuff's Seminole Ironmen was last with 103. McAlester won enough games to finish first in most other years. In 1951 they finished third at 91-48.

Hoscheit's fourth and final year at McAlester was dominated by the pitching presence of former St. Louis Brown, Dee Sanders, who completed each of the twenty-nine games he started and had decisions in thirty-one of his thirty-three appearances finishing with a 27-4 record and an ERA of 1.67; he also hit .331 in 139 at bats. With pinpoint control he set an Organized Baseball record between a May 26 win over Seminole and the Fourth of July game with Ada with seventy-five and one-third innings without a walk. He issued only twenty-four free passes all season. Remarkably, he only pitched in McAlester as he had a business to manage. The other starters combined with Sanders to lead the league with fourteen shutouts and a collective ERA of 3.76. Leo Evans appeared in forty games, started twenty and finished fourteen to wind up 17-12 and a 3.26 ERA. Roger Hanners was 19-6 with a 3.23 ERA in thirty-four games, twenty-six of which he was the starter and eighteen of which he finished. Frank Lucas had ten wins against six losses completing eight of his seventeen starts and tallied a 3.92 ERA in twenty-four appearances. Hoscheit again led the team in hitting with a .354 average. As a third place team the Rockets were second in batting .292.

Again the 1951 team was dominated by rookies and sophomores. Only Sanders and Tommy Evans, who played in thirty-nine games at home and a few nearby on the road due to his elected position as Pittsburg County Treasurer, were veterans. Catcher Ray Burtner, first baseman Ed Dickson, and pitcher Roger

McAlester native Dee Sanders was a star for OU in 1941 and threw his first professional pitch for the St. Louis Browns in 1945. Winding up in the Texas League after a sojourn in Mexico, Sanders joined the 1951 Rockets as a "home only" pitcher amassing twenty-seven wins with a 1.67 ERA. His control was pinpoint as he established an Organized Baseball record of 75 1/3 consecutive innings without a walk. He was elected Sheriff of Pittsburg County in 1952 hiring Pepper Martin as his deputy. He was a successful businessman, rancher, and philanthropist. (Ma-15)

Hanners were back from the playoff winner. The regular 1950 shortstop/third baseman Jennings began the season but was cut after twenty-seven games in which he fielded a miserable .867. Future Yankees Jerry Lumpe and Norm Siebern joined the team late in the season; Lumpe played twenty-nine games at third while hitting .355 and Siebern hit .331 in fifty games as an outfielder. Hoscheit shuffled players around to different positions trying to find the right combination. Ed "Arky" Dickson (.321) was solid at first base. Jerry Morgan (.287) held down second. Jim Carney (.289), Evans (.241), Hoscheit and Lumpe alternated at third. Doyle Chadwick (.305) beat out Jennings for shortstop. Jack Burris (.308) was the most frequently seen outfielder but Carney, Siebern, Ed DeGeeter (.268), Carroll Bryan (.284), and Hoscheit all saw duty.

In the 1951 playoff, the Rockets ruined Shawnee's debut in a three game sweep. Bennie Warren's Ardmore Indians dropped the first two finals games at McAlester. When the action moved back to Ardmore, the Rockets salvaged one game while the Indians were within one game of tying the series. Back at Jeff-Lee Athletic Park, McAlester took Ardmore 6-5 for the championship.

Coming off playing the 1951 season with the Yankees' Kansas City Blues AAA affiliate, Bill Cope had Vern Hoscheit's big shoes to fill and did so with pennants in 1952 and 1953. (Ma-16)

1952

Hoscheit was promoted after the 1951 season. The Yankees assigned infielder Bill Cope to manage their 1952 rookie crop. Conscription had taken its toll. Seven of the 1951 Rockets were drafted into the Army. The May 30, 1951 issue of *The Sporting News* reported that outfielder Nick Wilson, sent down from Baton Rouge, joined the Rockets on the road for three games, then reported for induction without ever seeing McAlester. Tommy Flack was back from 1951 after breaking an ankle on August 1. Dan Demby, who had tied with his team mate at Pauls Valley Donnie Williamson for the home run crown with thirty, came to the Rockets by a circuitous route. He was sold to San Angelo, Texas, with the understanding that if he

The small press box of Jeff-Lee Athletic Park. (Ma-17)

were sold to another team, he would receive half his price. In April, the Rockets bought his contract for $500. He refused to report when San Angelo reneged and then demanded that McAlester pay him $250 to report. It took National Association president George Trautman's ruling that McAlester could not pay him to get him to play; he showed up on May 3. Dick Foster, the regular third baseman, Jerry Kudajeski, who played at first base more often than anyone else, Al Weber, who spent most of his time in the outfield but also played first base and catcher, and outfielder Bob James all had one year of playing experience at the Class D level. Pitchers Dan Beck, Bob Dawkins, Wally Sparks, and Gene Bremer also had thrown in a professional game. Bremer had been a star in the Negro Leagues throwing for the New Orleans Crescents, Memphis Red Sox, and Cleveland Buckeyes. He joined the team shortly after Napoleon Daniels broke the color line at Sherman on June 25. He played two seasons in the minors.

McAlester led the league in hitting with a .286 average on 1,392 hits. McAlester would have been the best fielding team but for the left side of the infield. At third base, Foster handled balls at a .906 competence level while James bobbled at a .762 rate and Harbaugh made nine out of ten plays at shortstop. On the mound, Charlie Seymour owned the league. He had a 1.91 ERA, 292 strike outs, twenty-five wins, and winning percentage (.806). Don Gibbs (17-8, 3.33), Charles Madden (11-4, 2.58), and future hurler for the Pirates and A's, Jack Mc-

Mahan (9-7, 3.43), completed the rotation. The only pitcher with an ERA over 4.00 was veteran Gene Bremer at 5.80. After a first place regular season finish, the Rockets breezed through the playoffs. Once again, they eliminated Shawnee in four games and then went the distance against Pauls Valley to become the first team in Sooner State League history to win both the regular season and the playoff.

For several seasons, the McAlester Chamber of Commerce, which Crowl chaired in 1953-1954, ran a promotion called "Town Night." Several of the thirty-six small communities around McAlester would be selected for one of eight Town Nights. Free tickets would be distributed through merchants in those hamlets usable only on a specific evening by residents of the towns selected for that game. In 1952, for example, Town Nights brought in 2,458 fans. Weather could be a problem, of course. For a game against Shawnee, the temperature was 47° as fifty hearty free ticket holders showed up, outnumbering the forty-one paying customers.

Russ Snyder's 1953 .432 batting average earned him the Silver Bat award for being the highest in the minor leagues and a placed in the Sooner State League record book. He hit .271 in 1,365 games in eleven Major League seasons. (Ma-18)

1953

Just as Dee Sanders dominated the 1951 season, outfielder Russ Snyder terrorized Sooner State League pitching in 1953 to be the top Minor League hitter with a .432 average. The disparity between first and second divisions was apparent but not as marked as in 1952. With eighty-three wins, fourth place McAlester finished nineteen games ahead of fifth place Pauls Valley. Cope shuffled position players and pitchers. Only four players appeared in 100 or more games at the same position: Snyder, outfielder Carl Zellar (.317), second baseman Jim Schrank (.250), and catcher Donnie Saatzer (.220). Of the twenty-two pitchers who appeared, fifteen saw action in fewer than forty-five innings. As a group their record was 12-18. Bob Shipman (13-3, 2.70), Al Kipper, back from a 9-9 season in 1951, (13-9, 2.83), Ron Saatzer (17-11, 3.00), and Charles Kasden (14-7, 3.12) formed a sound rotation. The staff allowed 774 runs but the hitters scored only 801. More than a few close games were lost. The Rockets managed to continue their September mastery over Ardmore, eliminating the first place Indians in four games. They made quick work of old rival Ada in five games to retire the Governor's Cup with their fifth championship.

Ron, a pitcher, and Don, a catcher, Saatzer were twins from Minnesota who played as a battery in the Yankees' organization in 1952 and 1953. They were split up after their season at McAlester, playing until 1956. (Ma-19)

1954

To assure operations in 1954, Ernest Smallwood and Otto Copeland formed the "1,000 Rocket Booster Club" the goal of which was to sell one thousand season passes at $27 each. They were unsuccessful.

The Yankees held tryout camps annually at McAlester. Tom Greenwade, the Yankee scout who signed Mickey Mantle as well as Hank Bauer, Elston Howard, Bill Virdon and Bobby Murcer, presided except when Yankees Director of Minor League Operations, Bill McPhail attended. The McAlester manager assisted. Several players would be given the opportunity to perform in Rockets' pinstriped flannels. Most lasted only a few weeks. In a league with a fifteen player cap, there was never room to give a rookie a long look see. Ray and Roy Mantle were products of the 1954 tryouts. A special tryout was conducted before Greenwade and 1954 manager Bunny Mick at the Oklahoma State Penitentiary for Billy Joe Moore, a phenom in prison stripes, to see whether he might one day wear pin stripes.

A third place finish in 1954 was attributable largely to McAlester's regular season mastery over second division Ada, Seminole, and Pauls Valley winning fifteen, thirteen, and sixteen games out of the twenty game series. That fifth place Gainesville beat the Rockets fourteen games to six speaks for the balance among the second through seventh place 1954 league clubs.

Malcolm "Bunny" Mick received the charge of managing the 1954 Rockets. Like Cope, he shuffled players among positions and saw fifteen pitchers on the mound for him. Keith Mitchell (.318) was the only member of the 1953 club who completed the 1954 season; pitcher Charles Gageby pitched in eight and pinch hit in nine games before being cut to make the fifteen player limit.

Mick (.327) at first base, All Star Frank Ricco (.251) at catcher, third baseman and outfielder Tony Young (.312), and Mitchell were the only regulars on the club. Max Mantle, Mickey's cousin, played the first part of the season at second base until released on July 3, hitting .233 and fielding .906. He was succeeded by Bob Maness who hit .288. The club under Bunny Mick played a small ball game that really didn't fit the Yankee paradigm. While hitting a very respectable .288 as a team, the 1954 Rockets hit only fifty-two home runs. The first did not come until May 28, when pitcher Galen Hudspeth launched one at Lawton. The next night Mick hit a grand slam at Gainesville to contribute to a 19-3 win.

Future New York Mets favorite Rod Kanehl, who divided his time between the outfield, third base and shortstop, came close to scoring the first inside-the-park home run on May 8, but failed to step on third base; he was credited with a double

Rod Kanehl hit .313 as a 1954 rookie. He was an original New York Met in 1962 and a favorite of Casey Stengel. He observed "Baseball is a lot like life. The line drives are caught, the squibbers go for base hits. It's an unfair game." (Ma-21)

Malcolm "Bunny" Mick was a small ball advocate in an organization that thrived on home runs. Coming up through the Yankees' system, he was a playing manager at Independence, Kansas in the K-O-M and Joplin of the Western Association. McAlester was his last stop in flannels. He later owned and operated the Tampa Tarpons and coached the Soviet Union team in the Goodwill Games in 1990. (Ma-20)

and tagged out after he crossed home. The Rockets pulled off a triple play at Pauls Valley's expense on July 2. The Raiders' Deckman and Underwood had walked. Manager Bennie Warren lined to manager Bunny Mick at first who tagged Deckman for number two and threw to shortstop Johnny Young to nail Underwood on the force at second.

Mick got to handle the rookie Mantle twins, Roy and Ray. They hit well, .325 and .324, but fielded miserably with Roy at .878 and Ray at .833 in the outfield. The Yankees converted them to the infield in 1955. Another prospect Mick scouted was Billy Ray Moore of the Oklahoma State Penitentiary Outlaws. His report aided Moore to receive a sixty day parole to try out with independent Grand Forks, N.D. of the Northern League; the Yankees would encourage but not sign him.

Mick took the Rockets to their final playoff series. For the first time in six previous appearances, the Rockets were eliminated in the first round. They took Travis Jackson's first Lawton team to the fifth game but dropped the series. While Ricco was named to the All Star team, Mick should have been considered. His On Base Percentage was .424 and he scored 133 runs while batting .327. Instead Robert White of Ardmore with thirty-two homes runs simply dazzled the scorekeepers and other managers who selected the team.

1955

Following the 1954 season, the Yankees made a radical change in their approach to player development. They would no longer sign players to man minor league teams. Rather they would sign only genuine Major League prospects. Additionally, they shrunk their minor league system from its high of twenty-two teams, nine of which were owned, to nine, only one of which was owned. McAlester ceased to be the first line Class D club.

The caliber of player sent to McAlester declined resulting in sixth and seventh place finishes during the Rockets' last two seasons. This spelled the end for professional baseball in McAlester.

The Chamber of Commerce raised $15,000 in pre-season ticket sales before the 1955 season. A sixth place team drew 6,000 fewer fans than in 1954. The bottom line result was that the franchise lost $3,287 for the year and finished with an operating debt of $5,100. Paul Crowl, after ten years as McAlester baseball's main booster, resigned as president of McAlester Athletic Association to be succeeded by longtime officer, Matt Patterson.

Mick's contract was not renewed. Marv Crater was chosen to lead the last two McAlester nines. The Yankees began a pullback in their Minor League system. Instead of signing anyone with talent and then cutting or keeping after a Class D look-see, they began limiting signees to those with a reasonable prospect of playing in Yankee Stadium. The effect was to reduce the number of Class D Yankee farm hands. This was apparent in 1955 and manifest in 1956. Dennis Brenek, who would reappear at Shawnee in 1957, Hugh Craig, Paul Hinch, and pitchers Bob Bleyenberg, Lloyd McKinney, and Wally Sohn returned from the 1954 club. Sohn and Don Gilbert, an outfielder, had a season-ending car wreck in May. Brenek was cut after six games.

Unlike Mick, Crater found an infield early and stayed with them all season. Bob McClish (.254, .958) held down first. Tony Asaro (.298, .967

Like all McAlester managers since Hoscheit, Marvin Crater was a product of the Yankees' farm system. With a change in thinking about what their minor league operation should be doing, weaker rosters were sent down resulting in sixth and seventh place finishes in 1955 and 1956. Crater finished his time in baseball as coach of Wake Forest University. (Ma-22)

League best) owned second. Morris Millet (.300, .876) and Hugh Craig (.267, .897) formed the left side of the infield, third and shortstop, respectively. Vince Caradonna (.234, .941) and Les Miller (.242, .936) were in the outfield in most games; ten others joined them at one time or another.

In a season in which Dale Hendrickson of Lawton intimidated all hitters with a 1.26 ERA, McAlester's John Davilo may have outshined him had he not been promoted after nine starts to Modesto of the California League. He allowed only ten earned runs in seventy-five innings for a 1.20 ERA. His 4-5 record is attributable to the eighteen additional unearned runs his fielders allowed to score. The

Photios "Tony" Anthony played his sophomore season at third base for the last edition of the Rockets. He pursued the dream of all ball players in the Yankees' and Orioles' systems through 1963. Class AA was as high as he reached. (Ma-23)

staff posted a 4.08 ERA. In sixty-one innings, Lloyd McKinney, who was 19-9 for the 1954 Rockets, was 5-3 with a 2.06 ERA before he accompanied Davilo to Modesto. Bob Bleyenberg at 12-11 and 3.46 and Dave Kostenuk (11-9, 3.55) were the best of the rest. The sixth place team was third in hitting at .257 with a league low of thirty-one home runs. But for their left side, the Rockets would have led in fielding; they finished fourth in that category at .942.

1956

Six of the 1955 McAlester club members were promoted and four were back in 1956. Thirteen were out of baseball. Marv Crater's last team was plagued with poor pitching, bad hitting and sloppy fielding. Again, Crater played a set infield. First baseman McClish bested his 1955 performance at first base hitting .304. Joe Cintron at second base and outfield led the team in hitting with .312 until he was injured in August. Photios Anthony hit .259 while holding down third. Dave Irby had over half the season at shortstop adding a .278 bat.

Outfielder Bruce Swango was the big name on the club. Baltimore had signed him out of Welch, Oklahoma, high school for a bonus and salary in the $36,000 neighborhood and he immediately reported to Baltimore. He was so wild that the Oriole hitters would not let him throw batting practice. Paul Richards, the Orioles' GM who had called the 1955 O's a bunch of clowns, walked away from Swango before the end of the 1955 season without ever putting him in the lineup. The Yankees signed him to a minor league contract with hopes of making an outfielder of him. McAlester was their closest Class D team and there he was assigned. He played every game fielding .910 and hitting .246 when he quit the team in frustration on August 3. He came back three days later when Cintron suffered a season-ending injury. His batting didn't improve, finishing the season at .224 with only seven home runs. Crater did let him pitch the last game of the season. In his first professional start, Swango handcuffed Muskogee 11-4 for his first win in Organized Baseball. It was McAlester's last win in Organized Baseball.

Patterson announced that the Rockets would need $35,000 to $40,000 to operate in 1956. Pre-season ticket sales were disappointing at $3,775. Fence ad sales were $2,800. A weak team was fielded that was watched by only 32,302 paying fans. By the late fall of 1956, having exhausted all resources, McAlester Athletic Association returned its charter franchise to the league.

Bruce Swango of Welch, Oklahoma went from high school to Baltimore in 1955 as a bonus baby never to see action in a game because, while a hard thrower, he was so wild that the other Orioles would not even take batting practice from him. The Yankees tried to make a hitter of him when he was signed to a $250 monthly contract and assigned to McAlester. He returned to pitching and, after being sold to the Twins, reached the AAA level. Here he is shown with Fargo-Moorhead where he tossed a no-hitter in 1958. (Ma-24)

1956 McAlester Rockets. L-R Top row: Hoby Powell, Wes Wright, Bob Coscia, Duke Addis, Bob McClish, Jack Hoy. Middle row: Manager Marv Crater, Don Dallas, Ralph Tracey, Bruce Swango, Photios Anthony, Jim Pignatello. Front row: Joe Cintron, Red Irby, Duane Kinart, Fred Taylor, Roy West. National Service players did not count against the fifteen player roster limit. Phil Mudrock (not pictured) was the only member of the 1956 squad to appear in a Major League game: one inning for the Chicago Cubs. (Ma-25)

MIAMI BLUES 1946
MIAMI OWLS 1947-1949
MIAMI EAGLES 1950-1952
KANSAS-OKLAHOMA-MISSOURI LEAGUE

SEASON	ATTENDANCE	RECORD	FINISH	AFFILIATION	PLAYOFF FIRST ROUND	PLAYOFF FINALS
1946	49,266	69-54	Second	Brooklyn	Lost to Iola 1-3	
1947	53,119	76-49	First	Topeka (W.L.)	Beat Bartlesville 3-1	Beat Iola 4-1
1948	33,716	58-66	Fifth	Topeka (W.L.)		
1949	32,887	56-69	Seventh	Topeka (W.L.)		
1950	27,548	62-60	Fifth			
1951	23,500	67-55	Third		Beat Bartlesville 3-1	Lost to Carthage 0-3
1952	43,008	67-57	Second	Philadelphia N.L.	Beat Pittsburg, 1-0	Beat Ponca City 2-0

An opening day ticket from 1950.

1946

Miami attorney Hershel Beauchamp was an original organizer of the K-O-M along with baseball men Gabby Street, St. Louis Cardinals scout Runt Marr, A. H. Moorman, and Carthage publisher E. L. Dale. Beauchamp landed the franchise for his home town. The club's board included Beauchamp, R. O. "Hoot" Gibson, Wallace Millner, Bill Wing, Emmett Utter, Charles Fox, and Rex Renegar. They in turn appointed Ted Vernon as general manager. Accordingly to K-O-M expert John Hall, Vernon, an Amarillo native, was in fact the team's owner. Vernon was wary of working agreements and particularly suspicious of the Brooklyn Dodgers farm system then controlled by Branch Rickey. Nonetheless, he negotiated a loose arrangement with the Dodgers by which players were fed to the newly named Blues but Miami remained free to sign, develop and sell its own talent.

Games were played at the Miami Fairgrounds which was configured as a racetrack complete with light poles on the field of play. Among the regular attendees of Blues' games were the Mutt Mantle family from Commerce. Their oldest son, Mickey, would shag flies during batting practice. He particularly admired the fastest man in the K-O-M, "Jumpin'" Joe Pollock. Some of the players would harass young Mickey, tossing his glove over the fence. Not Pollock. Joe attended all of Mickey's high school games over at Commerce when the Blues were at home.

A member and later Chief of the Peoria-Miami tribe with a long baseball pedigree was hired to run things on the field. Guy Froman played in Organized Baseball from 1921 when he broke in with Coffeyville (KS) of the old Southwestern League as a first baseman through 1932 mainly in Classes B and C. He later was a fixture in local semi-pro circles playing through World War II for Eagle-Picher

The fairgrounds in Miami had a racetrack and grandstand that was adapted for baseball but not perfectly. There were light poles in the playing field. (Mi-1)

Mining & Smelting, one of the area's largest employers. Tasked with assembling a roster, he had a mix of rookies and pre-War pros and semi-pros, several with multiple years in the military service, with a decidedly local flavor. Brooklyn sent Joe Beran, Robert Brown, Dale Burich, Dave Dennis, Steve Jordan, and Red Pace plus a number of other prospects who didn't last long enough to show up with any statistics.

In addition to local Froman, Beran was from Odin, KS, Simon Bush from Vian, Bill Chandler hailed from Tulsa, the Dennis brothers were from Mapleton, KS, Oscar Engel shared a Meeker hometown with Giants' great Carl Hubbell, Ray Jordan called Dustin, OK home, Newt Keithley was a pre-War star second sacker for Eagle-Picher, quarterback for the University of Tulsa and head football coach for Miami High School, Ralph Marler was from Springfield, MO, Robert

Joe Pollock befriended a young Mickey Mantle. (Mi-2)

Montgomery shared Commerce with a high school boy named Mantle, Robert Pace was from Neosho, MO, Loren Packard called Helena, OK home, James Reddick was from across the line in Bentonville, AR, James Sooter was from Bluejacket, and Billy White from Grove. Dave Dennis, Ray Jordan, Harvey McKibben, and Joe Pollock had all played ball in the military.

The Blues' regular line-up had Dave Dennis behind the plate, Dale Burich at first, Keithley at second, Engel at third, and OU baseball alumnus William Chandler at shortstop. Bill Chambers appeared at second and shortstop until Salina (KS) of the Western Association bought his contract early in the season. Loren Packard, Jim Cooke, and Pollock, after being sent down June 20 from Muskogee following sixteen games there, appeared as outfield-

ers in roughly two-thirds of the Blues' games. McKibben, Montgomery, and Steve Jordan took their places there between starting assignments on the mound. Robert Carson, Joe Connor, Rodney Lewis, Elden McHugh, Wes Nettles, Pace, and White also saw duty in the outfield.

At least eleven players threw for the Blues. Bain Hatfield, Ray Jordan, Steve Jordan, Ralph Marler, Harvey McKibben, and Robert Montgomery formed the core of Froman's hurling staff. None turned in an ERA under 3.00. Steve Jordan, a Dodger property who would spend the next season at Ponca City, was the ace and workhorse with a 16-5 record and 3.25 ERA in 177 innings. Close behind with the same ERA was McKibben at 13-5 who threw 130 innings. Ray "Blue" Jordan split sixteen decisions in twenty-nine appearances with a 4.10

An Amarillo native, Joe Engel was surreptitiously signed by Ted Vernon the actual owner and operator of the Miami club. When the National Association learned of the arrangement, the season was over. No harm, no foul. (Mi-3)

Miami produced a scorecard that was elaborate by Class D standards. (Mi-4)

Jim Cooke and Joe Pollock formed two-thirds of Miami's 1946 outfield after being sent down from Muskogee. (Mi-5)

ERA in 136 innings. Ben Hatfield would return to Miami for 1947 after working 109 innings with a team best 3.14 ERA for a 8-8 record. Marler was 6-6 with a 3.60 ERA in 90 innings. Montgomery had a respectable 3.72 ERA in ninety-two innings but would up with a 4-5 record. William Morgan and Barney Zapf both threw in seventy innings. With a 3.34 ERA Morgan posted a winning 6-3 record while Zapf's 5.40 ERA put his season totals at 4-5. Dodger farmhand Joe Beran was 2-4 in eighteen appearances. James Reddick (1-1 12.24 ERA) and Coleman Riba (1-3 4.03 ERA) kept their rookie status as they pitched in fewer than forty-five innings.

Keithley, Pollock, and Dennis were named to the first K-O-M All Star team. Keithley's .346 batting average with 167 hits was the best in the league while Pollock topped all base runners with sixty-seven thefts. An odd K-O-M rule allowed players to sign with different teams for the playoffs. Miami inked Bartlesville's first baseman Jerry Cross. Dave Dennis left the Blues for the first place Chanute Owls. Dennis made the better choice as Chanute eliminated Pittsburg in the first round and then divided six games with Iola before bad weather and wet grounds dictated an end to the season.

The Blues disbanded. For many, it had been the first and last stop in Organized Baseball. Several returned to semi-pro work where the pay was as good or better than the K-O-M and the hours less arduous. A number just left the game. Eleven were in Organized Baseball in 1947.

1947

The Dodgers moved their affiliation to Ponca City for 1947. Miami entered into an unusual symbiosis with the independent Class A Topeka Owls of the Western League that would last three seasons. It was not a working agreement because Topeka did not supply all or even most of the

players who appeared for Miami. They did sends players to and call up from the K-O-M. The Blues would become the Owls. Topeka joined its new partner for spring training in Miami on March 28. Only Loren Packard and, briefly, Bain Hatfield returned from the inaugural season. Vernon hired a veteran minor league pitcher from the Yankees' organization, thirty-one year old William Davis, to guide the new crowd of faces at Fairgrounds Park. He even added five wins from the mound to help the Owls' cause.

The Owls were easily the oldest team in the K-O-M. Five had played before or during the War and two were veterans of the military. The team's only left-handed pitcher, James McGee, had only recently been released from the Texas State Prison at Huntsville after a stint there for armed robbery. The Owls had the best batter and top pitcher. They were destined to win it all in 1947.

Bob Davis led the independent Owls in 1947. He left the game after the season settling in Miami. (Mi-6)

1947 Miami Owls. Top row, L-R: Jim Morris, Walter Snider, Jim McGhee, Loren Packard, Curtis Darnell, Hank Kelly. Middle row, L-R: Jim Hansen, Irv Scheurman, Bob Hegwood, Marty Debish, Nathan Waterman, manager Bill Davis. Front row, L-R: Ray Mazzucco, Len Worthington, Tom Tarascio, Les Harris, Travis Kunce. (Mi-7)

Jim Morris tossed a no-hitter at Carthage on the opening night of the 1947 season. He is shown being congratulated after the game by K-O-M president Dale. (Mi-8)

Catcher, first base, second base, shortstop, and two outfield slots enjoyed regular occupants. The pitching staff had four hurlers with over 170 innings each.

A former football player at Iowa and Nebraska, Jim Hansen guided the team from behind the plate with occasional relief from Travis Kunce. Zeb Snider ruled first base. Diminutive (5'4") Tom Tarascio played 121 games at the keystone. Darnell, sent down from Topeka, appeared in most games mainly as an outfielder but also occasionally as a poor fielding (.757) third baseman and as backup for Snider. The left side of the infield was a weak spot. Joe Royner had seventy-five games at third but his .851 fielding was a hindrance

Loren Packard edged Bartlesville's Dixie Upright for the batting crown by .0004 point. (Mi-9)

albeit better than Darnell. The hot corner solidified only when Henry Kelley appeared fresh from Boston College and then Les Harris, who began the season at Fond du Lac, was sent down from Topeka to replace utility infielder Robert Kehoe. Kehoe's heart was in soccer; he was captain of the 1965 and 1972 U.S. World Cup teams. The Owls did not corner the market on stone-handed shortfielders; no 1947 K-O-M shortstop had a fielding average above .898. Ernest Schuerman joined the Owls on loan from the Cardinal's farm system on June 15 taking over the position from Preston German who had been released a few days before. Marty Debish and Loren Packard were regular outfielders with Darnell joining them half the time. Frank Babkiewich, who moved up to Baton Rouge, Pete Canaglia, sent down from Topeka then released on June 10, and limited service player Bob Hegwood filled in.

Four pitchers appeared in over thirty games. Two others were called up to Topeka, Fred Luciano and Leonard Worthington, neither with a decision. Joe Lescard was released on May 10 to emerge with Chanute. Nathan Waterman (3-2 4.78 ERA) was sold to the Boston Braves who converted him to the outfield at their Leavenworth club in the Western Association.

Jim Morris, at age twenty-three the youngster of the staff, threw in 274 innings of forty-five games to become Miami's first twenty-game winner (21-14) with a 4.20 ERA. He got off to a brilliant start when he no-hit Carthage on opening day. He also won three games in the play-offs. Ray Mazzucco (14-7 3.72 ERA) appeared in 203 innings of thirty-three games. In a six day stretch, he hurled three complete games. Worthington's 15-11 record in 199 innings and his giving up only 4.7 hits per nine innings earned him a promotion to Topeka. Joining the team late due to his Texas entanglements, James McGee tossed in thirty-five games to earn a 14-5 record with a 4.78 ERA. And, again, manager Bill Davis was 5-0 with a team best 2.87 ERA.

With combat veterans and a reformed robber on the squad, ring-led by manager Bill Davis the team's moonlight theft of some forty watermelons on a trip back from Ponca City doesn't come as a complete shock. Players received a little over $2.00 per day for meal money and were always hungry. The melons became "commodity currency" and trade to a local diner resulted in full meals for all.

The Owls took an early lead in the standings and never shared the top spot all season finishing six games ahead of the Cubs' prospects from Iola. Miami beat out the Pirates' farmhands from Bartlesville in four games to earn the right to face Iola. In a best-of-seven series, after dropping the first contest, the Owls prevailed in the next four to cop the 1947 pennant. Just as in 1946, Miami placed three members on the All Star squad. Hansen, Snider, and Packard joined the   K-O-M elite. Packard edged out Bartlesville's Dixie Upright for the batting crown by .0004 point. Packard's 184 hits and 124 RBIs set all time K-O-M records. The Owls were second in team hitting with a .275 average. They led with 234 doubles, 807 RBIs, and tied with Independence with the most home runs at sixty-two. More important, 53,119 fans from this blue collar town paid to see their local champions plus another couple thousand watched the Owls against the K-O-M All Stars.

1948

Henry Gornicki had a good career at the top on the minors going as he pitched three seasons for Rochester in the International League before the War. After a four-year detour in the military, he returned as a Pittsburgh signee in the Pacific Coast League for the 1946 Hollywood Stars. The next season was not as kind as he was released after a game with Indianapolis and fell to Class B Gainesville in the Big State League. Nonetheless, he signed on to try his hand as bench general for Topeka's Miami

affiliate for 1948. After selecting a ball club and running them through Spring drills, Gornicki walked away from baseball. Desperate for a field leader, Topeka turned to their twenty-six year old War veteran infielder Art Priebe to head the little Owls.

Until his forced departure on August 4, Priebe performed a juggling act with the roster he inherited and augmented after the season began. Three came on the bounce via the K-O-M's other independent, Iola: Ed Kababeck was at Miami for fifty games after just two at Iola; pitcher Ed Jaroch came in mid-May for seven outings; giant (6'7") Bernie Tye suited up for fifty-seven Owls' games after three at Iola and thirty-three at Chanute in May and June. Seven returned from the first-place 1947 club: veteran catcher Jim Hansen, third sacker Les Harris, fly shagger Henry Kelley, backstop Travis Kunce, keystone Tom Tarascio, and throwers Ray Mazzucco and Loren Worthington. Four rookies were signed after the season began: first sacker Duane Melvin and outfielder Earl Parker joined the Owls on

The long and short of the 1948 Owls. Bernie Tye (6'7") had been with Chanute before joining Iola. After slapping the team owner with a glove, he boarded visiting Miami's bus as its newest member. Tom Tarascio (5'4") was a carry-over from 1947. (Mi-10)

May 25, shortstop Guernsey Freeman on June 15, and pitcher Art Coleman on July 20.

Rookie Warren Liston divided his play among the positions of catcher, first base, and outfield. Others were not as versatile. Hansen and Kunce shared catching duties. James Manuel came to first base as a result of his play-or-trade contract with the St. Louis Cardinals' system; otherwise, he would have been at Carthage. Short-timers Charles Cooper and Melvin also guarded the first sack. Tarascio played 106 games at second base assisted by Freeman in twenty-one. Les Harris was at third base in nearly every game. Ed Kababek hitting .185 lost his place at shortstop. Priebe returned from the bench until Freeman arrived to handle the hot corner for the remainder of the season. Jim Reaugh was the sole regular in the outfield appearing in 121 games. When he arrived for the second half, Tye appeared in every game. Pitcher Roy Buffalo was called into service in seventeen games. Japanese-American Brooks Iwakiri saw action as did Kababek, Henry Kelley, Thomas Kappele, Earl Parker, as well as Liston.

Skinny rookie Ed Wilson was the star of the mound staff appearing in the most games (29), throwing the most innings (191), boasting the best ERA (2.83), and the best record (14-8). Rookie James Price had a 2.92 ERA in 157 innings finishing with a 8-11 record. Back from 1947, Ray Mazzucco was just behind Wilson in innings (183) winning nine of nineteen with a 3.69 ERA. Another rookie,

Rudy Neumann had a winning percentage (9-8) with a team-high 4.47 ERA in 151 innings. Sophomore Art Grieve was 6-5 in eighty-two innings. In sixteen games, Iola transplant Ed Jaroch was 4-6 with a 3.45 ERA. Rookie Robert Vogel had a 2.86 ERA with four wins against five losses in the sixty-six innings pitched before he was released on July 4. Latecomer Art Coleman was 1-3 in nine games. Manager Priebe got into the pitching act for the first and only time in his career. He posted three wins with only a single loss and a 2.42 ERA in seventeen appearances totaling fifty-two innings.

Miami dropped the opener to Carthage 6-1. The Owls started in fifth place at 10-10 on May 27. They rose to their only first division appearance on June 17 at 20-20 including Priebe breaking up Bartlesville's Pierro's bid for a no-hitter on June 9. A seven-game losing streak included the embarrassment of a single pitcher, Tom Smith of Carthage, taking the Owls in both ends of a doubleheader 5-1, 6-0 on June 17. Miami managed only three hits in the twin bill. The Owls fell to eighth. On July 27 at 27-36 the club was in seventh. By then with attendance far down general manager Ted

1948 Owls "sluggers" L-R Gus Freeman, Tom Kappele, Jim Hansen, Jim Manuel. Using the dead Worth ball, the team had ten home runs all season. Kappele led with two. (Mi-11)

1948 Miami Owls. Top row, L-R: Bernie Tye, Warren Liston, Jim Manuel, Ed Wilson, Gene Jaroch, Tom Kappele, Ed Kubabeck, Alex Grieves. Front row, L-R: Jim Price, Jim Hansen, Ray Mazzucco, Tom Tarascio, bat boy, Ray Newmann, Jimmy Reaugh, Les Harris, Guerney Freeman. (Mi-12)

Vernon had seen enough of Priebe. Vernon didn't have any desire to take over on the field and 1947 winning manager, Bill Davis who had settled in Miami, declined to return to flannels every day. On August 4, Priebe was fired and catcher Jim Hansen at twenty-three years took the reins; Davis did agree to assist the first-time leader. The Owls played winning ball under Hansen passing Carthage, Iola, and Chanute to finish the season twenty games behind pacesetter Ponca City at 58-66 in fifth place before 33,716 paying observers, a decline of 19,403 or nearly thirty-seven percent from 1947. Serious flooding of the Neosho River forced cancellation and rescheduling of home games in Miami, Chanute, and Iola. Additionally, the K-O-M region suffered through the hottest summer in decades.

Les Harris landed a spot on the mid-season All Star team that lost to Ponca City 12-11 in ten innings on July 8 before a packed house of 3,496. No Owls appeared on the post-season elite squad. The Owls managed only ten home runs with the dead Worth baseball and finished seventh in batting with a paltry .214 team average. Hope was that 1949 would be better.

1949

The 1949 season was doomed when six-year veteran Omar Lane was placed at the helm for the last season Miami was hooked up with Topeka. A huge man (6'5" 250+ pounds), Lane was big enough to play defensive line on any professional football team but he chose to bully in baseball. He ran off three promising pitchers from San Diego during the first three weeks of the season. Carl Hirlbach jumped the club on May 23. Billy Noel returned to the Miami semi-pros on May 28. Ike Robbins lasted the season but not as a pitcher. George Gibson left the team the first week because he was homesick. Loren Worthington, a 15-11 hurler for the 1947

champions, had his fill of Lane and quit the game. Pugnacious, he would challenge players to fights on bus trips knowing they were too sane to take him on. Managing by intimidation may have instilled fear but never respect or authority.

Only four 1949 Owls were limited service players including Jim Reaugh from 1948. Four regulars, Lane, John Bulkley, Ken Skaggs, and Casey Wonka, were professional veterans with at least three years in the game. The rest were rookies.

Skaggs and limited service player Robert Paulausky provided stability behind the plate. Lane rarely shared first base with Robbins. Joe Verbanic joined the club late after four years in the Marines. He covered second base more than half the time with Bulkley filling the rest. Future Major League utility player Harry Bright, whom the Yankees sold to Miami after he sat out the 1948 season, held down third base and also played twenty-two games at second. Duane Melvin, back from 1948, was the regular at shortstop with team problem child Casey Wonka filling in a baker's dozen times. Reaugh was again the stalwart outfielder usually paired with Wonka and semi-pro veteran Adam Thompson. Robbins, Earl Hays, Ed Brennan and Charles Dorman, both released on June 1, and Leo Downing were the fill-ins.

Hays was mainly a pitcher working 144 innings for a 9-10 record with a 4.75 ERA. Richard Butler was the best pitcher at 8-2 with a 3.94 ERA until he left the team over Lane's laxity; he finished the season

Omar Lane at 6'5" and over 250 pounds, down from Muskogee, managed the 1949 club by intimidation. It didn't work. The Owls' seventh place finish was the worst in franchise history. (Mi-13)

Harry Bright was released by the Yankees' organization after sitting out 1948. The Cubs' minor league office signed him after Miami. He went on to play in the Majors between 1958 and 1965. He managed in the minors for eleven seasons. (Mi-14)

Casey Wonka, who finished ahead of Mickey Mantle in the batting race, was the Owls' free spirit. After twice being fined, he quit the club with two weeks to go in the season. (Mi-15)

with Chanute. Joining the club on May 25, Jack Schaening had the most wins and best ERA (12-11 3.03 ERA) in 181 innings of thirty games. Ray Stockton was the workhorse with 191 innings in thirty-five games posting a 10-13 record with a high 4.73 ERA. Eddie Stephens of Tulsa belonged to the Red Sox but was optioned to Miami to prevent homesickness; his 4.74 ERA and 1-8 record made for a marginal baseball future. Judd Sommers assured that 1949 would be his only season with a 5.78 ERA and 2-7 record. Elmer Peacock, a Seneca from Wyandotte, signed July 23 from the Miami semi-pros, was 4-0 when he suffered a nearly fatal head injury at the hands of Joe Malott, Iola's pitcher from Big Cabin, on August 3. He gave up baseball after that although he appeared at the semi-pro level a few years later.

Nebraskan Casey Wonka was playing semi-pro ball when a team mate persuaded him to head for Los Angeles before the War. When he turned eighteen he got a job at Paramount and became friends with UCLA and future Rams' quarterback Bob Waterfield. Wonka doubled for Mickey Rooney in three movies. He was playing in an exhibition in San Francisco against a team of Japanese All Stars on

December 7, 1941. With the Americans in the lead, the game was halted when the news of Pearl Harbor arrived with police surrounding Seals Stadium. *Ripley's Believe It or Not* called it the United States' first victory of the War. The Boston Braves signed him after the War and had him toiling for two seasons with their Leavenworth (KS) Western Association club. Released, he joined independent Topeka in 1948 and found himself down at Miami in 1949.

The greatest internal turmoil during a season of conflict and dissention occurred on August 3. The Owls' best pitcher Richard Butler quit the team that day because his team mates weren't serious about training and before the preceding evening's loss to Chanute two Owls had been drinking contributing, according to Butler, to the defeat. The Miami board of directors called a players meeting to calm the waters. Outfielders Adam Thompson and, unsurprisingly, Wonka were the culprits. Thompson was tagged with a $50 fine and Wonka twice that—a month's pay when $25 was usual the cost for bumping an umpire. Management agreed to remit the fines if both played out the season without further incident. In second place in the K-O-M batting race with a .31374 average, Wonka walked away, returning to his Leavenworth home. Miami hit him with another $100 fine and a ban from baseball until he paid both. For 1950 he played semi-pro in Superior (NB) then appeared in twelve games for the 1951 Miami Eagles before hanging up his spikes for good.

A stunt proving that Lane's club by mid-July was not taking the game seriously was pulled off on July 18. In the second game of a doubleheader with the Independence Yankees, every player got into the game with all at the wrong positions. Lane, Wonka, and Melvin pitched. Independence rookie shortstop Mickey Mantle feasted on their servings batting seven-for-nine. K-O-M president E. L. Dale was outraged and fined the Miami franchise $100 for "conduct detrimental to baseball."

A record of some sort was set on August 25. Iola sent nineteen batters to the plate against Miami in an hour-long first inning resulting in fourteen runs and a 20-5 Miami loss.

Robert Paulausky batted a team best .322 but lacked enough chances at the plate to compete in the 1949 K-O-M batting race. Bartlesville's Dick Drury won the crown with a .317 performance. Despite his going AWOL, Wonka finished second edging out Mantle who finished the campaign at .31269. The last edition as the Owls finished in seventh place with a 59-69 record fifteen and one-half games behind the Independence club. They remarkably were second in team batting with a .253 average. The Owls swung away, receiving the league's fewest free passes. Fourth in team fielding with a respectable .940, Lane, Bright and Melvin put together a triple play.

Miami wound up in the K-O-M cellar in the most important category drawing 32,887, a poorer showing than the near-bankrupting 1948 season. The December 7, 1949 issue of *The Sporting News* reported that Topeka was dropping Miami. It would proceed as an independent.

1950

Ted Vernon couldn't handle owning a ball club after the disastrous 1949 and 1950 seasons. F. A. "Pug" Griffin, who broke into baseball with the 1917 Philadelphia Athletics and then after a brief trip to the Polo Grounds in 1920, batted .316 in thirteen minor league seasons mainly in the Texas League, Western League, and Southern Association, found himself a scout for the Cardinals after being relieved of duties with the Redbirds' Lynchburg (VA) club in late May, 1949. Griffin was no stranger to owning and operating a minor league franchise. Between 1934 and 1939 he was proprietor of the Lincoln Links of the Nebraska State League and

managed them on the field for two seasons. Fortunately for Vernon, Griffin felt he could still be a one-man show and took the faltering franchise off his hands. A new bird was selected for the Miami club's name. Henceforward they would be the "Eagles."

Griffin advertised in the March 15, 1950 issue of *The Sporting News* for a tryout camp at Miami April 1-10. He put the prospects through their paces during spring training at Miami that started at the end of tryouts and finished with the opener on May 5. Two days before the opener, Griffin selected his new shortstop, Jack Hodges, a twenty-three year-old product of the Browns' post-War farm system, to be the field leader. The season opened auspiciously with a 10-0 victory over host Carthage. Two weeks later the Eagles were playing over .500 ball in fifth place. Jack Hodges asked to be relieved of managerial duties so he could concentrate on batting and playing shortstop. It was also approaching cut time and he was understandably reluctant to issue pink slips to his team mates. Two cuts he did make were outfielder Maurice Mathey and weak-hitting Mike Stelma. Griffin obliged and found in his rolodex the name of James Oglesby who had spent the prior three seasons managing

Pug Griffin played in a few games for the Athletics in 1917 then the Giants in 1920. Between 1918 and 1932, he toiled in the high minors. He bought the Miami franchise in 1950 operating as an independent and walked away from it in the midst of the1951 campaign. (Mi-16)

Jim Oglesby led Griffin's 1950 Eagles from May 23 through July 4. He was fired as a cost-saving measured with Griffin taking over the helm. He toiled in the minors from 1926 through 1942 including a three game stint with Connie Mack's 1936 Athletics. (Mi-17)

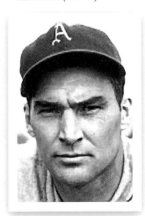

in the lower reaches of the Cubs' organization. He joined the club on May 23 and lasted until July 4 never emerging from the second division. Allowing Carthage manager Don Anderson to steal second, third, and home on a single in Oglesby's debut game set the tone. He added Jim Allicotti, on the bounce from the Browns' Sooner State League Club at Ada, then cut outfielders Max Burgett and Louis Salerno, catcher Jack Williams, first baseman Charles Mann, second sacker Dean Rorbaugh, and pitchers Gerald Beavers and Alva Cummings. When Oglesby received his walking papers on Independence Day as a cost cutting measure, owner Pug Griffin took over.

At a league meeting on June 18, Griffin surprised the other owners when he predicted Miami would fold. Competing against decent semi-pro clubs in Commerce and from the Eagle-Pitcher Mines and with television beginning to be available from Tulsa, the Eagles had drawn an average of 250 fans to the Fairgrounds; he needed 1,000 to break even. Needing revenue rather than kudos, Miami took on Iola in a doubleheader rather than let a date go by for the K-O-M All Star game in Ponca City. Griffin squeezed in another game on the day after the regular season ended. On July 27 in a game in Miami with the Eagles up 4-2 in the

sixth inning, Griffin confused a Carthage outfielder into tossing him the ball. Carthage protested and prevailed. The game had to be replayed beginning where the trick had been done. With the bases loaded with Miami batsmen, the Eagles managed another run to hold off their guests for a 5-4 win. The loss dropped Carthage to third moving Bartlesville up to the second spot. It was all downhill for Carthage after that.

With as many position players coming in as going out, there was remarkable fluidity in the field. Paulausky at catcher was one of two Eagles to appear in over one hundred (103) games. He had replaced Williams who, after he was cut plied his trade for Chanute and Iola. Early on, Mann and Stelma vied for first base but after giving rookie Don Fitzgerald a try, Gary Hildebrand ended up with the job. Jim McHugh, a member of the 1946 Blues and the 1951 and 1952 Eagles, owned second base with Gene Juanta appearing there in five contests. Bob Jenkins and Robert Kuykendall vied for third base after Bill Sartain took over the shortstop position. Sartain replaced former manager and weak hitting (.199) Hodges in the short field.

The fairgrounds grandstand from the playing field. (Mi-18)

An opening day ticket from 1950. Far too few of these were used to make Griffin's ownership a profitable proposition. (Mi-19)

Carl Zellar, released from the Yankees' McAlester farm club, saw the most action in the outfield with sixty games. Willard Winslow, John Gierek, Bob Jenkins, Allicotti, Bill Pace, Bernie Lee, Mathey, Max Buzzard, Lou Salerno, and Kendall Moranville, in that order, made outfield appearance.

While no 1950 Eagle ever saw a Major League game except as a spectator, two went on excel in other fields. Eldon Yung earned a Ph.D. and became a college professor. A two-game outfielder whom Griffin had cut went on to become a Navy flyer and later the Admiral commanding first the Third Fleet and then Sixth Fleet.

Neither Oglesby nor Griffin had time to develop young pitchers. They worked their pitchers hard. Limited service hurler Don McKeon tied for the most wins in the K-O-M throwing in 237 innings of thirty-six games to boast a 17-11 record and sterling 2.24 ERA. He missed a perfect game on June 21 when the same Iola batter first walked then stroked a single; he got the 4-0 win in any event. Veteran John Hanna was 9-10 with 139 innings and a 2.98 ERA. The rest of the mainstays were rookies. Bill Bunch saw action in 181 innings finishing with ten wins in twenty decisions and a 3.58 ERA. George Garrison was 12-9 in 192 innings of thirty-one games including a 3.31 ERA. Vernon Cray threw only ninety-one innings for a 4-8 record and 4.85 ERA. Charles Mann was winless when released and didn't improve much after finding refuge with Iola; he won one game for them.

Somehow, the Eagles staggered to the end of the season. A fifth place finish was a disappointment but a winning percentage was encouraging. Financially, the season was a bust with only 27,548 fans appearing for the season. However, the average gate ended up at 444, a big improvement over the 250 in the first month of the season. There must have been some thousand seat games. Griffin was back for 1951.

1951

Griffin called for players again and after spring training was ready to proceed with a Miami roster that returned only second baseman Jim McHugh and pitcher George Garrison from 1950. On the day of the season opener, owner Griffin introduced his new manager, Tommy Warren whose story is among the most interesting and tragic in the K-O-M and indeed Oklahoma baseball.

A Tulsa native, Warren had played semi-pro and Class D ball in the West Texas-New Mexico League before the War. He enlisted in the Navy on December 8, 1941 and on November 7, 1942 as a commando in Operation Torch, the invasion of Vichy French Morocco, was severely wounded in action against the Foreign Legion and evacuated to the United States. Following ten months' convalescence where his wounds both physical and mental—he suffered from what today is known as post-traumatic stress disorder—were treated, he was honorably discharged in September, 1943. He showed up at the Brooklyn Dodgers' spring training camp in red cowboy boots and a cocksure attitude and impressed Branch Rickey enough that he went north with the Dodgers and appeared in the season opener against the Phillies. He was up and down from Montreal but pitched in twenty-two games for the Bums with a 1-4 record and batted .256 as a pinch hitter. He has the distinction of being the first wounded World War II veteran to appear in a Major League game. Between 1946 and 1948, he was back at home toiling for the Tulsa Oilers and serving as a deputy sheriff.

Tommy Warren of Tulsa was one of the most interesting characters to appear in Oklahoma baseball. He is shown here with Brooklyn as the first returning veteran to appear in the Majors. (Mi-20)

The independent Miami Eagles' ragtag 1951 pitching staff. L-R Larry McComb, George Garrison, Kenneth Campbell, Roger Fulton, manager Tommy Warren, Ken Fentem. (Mi-21)

Gaspar del Toro of Havana introduced, as John G. Hall phrased it, "exotic smoking materials" to the K-O-M. He played for A. C. Gonzalez in 1950 and finished professional baseball in 1952 at Key West on his way back to Havana. (Mi-22)

Warren was a genuinely nice guy who worked with children but was addicted to gambling. He hatched a scheme to raise money for his habit by duping used car dealers out of cash with the promise he could get them new vehicles—quite a feat after the War as new cars were very scarce and expensive—due to connections he had in Detroit. Obtaining over $38,000 in the scam, he was caught, convicted of larceny by fraud and sentenced to three years in prison. He pitched for O.S.P McAlester losing a 15-1 decision to the McAlester Rockets on April 15, 1950. On December 27, 1950 the Oklahoma Court of Criminal Appeals in *Warren v. State* (1950 OK CR 162) reversed his conviction because he had not committed larceny but should have been charged with obtaining money under false pretenses. Free on $3,000 bail, Warren was available for employment albeit with the fraud charge pending. He remained free on appeal bond after being convicted on the correct charge on June 21, 1951.

Three weeks into the season, the Eagles were in third place with an 8-11 record. In fact, the only team with a winning record at that point was Ponca City which had won eighteen straight after dropping their opener. Between May 24 and June 21, Griffin, who was in bad health, told a meeting on league owners on June 2 that he was returning the franchise to them; a local group would be formed to operate. With a $1,000 loan from the K-O-M treasury, the Miami Baseball Association took over the Eagles and immediately began a campaign to raise funds to complete the season. A local fundraising campaign was put over the top when the two largest employers, Goodyear Tire and Eagle-Picher Mining & Smelting, chipped in to make the drive a success and assure Organized Baseball the rest of the summer.

With the details of the sale (or abandonment) up in the air, Griffin retired to Colorado Springs but not without making a claim against the new owner. The National Association conducted a hearing on Griffin's claim and the Miami club's counterclaim on September 26. Griffin's death on October 12 mooted things.

Amid the turmoil, baseball was played. Mired in seventh place on June 21, the Eagles rallied to hold third place on July 5. Winning twenty-nine of the next thirty-nine games, with one month remaining in the season Miami had a winning percentage and a firm hold on third place. Winning fifteen against twelve losses during August, Warren's charges were headed for a place in the playoffs for the first time since 1947.

When he wasn't taking away the players' money playing poker (and then loaning it back at usurious rates), Warren was running a ball club and doing a reasonably good job of it. He aided his own cause. On July 4 playing through an injury, he threw a seven-inning no-hitter at Iola with nine strike outs and only one walk. Ten days later, his grand slam at Carthage propelled the Eagles to a 12-4 win.

There was a lot of juggling in the lineup. Delbert Gay, who played 1950 at Seminole and began the season with Chickasha in the Sooner State League, caught 104 games replacing William Dennis who went on to Borger (TX). Rookie Bill Cheatham in his only season in Organized Baseball replaced Tom Tuttle on May 14 at first base. Jim McHugh, who would play more games for Miami than any other player, was the regular at second with Fred Gomez. Veteran Gaspar Del Toro of Havana was a reliable .300 hitting third sacker who appeared in 120 games there and supporting Meeres. Gordon Meeres, after his release from Ponca City, played a little second base and outfield but with sixty-nine games at the position was the usual Eagle at shortstop. Tom Guinn, who set a K-O-M record with three home runs in a game plus a fourth in the night cap of a twinbill at Ponca City on July 10, along with Warren and Altus native Jim Eldridge before his return to Borger (TX), were the most frequent outfield combination. Pitcher George Garrison appeared in the outfield forty-six times while Meeres, Del Toro, Cheatham, and Charles

Tuttle, who joined the Eagles after sojourning at Vernon (TX) and Chickasha earlier in the season, often roamed there.

Miami had three fourteen-game winners. Manager Warren pulled the laboring oar with 213 innings to his credit; his record was 14-13 with a 2.66 ERA. Bud Closs, who was a rookie with Bartlesville in 1949, was 14-7 with a 2.76 ERA. Closs was closing in on Ross Grimsley's 1946 single game strikeout record when Warren ran in from left field in the seventh inning to instruct him to stop throwing fast balls. Closs did not strike out another. Warren later explained that he didn't want Grimsley to lose his record. George Garrison, who was 12-9 for Miami in 1950, improved to 14-8 with a 3.73 ERA. Del Wichtendahl was 8-2 for Miami after being released by Ponca City. Another pitcher on the bounce was Richard McKinley who split eight decisions after coming over from Bartlesville. Ken Campbell had a bad start with Lawton of the Sooner State League and was given shelter at Miami. He rewarded the Eagles with three wins against a single loss. Tony Serpa went 6-3 with a 3.87 ERA in his only professional season.

Ponca City had run away with the regular season race but fell to fourth place Carthage with a losing record in the first round of the championship series. Miami eliminated Bartlesville. It was the Carthage Cubs' year as they swept the Eagles in three game to win a pennant that would never be presented because the Cubs moved to Blackwell for 1952.

The Eagles finished third in team batting at .258 while leading with forty-seven home runs. The battery of George Garrison and Delbert Gay were voted on to the All Star team and then drafted away. The fans again failed the test. Only 23,500 came out to the ballgame. But that was endemic in the 1951 K-O-M. Carthage, Pittsburg, and Iola drew even fewer.

John Davenport , having been a pre-War Giants property, played and managed in the Phillies system before assuming command of Miami for 1952. (Mi-23)

1952

For the first time, Miami secured a full working agreement with a Major League club. The Philadelphia Phillies sent a manager and a roster that gave the town its most competitive team. There was hope for baseball blossoming again among the fans. To lead the prospects, Philadelphia assigned John Davenport. Before entering the military in 1943, Davenport had played his rookie year in the New York Giants' organization and spent the 1946 season there. He became a Phillies' property in 1947 batting .317 with Salina in the Western Association in both 1947 and 1948. Moving up to Class B Wilmington (DE) for 1949, he returned to Salina as playing manager in 1950 and then led Phillies rookies in Class D at Bradford (PA) and Elizabethton (TN). Miami replaced the Tennessee town at the entry level of the Phillies' farm system for 1952.

McHugh signed a Phillies contract to become the only carryover from 1951. Davenport understood the minor league manager's job to develop talent for the parent club and used the twenty-eight prospects that passed through to accomplish that job.

He used three catchers focusing on Ed Sacks who played ninety-seven games behind the plate. Chet DiEmido got a look-see but couldn't hit and was released. Nick DeMiao filled in when he wasn't patrolling the outfield. Davenport appointed himself to cover first base in every game. McHugh again was the regular at second base until he was assigned to Bradford for further look closer to the home club. Gerald Dodds filled in but spent most games at third base or occasionally in the outfield. Poor performance at the plate doomed Billy Long's future at shortstop and third base. Dick Klingman eventually beat out Ed Rommel and Charles Estes for that slot. Don Ervin had a permanent place in the outfield after replacing Bert Convy who was kicked up to Salina. John Vossen, signed as a free agent after a season with the pathetic McDuff's Seminole Ironmen of the Sooner State League, played beside him in ninety-five contests. DeMaio, Dodds, and Robert Hardy also rotated through.

Two future Major Leaguers were among the Eagles 1952 pitchers. Seventeen year-old Seth Morehead threw in eight games with a 3-4 result after traveling down from Bradford and before moving up to Wilmington. The workhorse of the

Seth Morehead threw for the Phillies, Cubs, and Braves between 1957 and 1961. He was up and down from AAA through 1963. (Mi-25)

1952 Miami Eagles, the only Miami team with a Major League working agreement. Top row, L-R: Don Ervin, John Vossen, Raymond Von Hagle, Jerry Dodds, Jim Owens, Ed Rommel, John Davenport (manager). Middle row, L-R: Seth Morehead, Jim Melito, Jim McHugh, Denny Hamilton, Bob Bandelier, Dick McKinney. Seated, L-R: Billy Ray Long, Eddie Sack. (Mi24)

staff was Jim Owens with 245 innings in thirty-five games posting a K-O-M best 1.76 ERA with a 22-7 record as well as tying a league strikeout record with 300. Milton Melito in his only professional season threw in more games than Owens but mainly in relief for a 8-7 record but high 4.88 ERA. Long switched from infield to the mound finding better success with a 9-4 record in 113 innings. Gene Easterling, who would die in a Federal Penitentiary finishing a life sentence for murder, was 6-8 with a respectable 2.79 ERA in one hundred innings before being called to Bradford on August 5. He tossed a four-hitter and struck out twelve for a 4-2 win over Ponca City in his K-O-M swan song. Teresita (OK) product Wayne Doyle was 4-3 in eleven games. Dennis Hamilton got off to a rough start of 2-6 with Miami but was moved up to Salina.

The Eagles were in third or fourth place in the pennant race most of the season before overtaking Ponca City for second on August 28. Over the campaign, Ervin set the K-O-M record with twenty-four home runs. Sacks was hot in June knocking a grand slam on June 20 for a 20-5 romp over Bartlesville and overcoming a Bartlesville grand slam with a pair of three-run round trippers to make a 10-9 win. On June 30, the Eagles overcame Iola's Jim Hasten's grand slam for a 15-8 victory. Davenport had a single, triple, and home run to lead the Eagles over to a 10-4 romp over Independence on August 3. Owens posted five shutouts and one-hit Ponca City on August 7 for his nineteenth win 7-2. There was a new format for the playoffs. The first round was sudden death. Miami eliminated Pittsburg 4-0 on Owens' second one-hitter. The Eagles then breezed past Ponca City in two games by scores of 9-1 and 7-4 to capture the second pennant.

Sack (.299, 17 HR), McHugh (.281), Vossen (K-O-M best .335), and Owens (22-7, K-O-M best

Jim "Bear" Owens, with a 1957 detour in the Army, was in the Majors from 1955 through 1967, mainly with the Phillies and Astros. He had a brief sojourn in 1966 with the Oklahoma City 89ers. (Mi-26)

1.76 and 300 strikeouts tying Bill Pierro's 1948 K-O-M record) were named to the last All Star squad. Unjustly overlooked was John Davenport's performance. He was second to Vossen with a .333 average. He led the league in RBIs (116) and doubles (37) as well as posting the top slugging percentage (.560) and on-base percentage (.453). Don Ervin set the K-O-M home run record with twenty-four and finished second to Davenport with ninety-six RBIs and slugging (.475). Most importantly, the fans were back. Up nearly 20,000 from 1951, 43,008 paid to see the Eagles.

Thoughts for the 1953 season dampened when Philadelphia pulled out of Salina and Miami at the end of October. While five teams, Independence, Iola, Pittsburg, Ponca City, and Blackwell announced prepared to go forward, Miami was unable to secure any working agreement. With the financial drive for 1953 a failure, Miami Baseball Association notified the league office that it could not field a club. Because of that, the K-O-M League formally suspended on February 24, 1953. An attempt to revive the league the following October was stillborn. Professional baseball in Miami was gone forever.

Rookie Don Ervin had a good year at Miami. After a long detour in the military, he emerged at independent Grand Forks in the Northern League in 1955. (Mi-27)

MUSKOGEE REDS 1946-1950
MUSKOGEE GIANTS 1951-1957
WESTERN ASSOCIATION 1946-1954
SOONER STATE LEAGUE 1955-1957

SEASON	ATTENDANCE	RECORD	FINISH	AFFILIATION	PLAYOFF FIRST ROUND	PLAYOFF FINALS
1946	79,494	75-64	Fourth	Detroit		
1947	78,511	75-64	Third	St. Louis A.L.	Beat Salina 3-2	Lost to St. Joseph 3-4
1948	62,472	60-71	Fifth	St. Louis A.L.		
1949	84,903	77-62	Fifth	St. Louis A.L.		
1950	52,126	52-79	Seventh			
1951	56,032	61-63	Fifth	New York N.L.		
1952	61,391	73-66	Second	New York N.L.	Lost to Joplin 0-4	
1953	41,749	57-81	Sixth	New York N.L.		
1954	44,193	85-54	Second	New York N.L.	Lost to St. Joseph 2-3	
1955	47,485	74-66	Third	New York NL	Beat Shawnee 3-2	Lost to Lawton 4-2
1956	37,983	63-76	Sixth	New York NL		
1957	21,253	71-55	Third	New York NL	Lost to Ardmore 3-0	

The motive force behind baseball in Muskogee and the reason that, but for the War years when most minor leagues suspended play, the city had professional baseball from the revival of the Western Association in 1934 until the curtain fell on the Sooner State League in February, 1959 was Joseph Julius Magoto (1888-1969). Through the Great Depression, post-War boom, the advent of television and residential air-conditioning, Magoto remained as the president of the Muskogee Athletic Association often financing operations from his own pocket until the demise of the Sooner State League. An Ohio native, he graduated from the Cincinnati School of Pharmacy in 1911 and departed for the new State of Oklahoma where he went to work for Cardinal Pharmacy. He worked nearly around the clock during the Spanish Flu epidemic in 1918 preparing the best medications medicine could prescribe at that time. He saved and eventually bought his employer, renaming the enterprise Purity Drug Store and opening a chain of stores in eastern Oklahoma. His annual January baseball dinners at the Muskogee Country Club became legendary. Baseball luminaries such as Oklahomans Allie Reynolds, Dale Mitchell, Bobby Morgan, and Pepper Martin joined the likes of Lou Boudreau and Vernon Gomez who regaled the over 200 guests with a dose of mid-winter baseball fever. He was several times charged and several times acquitted of bootlegging during Oklahoma's Prohibition era (that only ended in 1959). No doubt medicinal whiskey flowed at such affairs.

Before the Western Association suspended for the War, the Muskogee ball club went by the monikers Tigers (1934-1936) and Reds (1937-1942). The ball clubs operated under working agreements with Detroit (1934), Cincinnati (1936-1939), Chicago Cubs (1941) and as an independent (1935, 1940, 1942). After Cincinnati pulled its support following the 1939 season, Magoto persuaded 115 Muskogeans to go on the line for $35 each to assure the

Joe Magoto was Mr. Baseball in Muskogee from 1934 through 1957. (Mu-1)

independent Muskogee Reds would finish the 1940 season. He kept the Muskogee Athletic Association alive during its wartime dormancy. In the last season of the Western Association, he twisted arms raising $10,000 in guaranties to keep the local team afloat. Magoto treated the ball club as a civic enterprise. He sunk thousands of his own dollars into the team over the years as well as all profits. He told *The Sporting News* in a 1957 interview that "I like to

Athletic Park looking toward left field. (Mu-2)

spend [my money] in baseball because it's still the grandest sport in the United States and we won't let it die."

One of the more expert leather-lungs and umpire baiters from his box seat behind home plate, Magoto exasperated a generation of umpires by rubbing up the balls himself and passing them through the screen behind the catcher one at a time as needed. After all, balls cost $2.50 each. Oklahoma newspaper legend Frosty Troy wrote of Magoto in 1955, when Muskogee joined the Sooner State League "Magoto can be expected to breathe fire into this portion of the revised Sooner State League. He is gruff but understanding, and if there are any breaks to be had, he wants them all. By the time [the 1955] season is through, the name Magoto will be ringing through the bleachers, either being blessed or cursed, but always respected as one of minor league baseball's all time greats." He hosted the final meeting of the Sooner State League on February 2, 1958. As reported in the February 19, 1958 issue of *The Sporting News*, Magoto as the league's first-vice-president announced the owners' unanimous decision to retire the last Class D league west of the Mississippi.

Athletic Park was the home of Muskogee's professional baseball teams for over fifty years. The municipally-owned ball park covered a city block. It was bounded on the north by Boston Avenue; entry was from that street. Fifth Street was on the west and Fourth Street on the east. The south wall was along Cincinnati. Originally a wooden structure erected around 1900, concrete bleachers were added in 1921. Lights came in the early 1930s. The covered grandstand extended from first base to third base. There were bleachers down the lines. It was a hitters' ball park with a short, 300 feet left field porch while the center field fence was 385 feet away and the right field line extended 325 feet. No one knows the number of windows broken in the

Dr. Pepper bottling plant that stood just beyond the left field fence. Athletic Park was finally torn down in 1962. The Muskogee Civic Center now occupies the site.

1946

The Detroit Tigers over the first post-War season sent their new affiliate at Muskogee a roster that included three older than thirty, ten with prior professional experience, and thirteen rookies. First time manager C. Ray Baker, who would be at the helm through 1948, was a returning World War II veteran from Ft. Smith who had gotten his start in the New York Giants' organization in 1937 and spent 1938 through 1942 in the Western Association with Muskogee and Topeka. The new season, then, was something of a homecoming.

C. Ray Baker led the Reds for three seasons 1946-1948. He later served as Mayor of Ft. Smith, Arkansas. (Mu-3)

He experimented early on with what was in his dugout. Experienced players quickly nailed down positions: veterans Pete Deem, who joined the club in mid-May after being discharged from the Army, at catcher, Shawnee's Kelly Wingo at second base, and Al Lawrence in the outfield also where Baker himself spent most of the season when not tending third base. Rookie Andrew Meyers quickly impressed and secured the first base position while his fellow rookies Robert Falk and Aubrey Davis would divide most of the contests either at shortstop or third base. An early starter at third base, Walter Holiday, was re-assigned to Jackson (MS). His successor, Joe Volk, was sent down from Ogden (UT) in early July. Outfielders Carl Del Grande and Joe Pollock were sold off to independents Bartlesville and Miami, respectively, of the K-O-M League. Two gray-beards joined later in the season seeing action in the outfield. Al McElreath had been in the game since 1931 and played at Muskogee in 1933. Ab Wright, who began his professional career in 1928 and had received his release from Oklahoma City, played 1935 with Cleveland and 1944 with the Boston Braves. Gene Ritzenthaler, backup catcher, played in the Northeast Arkansas League in 1937 but since had labored in the semi-pros and military; 1946 was his last season.

There were two veterans on the pitching staff, Kennon Black (3-6 5.56 ERA) and William Davis (5-7 3.51 ERA), but they did not see nearly as much action as the rookies. Fay Rossen was the star of the staff with a 20-9 record who threw a 2.89 ERA in 237 innings of thirty-six games. Gene Manzer also appeared in thirty-six contests for 183 innings posting a 16-9 tally with a 3.49 ERA. In spite of their auspicious starts, Manzer was drafted and returning in 1948 failed to progress beyond Class C while Rossen toiled in the Big State and West Texas-New Mexico Leagues for six more seasons. Robert Fritz was the only other hurler with a winning record at 12-11 with a 3.18 ERA and 212 innings in thirty-three games. Don DeArmond gave up the game after a 8-11 performance with a 4.42 ERA. Gary Grisham was cut after 101 innings in sixteen games with a 5-6 total and 4.81 ERA; he was picked up by Greenville (TX) in the East Texas League.

The season got off to a damp start. During the first seventeen days of play, twenty league games were postponed due to weather. The Reds dropped their May 2 opener at home 4-0 to rival Ft. Smith as their eight hits were scattered and opposing pitcher Paul Almonte aided his cause with a three-run round tripper. The Topeka Owls suffered their first defeat of the young season as the Reds took advantage of a pair of walks and a pair of errors to send three across the plate for a 4-2 victory. A seven-run

inning was not enough as Joplin extended the Miners' losing streak to seven as the Reds took their May 16 game 11-10. Ritzenthaler's two-run home run on May 20 capped a seven-run rally to propel the Reds to a 14-6 decision over the Hutchinson (KS) Elks on May 20. Rookie Gene Manzer shut out St. Joseph (MO) on two-hits taking a 4-0 win on June 5. Muskogee was on the wrong end of a 3-2 decision on June 26 as Hutchinson ended an eleven-game losing streak. As the first half of the season closed, the Reds finished third with a 36-33 record behind Leavenworth (KS) and Ft. Smith.

Ab Wright joined the Reds in time to see action in thirty games during the second half. The wheels fell off on July 19 as every Ft. Smith batter hit safely at least once as the Reds fell to the Giants 12-3. At July 22, Manzer's season record stood at 11-4 as Lawrence was batting .342 and Aubrey Davis .322. St. Joseph pitcher Larry Guelfo tossed a one-hitter at the Reds on July 28 but lost the game 1-0 as McElreath doubled in the winning run. To celebrate Manzer's marriage to a Muskogee girl the evening before, the fans planned to fete the couple after the game against Topeka he started on August 31. A scorching line drive off his shoulder in the first inning forced him to leave the field as veteran Kennon Black finished the game for a 7-4 win. He was recovered sufficiently by game end to accept the gifts. The second half ended with Muskogee again in third place at 39-31 resulting in a season finish of 75-64 four games behind pacesetter Leavenworth.

Al Lawrence was the Reds' sole representative on the All Star team batting a Muskogee best .319.

Ab Wright finished his nineteen season career with the 1946 Muskogee Reds. He spent 1935 with Cleveland and 1944 with the Boston Braves. He batted .324 in 1,981 minor league games. (Mu-4)

McElreath hit .354 with a .477 slugging percentage but didn't have enough trips to the plate to qualify for the title. Pete Deem led the Association with eighteen home runs. As a squad, Baker's Reds batted .261 for fourth place. They led the league in at-bats (4,677), total bases (1,728) and stranded runners (1,037). In the best season of his career, Deem's .483 slugging percentage edged out Lawrence's .469 and Don Meyers' .451. Muskogee again showed it was a baseball town as 79,494 fans supported the team Magoto brought to town.

1947

Magoto and the Tigers parted ways and the St. Louis Browns became the new parent organization. The Browns leased the old Army Air Force base, Grider Field, at Pine Bluff (AR) as its minor league camp with three hundred in attendance. Baker was back to head the Reds for 1947 but with the exception of Falk, Fritz, McElreath, Don

Al McElreath played in the minors from 1931, including 1933 with Muskogee, until being banned from baseball for attempting to rig a game in 1947. He played outlaw semi-pro ball after that. (Mu-5)

Meyers, and Wingo, all were new faces from a new organization but only four were new to baseball.

Al McElreath joined the Reds the previous season. He owned a lumber and roofing business and made his home in Muskogee. At age thirty-four he was the oldest man on the team, four years senior his manager. He was batting .389 on May 4 when he approached a fellow player about throwing a game at St. Joseph. The player declined, a double header was played and the next morning he reported the incident to manager Baker. It went up the chain to Western Association president Tom Fairweather then on May 10 to the office of George Trautman, president of the National Association, who investigated. Three weeks later he announced his decision that McElreath would be banned from Organized Baseball for life based on Major-Minor League Rule 21 that had its origins in the aftermath of the 1919 Chicago Black Sox scandal. McElreath appealed to the executive board of the minor leagues. That body affirmed Trautman's decision that his conduct was detrimental to baseball. The ban was final.

1947 Muskogee Reds. (Mu-6)

Baker put a stable roster in place. After Hubert Estridge was promoted to Rock Hill (NC) in Class B, Frank Benites handled the catching chores until rookie Dudley Carson arrived the last three weeks of the season. Omar Lane, a huge swaggering, pugnacious veteran, sewed up first base; he managed Miami in the K-O-M League in 1949. Kelly Wingo, who played and managed in the Sooner State League after seasons at Muskogee, was back at second base. Joe Kronberg was the Reds' third sacker until the Browns assigned him to their Globe-Miami club in Arizona. Charles King was sent up from Hannibal (MO) to replace. Sophomore Robert Falk had won the shortstop job for the season based on his Spring and 1946 performance at Muskogee. The outfield had a large cast. Baker played himself fifty-two times in the outfield after McElreath was banned. Veteran Jack McQuillin saw much action until he was called up to Springfield (IL) of the Three-I League. Charles King had been sent from Hannibal and earned a slot in the outfield. Robert Carroll roamed the outfield in 107 games but only eighty-three were for Muskogee. He began at Hannibal and after his sojourn with the Reds saw duty at the Browns' Class C farms in Aberdeen (SD) and Globe-Miami. Don Torres was rewarded with a promotion from Wausau (WI) near the end of the season and was a Red for twelve games. Paul Zubak came aboard in mid-June from Hannibal. Don Meyers from the 1946 club was sent down from Dallas of the Texas League. William Glenn, who spent 1946 with independent Bartlesville, played fifty-eight games for Muskogee before being sold to Salina where he played the second half.

Four hurlers were in double digits in the win column. Leading the staff was rookie John Crocco at 17-4 (.810) who threw 202 innings in thirty-eight games with a 3.61 ERA. He spent the rest of his career in Classes AAA and AA. Next was southpaw Hal Hudson at 16-12 in 223 innings of thirty-seven games with a 3.60 ERA. He was featured in a *The Sporting News* article in its April 9, 1952 issue about his superstition that he had to eat two chocolate bars before pitching. He had a cup of coffee with the Browns early in 1952 and, after being taken on waivers, briefly with the White Sox in 1953. Lefty Ed Zabotka, who would return in 1948, fashioned a 13-10 record appearing in thirty-nine games with a 4.60 ERA. Pitching in forty-four games, Buck Ross completed 207 innings with 12-11 totals and a 4.22 ERA. The hard luck story was Robert Fritz coming off a winning but wild 1946 year with the Reds. He improved his control but not his record limping to 8-11 in twenty-nine games with a 5.43 ERA. The other rookie thrower was Jack Houston at 5-4 and 3.60 ERA in eighty-five innings of seventeen contests. Joining the team late after being sent down from Springfield, Ed Yelkin pitched only forty-five innings in nine games for a team high 6.20 ERA and a 2-3 record. He was among the older players having played in 1941 and 1942.

Hal Hudson had brief visits to the Majors with the 1952 St. Louis Browns and 1953 Chicago White Sox. (Mu-1)

Rain and weather too cold for night baseball plagued the Western Association in April and May. The race early on became a dual between Topeka's pitching and power and Muskogee's balanced, experience club. On May 1, Hudson yielded five hits and fanned twelve for a 2-0 victory. He repeated the score against Topeka on May 17 on six hits and eight whiffs to go 5-1 on the young season. The Reds were fine ball handlers with fifty-five double plays in the first forty-five outings. On July 29, King was batting .312 while Lane in one hundred games hit the ball for a .304 percentage. Crocco had worked 137 innings with a 12-2 result. Yelkin won a four-hitter against Topeka on August 28 1-0 handing Owls' Lee Dodson, with the best ERA in the Association, only his fourth defeat and breaking an eleven-game string of wins. Ending the season ten and one-half games behind Salina with a 75-64 third place finish, the Reds were in the Shaughnessy playoff taking on the regular season champion. They upset the Phillies' farmhands winning three of five. Second place Topeka had fallen to St. Joseph to set up the finals. The seven-game series between the two St. Louis teams' prospects went the distance with Muskogee coming up short. Season attendance was 78,511 down slightly from 1946 but a good showing considering the early season cancellations. While the Reds produced no All Stars, they led the Association in team average at .276 along with being top in home run production with seventy-three.

1948

The bus to Muskogee from the Browns' minor league camp at Pine Bluff held only three rookies: pitchers Ed Carl and Hal McKinley and outfielder Don Harrell who was pink slipped after twelve games. The rest were mostly limited service players and veterans: Kelly Wingo, Jack McQuillen, Don Pope, Robert Barton, who began playing at age sixteen with the Siloam Springs Travelers in 1938, and manager C. Ray Baker.

Players on the 1948 edition of the Reds had to be versatile. Duane Carson, a catcher by trade who had seen limited action with the Reds the previous year, suited up for all the games but spent most in the outfield. Second sacker Kelly Wingo was in the outfield for a third of his appearances. Howard Wooster played second, third, and shortstop. Robert Klein divided his thirty games between second base and shortstop before being released to Helena (AR) in the Cotton States League. In his third season, Larry Bucynski usually was behind

the plate. Don Pope was the first baseman until he was promoted to Springfield (IL) on June 1. Lawson Williams was sent down from that club for more seasoning as Pope's replacement. When Robert Mainzer was sent down from Springfield, he assumed ownership of third base. Robert Falk became the regular shortstop as he had been in 1947. Carson, McQuillen, and Barton were the core of the outfield receiving help from Wingo, Baker and Paul Zubak before he was re-assigned to Aberdeen (SD).

Baker was no slave driver with the pitchers. The two top pitchers from the 1947 Ada club of the Sooner State League, Bill Donaghey and Woody Smith, came up on the bus but quickly were re-directed. Donaghey went to Globe-Miami (AZ) while Smith developed a sore arm and saw limited duty with the Browns' Aberdeen and Hannibal farms. He converted to third base and went on to win several Silver Glove awards as the best fielder in the minors. Sophomore Bill Bordt was both the ace and workhorse of the staff. He carried a 3.36 ERA in 177 innings in thirty-one games for a 14-10 result. Another soph, Jerry Barta, simply didn't receive support when he went to the mound. His 3.29 ERA does not portend the 1-9 record he finished with showing better control than others with similar innings pitched. Rookie Hal McKinley posted a respectable 11-6 tally with a 3.57 ERA in 141 innings of thirty-five games. Rookie Earl Carl saw action in twenty-two games but had decisions in only nine: a 5-4 record with a 4.43 ERA. Another second year hurler, Jack Houston appeared twenty-eight times but would up on the short end with a 7-10 result and 4.56 ERA. Bill David and Larry Doyle were sent down together from Springfield in exchange for Bob Freels who was having the best season on the Reds at 9-4 when called up. David finished 4-6 and Doyle had no decisions in eighteen games. Likewise, Mack Hyde who had been throwing well at Ada saw little action with no re-

With the Reds coming into the Browns' fold in 1948, promotions from Class D Ada were up to Muskogee. Pitcher Mack Hyde was the first Hereford to become a Red. (Mu-8)

sults. Buck Ross from the 1947 Reds was off his past season's performance finishing with a worse record, 6-8, and ERA, 4.89. Lefty Jack Wilson, also from the 1947 Ada squad, was only 2-3 in fifty-five innings.

The team finished third in batting in a hitter's year. The Reds' .264 would ordinarily have been an accomplishment but the top team, Leavenworth, batted .281. The Reds did have the long ball finishing second with seventy-five home runs. There were no All Stars. It was the first losing season for the Reds since the War, 61-70 and twenty-five and one-half games back, and the fans stayed away. Attendance was down to 62,472. The fact that seven contests were rained out does not explain a twenty-one per cent decline. Magoto was hoping for a better crop from St. Louis in 1949.

1949

Ray Baker managed a pair of independents in 1949. Magoto and the Browns turned to a utility infielder for the 1938-1941 Phillies and minor league veteran, Emmett "Heinie" Mueller. He had managed a Browns' farm in 1946 and had been out of the game for two seasons. Four rookies wore Reds' flannels. There was little of the shuffling and promotion among farm clubs as in past seasons in the Browns organization.

The Western Association was unusual in its balance at the top. The Reds finished fifth with a winning

77-62 (.554) record while sixth place Salina played .500 ball. Two independents were the doormats. Leavenworth at 25-112 had one of the worst seasons in baseball history; the franchise moved in 1950. Hutchinson in central Kansas did better but not by much: 41-93 (.306) yet drew more fans than second place St. Joseph; that town had baseball in 1950 as the franchise was owned by the local Elks Club.

Heinie Mueller led the Reds in 1949 and 1950. (Mu-9)

Mueller had a different philosophy than Baker. He picked his starters and varied little. Carson played most of the time as the catcher. When he was outfielding, Tommie Robertson relieved. Harvey Christenson, a rookie, held first base. Howard Wooster owned the keystone. Konyar divided third base with manager Mueller two to one. Falk as in the prior two seasons was the Reds' shortstop. Robert Masser, enjoying what would be his career season, and McQuillen held down two outfield spots. Dan Kantor was beside them for the first month but when he was sent down to the K-O-M farm at Pittsburg (KS), Ed Bucynski stepped in most evenings. Carson also saw outfield duty. Jake Crawford, a recent University of Missouri star, joined the Reds at the end of the season. The Browns called him up in September 1952 for the proverbial cup of coffee.

Bob Norden had the best ERA, 2.18, in the Association but with 103 innings in sixteen games did not qualify for the league crown. He finished the season at 9-3. Ed Carl made up for all the action he didn't see as a 1947 rookie. Mueller sent him to the mound forty-one times where he threw more innings than any other Western Association

Bob Norden had a good 1949. He had slipped to Class D by 1953. (Mu-10)

pitcher, 260. His 14-16 record does not reflect his 3.63 ERA. Ed Lubanski had the best percentage (16-5 .762) and a respectable 3.53 ERA; he gave up the game after this third and final season. Lou Vavro was 4-2 with a 3.00 ERA in seven games when he was re-assigned to Marshall (TX) in the East Texas League. Rex Simpson parlayed a 4.11 ERA into a 12-9 season throwing a runner-up 173 innings in thirty-nine appearances. Mack Hyde got a full season in Class C between Pine Bluff and Muskogee and acquitted himself well for the Reds on winning (7-4 .636) but his ERA was wanting: a team high 5.65. Robert Grunwald arrived from Globe and after a few appearances was exiled to Leavenworth for the balance of 1949. Robert Lindquist was 8-9 with a 5.24 ERA in 161 innings of twenty-four contests. Larry Doyle and Charles Kohs had fourteen and eleven appearances, respectively, with no decisions and under forty-five innings. Even manager Heinie Mueller touched the pitcher's plate twelve times, a first in his career stretching back to 1928.

Mueller put the Reds back in the winning column and led them through a tight race for the first division and the playoff. His team fell short by one-half game. The Reds batted .278 as a team. In most years that would be the highest in a league. In 1949, it was good for fourth. Muskogee did lead the Western Association with eighty-nine home runs.

Minor league baseball reached its zenith in 1949. Organized Baseball had 448 minor league teams competing in fifty-nine leagues. A twentieth century record 41,872,762 paid to watch their local ball clubs. The Muskogee patrons did their part. August 17 was Heinie Mueller Appreciation Night. A record 3,016 fans packed Athletic Park to present the Reds' manager with cash for a new car. Those fans were part of a record Muskogee season attendance of 84,903.

1950

The St. Louis Browns took a meat-ax to their nineteen-member minor league organization by terminating eight working agreements for the 1950 season. One of those was Muskogee. Magoto had seen this before and knew how to field an independent ball club if only for a single season until affiliated with a new parent club. He brought back fan favorite Heinie Mueller and began assembling a roster. Fortunately, the relations between the Browns and Magoto remained cordial.

The 1950 edition of the Reds was a collection of recently released free agents, players on optional assignment from their parent organizations, and Muskogee locals. The Browns also directed their castaways from Pine Bluff in the direction of Muskogee. As a consequence, unlike the past season, there was a good deal of fluidity at the positions. Mueller had to make do with what he had in the dugout at any point of the season.

Behind the plate, Robert Evert saw early action. Joe Petrongolo, cut from the Detroit system, found a home there for much of the remainder of the season with Ken Stange, released from the Cubs' farm at Carthage (MO) in the K-O-M, providing relief. Charles Mann started at first but after a month was sold up the road to Miami in the K-O-M. Ray Cucchiarini, on option from Brooklyn, played the full season rotating from second base then to first base after Mann's departure, and into the outfield as needed. Muskogee resident Jim McQuillen in his third season with the Reds played fifty-one games at first base and seventy-eight in the field. Frank Santora, a free agent with experience in the Cincinnati and Giants' systems, was principally a second baseman but served at shortstop and third base. Thirty-nine year old Sammy Bell was picked up to play some second base after he was relieved of his duties

Tony Costa joined Bob Norden down on the Ada farm in 1953. (Mu-10)

Joe Trimble had short stays in the Show with Boston in 1955 and Pittsburgh in 1957. (Mu-12)

The 1950 scorecard featured manager Mueller. (Mu-11)

as manager of the Morganton (NC) Aggies of the West Carolina League. Santora was playing out of position as a third baseman as the season started but Jack Cooley was signed and handled the hot corner. Robert Selecy was optioned from the Browns and covered shortstop into late July. His departure forced Santora to cover that position. Mueller was the gap filler in eleven games. The Browns kept Jake Crawford in Muskogee for 1950 and he anchored the outfield. Another Browns' property, Tony Costa, was an outfield regular along with Jack McQuillen when he wasn't covering first base. Bruce May was undergoing the conversion from pitcher to outfielder; he left the game after the season ended. Richard Carr, a member of the infamous 1949 Leavenworth Braves, got a dozen-game look-see but didn't stick with the Reds.

Jim Post, a veteran optioned from the Browns, was the only Reds hurler to enjoy a winning season: 12-6 with a team low 4.16 ERA in 158 innings of twenty-four games. Post would play at the AAA level into 1959. Joe Trimble, a Cincinnati property, had a 9-10 year working 173 innings in thirty-three outings while posting a 4.79 ERA. Trimble would have two brief visits to The Show first with Boston in 1955 and then in 1957 with Pittsburgh. Ed Kruer, a free agent after being released from the Columbia (SC) Sally League club, saw the most activity of the staff. He threw 218 innings in thirty-three games with a 4.33 ERA and 12-17 result. Muskogeean Buck Ross, a member of the 1947 and 1948 Reds, posted a 5-7 record with a 5.55 ERA in

twenty-seven games. Another returnee from 1947 and 1948, Jack Houston, appeared in ten games but threw under forty-five innings. Robert Radomski was released by the Browns' Class D club at Appleton (WI) and signed by Muskogee. He received his walking papers after yielding eleven walks per game, allowing 9.28 earned runs per contest and losing seven decisions without a win. Billy Creech, with experience at Ardmore in the Sooner State League and Iola in the K-O-M, was 5-6 with a 4.24 ERA in 104 innings. Calvin Moore won five of thirteen decisions in twenty-two appearances allowing 5.50 earned runs per nine. Fred Lietz worked forty-eight innings to post a 6.75 ERA and 1-3 record.

Muskogee finished the campaign in seventh place with a 52-79 record, thirty-five and one-half games behind Mickey Mantle's Joplin Miners. They played six fewer games than any other club. Collectively, the Reds had the worst gloves in the Association with a .938 fielding average. They were .259, fifth in the league, at the plate. They had the fewest number of hits but also the fewest trips to the plate. Frank Santora's multitasking did not go unnoticed. He was selected as the second sacker on the 1950 All Star team. Attendance was down thirty-six percent to 52,126. Muskogee needed a higher quality baseball performance on the field. Magoto needed a new working agreement.

1951

With one of the larger farm systems, the New York Giants had owned the Western Association franchise in Ft. Smith for a number of seasons. Frustrated over local officials' broken promises, the Giants packed up their operation and moved it to Enid for 1950. That experience was a disappointment. The Ft. Smith territory was open but they had had their fill there. The little Giants needed a new home and Muskogee had one. New York appointed Magoto its agent to sell its Enid franchise and he did so for $1,000 to a group from Ft. Smith. The Giants then signed a full working agreement with the Muskogee Athletic Association aka Joe Magoto in October, 1950. Muskogee would be Giants' territory for the rest of its baseball life.

The Western Association winter meeting was held in Enid, home of the only independent in the circuit. Magoto missed it due to a car wreck on icy roads that landed him in the hospital temporarily. In his absence, the owners shortened the season to 126 games.

Spring training was held at the Giants' minor league campus in Sanford, Florida. There a post-War veteran who had performed at the AAA and AA levels was selected to guide the Giants' prospects. Hal "Dutch" Bamberger appeared in seven games at the Polo Grounds at the end of the 1948 season and seemingly had a good baseball head. With an average age of twenty-two, the squad he brought to Muskogee was younger than had been seen in a few seasons. There were four rookies and four veterans. The rest were players with one or two seasons under their belts. That is what a Class C team should look like.

There are two ways to handle a team of prospects. One is to identify one with potential and have him play a single position all season. The other is to do a series of figurative tryouts and keep the ones who do best. Bamberger did both. With the parent club owning the contracts, call ups were inevitable and the manager had to plug holes.

John Cooney, Wayne Yoder, Al Malewski, and Ray Johnson were at, respectively, first, second, shortstop, and center field all season. James McArdle had won the catching spot from Don Stange, a member of the 1950 Reds. When McArdle was promoted to Sunbury (PA), the Giants borrowed Bill Bowman from the Cincinnati organization to fill the gap. Frank Santora, from the 1950 Reds, belonged to the Browns who sent him to their Class C farm at Aberdeen SD after twenty-six games at Muskogee. Ted Drakos was called in for about thirty contests but the parent club sent him to Idaho Falls. Sophomore outfielder Mel Lightner was forced to learn a new position for the balance of the season. With Lightner

In the first year of being a part of the New York Giants system, Dutch Bamberger was called on shape the 1951 Class C prospects. (Mu-13)

1951 Muskogee Giants. (Mu-1)4

at third, Bamberger called his own number to play outfield. Bob Hallman was a regular in the outfield until after 101 games he was called up to Sunbury. An acquisition from the Braves system, Charles Schuck filled gaps in the outfield.

In his third season, southpaw Fred Sherkel easily outperformed all but four pitchers in the Western Association with a 17-5 (.773) season record and a 3.06 ERA, hurling the most innings (191) among the Giants' staff. Only one other had a winning percentage, lefty Bob Reich at 8-5 with a 4.84 ERA in 119 innings of nineteen games. He accomplished something no other pitcher in the league attained: a no-hitter on August 24. Reich was making his first start after spending over a month on the disabled list with a sore arm. He walked two and struck out seven on the way to a 6-0 eighth win over Enid that snapped an eight-game losing streak for the Giants. Jim Tracy was 10-10 with a 3.54 ERA while rookie Robert Wilkinson was 6-10 with a 3.59 ERA, both appearing in twenty-nine contests. Thomas Broadway, another lefthander, was 4-5 in fifteen outings with a 3.72 ERA. Walt Hoefscher, with the Giants at Enid in 1950, was 3-3 in fifty-three innings of seventeen games allowing 4.75 earned runs per nine. Don Mireau, down from Sunbury on June 20, was 3-5 with a 4.91 ERA. Rookie Robert Benning, assigned from the Giants' club at St. Cloud (MN), was 1-4 in eleven games yielding seven walks per nine with an ERA of 4.68. Warren Ley, up from the Springfield (OH) farm, and local player Buck Ross each appeared in ten games but lacked forty-five innings and figured in no decisions.

With the Korean War at a fast boil, Wilkinson, Reich, and McArdle were soon taken in the draft that, like the case with so many prospects, effectively ended their Major League hopes. The Giants were fourth in hitting with a team average of .268. They were a swinging lot, leading the Association in batters striking out and hits wrongly timed, leaving the most runners

(1,133) on base. Cooney at first base with a league best .344 batting average, a .473 slugging percentage and .425 on base percentage justifiably was selected for the All Star squad. Attendance was up to 56, 032.

1952

The Western Association contracted to six teams for 1952 with St. Joseph and Enid dropping out. For 1952, New York assigned perhaps its best minor league manager to guide the prospects at Muskogee. Andy Gilbert entered the game in 1937 and came into the Giants' organization in 1947 by way of a trade from the Browns' Toledo AAA operation. He had enjoyed brief cups of coffee with the Red Sox in 1942 and 1946 appearing in a total fifteen games. He played at the AAA level from 1946 through 1949. He added managing to his resume in 1950 at Springfield (OH) in the Ohio-Indiana League. He returned from camp at Melbourne, Florida to Muskogee with a young, average age twenty-one, typical but talented roster of limited service players with a couple of veterans and rookies.

Gilbert arrived in Muskogee with a fairly well set roster. Dick Urlage was his catcher. Earl Hemberger would handle first base until Gilbert took over in

Andy Gilbert, shown here with Louisville in 1942, was among the best minor league managers the Giants had under contract. He led Muskogee in 1952 and during the city's last campaign in 1957. (Mu-15)

the second half of the season. Jack Varnado would take second and Ron Parente third with Mel Collins at shortstop. Jack Lewis would anchor the outfield with John Joyner beside him most evenings. Reserve catcher Ralph Onnasch, Dale McMullin who was up from Kingsport (TN), Robert Hallman, a veteran who arrived via Sioux City (IA) in Class A and Knoxville (TN) in Class B, and Frank Szekula as well as Gilbert himself covered the third outfield slot.

The pitching staff, on average, was old enough to be drafted but too young to vote. Jerry Schultz at twenty-two was the "old man." Larry Paladino blossomed after his 1951 rookie year at Muskogee posting a team best 3.43 ERA and 16-8 (.667) record with the most innings pitched (197) and most games (33). Selecting the All Star squad at season end, the sportswriters and scorers overlooked his performance for that of team mate Jerry Schultz. Schultz threw nearly the same number of innings (194) in the same number of games with a 4.10 ERA and wins in thirteen of twenty-three decisions. Returnee Tom Broadway had a 3.99 ERA with a 5-7 record in 106 innings of sixteen appearances. Jim Mazzola, assigned from the Giants' club at St. Cloud, was .500 in eight decisions posting a 4.58 ERA in fifty-five innings. Rookie James McDonald was off to a rough 4-9 start in eighty-two innings but kept his ERA relatively down at 4.06. Al Neville threw 141 innings in thirty-two games for a result of wins in eight of fifteen decisions but a team high 5.36 ERA; his control was good with just over four walks per nine. Rookie Bob Raymond had a winning 6-5 record in 134 innings of twenty-nine outings with a 4.84 ERA. Another rookie, Ed Sassone was the workhorse of Gilbert's mound crew appearing in forty-five games for 165 innings, a disappointing 9-11 tally but a fine 3.60 ERA and the best walks/nine inning ratio, 4.1. John Boyd joined the club from the Pauls Valley Class D farm in time to see action in thirteen games and to compile a 4-3 record and 3.57 ERA.

Ron Parente got off to a fast start in the April 27 opener against Ft. Smith with back-to-back home runs and three more hits but the Indians prevailed 15-12. The Giants won the next thirteen until they ran into Jack Brown of Hutchinson (KS) on May 11 who collared them on three hits for an 8-3 Muskogee loss. Schultz was wild on May 14 when he forced in three runs on walks to give Joplin a 5-3 win. Nonetheless, at May 22, the Giants were in firm possession of the top spot with a 19-6 record. The Giants went on another winning streak, this time for nine games that Ft. Smith snapped on May 28. Jack Varnado ruined Jerry Murphey of Salina's no-hit bid on June 23 with a fifth inning single.

Unlike Muskogee, Ft. Smith was mired in the cellar at 16-30 with fan interest dissipating and no hope to be competitive unless there was a restart. President Howard Goetz explained to the owners that they had two choices: either adopt a split season or "blow up the league." With Topeka dissenting, the season was split and a second half would begin July 1. The Shaughnessy Playoff was abandoned and the winners of the halves would battle for the pennant.

The Giants cruised to the first half title finishing 40-24 to assure a post-season berth. Ft. Smith jumped out to a 6-4 second half start including a 12-4 win over Muskogee on July 8. The Indians maintained their first place position until August 28 when Joplin overtook them. Meanwhile, the Giants were stumbling.

There were high points. On July 16, Gilbert hit a grand slam for an 11-9 win over Topeka. Ralph Onnasch's grand slam at Hutchinson on July 20 gave the Giants a sweep of the twin bill. At month end, Muskogee was in fifth place with a 14-18 total. In the July 24 game, Joyner gave Joplin infielder and future Yankee, Jerry Lumpe, his lumps when his batted ball took an odd bounce and hit Lumpe in the face. On August 1, Jerry Schultz was in trouble, and manager Gilbert called for a pinch hitter when the pitcher's turn at bat came. The umpire declared that the hitter, Earl Hemberger, was not on the roster presented and was ineligible. Schultz went to bat and singled in the tying run then in the ninth got his second RBI to win over Topeka 6-4. Gilbert's twentieth round tripper was not enough to prevent Topeka from gaining revenge on August 8 by a score of 8-5. Meanwhile, the Giants had climbed to fourth place with a 22-24 record. James McDonald was within two outs of a no-hitter when Joplin's Norm Siebern, a future Yankee and Western Association Rookie of the Year, cracked a double. The second half found the Giants in fourth with thirty-three wins against forty-two losses. The Giants' prospects faced off against the Yankees' future in the playoffs. Like the 1951 subway World Series, the Bronx's Joplin Miners topped Manhattan's Muskogee Giants.

There were plenty of accolades at season end. Gilbert was named the Most Valuable Player. He led the Association in hitting with a .357 average, slugged at a .578 percentage and got on base 44.8% of the times he came to the plate. Mel Collins with 115 scored the most runs. Jack Lewis was best with 156 hits. Gilbert was an All Star as were Jack Varnado, Jack Lewis, and pitcher Jerry Schultz. The club finished 73-66 on the season good for second place fourteen games behind Joplin had it not been split. Attendance was up to 61,391, bucking the trend in the minors.

Action at Athletic Park. (Mu-16)

1953

The Giants dipped into their barrel of minor league managers and brought out Harold Kollar, a thirty year-old with four seasons of playing-managing under his belt. He was no stranger to the Western Association, having managed Ft. Smith in 1949 and Enid in 1950. He spent 1951 at the Giants' Class C affiliate in St. Cloud (MN) and 1952 teaching rookies at Shelby (TN).

The squad be brought back from spring training in Melbourne, Florida looked much like Andy Gilbert's 1952 crew and actually had two future Major Leaguers. Only one rookie was among the group that touched down in Muskogee. Seven had "National Service" status meaning they were returning from military duty in the Korean War and did not count against league-imposed limitations on veteran and limited service players. Two, pitcher James McDonald and catcher LeRoy O'Neill, were picking up their careers that had last been under Kollar's tutelage at Enid in 1950.

Walt Wrona came out of retirement from the Tulsa Oilers four times to act as backstop when the regulars were on the disabled list. (Mu-17)

Only three players saw action at the same position in over one hundred games. Two were in the lineup every night but at multiple positions. Ed Opich played every infield position. He began at first base then filled in at third until help arrived from Danville (VA). He covered second for most of the season while the regular was on the disabled list. He substituted at shortstop between prospects sent up and down at the whim of the Giants' minor league development office. Ed Mueller's regular billet was in the outfield but he plugged gaps at third and shortstop. O'Neill was the regular catcher but was relieved by John Skarzynski, a third baseman by trade, who was sent down from Danville. Additionally, Kollar turned to former Texas League catcher Walt Wrona, an electrician in Tulsa, who commuted to home games to provide help behind the plate. Kollar took over first base when Opich moved.

Clell Callaway during his 1952 rookie season at Pauls Valley. (Mu-18)

Clell Callaway, who had spent the past season at Pauls Valley in the Sooner State League, played ninety games at second base. In June, the starting third baseman, James Madelone, was called up to Andy Gilbert's Class B club at Danville and replaced by Skarzynski with Mueller and Opich filling in during the interim. Mueller began at shortstop but moved to the outfield when Russell Stuart was called up from Pauls Valley then, after batting .148, replaced by rookie Robert Koperwhats optioned down from Class A Sioux City. Again, Opich and Mueller filled in between starters.

Dan Chepkauskas, a veteran of Pauls Valley in 1949 and most recently the Army, was in the outfield every night. Dan Toma, also down from Danville, quickly secured an outfield position. Mueller would have been a third but for his versatility in the infield. Glenn Gostic, up from Mayfield (TN), George Reid, up from Pauls Valley, and John Joyner, a member for the 1952 squad, rotated through the outfield.

Kollar worked his pitchers hard. During spring drills, the Giants' Class A Sioux City (IA) Soos assigned Dom Zanni, a twenty-game winner at Pauls Valley in 1952 who would spend seasons in The Show with the Giants, White Sox, and Reds, to Muskogee for more seasoning. And work he got. Zanni appeared in a team high fifty-five games for 236 innings producing a 15-15 record with a 3.66 ERA. National Service player Jack Gruell was 12-11 in 206 innings of forty contests posting

a 3.50 ERA. Rookie Alex Murawski received his introduction to professional life in 214 innings of thirty-eight games to finish with a 15-14 tally and 3.70 ERA. Hard luck hurlers were National Service Carroll Mattson, one of the Enid 1950 alumni, and 1952 Muskogee Giant James McDonald. Mattson's 5-10 record is attributable to wildness, ten walks per nine, and a 5.12 ERA. Sophomore McDonald at 5-13 in 200 innings of thirty-six games yielded 4.64 earned runs per nine innings. Rookies Alex Schmidt and Sherman Jones down from St. Cloud arrived late. Schmidt threw 112 innings in twenty-six outings as he split six decisions with a 4.10 ERA. Jones, one of the original 1962 New York Mets, gave up fifteen walks per nine innings and nine earned runs per nine explaining his 0-6 performance in thirteen appearances. Ed Sassone from 1952 had no decisions in three games when he was drafted. Gus Bergemann was cut after a 1-2 start. Up from Oshkosh at season end, Joe Burke was 0-4. Victor Vick up from Pauls Valley in September was 0-1. Mueller was even called to the mound once.

Muskogee quickly fell into the second division, arriving where the Giants would finish in fifth place in mid-July. The Giants dropped a 15-5 match to Joplin on May 15 when in a single inning they gave up five hits, four walks, hit a batter, and make two errors. The May 22 game went seventeen innings and was finally called a 7-7 tie. Ten days later, Zanni showed some brilliance as he scattered nine hits, whiffed thirteen St. Joseph batters, and aided his cause with a home run on the way to an increasingly rare 7-3 win. June 8, the Giants were victims of a triple killing at Hutchinson. Attendance was lagging at Muskogee attributable, according to new Western Association president George Barr, to early bad weather. The Giants overcame Hutchinson's Joe Beran's grand slam to hold on to a 6-5 win on July 13. Zanni lost a no-hit bid against Joplin on a fifth inning single but got the 5-0 shutout. After a particularly nasty rhubarb at Muskogee, frightened umpire Eldon Bushong fled for his home in Henryetta and failed to show up for the next night's game; Barr fined and suspended him for the season. Muskogee dropped a 3-2 heartbreaker to Hutchinson on August 17 when in the same inning the Giants allowed two runs and turned a triple play. After the runs had scored, Hutchinson had runners on second and third. The batter hit a grounder to second baseman Clell Callaway who chased the runner coming from second and tagged him for out one. The runner on third headed for home but Callaway's throw to O'Neill beat the runner who was tagged for out two. The batter meanwhile was running the bases trying to stretch a double to three bases as O'Neill fired to Madelone who applied the tag for out three. James McDonald's bid for an August 19 no-hitter was thwarted when the Hutchinson pitcher tapped a single; McDonald got the 4-0 shutout for one of his five wins.

Twenty-five games behind pacesetter St. Joseph, the Giants finished the 1953 marathon in fifth place with a 57-81 finish. While third in overall batting at .241, the Giants led in no categories. Dom Zanni was named the Western Association's most Valuable Player and Toma joined him on the All Star list. The 1953 season was a bust at the gate as only 41,749 fans paid to see the Giants.

Dom Zanni was the 1953 Western Association MVP. He threw in 111 Major league games between 1958 and 1966. (Mu-19)

1954

At the annual meeting in November, 1953 president Barr reported that the Joplin, Ft. Smith, and Muskogee franchises were in trouble. Magoto announced that he was actively searching for a place to move this operation. The prospects for 1954 were grim. He did hold his annual Baseball Evening at the country club and there extracted guaranties from community leaders totaling $10,000 to assure the Giants would be back for another 140-game season beginning April 26 at Ft. Smith. Joining the Association were two new franchises, Blackwell and Ponca City. For the first time, Magoto hired a business manager, George A. Lawson. He celebrated his twenty-first anniversary of heading baseball in Muskogee.

John Davenport, who led Miami to the 1952 K-O-M pennant, took the 1954 Giants to a second place finish and the first round of the last Western Association playoffs. (Mu-20)

A fourth manager in as many years was at the helm of the Giants when they set foot in Muskogee. John Davenport, originally in the Giants' organization before the War and then in the Phillies' system since 1947, had been a player-manager since 1950 and took the 1952 Miami Eagles to the K-O-M pennant. Davenport was no stranger to the Western Association, having spent 1947, 1948, and 1950 at Salina. He was determined to field a competitive, first division club.

The final edition of the Western Association Giants was loaded with nine National Service players as well as six rookies, five of whom were pitchers. Only two, outfielder Dan Chepkaukas and third baseman Jim Madelone, were back from the 1953 squad. Rookie Cedric Woods in his only professional season shared the catching duties with Chuck Schuck returning from the military.

Bill Sells, optioned from Nashville of the Southern Association, divided first base equally with manager Davenport. Sophomore Pete Traina was at second ninety-five per cent of the games with brief relief from third sacker Madelone. Madelone usually held down the hot corner but when disabled or covering for the shortstop, Sells moved over. Cuban veteran

Dominican rookie Rudy Hernandez was 15-4 for Davenport's Giants. He later played for both the 1960 Washington Senators and expansion 1961 Senators. He played at the AAA level through 1964. (Mu-21)

Raul Fundora was the regular shortstop with Madalone subbing on occasion. The outfield was fixed early in the season. Chepkaukas and Walt Fishburn saw action in nearly every game. National Service hand George Svotovsky replaced fellow veteran Jerry Lindley, sent down to Orlean (NY) a month into the season. Bert Briscoe, from the 1953 Pauls Valley roster, quickly returned to Class D at Shelby (TN) after two games.

A dozen pitchers, including manager Davenport, made appearances. A rotation of Malcolm Landry (30 starts), Don Tkacsik (27 starts), Rudy Hernandez (24 starts), and Harvey Dupuy (16 starts) emerged. At 226, Landry threw the most innings emerging with a 17-8 record and 3.27 ERA. Tkacsik was 13-9 in 191 innings posting a 4.34 ERA. Hernandez allowed 3.57 earned runs per nine coasting to a 15-4 season total. Theobold had fewer innings, 133, but tied Dupuy for the most appearances with thirty-five. He was 10-7 with a 4.65 ERA. Dupuy was 11-8 with a 4.61 ERA in sixteen starts. John Boback, a veteran and National Service player, was 2-6 in ten games; he was released. George Olsey appeared mainly in relief but started ten winding up with a 5-3 record and 4.65 ERA. Chris Theobold was the fifth starter with thirteen but came in relief in twenty-two. He

was 10-7 with a 4.26 ERA. National Service hurler Ed Kosior in his third season started in only one of his thirty-one outings going 4-5 with a team high 5.16 ERA. Jim Waldrip was released on August 1 after twenty-one appearances and was immediately signed by Ed Carnett's independent Ponca City Jets; he finished with a 7-9 total for the season and a 6.42 ERA. John Lytle was sent down to Orlean after eight appearances. Norm Faulconer joined him there after five games. Davenport had no decisions in two games.

The Giants quickly set the pace and won thirty-seven of their first forty-four games including win streaks of ten, eleven, and eight games. Fishburn hit two homers including a grand slam to lead the Giants to a 21-9 rout of Iola on May 6. Fundora cussed out umpire Rocky Sgro in Spanish and was surprised to receive a fine; Sgro spoke Spanish. Traina hit his fourth single in the contest with Blackwell on May 19 for an 11-10 win. Two days later he banged a grand slam and batted in two more runs as the Giants took Hutchinson 11-8. As part of President Barr's anti-profanity campaign, Lindley and Madelone drew fines in mid-May. On May 26, Landry twirled a four-hitter and singled in the sole and winning run in a twelve inning duel with Ty Braziel of Topeka.

On June 1, a ten-run third inning propelled the Giants to a 17-7 win over Ponca City. The next evening, Tzacsik struck out eighteen Iola batters on the way to a 5-4 victory. Two days after joining the Giants, George Olsey tossed a three-hitter at Iola and added his home run to a 3-0 win. The next day, Landry went to 6-0 on the season and extended his string of scoreless innings to twenty-six as the Giants embarrassed Iola once again by a 16-0 score. Fundora and Davenport both earned $50 fines on June 10 when the player bumped umpire Sgro and Davenport vociferously took up his cause. The Giants had to rally on June 13 to save Landry's seventh victory at

Hutchinson 13-12. His string came to an end in his next start at Blackwell on June 21 as the Broncos sent him to the showers in a 7-2 Muskogee defeat.

Proving the world is round, Iola hit five homers, a triple and seven doubles on July 15 for a 14-0 win over the Giants; it was only the second victory over Muskogee in fifteen tries. After ninety-four days in first place, on August 4 Muskogee fell to second by one-half game as Topeka beat Joplin and the Giants fell to St. Joseph 12-4. The next night Landry got a measure of revenge tossing a three-hitter against the Saints for a 2-0 win and his seventh shutout of the season. By August 12, the Giants were back in first at 71-39 and were still there on August 28 at 78-47. On the last day of the season, Topeka had crept back into first one and one-half game ahead of Muskogee. The Owls split a double header with St. Joseph. Joplin ruined the Giants' season by taking both ends of the twin bill, 2-1 and 3-1. The season ended with the Giants at 85-54, two games behind Topeka. The Giants squared off against St. Joseph in the first round. The series went the five-game distance with the Saints sending Muskogee home.

The 1954 Giants finished fifth in team batting at .262 but were swingers as they led with ninety home runs and struck out 922 times. Dominican Rudy Hernandez at 15-4 led the Western Association in winning percentage at .789 and his 3.57 ERA was seventh. Additionally, he was a good hitter batting .425, slugged .750 and had five homers, three triples and twenty-three RBIs. The writers and scorers overlooked this and placed team mate Mel Landry on the All Star list along with slugger Walt Fishburn. Hernandez's satisfaction would come later as he joined the Washington Senators. The fans apparently were enjoying their air conditioning; television didn't come to Muskogee until after the season ended. Attendance was up but just slightly to 44,103.

In addition to the Western Association, George Barr had served as president on the K-O-M League

that disbanded in 1953. As the annual meeting time approached, only Hutchinson, Ponca City, and Muskogee had working agreements. St. Louis had dropped Joplin and the Athletics' move into St. Joseph's back yard eliminated those towns. Blackwell had surrendered its franchise. Salina was unable to make a deal with any other Major League club. The oldest Class C baseball league dissolved on January 19 and officially disbanded on February 1, 1955. This was the second time Barr had presided over a baseball funeral.

1955

After fifty-two years of play, the Class C Western Association had ceased operations. The Muskogee Giants, Blackwell Broncos, and Ponca City Jets were faced with either finding a new home or becoming extinct. In the circles of the Sooner State League, it was assumed that the Seminole franchise would be for sale and that Ponca City would likely land it. As things turned out, Ada and Pauls Valley folded.

The headline in the December 26, 1954, *Ada Evening News* was "Sooner State League May Fold." Ardmore's Waco Turner and Lawton President Cy Stewart insisted that a return of baseball to Duncan was the only salvation for the Sooner StateLeague and were planning a coup against President Ucal Clanton. Stewart objected to moving the Ada franchise to Paris and Shawnee vetoed granting a franchise to Vernon, Texas. Nonetheless, the move of the Ada franchise and its working agreement with Baltimore to Paris (TX) was approved. With the failure of the Pauls Valley operation on January 23, 1955 and a perceived strong player looking for a home, Muskogee was invited to join the Sooner State League. With New York agreeable to staffing a rookie team there, Joe Magoto accepted. Blackwell and Ponca City were left in the cold

Dick Klaus was among the stable of Giants' minor league managers who specialized in handling rookies. His playing experience had been in Class A and Class B. His first managing job had been at Sanford (FL) then Moultrie (GA) before taking over the Pauls Valley Raiders from Lou Brower. When the Giants ended their working agreement with that town, he moved on to teach the Giants' newcomers at Danville (KY) in 1954.

Klaus arrived in Muskogee in mid-April, 1955, with a squad of two veterans, himself and a National Service player, five limited service players, and a dozen rookies under contract to the New York Giants. The fans in Muskogee were not accustomed to so many rookies and the kinds of mistakes they often repeatedly make on the field. The team's average age including Klaus and the National Service players was just twenty.

The process of creating a line up began with the usual weeding. Pitcher William Hill was soon released and Del Burns was shipped off to Salem (VA). Joe Beaulieu and Tommy Lynch got trials at catcher and soon were cut. Limited service player Al Kasper had the job until Sid Harvey arrived in mid-June from college. Kasper was released on July 15. Veteran Earl Hemberger lost out to rookie Malcolm Kingins at first base. Nick Tedesco won second base almost immediately. Daryl Robertson began at third base but with a weak glove was moved to shortstop and replaced by Eugene Johnson. Manager Kaus had played shortstop until Robertson moved over. Al Cruz (Rodriguez) arrived from Cocoa (FL) to complete the last forty games of the season. John Lennon and Billy Caye seized

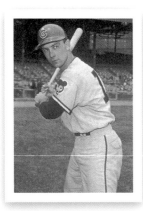

Daryl Robertson toiled in the minors from 1954 through 1962 where he finished with Tulsa. He spent two weeks with the Cubs in May, 1961. (Mu-22)

two of the outfield positions. Norm Gant and Ed Parrimon were soon eliminated from the competition for the third slot. Artie Dillon and Hal Entenmann vied for that place. Entenmann's bat gave him the edge.

Starters were Leonard Bacon (15-11), Joe Madaris (10-13), Bill DeJesus (12-9), Paul McAuley (11-8), and Stan Denny (5-7). Robert Laumann (12-6), who appeared in forty-four games, and John Mitchell (2-4) were used mainly in relief. The pitching competition in the Sooner State League was particularly fierce. Laumann's 2.14 ERA would often be the league best; in 1955 it was fourth. Bacon was the workhorse with 235 innings in thirty-two games. He, additionally, led the league with twenty-four wild pitches. A limited service pitcher who had hurled for three other teams in 1955, Cedric Wolfman, turned in the best performance when he twirled a no-hitter on August 17 to vanquish the Ponca City Cubs 9-2.

The campaign got off to a good start when Bacon threw a five-hitter at Seminole for a 5-0 win before the home crowd at Athletic Park. Following a rainout, the April 23 game was cancelled because of a dust storm. Paris handed the Giants a win on May 9 by a score of 5-4 with all of the Muskogee runs coming on Oriole errors. John Lennon got his fifth round tripper of the young season on May 14 against Ardmore boosting his RBI total to thirty for his first twenty-four games. Magoto observed on June 22, 1955 that the club would finish $7,000 in the red if attendance did not pick up.

Catcher Sid Harvey set a league record on July 5 with back-to-back grand slams for an 11-2 win over the Yankees' McAlester farmhands. The next night Lennon ended high-flying Lawton phenom Dale Hendrickson's seventy-five innings without an earned run with two home runs to send the game into extra innings and then scored in the twelfth on two walks and an error for a 3-2 victory over the league's toughest (1.26 ERA) thrower. Bacon tossed a fifteen inning complete game for a 4-3 win over McAlester on July 18; he gave up five hits and fanned ten but walked fourteen. Muskogee overcame Ponca City's Ed Proud and his twenty-two strike outs on July 20 to take a 2-1 win; the Giants had only four hits. Paris again handed the Giants a 16-8 win on August 8, committing fourteen errors, one short of a league record. Bill DeJesus shut out McAlester 5-0 August 2 giving up but a single hit. In the 24-5 romp over Shawnee on August 10, outfielder Bill Caye went to bat in every inning. He tallied six RBIs on seven walks and a grand slam home run. Third sacker Johnson was lost for the playoffs when a pitch broke his wrist. The Giants finished 74-66 in third place. Muskogee eliminated Shawnee in five games but lost to Lawton's Braves in the finals four games to two.

No All Star team was chosen in 1955. Klaus led the team in hitting with .315, the only regular to hit above 300. The Giants collectively had a .240 batting average, seventh in the Sooner State. They were swift with a league top 111 stolen bases. Despite the lower quality of play, the fans were back as 47,485, more than 1954, paid to see the baby Giants. That was the highest attendance in the Sooner State.

1956

The quality of play was much poorer than Muskogee fans were accustomed to seeing. An average Sooner State League game in 1956 saw twelve runs, fourteen strikeouts, eleven walks, and 4.6 errors. Klaus' second season would not be pretty.

Klaus returned to Muskogee with three of his 1955 team: pitcher Leonard Bacon, first baseman Earl Hemberger and first sacker Malcolm Kingins. The Giants shuffled prospects leaving Klaus' lineup in a state of uncertainty. Howard Gershberg was sent to the Class D club at Sandersville (GA) after

ten games. Pitchers Mike Coffy and Cedric Wolfman as well as 1955 slugger John Lennon were returned by St. Cloud. Pitcher John Hageman was followed by William Hatcher who arrived late in the season from Sandersville. Orland Johnson was down from Class B Danville (VA). Pitcher Stan Denney, a 1955 alumnus, arrived from Lake Charles in a trade for outfielder Don Cassidy.

The Major Leagues backed the first short season, sixty-three game rookie league in 1956. The reconstituted Nebraska State League had eight teams including the Giants' club at Hastings. The idea of the circuit was to "draw the creams of the high school talent over the country with a sprinkling of college talent" according to Phil Piton of the National Association office as reported in *The Sporting News*. The season would run July 1 through Labor Day. Eight Muskogee players would up there, clearing Klaus' roster. Pitcher James Fleming and outfielder Gordon Bretzing arrived via Michigan City (IN). Pitchers Gary Bogatay, George Kochis, who had been sent to Muskogee from Sandersville (GA), and Ronnie Green and position players Nick Popravak, Don Jones, and Norman Watson were sent directly to Nebraska. The Giants' Hastings club finished last among the rookies in batting, fielding, and pitching. The Giants didn't find much cream.

Preston Carpenter, former University of Arkansas football star, had the catching position until he left to play football and rookie Neil Wilson arrived on the scene. He held the post

Dick Klaus managed in and scouted for the Giants for over twenty years. He headed Pauls Valley in 1953 and Muskogee in 1955 and 1956. (Mu-23)

Neil Wilson was a member of the Giants' organization his entire career. He played at Candlestick Park at the beginning of the 1960 season. (Mu-24)

173

until Hatcher arrived from Sandersville for a dozen games. Hemberger beat out his 1955 team mate Kingins for first base. Don Booher started at second but his weak back forced his release; he signed up with Roswell of the West Texas-New Mexico League. His replacement, Joe Boring, was drafted after fifty games. Poprovak filled in until assigned to Hastings. Klaus played third, with a .822 fielding average, and a baker's dozen games at shortstop. Ken Stevens, alternating between second and shortstop, finished the season at the keystone. Charles Clark divided his time between third base, a foreign position judging by his .855 fielding average, and shortstop. Bob Perry and John Stockton were mainstays in the outfield. John Lennon made a trio when he arrived. All the other outfielders had been sent to Hastings.

Gene Calder, Bacon, Chris Riddell before leaving for Michigan City, and Wolfman after

Main entry to an abandoned Athletic Park. (Mu-25)

he arrived were the starters. Mike Coffy, Robert Miller, Robert Reed, and James Fleming, before shipping out, formed the corps of relievers. With the most professional experience, Calder led the club with 235 innings, an even division of twenty-six decisions and at 3.52 the best ERA. Reed and Miller had the only positive percentages, .524 on an 11-10 record and .533 on an 8-7 performance. Reed showed the best control yielding 3.8 walks per nine innings. The staff was an easy touch for hitters. Wolfman (6-6 5.32 ERA) at 8.4 gave up the fewest hits per nine. Denny was the hard luck story with a 5-10 effort giving up one hit per inning with a 4.72 ERA.

The 1956 season opened at Muskogee on a windy, chilly fifty-five degree evening before two hundred hardy fans as the new Giants scored all their runs in the eighth inning for a 7-3 win over McAlester. The Rockets turned the tables the next evening as former Orioles' bonus baby

Bruce Swango attempting a return as an out-fielder homered to give his team a 4-3 win. In for a tryout on May 2, Dick Hilland homered with one on in the first and posted a grand slam in the ninth to hand the Giants a 10-7 win over Ardmore; he didn't get a job. Manager Klaus ruined Lawton twin Don Eason's twenty-five inning start without an earned run on May 10 by knocking two homers for a 2-0 Giants win. A few days later, Nick Poprovak was hit by pitches three times in a double header. That weather and those bruises were an omen for the season.

By May 17, the Giants settled into seventh at 9-13 and attendance was projected to be down by 9,500, a huge number in Class D. After giving up nine stolen bases to Ponca City on May 17 in a 9-3 loss, and dropping the next contest, Muskogee got a measure of revenge with a 10-7 triumph against the little Cubs. The jinx of County Memorial Park in Lawton came to an end on May 22 when Bob Miller overcame six hits and ten walks to trump the Lawton Braves 5-3. Theretofore, in fifteen appearances since joining the league, the Giants had not won a game in Lawton. Preston Carpenter's two-RBI double provided the 5-3 measure of victory against Ponca City on May 31. The Giants and McAlester went sixteen innings in four hours, thirty-eight minutes before a home run by the Rockets' Photios Anthony ended the contest 4-3. It was the longest game in league history. Muskogee fans got to see second year hurler Cedric Wolfman one-hit Lawton in the seven inning night cap of the June 10 twin-bill. The next night, Shawnee was in town and treated the fans to a triple play as the Giants fell to the Hawks 6-3.

Muskogee had climbed from the seventh place it had occupied all season to fifth by July 19 one-half game away from the first division. Catcher Preston Carpenter departed the Giants on July 15 to prepare for the College All

Star football game then report for pre-season drills with the Cleveland Browns. The Giants climbed to a tie with Paris for third place on August 2 with a 47-53 season record. As Seminole began its late summer charge from the cellar to the playoff, the Oilers smashed three homers in an inning to take the Giants 8-6 on July 29. Bob Reed aided his own cause hitting a grand slam to ice his five-hitter over Shawnee for a 11-0 August 20 win. The wheels were beginning to fall off as Lawton swept a double header on August 25. The Giants fell to sixth. They dropped the season finale at McAlester 11-4 on September 3 as Bruce Swango made his professional pitching debut for the Rockets.

The team was seventh in batting (.247), last in fielding (.9297 with 372 errors), and in the middle of the pack on the mound (4.62 ERA). No 1956 Giant hit over .300. Bob Perry, who led the team with twenty-three home runs, and Neil Wilson both were headed for the Show.

The 1956 Giants finished a disappointing sixth with a 63-76 record, twenty games behind first place Ardmore. It was reflected in the box office with attendance off by nearly 10,000 to 37,983. Actually the 1956 club had a better-games behind number than 1955 when the third place Giants were twenty-one and one-half off the pace. The 1956 League was well balanced; no team over .600 and none below .400.

Razorback All-American Preston Carpenter had a short stay with the 1956 Giants before departing on July 15 to begin his professional football career with the Cleveland Browns. He was back at Athletic Park for four games in 1957. (Mu-27)

Bob Perry played between 1953 and 1970 including two trips to the Majors with the Los Angeles Angels in 1963 and 1964. (Mu-26)

Andy Gilbert was back in 1957. Known for being level-headed and even-tempered, he had not been ejected from a game until 1957 after repeatedly experiencing poor umpiring in the Sooner State League. (Mu-29)

1957

Muskogee's appearance in the Sooner State League looked doubtful when 1957 began. The City of Muskogee wanted to raze Athletic Park for public parking. The decline in attendance in 1956 badly affected operating revenue. On January 28, however, Joe Magoto announced that local businessmen had committed financial assistance to the tune of $10,000 in guaranties and the parent Giants had also promised to help out more than in past years. *The Sporting News* featured Magoto in its June 12, 1957 edition in a story "Hobbyist Magoto in 25th Season as Muskogee Backer."

Gentleman Andy Gilbert, who had hit .357 for Muskogee in 1952, made a reprise this time leading from the dugout. The roster he brought back from Florida was mainly limited service players. Five of the rookies who made the trip north, were essentially warehoused until sent to the all-rookie Nebraska State League affiliate for its season beginning July 1. One of those, Bob Ronan who had been sent over from the Giant's Class C affili-

Verle Tiefenthaler broke in with Muskogee in 1955 before being drafted. On his return in 1957, he began progressing through the Giants' system reaching the AAA level in 1962. Traded to the White Sox he appeared in three games yielding a grand slam in his debut. (Mu-28)

ate at St. Cloud (MN), played fifty-three games at first base until shipped north. Richard Vogel and Al Geyer also got in playing time before leaving for Hastings. Russ Buhite and Aubrey Grigsby rode the bench. Outfielder Alvin Conway was a veteran and National Service player who had begun is career in 1951. Two carryovers from the previous season were regulars Neil Wilson and Charlie Clark. Although classified as a rookie, Verle Tiefenthaler had National Service status; he had appeared briefly with Muskogee in 1955. Two appeared very briefly in Muskogee. Emmett Hungate went to the Giant's farm at Selma (AL) after six appearances. James Fleming was off to Michigan City (IN) after three. Preston Carpenter, a 1956 alumnus, quit baseball to concentrate on his NFL career after four games.

Like Gilbert's 1952 club, he selected a line up and kept it intact for the season. Wilson caught most games although Pearson covered a stretch when Wilson was injured. Ronan was the first baseman until sent to Hastings. Rookie Mario Tamayo who had been an outfield starter shifted to first for the rest of the campaign. Clark once again held the keystone. Arturo Martinez was at third all season. Ainsworth "Buddy" Yeomans played every game between Clark and Martinez. The original outfield was composed of Johnny Weekly, rookie Herman Williamson, and Tamayo. Alvin Conway and third year player Dino Messina finished the season in Tamayo's slot.

The pitching rotation was Tiefenthaler, who worked 218 innings, Robert Wales (13-10 3.91 ERA 198 innings), Hector Cruz (14-9 4.06 ERA 193 innings), and Richard Tyndall (9-9 4.67 ERA 135 innings). Joe Griffiths (10-8 4.31 ERA 142 innings) had fifteen starts in his thirty-eight appearances. Tiefenthaler was the ace, leading in winning percentage (16-8 .667), ERA (3.47), and had the best control, yielding only 3.8 walks per game. James Tucker (4-5 5.74 ERA 58 innings) served as a short reliever in twenty-nine of his thirty appearances. Aubrey Grigsby split four decisions with a 2.48 ERA in forty innings before leaving for Hastings. Another who saw limited action before heading for Hastings was Richard Vogel (1-3 6.00 ERA 42 innings).

For the first time a Sooner State League game, the season opener, was cancelled because of television. Owner Joe Magoto decided to stay home with the rest of the country on May 1, 1957, and watch Sugar Ray Robinson knock out Gene Fullmer in the fifth round of the middle weight championship rematch. As things turned out, the game would have been called due to a deluge that hit Muskogee that evening. In fact, rain played havoc across the league as ten games were postponed during the first four nights of the season. After thirty-five days, fifty-nine games had been postponed because of rain or wet grounds. Ironically, the season had been shortened to 126 games with a delayed start in order to avoid the many early rainouts experienced the past two seasons.

The Giants picked up their third win on May 6 on Wilson's squeeze bunt in the ninth, 2-1 over Shawnee. Two nights later, Cruz got the honor of pitching the first Sooner State League shutout with a 1-0 victory over Shawnee. On May 12, Weekly hit the first Giants' home run at Athletic Park as they cruised to a 7-4 triumph over Paris. In spite of being held to six hits, Muskogee won a twelve-inning test against Ardmore ace Don Mitchell 4-3 on May 27. The Giants received a forfeit the next night. Ardmore manager J. C. Dunn had been ejected for delaying the game during a pitching change and when he refused to leave the field the umpires awarded the home team a 9-0 win. After a month of play, Yeomans was hitting .314 while Wales, Cruz, and Tiefenthaler were among the top eight hurlers. The Giants were leading the league pack. The Giants' staff had a combined 2.78 ERA which made up for the team batting average of only .238.

The Waterproof, Louisiana native was a Sooner State League All Star in 1957. Johnny Weekly shuttled between Houston and AAA clubs from 1962 through 1965. Houston traded him to Baltimore for cash and a player to be named later. Later, Baltimore sent Weekly back to Houston as the player to be named. (Mu-30)

Cruz polished his statistics on June 9 with a 4-0 one-hitter over Lawton. Ardmore slipped past Muskogee in the standings on July 4 to take over sole possession of first place. The wheels began falling off when Ardmore took five of six in a series between July 17 and 21. The Cardinals feasted on Muskogee pitching as they scored sixty-six runs; Ardmore's Jim McKnight slugged six round-trippers. By August 9, the Giants had fallen into the second division with a still-winning 50-45 record. A week later, they were back in third place. The Giants took a seventeen inning nail-biter from Shawnee on August 22 by a 7-6 tally. Back from Hastings, Ronan scored an inside-the-park home run in the eleventh. Another Hastings returnee, Grigsby relieved Tiefenthaler in the twelfth and grabbed the win with his own inside-the-park four-bagger in the seventeenth. Wilson nearly hit for the cycle with a single, triple, and home run to add five RBIs to his totals. History was made on August 28 when Andy Gilbert was ejected for the first time during his twenty-year baseball career.

The Giants held on to third place as Paris inched past Ardmore to win the regular season race by one-half game. In the first round, Muskogee handed Ardmore its only playoff loss as the Cardinals coasted past the Giants in four games and then swept Paris for the last Sooner State League pennant.

The 1957 squad was much better team at the plate (.261 average, .375 slugging percentage) than 1956, and superior with the glove (.949, 233 errors), the mound staff allowed a collective 4.16 runs per nine innings. Ainsworth Yeomans and

Johnny Weekly, a future Houston Colt .45 and Oklahoma City 89er, took advantage of the short left field fence at Athletic Park to finish in the top ten league batters. Only 21,253 fans saw the last Muskogee squad finish third.

Muskogee hosted the final meeting of an operating Sooner State League on February 2, 1958. Greenville's franchise had been revoked and Lawton was dropped because the Milwaukee Braves would not send players to a facility as dilapidated as Memorial Park. Vernon, Texas, and Ada were awarded replacement franchises. A few days later, on February 5, Joe Magoto, presiding in the absence of League President George Barr, announced that with Ada, Seminole and Vernon having been unable to secure working agreements, the owners had voted to suspend operations in 1958. The Sooner State League never played another game.

A skeletal Athletic Park served as a car impoundment center before demolition to provide space for the Muskogee Civic Center. (Mu-31)

PAULS VALLEY RAIDERS
SOONER STATE LEAGUE 1948-1954

SEASON	ATTENDANCE	RECORD	FINISH	AFFILIATION	PLAYOFF FIRST ROUND	PLAYOFF FINALS
1948	27,071	56-81	Seventh			
1949	61,085	88-52	First		Beat Ada 3-2	Lost to Lawton 1-4
1950	25,848	68-72	Fifth			
1951	27,580	90-50	Fourth		Lost to Ardmore 0-3	
1952	34,500	80-59	Second	New York NL	Beat Chickasha 3-1	Lost to McAlester 3-4
1953	18,453	63-74	Fifth	New York NL		
1954	29,468	41-99	Eighth	Cleveland		

Both the smallest city in the League as well as one of the oldest in Oklahoma, founded in 1857, 61,085 Garvin County residents paid admission to see the 1949 team on its way to a regular season pennant; but never on Sunday. The ministerial alliance held sway over a city council that refused to create a baseball exception to the local Blue Law. Schedules drawn for the Sooner State League had to put the Raiders away on Sundays or give a day off. Named the Raiders by Paoli schoolboy James Anderson in a contest before the 1948 season began, the Pauls Valley club was an independent signing and developing its own players for each year of its existence with the exception of the seasons with working agreements with the New York Giants in 1952-1953 and Cleveland Indians in 1954. The Raiders had a disproportionate number of All Stars and sent several players to the Major Leagues.

1948

Meeting at Worley's café on December 4, 1947, Banker Pete Grimmett, dentist Dr. G. D. Smith, funeral director J. H. Stufflebean, entrepreneur Eph Lobaugh, who was a three year letterman at the University of Oklahoma, and Dutch Prather formed the board of directors of Pauls Valley Baseball Club, Inc. along with Jerry Johnson as president, John Dowd vice president, grocer Jim Tom Kendall secretary, and R. W. Driskell treasurer. Prather, a native of Stratford, Oklahoma, had secured release from his contract with Ardmore so he could become the business and field manager of the new Pauls Valley club. Jack Grimmett of the banking family and civic leader served as business manager after Prather left the

Murl A. "Dutch" Prather played and managed in the minors for twenty-four seasons with twenty-two teams in fifteen leagues. He twice reached the AAA level, first in 1931 with Kansas City and again in 1937 with Sacramento. He managed or played for Ardmore, Chickasha, Duncan, Pauls Valley, and Seminole in the Sooner State League. (Pv-1)

organization midway through the inaugural season. Baseball was played at Wacker Field in 1948 but the grandstand was incomplete, there were no box seats, and the dugouts were wooden. With a seventh place finish after the hole Prather dug, it should come as no surprise that only 27, 071 went through the gates, nearly the worst attendance in the league, only twenty-one more than Ada and five more than Duncan. Prather was fired on July 29. The firing was accompanied by Jerry Johnson's resignation as club president.

Pauls Valley won a Sooner State League franchise over several other larger cities in December, 1947. It was the smallest city in the league and with a population around 6,500 one of the smaller cities in Organized Baseball. Its central location equidistant from Chickasha, Ardmore, and Ada gravitated in its favor. The Raiders made the playoffs twice in the four years as an independent. The top people in town were involved with supporting the team and they sunk a good deal of their personal money into the Raiders. After the 1954 season, the club's godmother, Mona Wacker, simply would not tolerate further losses. After trying to find a local buyer, the franchise was returned to the league.

Beginning from scratch in 1948, the Raiders signed six of its first players directly from the Rogers Hornsby Baseball School including first baseman and future Washington Senator Richard Hawes.

Roy Hawes spent 1948 and 1949 with the Raiders. He was among the all-time Pauls Valley favorites, living with the Wacker family. He was the first Raider to appear in a Major League game as a member of the Washington Senators. (Pv-2)

Oscar Kuver, who set a league record for runs and earned run as well as shattering his 1947 mark with 182 bases on balls, and catcher Colonel Stephens, followed Prather from Ardmore. Thirty-one players were signed to contracts and appeared at one time or another during the season. The roster limit was sixteen so the clubhouse needed a revolving door. The first season was ill-starred. Manager Dutch Prather was nonplused when his catcher, Percy Huff, walked off the field in the middle of a game explaining that he refused to catch if Bob Henderson was plate umpire; fortunately Colonel Stephens was well so the Dutchman did not have to personally fill in.

In what is thought to be an all-time Organized Ball record, Jimmy Cobb gave one of the worst pitching performances in professional baseball. He balked nine times in two and two-thirds innings as well as being tagged for nine runs on five hits, nine walks, a hit batsman, and three wild pitches. After facing twenty-three batters, Cobb tossed down the ball, walked off the field, past the dugout, past the dressing room, and into the parking lot and drove away, never claiming his pay check. The team was in last place at 35-60 (.368) when Prather left to take a playing job at Chickasha on July 29.

Pauls Valley native and retired Red Sox and Phillies pitcher Jennings "Jinx" Poindexter was called into service and in his first outing on August

1 beat Ada 14-7 on four hits. The Raiders played .500 ball for him winning and losing twenty-one, good enough to escape the cellar by two games over hapless Duncan. As a team they batted .258 but scored the fewest runs.

Local baseball hero Jinx Poindexter picked up the pieces Prather had left behind. He had pitched a few games for the Boston Red Sox and Philadelphia Phillies. (Pv-4)

A. B. Pearson was the eldest of three brothers to play for the Raiders and the most popular of those who played in Pauls Valley. He was a member of the 1948, 1949, and 1951 Raiders and would have been none in 1950 had not the National Association disqualified him, forcing him to play for Chickasha. (Pv-1)

They tied Duncan for worst fielding at .930. In a year of good pitching in the league, Dean Franks' 4.39 was the best ERA on the team. Rodney Province, picked up from Ada, led the league in wild pitches with twenty-three and managed to hit eighteen batters while posting the second best team ERA at 4.48. Local favorite and team MVP, A.B. Pearson, hitting .328 and Robert Hyatt .301 were the top batsmen. Excepting an involuntary one year detour to Chickasha in 1950, Pearson made a career at Pauls Valley. Hyatt would make it to AAA.

1949

Built for the Raiders, municipally-owned Wacker Field was dedicated on the 4th of July of 1949, Pauls Valley's pennant year. A concrete and cinder block structure, the club houses were in either end of the grandstand. The grandstand was a single building with one row of four-seat boxes and twenty rows of benches in three sections. Originally, entrance was through an arched metal gate with the word "Raiders" above it up a ramp in the middle of the grandstand; there was also access from either end. The row of boxes was seven feet above the playing field. There were bleachers down the base lines to increase capacity to around 2,000. Center field was 380 feet away while it was 320 down the left field line and 315 to right.

61,085 saw the 1949 Raiders edge Lawton's Giants by one-half game to win the regular season pennant. The largest crowd of the season, 2,532, watched the Raiders advance to the playoff finals with a 3-2 win over Ada. After eliminating Ada, the Raiders dropped the final series to Lawton four games to one. The front office also had a change. Developer and oilman E. P. Diffie became business manager.

Exterior of Wacker Park. (Pv-5)

The original entry to Wacker Park. (Pv-6)

View of the grandstand from the field. (Pv-7)

Clarence "Red" Phillips took the 1949 Raiders to their only first place finish and a place in the play-off finals. He had pitched for the 1934 and 1936 Detroit Tigers. (Pv-8)

Lounging on the dugout roof, L-R A. B. Pearson, Daryl Spencer, Ken Hemphill. (Pv-10)

The 1949 team made a complete about turn. The core of the team was the nine returnees from the 1948 club plus five players new manager Red Phillips, another Pauls Valley native, brought with him from the semi-pro ranks in Wichita as well as another Pearson brother, Lonnie. Phillips was a fine field leader who had pitched since 1933 and had a 4-4 record for the Detroit Tigers in 1934 and 1936. The Raiders rode excellent pitching that allowed only 617 runs to a half game finish over a good Lawton team to claim the regular season crown. With a .262 team batting average, the Raiders led the League in runs (863), hits (1,269), home runs (83), RBIs (718) and total bases (1,836). No member of the pitching staff had an ERA above 4.50 and two came in under 2.00, Willard Eppler (1.88) and manager Phillips (1.98). Pauls Valley local Rube Melton won twenty-three games while Washington, Oklahoma's Ken Hemphill won seventeen.

Rookie Jim "Rube" Melton won twenty-three games for his home town Raiders in 1949. He played nine more seasons finishing with a brief stint with the 1961 Ardmore Rosebuds. (Pv-9)

With a fielding average of .946, the players knew how to use their gloves. The star of the team was Daryl Spencer who came with Red Phillips from the Wichita semi-pros of Boeing. While his batting average of .286 was respectable if not extraordinary, his Slugging Percentage was .487. He was tops in home runs knocking twenty-three Worth baseballs –the cheapest and deadest balls sold—out of the park for a then league record. At the suggestion of Oklahoman Carl Hubbell, the Gi-

ants' chief scout, Mel Ott, traveled to Garvin County to watch him play. Ott was not the only scout looking. At the end of the season, New York won the bidding contest and paid $10,000 plus five minor league players for Spencer's contract. The Raiders eliminated fourth place Ada in five games and then felt Lawton's vengeance winning only one game in the finals.

1950

The controlling ownership of the team changed hands following the 1949 season. Jim Dulin of Paoli purchased a sixty-five percent stake. Stufflebean, Kendall and Dr. Smith remained on the board. Newcomers were Barney Paris, Diffie, B.A. Vaughn, Clifford Hanley, and Bill Humphrey. After the 1949 performance, it looked like a sound investment. The 1950 Raiders finished a disappointing fifth while attendance dropped to 25, 848 and, even worse, the club lost $13,000. Sale of Daryl Spencer for $10,000 and five Minor League players lessened the sting of the 1950 campaign and made the season financially break even. A player like Spencer didn't come along often and, in the Raiders' case, never again.

With Red Phillips at the helm, he welcomed back seven members from the 1949 team plus four 1949

Dick Von der Haar came over in the Spencer deal after three seasons in the Giants' Class D camp. 1950 was his last season. (Pv-13)

Joe Jacobs took over when Red Phillips stepped down during the last month of the 1950 season. (Pv-11)

The New York Giants paid the Raiders $10,000 and five players for Daryl Spencer. It was a good investment launching a career that saw him play eight National League seasons plus four more in Japan. (Pv-12)

Lawton Giants who came in the Spencer deal. Of the twenty-four who wore Raiders flannels in 1950, ten were rookies who were signed and released during the season. On May 4, the Raiders participated in one of the sloppiest games ever played in professional baseball. In losing to Ada at Wacker Field, the two teams committed fourteen balks (seven that scored runs), allowed eighteen walks, gave up thirty hits, hit five batters, unleashed two wild pitches, and made ten errors. Ted Szymanski, earlier released by Ada, committed seven of the balks. Phillips resigned on

August 3, with the team at 49-49 and was replaced by one of the Wichita group of players, Joe Jacobs, the thumbless catcher who had been released after the 1949 season and re-signed on June 19, 1950. The Raiders went 19-23 for him finishing a distant fifth place. Hemphill, Clark and rookie Andy Pane were the heart of the pitching crew logging forty-nine of the Raiders' sixty-eight wins. Joe Thomas hit .303 as a part timer while Jim Dionasotis was the top regular batsman at .292 and Dick Von Der Haar, who came over in the Daryl Spencer sale, next at .280. The 1950 Raiders were butterfingered committing 406 errors for a seventh place .923 percentage.

1951

Pauls Valley operated as a pure independent for the last time in 1951. To revitalize the Raiders, Dulin hired Lou Brower, the dean of Sooner State League managers, who had completed four years at Lawton. Brower was paid $300 per month plus a bonus if the Raiders made the playoffs. Unable to afford the financial hit of a money-losing season, on May 30, 1951, at a shareholders' meeting Dulin, explaining he had lost $13,000 in 1950, was $1,000 in the red for 1951, wanted out by June 5, and offered his interest in the team for sale to anyone local in an attempt to keep the team in Pauls Valley. Only eight of sixty-four shareholders attended.

Mona Wacker, widow of G. F. Wacker a prominent merchant and civic leader, purchased Dulin's shares for $7,000 in tandem with a public drive to raise $5,000 to cover the coming payroll, stadium rental, league dues, electricity, bats, and balls. She commended Dulin for holding on as long as he did. As new majority owner, she appointed club director Leo Tripp as business manager. New officers were Mrs. Wacker as president, Barney Paris as vice-president, Bill Humphrey secretary, and Dr. Smith treasurer. Newly elected directors in addition to the officers were Tripp, Floyd Rabon, Jim Blanton, restaurateur Julian Field, Stufflebean, Dowd, and Johnson. While manager Brower received his bonus for a fourth place finish, the fans didn't reward the owners at the ticket booth. Only 27,580 attended in 1951.

The 1951 team, the last as an independent, finished fourth with a 90-50 record losing to Ardmore in the first round of the playoff. They were called "Dulin's Durables" because the roster was always shorthanded. Only nineteen players appeared all season. The 90-50 season was the Raider's best winning percentage (.643) despite the fourth place finish, surpassing the champion 1949 team (88-52) and the second place 1952 entry at 80-59. The star of the team was sophomore Andy Pane. He started thirty-five games, relieved in four, and completed thirty-one for a 26-9 record with a 3.16 ERA and a berth on the All Star team. On the way he threw a no-hitter against Lawton on July 2, winning 5-0. His 305 strike outs were tempered by his twenty-five wild pitches. It has been estimated that he threw 5,295 pitches that season, eighth among all minor league hurlers between 1951 and 1955. Pane played outfield in twenty-two games and pinch hit in a dozen more. His .348 batting average and .472 Slugging Percentage were the best among the Raiders. The club batted .278 and, with the new official Rawlings ball, led the League in home runs (117). Dan Toma tied with Ardmore's Manuel Temes for the most hits with 195 while Donnie Williamson and Dan Demby tied for the lead in home runs with thirty each. With the fewest errors (261), the Raiders averaged .951 in the field. Kennesaw Mountain Landis Hemphill actually had a better season on the mound than Pane, winning twenty-seven and losing ten with a team best 2.91 ERA. Pane and Hemphill were the Pauls Valley version of the Boston Braves' "Spahn and Sain, and pray for rain." Their feats were, however, surpassed by McAlester's Dee Sanders who had a 27-4 record and 1.67 ERA and Ardmore's Armin Somonte's 341 strike outs with twenty-four wins. The team produced four All Stars and the two who tied for the league's home run title.

Mrs. Wacker's team bus was discovered in a field outside of town in the early 1980s. (Pv-15)

Mona Wacker was the only woman in America to own a baseball team. She saved the franchise when she bought Jim Dulin's interest in 1951 and kept the Raiders afloat through 1954. (Pv-14)

1952

Season box seat prices were lowered to $10 for 1952. With free agents and talent supplied by the Giants, and sporting new uniforms following the parent Giants' orange and black, the Raiders fielded a very competitive team finishing second with an 80-59 record six and one-half games behind McAlester.

Lou Brower's second season at Pauls Valley was the first that the franchise operated with any form of Major League working agreement. The Giants would option a few and release outright other prospects to the Raiders; the club had to beat the bushes for the rest. Fielders Donnie Williamson at first and Clell Callaway at second were the only returnees from 1951.

Pauls Valley infield in new Raiders flannels. L-R: Orland Johnson, Kimberg, Clell Callaway, Donnie Williamson. (Pv-16)

The third Pearson brother, Lloyd, joined the team as a free agent. Five —Don Deatherage, Gene Valloni, Jack Boyd, Harrell Thacker, and Bill Wedeking— had spent 1951 with the weak-hitting, seventh place Lawton Giants. Future San Francisco Giant Dom Zanni began his second year with the Raiders. The rest were the Giants' rookie prospects.

The 1952 season got off to an auspicious start as Williamson hit three doubles and two singles to whip Sherman 17-7. The Raiders for the season hit a huge .281 along with scoring the most runs (972). Williamson again tied for the most home runs with twenty-two and led the circuit with 148 RBIs. Rookie Burke Probitsky hit a solid .327, stole fifty-eight bases and compiled a strong .486 On Base Percentage. He had the best glove in the league among outfielders, fielding a sterling .977. The Raiders bested their 1951 fielding with a .952 percentage even though suffering a shortstop who bobbled the second half of the season at a .895 level. They missed Pane and Hemphill on the mound but Thacker (24-6, 3.42), Zanni (20-8, 3.10), and Wedeking (9-7, 3.61) more than compensated. The first affiliated Pauls Valley club finished second at 80-59.

Canadian Irvin Kimberg models an old Raiders road uniform during spring training in 1952. As the only Jew in Pauls Valley, Kimberg was a novelty. He finished the 1952 season with Ardmore and toiled for Seminole in 1954. He left baseball behind for a performance career as Kim Irvin. (Pv-17)

The Raiders vanquished the orphaned Chickasha Chiefs in four games and took the McAlester Rockets the distance in the playoff finals winning the first three before losing the next three and all important game seven. Only 34,500 fans saw Pauls Valley's last first division team. The bottom line for the 1952 campaign even with a full working agreement was a $4,000 loss. Mrs. Wacker published a letter to the fans and team on September 4, thanking them.

On behalf of the Pauls Valley Baseball Club, Inc., I want to thank manager, Lou Brower and the baseball fans of Pauls Valley and surrounding communities for making the team that we have possible. The loyalty of you people here is unsurpassed. You proved that Tuesday [September 2, 1952] night when you donated so much to the boys.

In my opinion, manager Brower's work has been instrumental in placing the Raiders in the play-offs more than any other factor, but of course the spirit of good play of the boys, and the work of business manager,

Bruce Probitsky despite having the best outfield glove in the league and batting .327 with a .486 on base percentage inexplicably was not named an All Star. Drafted after the season, he played in Class D in 1955 but without the numbers he put up as a rookie. (Pv-18)

Leo Tripp were indispensible.

There aren't enough words of praise for the kids who played and I want to go on record as saying that the players here this year were the cleanest and most sincere we have had.

However, I believe that nowhere else would citizens of a city this size throw as much support to a baseball team as the people have here.

1953 Pauls Valley Raiders. (Pv-19)

*1953 scorecard cover.
(Pv-21)*

1953 scorecard inside. (Pv-20)

1953

The New York Giants supplied most of the talent at Pauls Valley in 1953. Indeed, there were only two carryovers from the 1952 team. Player development trumped winning. Richard Klaus' Raiders produced one Major Leaguer, Dom Zanni, who came up with the Giants in 1958. Attendance slumped to 18,453 for the fifth place Raiders resulting in a financial setback that ultimately sounded the death knell for the club.

Predation by the Selective Service hampered 1953 manager Dick Klaus' efforts to field a competitive team. Valloni, Bob Reitz, John Boyd, along with four prospects tagged for Pauls Valley had been drafted. Pitcher Charles Bennett and second baseman Dan Marotta were back from the military as was shortstop Andy Durika, an All Star in 1950, whose two year hitch included captaining an Army team for eighteen months. As National Defense players, they did not count against the fifteen player limit. Williamson, who was questionable after not attending spring training in Florida, showed up in shape for the season opener as did Lloyd Pearson. Glen Groomes who appeared briefly in 1951 had also been signed but was quickly cut after eight games with no hits. Limited service outfielder Tex Seymour and pitcher Victor Vick were signed as a free agents and rookie Joe Moran was picked up after Shawnee cut him. Pitcher Virgil Brisson was sent over by the Giants from the Kitty League. Twenty-four rookies passed through the Wacker Field clubhouse in 1953. For ten it was to be the end of the line.

The talent New York sent was not equal to the previous year. A 63-74 finish was good enough to place a distant fifth. While the best glovesmen in the League at .948, at the plate they led the Sooner State in runners left on base (1,193) for which the .251 team batting average with only sixty-one home runs, the fewest in the league, is an explanation. Catcher Al Steignitz had the best average at .319. George Reid hit .302 with fifteen home runs. Don Williamson had a subpar (for him) year hitting .309 with only nine home runs. Tex Seymour contributed thirteen round trippers. Rookie Bob Loftin hit a grand slam home run in his first professional at bat. Veteran Lloyd Pearson turned in the best pitching performance from the Raiders' staff. His 2.92 ERA was seventh in the league and he had a positive 12-8 record. The next Raider regular was Bob Reime who posted a 4.28 ERA with five wins. Victor Vick was anchor man with a 5.89 ERA and 4-8 record. Things would get worse.

1954

Ownership assessed the cost of operating a team in 1954. Based on past experience, the organization was $10,000 short. The Giants cancelled the working agreement for 1954. That sent business manager Leo Tripp scrambling. A weak agreement was signed with Cleveland that provided only seven players. Lloyd Pearson at age twenty-eight was called on to assemble the 1954 Raiders and lead them on the field. Too much stress and too little money contributed to his resignation on June 27. Pitcher Glen Groomes, returning after being released in 1951 and 1953, took over in the interim until Bennie Warren, who had been looking for a job since being fired by Ardmore, came aboard. The old Phillies catcher couldn't make the motley crew of players gel. Jerry Johnson, the new business manager, couldn't give away seats. Near the end of the campaign, the club

Lloyd Pearson threw for the Raiders in 1953 and managed part of 1954. (Pv-22)

opened the gates to Wacker Field, set barrels out front, and hoped people would toss in enough to get the Raiders through the season. Johnson remarked "I would like to see 1,000 in the stands just once this season." He would be disappointed. Six hundred—the largest crowd of the year—showed up and left $171 in the barrels. The final Raider team finished fifty-one games out of first place. Attendance, surprisingly, rebounded to 29,468. Nonetheless, the Raiders lost $21,000.

With only three carryovers from 1953—Andy Durika, Victor Vick, and manager Pearson—the

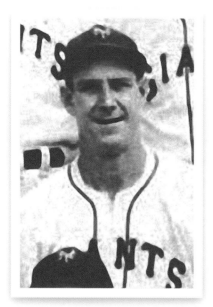

Bennie Warren had been unemployed since Gus Mancuso replaced him as Ardmore's manager. With Pearson leaving the Raiders for work in the oil patch, Warren assumed command for the rest of the season. He did not return to baseball. (Pv-23)

1954 squad was an assembly of castaways. At some time during the season sixty-one players appeared on the roster. Sixteen of the twenty-two who didn't stay long enough to appear in ten games were pitchers. Included in that number was John Lovallo who had no decisions in nine games for the Raiders; he was 1-1 for Seminole after he was cut. Before they signed with Pauls Valley, twenty-six had been released by at least one other team. For forty-one, including managers Pearson and Bennie Warren, Pauls Valley was the end of the baseball trail. Midway through the season, Pearson threw in the towel for the better money that oil field work offered and was replaced by Bennie Warren who had been

Rocky Johnson spent all or part of eleven seasons in the Major Leagues after making his debut with the Kansas City Athletics in 1960. (Pv-24)

fired by Ardmore's parent St. Louis Cardinals that June. He was unable to turn around the team which limped to a last place finish at 41-99 (.293), twenty games behind the league's last independent, seventh place Seminole. The club posted the highest ERA of any Sooner State League member, 6.71, allowing 1,156 runs against the 762 that Pauls Valley scored. The batters managed an eighth place .248 hitting percentage and a puny .375 Slugging Percentage. At .935, the last Raiders' performance in the field was at best average. Mrs. Wacker pulled the plug on this patient after this last pitiful season. Muskogee would take the Raiders' place.

Mona Wacker had been the godmother of Pauls Valley baseball directly subsidizing the team since 1951. In March, 1954, she put the team up for sale for $10,000. There were no takers, but the club's first president, Jerry Johnson, returned as business manager. Long time director Dr. G. D. Smith managed to raise $7,500 to underwrite most of the last half of the 1954 season. On December 1, 1954, Mrs. Wacker washed her hands of the enterprise, returned the franchise to the league and gave her stock to the city.

Jerry Johnson was scrambling. He told a January 6, 1955, meeting that it would cost $5,000 per month to field a team; that the club had $2,000 in the bank but league dues would wipe out that balance; that the Phillies had offered a limited working agreement with four to six players and $750 cash. Johnson published a plea in the *Pauls Valley Democrat* :

> This will probably be the last appeal I will be able to make to you to save the Raiders for 1955. . . Several days ago we called a mass meeting in the city hall to try to keep the club and at the meeting it was suggested   that we appoint a citizens' committee to call on Mrs. Wacker to see if they could work out a 50-50 deal with the president for this year. Dr. G. D. Smith was

appointed chairman of the committee, but after Dr. Smith talked to Mrs. Wacker and several men on the committee, it was decided to give up the charter and call it quits for the Raiders.

I attended the league meeting in Ardmore on Sunday, January 9, to report to the league, but the league refused to accept our charter at the time. They adjourned the meeting until Sunday, January 23, to give us another chance to save the club. This will be our last chance to go or quit.

This club is in good shape this year financially. We don't owe money to anyone. We have a promise of a good working agreement with the Phillies who will furnish us a good first division team and their own manager. They will train the players at their expense and send them to Pauls Valley. They will pay us $3,000 cash and all over $25 on each travel expense on players sent to us during the season.

We have been asked by hundreds of baseball fans, What about the club? They all regret to see us lose it. These summer nights will be long ones this year since we have had the club in Pauls Valley since 1948. But these are the facts and unless we can save it by the 23rd of this month [January, 1955] it will be curtains for professional baseball in Pauls Valley. Mrs. Wacker said she would go along with a group of twenty or thirty men who will sign to pay their part of any loss if we have a loss in 1955.

It was all too little, too late. Mrs. Wacker reiterated that she would not be involved with the team in 1955 and, further, denied a story published in the *Oklahoma City Times* that she would make a gift of $5,000 to whoever operated the club. "No one hates to see the Raiders leave more than I do," she said. She agreed to turn over the club's remaining assets to the city if a team was fielded. Pauls Valley Baseball Club, Inc. had been dissolved in December, 1954. The hope for baseball in Pauls Valley for 1955 expired on January 23. Jerry Johnson said the inevitable: "There is nothing else to do but tell the league we can't operate a baseball club this year."

PONCA CITY DODGERS
1947-1952
PONCA CITY JETS
1954
PONCA CITY CUBS
1955-1957

KANSAS-OKLAHOMA-MISSOURI LEAGUE 1947-1952
WESTERN ASSOCIATION 1954
SOONER STATE LEAGUE 1955-1957

SEASON	ATTENDANCE	RECORD	FINISH	AFFILIATION	PLAYOFF FIRST ROUND	PLAYOFF FINALS
1947	55,554	61-62	Sixth	Brooklyn		
1948	78,305	79-47	First	Brooklyn	Lost to Pittsburg 2-3	
1949	62,082	66-59	Fourth	Brooklyn	Lost to Independence 1-3	
1950	63,313	80-42	First	Brooklyn	Beat Pittsburg 3-2	Beat Bartlesville 3-1
1951	44,960	85-39	First	Brooklyn	Lost to Carthage 2-3	
1952	55,792	68-58	Third	Brooklyn	Beat Iola 1-0	Lost to Miami 0-1
1954	33,962	62-76	Sixth			
1955	21,477*	45-68*	Seventh	Chicago NL		
1956	20,674	70-70	Fifth	Chicago NL		
1957	21,253	52-74	Seventh	Chicago NL		

*Attendance and record after Gainesville moved to Ponca City on May 21, 1955.

WESTERN ASSOCIATION CHAMPIONS, 1936

1936 Western Association champion Ponca City Angels. (Pc-1)

Ponca City, founded as New Ponca in 1893 with a lottery for town lots, experienced a huge boom following E. W. Marland's company bringing in the Willie-Cries-for-War well on the Millers' 101 Ranch in 1911. The boom continued in the 1920s until the bloom fell off the price of oil and the Great Depression set in. Ponca City became increasingly a blue- and gray-collar town and by 1949 the headquarters of Conoco moved to Houston. Ponca City had grown by twenty percent during the War as Conoco and Cities Service Company's refineries produced high octane aviation fuel.

Ponca City was always a good baseball town. As early as 1914 its semi-pro club was winning border league championships. Professional ball came in 1922 when the Drumright Oklahoma State League ball club moved to town and a Southwestern League ball club competed in 1926. From 1934 to 1938, the Ponca City Angels, a downstream affiliate of the Pacific Coast League's Los Angeles team, the top farm club of the Chicago Cubs, competed successfully in the Western Association. The little Angels won pennants in 1934, 1935, 1936, and 1938 before decamping for St. Joseph (MO). Prior to the arrival of the K-O-M, the Ponca City Aviators, under the aegis of the makers of the Piper Cub aircraft there, appeared in the National Baseball Congress tournament.

Local Ford dealer Ted Parkinson was the driving force for professional baseball in Ponca City after the War. He would be involved with the franchises in the three leagues in which his home town competed.

1947

Disillusioned with the arrangement with Miami, Brooklyn was looking for a new home for its many rookie prospects, most fresh-faced high school boys and a few War veterans. The K-O-M expanded to eight teams for 1947 with the addition of Independence (KS) and the home of Continental Oil Company ("Conoco") and 20,000 potential fans, Ponca City.

Parkinson's organization hired Owen Martinez, who would have a long career as a baseball executive including serving as the first general manager of the Oklahoma City 89ers, to launch the new franchise named, like all the lower level Brooklyn farm clubs, the "Dodgers." The first task was to find a place to play. The old ball park where the Angels played had been demolished during the War. WPA-built Blaine Stadium was suitable only for football. It should come as no surprise that Conoco underwrote the K-O-M League ball park that bore its name, Conoco Park. It was erected on the site of the

Moses Yellowhorse, a member of the Pawnee tribe, threw for Pittsburgh in 1921 and 1922. He was groundskeeper at Conoco Park. (Pc-2)

1946 Cherokee Strip rodeo to house the little Dodgers on the north side of West South Avenue across from Conoco's headquarters. Begun in mid-March, the grandstand was partially roofed and made of closed concrete and steel with three dressing rooms. The stands sat 1,800. The distances were short: only 315 down the left field line, 302 to right, and 350 to straight away center. The outfield fence was made of $1/8"$ structural steel, the kind used to make oil tanks. Near the refinery, the fans simply got accustomed to the smell that pervaded the area. Martinez needed a batting cage and handed a set of schematics to a local welder for construction on site. When he went to inspect the product, the welder had indeed built a completely enclosed cage. It was literally back to the drawing board. Before the 1947 team arrived from spring training at the Dodgers' minor league camp at Thomasville (NC) the problem had been corrected. For the duration of the Dodgers' tenancy, 1921 and 1922 Pittsburgh hurler Moses Yellowhorse, a member of the Pawnee tribe, groomed the Conoco Park grounds.

If Conoco was the driving force in Ponca City, Branch Rickey, inventor of the farm system during his tenure with the St. Louis Cardinals, was the absolute master of the Dodgers' organization from Ebbets Field to Ponca City. With twenty-four mem-

Conoco Park was home to baseball 1947-1957. (Pc-3)

bers, Brooklyn had the largest player development system in all baseball. Rickey selected Boyd Bartley, a returning veteran who enjoyed a brief stint with the parent Dodgers in 1943 and, while lacking the talent to stay in the Major Leagues with all the pre-War stars, including shortstop Pee Wee Reese, had a good baseball head and could teach the game. Rickey was perhaps the best judge of talent in the history of the game.

Signed out from under the noses of the Chicago Cubs in May, 1943, the star University of Illinois shortstop went directly from campus to Ebbets Field. After fielding well in about ten games but hitting only .048, manager Leo Durocher optioned Bartley to the Dodgers' top farm club at Montreal. He spent the seasons of 1944-1946 in the Army where he was injured in a jeep accident. He was Ponca City's player-manager for three seasons, 1947, 1948, and 1949, where he batted respectively .330, .343 and .272. He was a bench manager there in 1950. He was called to the service during the Korean Conflict managing baseball operations at Ft Chaffee, Arkansas. After his discharge, he returned to manage the 1952 edition where he appeared in nineteen games as a pinch hitter. He was a superb teacher of the game with many successful alumni. He also had a temper and was fined and suspended more than any player or manager in the K-O-M's six seasons of operation.

The average age of the team was under twenty-one. There were no veterans; Bartley himself

was a twenty-seven year-old limited service player. Pitchers Steve Jordan and Joe Beran were carryovers from the 1946 Miami Blues. There were several sophomores but by and large Bartley's charges were very young rookies, many away from home for the first time. K-O-M members could begin the season with twenty players but had to cut to seventeen by May 21. Bartley axed three pitchers, Don Tisnerat, Robert Hitchens, and Ken Wherry by the deadline. Beran, who had been called up to Abilene (TX), was replaced by Keith Baker, down from Danville (IL) of the Three-I circuit. Clark Taylor was signed to plug the holes left by the release of outfielders Nicholas Kucher and George Nichols. By June 1, Bartley had a line up.

Art Billings became the regular catcher with Hill relieving and Jack Blaylock, who would become the parent Dodgers' bull pen catcher in 1948, seeing late season action. Twenty-six year old rookie Bill Boudreau played all the games at first base. Larry Tarbell held down second until released on July 27

Acknowledged as one of the top baseball teachers, Boyd Bartley guided the Ponca City Dodgers during its years in the K-O-M with the exception of 1951 when serving in the Army. (Pc-4)

1947 Ponca City Dodgers. Top row, L-R: Gale Wadem George Fisher, Tony Brzezowski, Herb McCoy, Mel Waters, Biff jones, Bill Hodges, Bill Boudreau, Dale Hendricks, Jim Baxes. Front row, L-R: Ted Parkinson (president), Phils Adams, Roland Wiblemo, Art Billings, Boyd Bartley (manager), Howie Fisher, Jack Blaylock, Keith Baker, Owen Martinez (business manager). (Pc-5)

and replaced by Bill Hodges. Howard Fisher guarded the hot corner in nearly every game. Jim Baxes, a future Major Leaguer, was regular at shortstop until he was called up to Santa Barbara in the California League. Bartley had to finish the season at that position. Like many clubs in the lower classifications, there was a surfeit of outfielders. Dale Hendricks appeared in 117 games. Future Chicago Cub Gale Wade was signed as a pitcher but was transitioned to the outfield at Ponca City. Likewise, Ken Baker spent only ten of his sixty-seven games as a pitcher; the rest were in the outfield. James Cahill, who came down from Kingston (NY) saw action in eighty-six games while late signee Taylor played in fifty before he was released on August 24.

Ten pitchers saw action in forty-five or more innings. The other pitchers had a combined record of nine wins and nine losses. A number more rotated through on brief assignments including Walter Harris, a member of the Otoe tribe with some pre-War Texas League experience, who would

Dimitrios Speros "Jim" Baxes played his rookie season for Boyd Bartley. He divided 1959 between the Los Angeles Dodgers and Cleveland Indians. He played from 1948 through 1961 at the AAA level batting a career .325 average. (Pc-7)

fill in when the Dodgers were short-handed. Like the position players, the pitchers predominantly were rookies with an average age of just nineteen. Melvin Waters appeared in the most games (33) and threw the most innings (195) compiling a 14-8 record. Gale Wade at 10-9 was not far behind with 181 innings in twenty-eight games. Wade would soon be out of pitching, making his way to Wrigley Field as an outfielder. Tony Brzezowski was the other pitcher with over one hundred innings (148) winning fourteen of twenty-one decisions with a team best 3.53 ERA. Bob Hughes was 1-2 in six appearances before moving on to Abilene. Steve Jordan threw eighty-nine innings posting a team high 6.27 ERA and a 6-4 record. Don Hall was 3-7 in eighty-eight innings while George Fisher was 5-6 in eighty-three.

By May 27, the Dodgers were playing just over .500 ball with a 11-10 record. They battled to a rare 6-6 tie on May 23. Rain ended the ten inning spectacle as Bartlesville's Ralph Liedendorfer fanned seventeen Dodgers while walking fourteen. Ponca City embarrassed the Yankees' prospects at Independence on May 26. Trailing by five runs, the Dodgers got seventeen hits and coaxed twenty-one walks from the home team's exhausted mound staff in the final four and one-third innings for the win. For the mid-season All Star game, only Tony

Ponca City's bus. (Pc-6)

Brzezowski appeared to represent Ponca City at the contest in Miami. By late August the Dodgers had settled into sixth place where they would finish. They did have strength left, however. In a wild fifth inning on August 22, the Dodgers exploded for eleven runs on eleven hits capped by Clark Taylor's two-run round tripper to vanquish Iola 13-7.

The final season tally was sixty-one wins against sixty-two losses. The club was third in batting with a respectable .271 including a K-O-M best 960 hits. There was no post-season play. The new team in town attracted 55,554 paying fans, better than 900 per outing. Shortstop Jim Baxes, who batted .343 and hit for a titanic .636 slugging percentage before being promoted, was the only 1947 Ponca City representative on the post-season All Star squad.

1948

The 1948 Dodgers were a slightly younger team than 1947, averaging just under twenty-one years. Outfielder Dale Hendricks, Joe Beran, now an outfielder, pitcher Don Hall, and converted pitcher Gene Wade were back from 1947. All of the limited service players were sophomores. The fastest man in the Dodgers' minor league camp, James Carney, an outfielder, was soon cut after fourteen games and joined independent Chickasha of the Sooner State League, following team mate pitcher Claude Wurman who was cut on May 20. Other first month casualties were outfielder John Wilson, first baseman John Knott and pitcher Cecil Gregory. They made room for latecomers outfielder Al Endriss, who later played pro football in the NFL and Canadian League, pitcher Dick McCoy, and outfielder Ewing Turner. As always the Dodgers shuffled players. Beran moved up to Abilene, first baseman Bill DeGeer and shortstop Don Fleisch went to Cairo (IL), Knott was reas-

1948 program. (Pc-8)

PONCA CITY
Dodgers
EVERYTHING HAPPENS AT
CONOCO PARK

Official 1948 Souvenir

Larned, Kansas native Joe Beran broke in with Miami in 1946 and divided 1947 and 1948 between Ponca City and Abilene. Brooklyn sold him to Pittsburgh in 1950. He finished his professional career with Hutchinson in the Western Association in 1953 and 1954. (Pc-9)

Gene Castiglione spent his first two seasons at Ponca City. He moved up to Class A in 1950 before a tour in the Army. He remained a Brooklyn property the rest of his career, retiring in 1954. (Pc-10)

signed to Cambridge (MD), pitcher Bill Olsson was on the bus to Pulaski (KY), and pitcher Bill Morris returned to the site of spring training, Thomasville (NC). Utility player Don Copps was signed and given a look-see on June 12 but didn't make the squad;

Dick Spady split his signing bonus with his hometown American Legion team. (Pc-11)

he wound up with independent Del Rio. Catcher Tom Kubat received his walking papers June 24 after losing the contest for the catching position.

Bartley gave a lot of playing time to his regulars. After mid-June the lineup had Leon Irwin behind the plate, Ray Schershligt, who had beaten out Tulsan DeGeer and Knott, at first, Gene Castiglione at second, Bill Delich at third, Al Muirhead at shortstop, and Beran, Hendricks and Turner in the outfield. Bartley substituted at second and shortstop when needed. In the outfield, Ponca City native Bob Casey, and Gene Wade in addition to those position players cut all saw playing time.

Pitching carried the 1948 Dodgers to the regular season championship. Seven accounted for all the decisions. With the exception of William Hall,

with eighty-three innings, all of Ponca City's hurlers had over 138 innings. All but Ed Grove had ERAs under 3.00. Setting a K-O-M record, Canadian Joe Tufteland won eighteen and lost only two for a .900 percentage in 185 innings of twenty-seven games with a team best 2.29 ERA. The plough horse was 1947 alumnus Don Hall who threw 215 innings in the most appearances, thirty-one, with a 2.39 ERA and 14-8 record. Gene Rogers was 12-9 in 171 innings of thirty games with a 2.68 ERA. Dick McCoy had 142 innings in twenty-two games posting a 9-7 record and 2.98 ERA. Ed Grove had the highest ERA, a respectable 3.45, in 141 innings for a 11-7 record. The youngest player straight from American Legion ball was Nebraskan Dick Spady who won eight of twelve decisions in twenty-three games with a 2.80 ERA. William Hall appeared mainly in relief and, while posting a 2.82 ERA, had the only losing percentage on the staff with a 6-7 record.

On the strength of Muirhead's ninth inning RBI, the Dodgers won their season opener 10-9 at Bartlesville. They never fell out of first. After giving half his signing bonus to American Legion ball in his home town, on May 19 Dick Spady won his professional debut shutting down Independence 8-1 on five hits. From the bench, Bartley earned his first suspension of the season and a $10 fine on May

1948 Ponca City Dodgers. Top row, L-R: Bob Casey, Dick Spady, Gene Rogers, Dale Copps, Ray Scherschligt, Joe Beran, Don Hall, Dick McCoy, Joe Stanek, Dale Hendricks. Front row, L-R: Ted Parkinson (president), Ewing Turner, Gene Castigleine, Alex Muirhead, Boyd Bartley (manager), Ed Grove, Leon Irwin, John Hall, Bill Delich, Owen Martinez (business manager). (Pc-12)

14 after arguing too violently with the umpire over whether a ball was fair or foul. He watched games through May 17 from the stands. Injuring his wrist in the opening series, manager Bartley returned to shortstop on May 22 wearing a cast and banging out a double and a pair of singles to lead his team to a 5-2 win at Carthage. Lou Ott's first inning single was the only hit Don Hall gave up on June 9 as he retired twenty-five consecutive batters for a 5-1 win over Carthage. By the third week of June, Ponca City filled its own hospital ward. Bartley had a broken rib, Wade a cracked shoulder bone, Scherschligt an infected toe, Tufteland a broken jaw, and DeGreer a pulled shoulder. The injuries did not prevent the Dodgers from whipping the All Stars on July 9 before 4,000 Dodgers fans, the largest crowd ever there until 1952. The Dodgers came from behind three times on home runs by Turner, Hendricks, and Beran and erased a four-run deficit in the ninth before Gene Castiglione's tenth inning single drove in Muirhead for the 12-11 win. Spady threw a fourteen inning complete game on August 30 including ten hitless innings after giving up a first inning single. Muirhead capped the season by putting the last pitch of the season over the fence. He prevailed over Pittsburg 2-1. With a 79-47 season behind them, the Dodgers ran out of steam in the playoffs losing to the Browns' fourth place farmhands from Pittsburg in five games. It had been a very successful season. The 78,305 paying fans that followed their Dodgers set a city and K-O-M record. The season earned Bartley a reprise for 1949. Branch Rickey was pleased.

1949

Brooklyn consolidated all its system's spring exercises at a new Dodgertown in Vero Beach, Florida. Bartley along with the minor league development staff sorted and assigned. He welcomed back six from his 1948 champions: first sacker Bill DeGeer, third baseman James Carney, bonus baby Gene Castiglione, and pitchers Ed Grove, Dick McCoy and Gene Rogers. The 1949 edition was another young team with an average age of twenty years and eight months. The pitchers were a kiddy corps averaging nineteen. The annual early bloodletting was done by early June. Sophomore Bill DeGeer didn't make the club after a brief 1948 with Ponca City and an extended stay with Cairo (IL). Catcher Burl Atchley was signed May 24 but quit the game a week later. Pitchers Richard Hames, David Williams, and Richard Tretter each received a release as did outfielders Charles Damberti, Jack Nixon, and Dan Chepkaukas. Pitcher Paul Oakes was being given a second chance when transferred from the Dodger's Sheboygan (WI) farm but he failed. They made room for post-spring signees catcher Omer Ehlers, Stan Gwinn, a recent Oklahoma A&M graduate, pitchers Connie Swensson and Ernie Nichols, hurler Charles Lamberti who joined the club on June 24, and later in the season, John Kustich sent down from Trois-Rivieres to recover from fright of a pitched ball after getting beaned three times in Canada (he didn't). Bob Beran of Larned (KS) made a brief stop with the Dodgers at season end. He was the third Beran along with Joe and Gene to appear in the K-O-M. Regular shortstop Bill Hodges and outfielder Nick Zender were called up to the Class C level in July and early August forcing Bartley to the playing field and shuffling his line up more often than a manager likes.

The pitching was not as keen as the Dodgers enjoyed in 1948. Connie Swensson who arrived on June 5 led the team and league in pitching percentage with a 12-3, .800 won-loss performance. His ERA of 1.69 in 149 innings of twenty-one games put him in the K-O-M record book. He also blanked opponents four times. All the other hurlers had ERAs above 3.30. Another who missed spring drills was Ernie

Conrad Swensson had a 28-6 record for Ponca City in 1949 and 1950. In his rookie season, he set the K-O-M mark with a 1.69 ERA. (Pc-11)

Nichols who arrived just after the season began. He threw in thirty-one games in 174 innings compiling a 14-9 performance with a 4.29 ERA. Ed Grove threw more innings that in 1948 but had a slightly higher ERA, 3.87, as he took twelve of twenty-two decisions. Dick McCoy failed to match his 1948 performance in 150 innings of twenty-eight games finishing with eleven wins against nine losses with a 4.32 ERA, well above the prior year's 2.98. Gene Rogers saw much less action in 1949. He had decisions in seven of his eight starts finishing with a comparatively low 3.71 ERA and a 5-2 tally. Charles Lamberti didn't join Ponca City until the mid-point of the season and then performed as a reliever. He posted the only losing percentage winning but two of six decisions in twenty appearances. Louis Hula, not from Hawaii, was another limited performer. In his only professional season, Hula

Loren Doll held down first base in 1949 and 1950. He moved up to the Cotton States League in 1951. After the Army, he finished with Hutchinson in 1953. (Pc-14)

finished in relief with a record of three wins and two defeats with a 4.41 ERA. Rookie Joe Stanek make thirteen appearances fielding flawlessly but without a decision or enough innings to earn a statistical place. He would eventually reach the top of the Brooklyn system at Montreal and St. Paul.

The position players were the K-O-M's best glove men with a .950 fielding percentage. Doll, Castiglione, and Carney teamed up for a triple play. Keeter was behind the plate twice as much as Omer Ehlers but the latter was the best defensive catcher in the league. Loren Doll, whose memory of his time at Ponca City was long "bus ride, hot hotel rooms and bad food," had won a place on the club through a tryout camp; he played all the games at first base. Castigione retired Bill DeGeer and owned second base. James Carney beat out Walter Dunsford for third base and then was benched when Ted Dean was sent west after spending most of the season at Valdosta (GA). Until promoted, Bill Hodges was the regular at shortstop. Manager Bartley and Bob Bonebrake, pulled from the outfield, filled in the rest of the season. Bonebrake was the regular in the outfield. Gwinn, Zender, until promoted, and Hopkins with help from Mike Witwicki and early casualty light-hitting Jack Nixon who both had twenty-eight games, filled in the outfield

After spring training, the Dodgers returned to post five wins against a single loss as the first week of play ended. The third was their lucky inning. Against Bartlesville on   May 6 the Dodgers exploded for eleven runs en route to a football score 16-14 win. Three days later, a ten-run third produced a 14-4 triumph over Independence. After dropping a Memorial Day twinbill at Independence, Ponca City found itself in the second division for the first time since May, 1948. When Tulsan Don Keeter was behind the plate for Earl Nichols, he presaged Kevin Coster's psychological stunt in the movie *Bull Durham*. During warm up Nicholds would exercise

1949 Ponca City Dodgers. Top row, L-R: Dick Tretter, Dave Williams, Dick McCoy, Ernie Nichols, Jack Nixon, Richard Loeser, Jack Lewis (business manager). Middle row, L-R: Bob Beran, Wally Dunford, Richard Hames, Bob Bonebrake, Don Keeter, Gene Castiglione, Boyd Bartley (manager). Front row, L-R: John Mamerow, Louis Hula, Loren Doll, Nick Zender, Jim Carney, Ed Grove. (Pc-15)

fine control but the first pitch of the game invariably was a fast ball directly at the batters head but several feet over. Keeter would retrieve the ball and empathize with the hitter and remark that Nichols was really wild that evening. As Nichols couldn't pitch every game, Keeter developed a distracting and disgusting technique for batters who dug in too firmly: he would spew a stream of tobacco juice on to the hitter's shoe. The man at the plate would naturally protest to the umpire. That was the exact disruption in concentration the act was designed to elicit.

Bartley learned not to slug an umpire when K-O-M president E. L. Dale was in the stands. Umpire Harry Duncan was felled at Miami on July 24. Dale immediately fined Bartley $100 and barred him from the field for fourteen days. Duncan apparently thought he was impervious to challenge after that and developed a reputation for taunting not only players but fans, often challenging them to fight him. This was too obnoxious for even the K-O-M and Dale fired him on August 22.

The Dodgers pulled themselves out of the second division by closing day to find the club one game ahead of Chanute—a rare fifth place team with a winning record—and five and one-half games behind Mickey Mantle's Independence Yankees. Surrogates for the World Series participants that year, the first round of the K-O-M playoffs had the Yankees besting the Dodgers.

Batting a team average of .240 placed them in a tie for fifth with Carthage. They were speedsters, leading the K-O-M with 200 base swipes. Castiglione and Swensson were named All Stars. Carney in spite of a .216 batting average managed a .421 on base percentage. There were no long ball hitters. Stan Gwinn's seven home runs topped the team. While there was a hot batting race, none of the Dodgers were in it. For the first time, no one batted .300. The fans came but not in 1949's record numbers. Through the turnstiles passed 62,082, best in the K-O-M. Again, the players scattered in anticipation of the second half of the twentieth century.

1950

The ride to Ponca City from Vero Beach could have been a reunion of the 1949 club. Bob Bonebrake, Loren Doll, Don Keeter, Charles Lamberti, Joe Stanek, Connie Swensson, Canadian Mike Witwicki, and Norm Furgal, who was soon re-assigned to Sheboygan (WI), were on the roster. Others who made the club were soon released and found their way to independent teams in the Sooner State League. After eighteen games, Roland Alexander found a job at Duncan. Shortstop John Franchi and pitcher Billy Wayne Hollis joined the Pauls Valley Raiders. Pitchers Charles Key and Mike Wallin augmented the Ardmore Indians'

Willie Davis had a private contest with Harry Crandall as to who could strike out the most. Davis won with 169. He began 1951 at Ponca City before being promoted to Class C. He reached the top of the Dodger's farm system with St. Paul in 1955. After beginning 1956 with Dodgers' club at Pueblo, he was traded to the Braves' affiliate at Topeka. He retired after that season. (Pc-16)

moundsmen. Infielder Dwain Mintz struck out in his first four trips to the plate and was given a full release. Shortstop Lloyd Moore batting .171 lost his place. Catcher Clyde Girrens lost out to Keeter and returned to the semi-pro ranks.

Some sophomores kept their old positions and rookies filled others. Keeter was still the regular catcher after Rafel Fernandez was transferred to the Dodgers club at Hazard (KY). Doll once again owned first base. Newcomer Don Hunter held down second base also giving third a whirl. Don Blackman, acquired from Paris (IL), filled in at second. Slugging rookie Willie Davis was the regular at third but, with a weak glove (.877 fielding) was given a shot at shortstop appearing in twenty games (with a .835 fielding average). Bartley had a strong

shortstop in Jasper Spears but an injury made him scramble again moving Bonebrake from the outfield; his glove there was over .100 worse than Spears'. The outfield was stable with Gwinn, Robert Henne, and Harry Crandall, sent down from Pueblo, starting most games. Witwicki and Bonebrake roamed the big pasture from time to time in about one-third of the games.

The pitchers all had at least one season of experience with the exception of rookie Joe Stanka of Hammon (OK) who joined the team late after his employer, Otto Utt of the Sooner State League Duncan Uttman, moved the franchise to Shawnee. In forty-three games, Lamberti became the fireman with a 2.29 ERA and eleven wins against six losses. Swensson again was the workhorse compiling a 16-3 record in 181 innings of twenty-four games with a respectable but not record-making 3.58 ERA. Stanek came into his own hurling twenty-five games in 138 innings with an 11-2 showing and 3.39 ERA. Nichols had another good year posting a 12-6 record in 148 innings of twenty-one games with a low 2.86 ERA. Rookie Mike Werbach showed he was ready with a 2.58 ERA in 122 innings of twenty-seven games for a 8-7 record. Rookie Ernest Jordan earned a promotion to the Dodgers' Class C desert camp at Bisbee-Douglas (AZ) with his 3.13 ERA and 8-5 record in sixteen stars. Stanka threw in only five games with a 1-3 record and 3.54 ERA. This was a big improvement over his 1-8 Duncan debut with a 8.71 ERA.

1950 Ponca City Dodgers. Top row, L-R: Jack Lewis (business manager), Boyd Bartley (manager), Willie Davis, Don Brate, Don Hunter, Chuck Lamberti, Stan Gwinn, Bob Bonebrake, Harry Crandall, Don Keeter, Ted Parkinson (president). Front row, L-R: Ernie Nichols, Bob Henne, Mike Witwicki, Ernie Jordan, Joe Stanek, Mike Werbach, Loren Doll, Connie Swensson. (Pc-17)

Brooklyn saw potential and they were prophetic. Stanka was the only member of the 1950 Ponca City Dodgers to reach the Major Leagues.

The Dodgers broke Bartlesville ace Dave Elliott's string of thirty-four scoreless innings on May 24 in the eighth inning with the help of six errors but still dropped the contest 11-6. After thirty games, Hunter was hitting .326 and Gwinn .316 while Swensson and Brake were undefeated. Two weeks later Ponca City was trailing Pittsburg, Chanute, and Bartlesville in fourth place with a 26-14 record. Harry Crandall learned on August 5 that while hitting one of the Conoco signs above the outfield fence was good for $100, sailing one over the sign drew an award of just $5.00. By August 10, the Dodgers had taken over first and remained there through the September 4 finale for an 80-42 season. At-

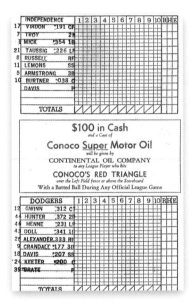

1950 scorecard advertising $100 prize for hitting Conoco sign. (Pc-18)

tendance was up slightly to 63,313, another league best. In the playoffs Pittsburg took the Dodgers the distance before falling in five games. In the finals against Bartlesville, Ponca City had the battery of Nichols and Keeter in what would be the last game of the series at Ponca City. The home club ran out of balls so had to finish the games with batting practice balls. The Dodgers prevailed to capture their first, and as it turned out only, pennant.

As a team the Dodgers led in average (.258), hits (1,080), and stolen bases (186) as well as batters striking out (957) and stranded runners (1,103).

There were several individual league leaders. Gwinn's 320 at-bats and fifty-three stolen bases were tops. Hunter and Doll tied for the most hits with 152 each, Davis led with 21 home runs. On the mound Stanek's .846 was the best winning percentage. With Davis at third base, he combined with Hunter and Doll for a triple play. Crandall and Davis had a private contest going for who could strike out the most. Crandall lost with 149. Davis led the league with 169.

The Korean War began on June 24, 1950. Conscription kicked in and by 1951 many minor league players found themselves in olive drab. One of those was Boyd Bartley who was called to the colors although he spent his service this time running the baseball program at nearby Ft. Chaffee, Arkansas.

A product of Oklahoma A&M, Stan Gwinn spent 1949 and 1950 with Ponca City. After moving up to Class A Pueblo in 1951, he retired from the game. (Pc-19)

1951

The big news in Brooklyn was that the front office battle between Walter O'Malley, who came to control the stock of the Dodgers as estate attorney, and one-quarter owner Branch Rickey. O'Malley won but had to pay Rickey $1,000,000 for his interest. Rickey quickly landed the same job for the hapless Pittsburgh Pirates and became the head of the organization that owned the Bartlesville franchise. Buzzy Bavasi was the new Dodgers general manager. As the season began, with a few exceptions all the players on Ponca City's 1947-1950 rosters

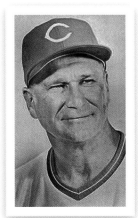

George Sherger led the Dodgers in 1951. He is pictured here as part of Cincinnati's Big Red Machine. (Pc-20)

Steve Cavlovic played both of his professional seasons with Ponca City. (Pc-21)

Joe Stanka had been optioned to Duncan in 1950. He spent the 1951 season in Ponca City then began his rise up the baseball ladder that reached to Comisky Park in 1959 and then six seasons in Japan. (Pc-22)

were *up* to a higher classification, *out* of baseball, or *in* the military.

With Boyd Bartley in the Army, the Dodgers turned to an experienced minor league manager from their system, George Scherger. He began as a pre-War Brooklyn player in Classes D and C and on return from the military from 1947 after was a player-manager in those classes at Thomasville (NC), Orlean (NY), and Trois-Rivieres (CAN). He continued to scout and manage as late as 1988. His proudest times were as a coach for Sparky Anderson's Big Red Machine at Cincinnati between 1970 and 1978.

Most of the riders on the bus trip back from Vero Beach had never laid eyes on Ponca City. The only returning Dodgers were regular outfielder Robert Henne who quickly lost his job and was released after sixteen games and three 1950 latecomers, Steve Cavlovic who had been seen in ten games in 1950 and was gone from the 1951 squad after thirty-one, Gene Hines who threw in a dozen games in 1951 and Joe Stanka who had escaped from the Sooner State League in late August. Roland Alexander who had been sent to Duncan for most of 1950, and Don Blackman who had come late in 1950 from Paris (IL) also had seen limited action in 1950. Alexander and Blackman were quickly cut. All the other players were fresh faces and all but four were under age twenty-one.

The manager and Brooklyn's minor league development office made a number of other cuts during the

first month of the season that began on May 3. Eight pitchers felt the ax: Frank Alessandro, Dick Collins, George Foreman, John Graves, Mike Krmpotic, Leonard Tapia, Frank Herring, trying a comeback after five seasons away, and Bernard Winslow who then signed with independent Pauls Valley in the Sooner State League. Outfielders William Stone and catcher Brad Smith also got pink slips.

Scherger rotated catchers with Gerald Boldt and Jack Wolfe being the regulars and George Singer dividing his time behind the plate and in the outfield. Stanley Santo played every game at first base; he was drafted into the Marines shortly after the season ended. Scherger made himself the regular at second base with Wiley filling in ten times. Morris "Mo" Mack was the regular at the hot corner. Shortstop was also a rotating position after Bobby Dolan left for the Army on July 5. Joe Gravino, and Wiley shared duties the rest of the season. In the outfield, Jack Denison and Canadian rookie Don Stewart each appeared in over one hundred contests. Early on Henne and Cavlovic joined them. Herman Humble saw limited action before he departed the club in mid-July for Bisbee-Douglas in Class C. Hal Zimmer, younger brother of the late Don Zimmer, spent his time at Ponca City in the outfield until re-assigned to the Hazard (KY) farm club. After twenty-six games at Brooklyn's Hornell (NY) Class D operation, Ralph Cascella was transferred to Ponca City to get more playing time in the outfield.

Joe Stanka led the pitching staff appearing in the most games (33), throwing the most innings (196), posting the lowest ERA (2.53), and tying Eldon DeRoin and Diedrich Wiegand with sixteen wins. Stanka and DeRoin had identical records (16-5 .762). Eldon DeRoin, a product of the Chilocco Indian School near Ponca City, had an outstanding rookie season pitching 154 innings in twenty-three games with a 2.92 ERA and yielding only forty walks all season, the club best. Wiegand threw 161

innings in thirty-one games posting the best winning percentage (.800 from a 16-4 record) but was wild with 121 free passes and a 4.14 ERA. Cliff Ohr was the fourth in the rotation winning eleven of eighteen decisions in twenty-seven games in which he was of record in 166 innings; his ERA was a low 3.14. Gene Hines was 3-2 in twelve outings but wild. Latecomer Don Smith was 0-4 in nine starts and earned his walking papers. Wichtendahl had no decisions in his six appearances for the Dodgers; he would be 8-2 for Miami. Rookie Lloyd Brazada was 8-5 with a 3.66 ERA that would assure him an invitation back in 1952. Con Causy at 4-2 in fewer than forty-five innings was not so lucky. He would be out of baseball before the season was over.

Following an opening day loss to Bartlesville, the Dodgers cranked out eighteen consecutive wins before falling to the Pirates at Bartlesville on May 24. By then the Dodgers were in first place and would there remain the rest of the season. The season ended with a Labor Day double header against Carthage. What gave excitement to the twin bill was Jack Denison's quest for the batting title for 1951 and perhaps becoming the all-time K-O-M record holder. He needed to get at least three hits to finish ahead of Miami's Jim Eldridge who had finished at .364. If he could finish at .365 he would eclipse

Miami's Loren Packard's .3642 record set in 1947. Denison got a pair of singles in the first game as Carthage pulled a 4-2 upset. In the nightcap, the Dodgers were again in the hole as Weigand relieved Smith in the ninth. He held the line. Denison had been hitless. In his last plate appearance, he ran out a slow grounder. That lifted his average to .3646 giving him the 1951 batting crown as well as the league record by .0004. The game ended with Don Stewart's walk-off single that drove in the winning runs for the Dodgers. Ponca City finished with a final record of eighty-five wins versus just thirty-nine losses, a .685 percentage. A day later, the Dodgers squared off again against Carthage in the first round of the playoff. The series went the five-game distance but when the dust settled the Cubs' farm hands were on top, advancing to the finals where they would win in a sweep of Miami.

While the team's batting average, .258, was second behind Bartlesville's .261, the Dodgers led the K-O-M in most categories: at-bats (4,139), hits

Jack Denison set the K-O-M record for batting average with .365. He spent his professional career in the Dodgers' organization. He retired after a 1955 season at Bakersfield. (Pc-23)

1951 Ponca City Dodgers. Top row, L-R: Phil Vickery (business manager), Eldon DeRoin, Jack Wolfe, Joe Stanka, Cliff Ohr, Dedrich Weigand, George Sherger, Ted Parkinson (president). Middle row, L-R: Ralph Cascella, Don Smith, Lloyd Brazda, Don Stewart, Stan Santo, Jack Denison. Front row, L-R: George Singer, Bob Dolan, Morris Mack, Wayne Wiley. (Pc-24)

(1,067), runs (772), total bases (1,485), doubles (190), stolen bases (222), RBIs (633), and stranded runners (1,042). They were the best fielding team with a collective .953 percentage. They also turned a K-O-M best 120 double plays. Individually, Denison was the story. In addition to posting the highest average, he led in hits, runs, RBIs, and On Base Percentage (.471). Not surprisingly, the Dodgers dominated the All Star team. Santo, Morris, Denison, Stanka , and Dolan –despite playing only a half season– were named to the elite. With television now beaming in from Wichita, the fans were finding their excitement at home. Attendance plummeted to 44,960.

1952

With the collapse of the Carthage franchise, the K-O-M shrank to six teams. There was no longer an "M" in K-O-M. Oklahoma boasted four of the six K-O-M teams as 1952 began: Ponca City, Blackwell, Bartlesville, and Miami. That would shrink to three on July 7 when the Bartlesville franchise set up shop in Pittsburg (KS).

Captain Boyd Bartley had been released from active duty and reported to Vero Beach where he was given charge of the 1952 edition of the Ponca City Dodgers. He wanted to take another look at some players who were around in 1951 but whom he hadn't seen. Pitchers Charles Key, Lloyd Brazda, and Bernard Winslow were quickly dismissed. Don Stewart and Lyle Wiley made the squad. Morris Mack began the season at Class B Lancaster (PA) but couldn't cope with the pitching. He was sent down to play regularly until Bartley fired him in early August. Pitcher Gene Hines was called up to Great Falls (MT) early on. With Clyde Girrens handling the plate well, 1950 and 1951 Dodger Keeter released to Blackwell after eighteen games. Early cuts involved pitchers. Harold Burton, and Ken

Reigel, joined Key, Brazda, and Winslow among the unemployed before the end of the first month. Infielders Charles Holliday and Joe Parisi also felt the ax. After that a line up began to gel.

Keeter began the seasons as catcher but it was apparent soon that with Girrens competing, he had to go. Girrens won the contest. When Girrens was drafted, Russell Greenbush took over until he was drafted in mid-August. John Mc-Dermott was brought in to fill the gap. Al Jarvis was the first baseman from day one. Mack and Wiley divided duties at second and third. Larry Smith and Bartley filled in for Wiley when he was on the disabled list. Tom Sleeper was sent down from Sheboygan (WI) to assume Mack's duties after his suspension. Elkins was given a shot at shortstop and third base. Ray Mladovich had been sent down from Class B Newport News for playing time. The Dodger brass had done the same thing with Robert Carlson re-assigning him from Class D Union City of the Kitty League. Between them they covered shortstop. The outfield was steady. Ron Stuart and Don Stewart—the *idem sonans* caused no small amount of confusion—joined Wayne Parsons as the regular trio. Les Machen was given some time before receiving his pink slip and finding work with Sherman-Denison in the Sooner State League.

As always, Bartley worked his pitchers hard. He carried five starters and a reliever. Canadian Ralph Vold worked 227 innings in thirty-seven games compiling a 12-9 record and 3.53 ERA. Mike Ruan worked more innings, 233, in fewer games allow-

1950 rookie Clyde Girrens took 1950 and 1951 Dodger Don Keeter's catching job in 1952. Keeter joined newcomer Blackwell. Girrens remained in the Brooklyn system through 1955. He had a brief comeback with Hawaii in 1964. (Pc-25)

Billy Cornsilk of Stilwell, Oklahoma was called the "Cherokee Kid." He started the 1952 All Star game. After a season in Class C, Cornsilk joined the Army where he made a career. (Pc-26)

ing 2.94 earned runs per nine resulting in a 15-13 tally. Billy Cornsilk had the lowest ERA, 2.24, for fifteen wins in twenty-five decisions in 200 innings of twenty-eight games. Tony DeVelis was on his way to a strong year until a cracked rib and sore arm ended his season on August 5. His numbers included a no-hitter and two one-hitters winning seven of twelve decisions in thirteen starts with a 3.94 ERA. Rookie James Peterson, who would be with Bartley at Shawnee in 1953, split sixteen decisions with 144 innings in twenty-nine appearances and a 3.88 ERA. Syl Zacher was the fireman in twenty-three games with a 3.00 ERA and 6-2 result.

By May 15, the Dodgers were in their accustomed first place with a 12-4 record. Ronald "Duke" Stuart began the season with a ten-game hitting streak that ended when Independence two-hit the Dodgers on May 9. Stuart began a new streak the next evening with a single and home run and on May 12 at Miami knocked a single and pair of triples to raise his RBI total to twenty-two in fourteen games. That night behind seventeen hits Mike Ryan got his fourth win with no defeats 10-5. On May 14, the Dodgers played nearly four hours before dropping a twelve-inning affair to Bartlesville 9-8. Mack was the base thief-in-chief as he swiped three at Bartlesville on May 28 and the next night swiped two against Blackwell raising his season to total to nine and his   K-O-M record from 1951 to eighty in eighty-two attempts. A second inning single by Tom Guinn cheated rookie phenom Tony DeVelis of a no-hitter at Iola on June 1 and his throwing

error prevented a shutout. Clyde Girrens' K-O-M record twenty-two game hitting streak came to an end on June 21 at Blackwell as he walked once and went hitless in four at bats. Tom Paddock stole an extra base hit from him by making a catch with his back to the wall. The same Tom Guinn of Iola couldn't save Iola from DeVelis again as he no-hit the Indians on June 16 for a 8-0 shutout win. A fast ball broke Lyle Wiley's wrist on June 22. Bartlesville catcher Chico Bernal single-handedly dismantled the Dodger on June 26 with a pair of home runs. At mid-season, the Dodgers remained in first place at 38-24 and prepared to host another All Star game. The Stars whipped the Dodgers 12-4 on July 10 before 2,203.

DeVelis tossed another one-hitter the night before the All Star game on July 9 against Independence with Jim Murray's second inning single spoiling the outing. It was a Phyrric victory as DeVelis broke a rib. That injury coupled with Girrens reporting for military duty on July 15 deprived the Dodgers of their best battery. Billy 'the Cherokee Kid' Cornstalk from Stillwell notched his eleventh win on July 19 against Iola as Al Jarvis banged out a pair of doubles and singles plus a home run for a 12-5 victory. The Dodgers smacked Blackwell 8-2 on July 23 fueled by Ray Mladovic's first inning grand slam. Iola was coming on strong and on July 31 moved into a tie with the Dodgers for first place. The Dodgers' brass sent DeVelis home on August 5 to recuperate removing any hope for him helping Ponca City in 1952. Iola took over first place on August 7 after sweeping a three-game series at Ponca City.

The Ponca City free spirit was Morris "Mo" Mack. He failed to show up for the All Star game costing him $25, a suspension, and manager Bartley's ire. He returned and was batting .328. Fed up, notwithstanding Morris' bat Bartley suspended him for the remainder of the season for failing to hustle.

"Mo" Mack had his own baseball card produced. Manager Bartley suspended him for the balance of the 1952 season after Mack skipped the All Star game. Play-by-play man Bill Platt was temporarily pressed into service at the hot corner until a replacement could be sent from the Dodgers' minor league camp. (Pc-27)

MORRIS MACK

Compliments of
Midwest Creamery

The Dodgers' radio play-by-play man, Bill Platt, was enlisted to fill Mack's position until Tom Sleeper could be brought in from Sheboygan to replace the errant Mack. The wheels had fallen off. Miami overtook the Dodgers for second place and finished the season .0007 percentage points ahead.

The playoff format was changed for 1952. The first and third place and second and fourth place clubs would face off in a sudden death, single game first round with the winners going to a best of three final. Ponca City eliminated nemesis Iola in the first round. Miami then swept the final series for a pennant that would never be awarded.

The Dodgers lead the K-O-M with 4,373 at-bats, 790 runs, 1,133 hits, and 672 RBIs although finishing second at .250 in team batting. Jarvis, Don Stewart, and Zacher were named to the last K-O-M All Star squad. The fans were back. Counting a special promotion on July 31 when 7,125 fans, who each received a bag with $2.00 worth of swag, set the all-time Class D single game attendance record—the fire marshal's comments have not been preserved—the last edition of the Dodgers attracted 55,762, an increase of over 10,000 from 1951.

The K-O-M failed in February, 1953. Brooklyn, which owned the little Dodgers, moved its Class

D operation south to Shawnee in the Sooner State League. Boyd Barley would again start a ball club in Oklahoma accompanied by pitcher Jim Peterson and infielder Tom Sleeper from his 1952 Dodgers.

The lights went out at Conoco Park after Ted Parkinson announced that Ponca City would sit out 1953 in hope of reviving the K-O-M for 1954. That attempt was stillborn. If baseball was to return to Ponca City, it would be either through the Western Association or Sooner State League. As events proved, it would be through both.

1954

Within a fortnight after the effort to resurrect the K-O-M was abandoned, the Western Association directors extended an invitation to join the old circuit as it was expanding to eight members. Rumors of the leagues demise were refuted. In January, Blackwell and Iola, replacing Ft. Smith, were welcomes as the new franchises. The Ponca City Baseball Association that had run the K-O-M club had remained intact. Ted Parkinson again was elected president with Harry Cragin first vice-president, L. W. Prunty second vice-president, and C. D. Hull secretary-treasurer. Bill Platt, former Oklahoma A&M ball player and the sports director of a local radio station, was named business manager for the club. At the same meeting, Ed Carnett, a Ponca City prep phenom who played with the Cubs, White Sox and Indians and had managed in the West Texas-New Mexico League was hired to pitch for and lead the team on the field. When a working agreement with Brooklyn failed to materialize, the management decided to go the first season back in baseball as an independent. Through a contest, the name "Jets" was selected. Work was begun restoring Conoco Park to playing condition. All the Ponca City Jets needed were players.

The year 1954 was effectively the last for independent minor league teams. The Majors were

Don Keeter had caught for Ponca City in 1950 and 1951 and for Blackwell in 1952. He joined Ed Carnett's Jets for 1954. (Pc-28)

abandoning the "catch and release" philosophy that had governed player acquisition in the past. Rather than feed from local teams that scouted, grew, sent back the prospects that didn't pan out and sell upstream those with potential, the Big Leagues were shrinking their farm systems and staffing them with players who, as small as the odds were, had the raw ability to become members of Major League rosters. For 1954, only Ponca City and Art Willingham's Seminole club in the Sooner State League were true independents. Blackwell began the campaign as an independent but, saved from bankruptcy by David Morgan, secured a full working agreement with the Chicago Cubs in late June. After 1954, there were no more independents in Oklahoma save for the Oklahoma City Indians who succumbed in 1956 by affiliating with the Boston Red Sox.

Carnett used his extensive connections to begin rounding up a roster. He had close associations in the West Texas-New Mexico and Longhorn Leagues as well as the Evangeline League and began taking players on option or purchasing outright. His first buy, from Lake Charles (LA), was a huge success. Larry Cagle went on to play in every game and hit .320 for the Jets. A tryout camp was conducted March 27-29 and advertised nationally in *The Sporting News.* Several players were obtained from the Oklahoma City Indians as they broke camp for the Texas League campaign. Veteran catcher with Ponca City ties, Don Keeter, was purchased from Crowley (LA).

By early April, Parkinson announced that 17,850 tickets had been sold toward a pre-season goal of 60,000. The Jets got a break when they received a bus from the Brooklyn organization in exchange for chairs belonging to the locals the Dodgers had purloined when they packed up after the 1952 season. New ticket books had to be printed when Congress repealed the amusement excise tax on ducat sales. The Jets kept the price the same, pocketing the revenue that had been budgeted for the tax.

Ed Carnett was a high school star at Ponca City where he played with the Cubs' Western Association club. Originally a pitcher, he converted to outfield. After action with the White Sox and Indians, he managed in the minors. The Sporting News called him "Mr. Five Jobs" because he pitched, played first base, managed, served as business manager, and drove the bus while at Borger, Texas. He was also a sports writer for his hometown paper. He was the logical leader when Ponca City won a Western Association franchise for 1954. (Pc-29)

The first dilemma Carnett faced was the veterans on his team. The Western Association allowed five. He had six. In addition to himself, Bartkowski, Cagle, Eldridge, Keeter, and Pemberton all had more than three seasons in Organized Baseball. Bartkowski was lame but insisting on playing.

PONCA CITY JETS Vs IOLA INDIANS

Today — 2 P.M. — Direct from Iola
The name's been changed but they're still our Ponca City "Nine"

and Bill Platt Hasn't Changed . . .

He'll be back at the mike again this year bringing you every game of the Ponca City Jets over WBBZ —
"The Sports Voice of North Central Oklahoma"

WBBZ
1230 Kcs.

Bill Platt — Will call every play at home or away for the Jets

Eddie Carnett, Mgr.

Patronize these friendly folks who bring you the games:

- **CASEMORE'S**
  Plumbing Dept. Store
- **SECURITY ABSTRACT**
  of Newkirk
- **MID-WEST CREAMERY**
- **FIRST NATIONAL BANK**
- **HAMM'S BEER** From the land of the Sky Blue Waters

Promotion for season opener. (Pc-30)

Whom did he cut? They were the heart of his team. The league owners came to the rescue on May 4 and increased the number to six.

For the season opener at Iola on April 25, Carnett carried seven pitchers. His lineup had Keeter at catcher, Larry White—on option from Oklahoma City—at first, Cliff Pemberton from the Evange-

line League at the keystone, Ron Slawski from the Browns' 1953 Ada club and rookie Bill Linneman were battling for third, Gene White—a free agent previously from the A's organization—at shortstop, Stan Bartkowski—a veteran most recently in the Big State League—in left, Lamar Cagle in center field, and Jim Eldridge who had played for Carnett at Borger in right. A knuckleballer bought from Crowley, Chet Younger started and earned the first win holding the hosts to five hits as the Jets tagged the Indians for eleven.

Shirley Poff, a rookie from Elk City, was chosen to open the Jets' home season and once again the Jets vanquished Iola. With weather-related cancellations—the Association did not play a full slate of games until May 4 with May 1 and 2 being league-wide rainouts—the Jets were undefeated and then discovered that league doormat Iola wasn't the only opponent in the Western Association. They dropped the next nine outings before taking both games of a series on May 14 and 15 at St. Joseph behind the pitching of Poff and Walt Novak. Don Chamberlain, newcomer Bruce Ennis, and Wayne Doyle combined on May 19 to throw a one-hitter at St. Joseph. The next night, three Ponca City pitchers gave up twelve hits, eighteen walks, and ten errors to hand the host Saints a 21-6 gift. Carnett worked on his team chemistry. He released Slawski and Linneman when it turned out Cagle would play third base well; he was there the rest of the season. When Gene White left the club dues to a family illness, James Robinson, previously cut from Seminole of the Sooner State League, took over as a stop gap. Larry White was cut. Pitching help came when Cincinnati released bonus boy Buck Bradberry and he signed with the Jets. On May 18, Detroit sent Bob Ward from Idaho Falls of the Pioneer League, and Oklahoma City sold Bruce Ennis, who was released on May 30. A rookie from Jacksonville (FL), LaVerne "Trick Shot" Washington was inked.

A seven game road trip wrapped up in Joplin. Will Rogers Wheless, on option from Oklahoma City, in his first start lost a 6-4 first end of a twin bill. Trick Shot Washington was saved in the nightcap by Bob Ward for the only win of the journey by a score of 8-6. Dropping the home opener to Topeka after blowing a lead in the ninth inning, the Jets came back to please the home crowd with a 10-4 win as Shirley Poff blanked the Owls with six relief innings. Washington had to relieve Carnett at first base after the boss was ejected in the ninth. Following dropping both ends of a Memorial Day doubleheader at Muskogee, Bartkowski, who had been hobbled by injuries since spring drills, jumped the team, never to be heard from again.

A thief stole $145 from Jets' wallets in the locker room during the first June homestand; the fans passed the hat to make the players whole. Carnett shook up the lineup. Robinson was released. Brooklyn sent first sacker Don Currie from Shawnee and second baseman/shortstop Dale Johnston from Bakersfield. On June 6, Currie got a grand slam at Muskogee. The next day the Jets romped to a 17-0 football score over Iola; Bob Ward's two-hitter was augmented by eighteen hits, eleven walks, and five Iola errors. Cagle batted twice in the sixth inning earning four RBIs with a single and triple. Revenge came on June 8 as Iola's Bob Matthison beat Ponca City twice, 3-2 and 7-0. Charles Way, by trade a catcher, had played third base, left field and right field in addition to backstop throughout the season. Carnett discovered that he could play every day and cover for injured players.

The last ten days of June saw more help. Hard hitting Walt Buerger came aboard after a new manager took over in Blackwell. Frank Bronk, a shortstop, was sent up from Shawnee freeing Johnston to play second. The Braves' organization optioned outfielder Tom Ballinger from their Boise club. Pemberton was shown the door. From then on, a stable nine was in

Ron Slawski had spent 1952 and 1953 with Ada. He joined the Jets as a free agent. (Pc-31)

Jim Eldridge of Altus, Oklahoma had played at Miami for Tommy Warren before joining Carnett for 1951-1953 at Borger. He followed him to Ponca City for his last season in Organized Baseball. (Pc-32)

Shirley Poff was 12-12 as a rookie for the Jets. The Yankees signed him to a minor league contract. He spent the next two seasons at Quincy, Illinois under Vern Hoscheit. (Pc-33)

Wayne Doyle was 4-3 at Miami in 1952. His 13-10 record with the Jets earned him a Yankees minor league contract for 1955. He left the game after that season. (Pc-34)

Having gotten his start with Duncan in 1950, Ponca City was the end of Will Wheless' baseball road after a 4-12 season. (Pc-35)

Charles Way was the utility player. He had come over from Borger. 1955 was his last season appearing with four teams in two leagues.(Pc-36)

Dale Johnson came from the Dodgers' organization. Ponca City was his last baseball stop. (Pc-37)

Lamar Cagle had been in the game since 1946. He had played the three prior seasons at Lake Charles in the Evangeline League. After sitting out 1955, his comeback try with Pampa in 1956 fell short.(Pc-38)

Rookie Frank Bronk came over from Shawnee. He played in the Brooklyn system in 1955 before retiring. (Pc-39)

Don Currie was a Brooklyn property on loan to the Jets. (Pc-40)

Bob Ward was on option from Detroit's Idaho Falls farm. He returned there for 1955. (Pc-41)

place that would remain the rest of the season: Keeter, Currie, Johnston, Cagle, Bronk, Eldridge, Ballinger, and Buerger. When Eldridge went on the ten-day disabled list, Way stepped in without missing a beat.

Having won fourteen of sixteen, the Jets climbed to fifth place for the first time on July 4 after sweeping Blackwell there and then repeating the feat at Iola. They remained there on July 21 with a 41-45 record but slipped to sixth on July 29. Currie got his third grand slam on July 31. Carnett was hit by a pitched ball on August 6, splitting a knuckle on his throwing hand. Eight days later, he threw the Jets to a 5-3 ten inning win over pacesetter Topeka. During the month after seizing fifth, Ponca City dropped twenty-one while winning only ten. They won eleven of the remainder to finish the first season in Class C since 1938 with 62-76 totals for 1954.

The Jets batted .258, seventh in the Association. Their fielding was also seventh. Lamar Cagle was the top batter with 166 hits including thirty-four doubles for a .320 average. Jim Eldridge matched his .320 average in fewer trips to the plate but boasted a .535 slugging percentage. Buerger had twenty-five round trippers but many came while at Blackwell. Eldridge had all seventeen of his for Ponca City.

Pitching was the Jets' Achilles heel. No regular had an ERA below 4.00. Not surprisingly, Ed Carnett was the best pitcher with a 4.05 ERA and a 7-3 record in eighty innings of fourteen games. Wayne Doyle, an alumnus of the 1952 K-O-M Miami champions, threw 199 innings for a 13-10 record and 4.30 ERA. Rookie Shirley Poff was the best surprise. He appeared in 206 innings of thirty-four games as a starter and in relief. He divided twenty-four decisions and turned in a team best ERA among the regulars, 4.24. After the military, the Yankees signed him to a minor league contract. Bob Ward was 11-11 in 181 innings of thirty games with a 4.38 ERA. Wheless with a 6.97

1954 Ponca City Jets. (Pc-42)

ERA in 164 innings not surprisingly had the worst won-loss record, 4-12. James Waldrip also posted a losing 7-9 record on a 6.42 ERA. Nineteen others took the mound for the Jets including position players Buerger, Currie, Keeter, and Way.

The Philadelphia Athletics moved to Kansas City for 1955 which spooked traditional Western Association locales as Topeka, Joplin, and St. Joseph. The Oklahoma clubs, Muskogee, Blackwell, and Ponca City, along with central Kansas town Hutchinson, were ready for 1955. Blackwell's funding drive failed. The center did not hold. The Western Association was officially put to rest on February 1, 1955. George Barr had presided over his second league failure.

Ponca City, Muskogee, and Blackwell all made overtures to the Sooner State League. Pauls Valley and Ada had folded. With Joe Magoto's long, favorable relationship with the New York Giants, he easily obtained a Class D working agreement for Muskogee which received the Pauls Valley franchise. The Sooner State owners were extremely cost sensitive to travel and nearly blocked the moved of the Ada franchise to Paris, Texas. They clearly were opposed to adding cities so far away as the Kansas borderland. The prospect for professional baseball returning to Ponca City was grim.

1955

Ponca City had sent a delegation to the winter January, 1955 Sooner State League meeting. The conventional wisdom there was that Art Willingham would put the independent Seminole franchise up for sale. The Gainesville club was thought reasonably solid with the civic financial infusion the past season and a strong working agreement with Chicago. There was opposition to Ponca City's entry because with Paris, Texas, now in the league the travel time and expense was significantly increased with no additional revenue. Paris, Lawton, Gainesville, and Muskogee formed the Sooner State League perimeter with Seminole, McAlester, Shawnee, and Ardmore in its interior. There was no appetite then for expanding north.

The Gainesville franchise was ill-starred after a former umpire Ernest Shadid bought the Chickasha operation and moved it to the north Texas town for the 1953 season. As related in *Baseball in the Cross Timbers* (pp. 75-76, 255-260), Shadid soon lost the ball club over a temper tantrum. A local civic group took over with a working agreement with the Chicago Cubs. The Owls drew 20,000 in 1953 with the worst team record in Sooner State League history. Attendance declined thirty per cent in 1954

Ed Carnett was hired by the Cubs to manage their 1955 Gainesville, Texas club in the Sooner State League. When the franchise was moved to Ponca City at the end of May, Carnett was back home.

even with a much improved fifth-place performance on the field. As noted, there had been a cash infusion for 1955 and outwardly Gainesville looked stable. The business manager of Gainesville had confided to the local sports editor before the season that if the ball club didn't draw fans in 1955, it would be quickly and quietly moved. Averaging fewer than 120 paid admissions in fourteen home dates and the bank account overdrawn $2,000, the die was cast.

The Conoco sign was atop the Conoco Park fence at the power alleys. As few players owned cars, the case of motor oil won for hitting the sign usually was sold. (Pc-43)

The Owls' owner wanted to place the team in a place that the other owners would approve of and that was acceptable to the parent Cubs. The Cubs had already planned to move their Western Association working agreement from Blackwell to Ponca City for 1955 and indicated to the league that Ponca City would be a good place for the Sooner State League. The Ponca City Baseball Association had stayed in business hoping for a new ball club and was in a position to immediately take over the operation. The other owners quickly approved the transfer followed by the blessing of George Trautman, president of the National Association, minor league baseball's governing body. The Ponca City Baseball Association bought only the Owls' balls, bats, equipment and bus. The team would be re-named the Jets and use the uniforms from the previous season. The only hitch was the Continental Oil Softball League which called Conoco Park home. When its members yielded, the second edition of the Ponca City Jets would open at home on May 21.

The working agreement inherited provided that the parent Cubs would provide a manager and all the players. The locals would receive a $500 per month stipend and partial reimbursement for travel costs when a player was bought or sold. Beyond that, the Ponca City Baseball Association was on its own.

Frank Renko spent both his professional seasons with Ponca City. (Pc-45)

Ed Carnett, who had been a sports writer for the *Ponca City News* in addition to his baseball duties managing the 1954 Jets, was again returning to his home town. The Cubs had hired him to manage the Gainesville farm club. With the suddenness of the franchise move, the club had only what was left over from the Western Association team to operate plus what was brought along from Gainesville. The former Owls proceeded directly to Ponca City from their road trip. Their record stood at 11-15 in sixth place. The scheduled opening was rained out.

Carnett brought eighteen players from Gainesville. Tony Migaiolo was the regular catcher and filled in the outfield. Pete Plyler, who spent 1954 at Blackwell, was reserve catcher. Don McCorkle, who spent 1954 at Gainesville, held down first. Rookie Joe Cascino and 1954 Blackwell alumnus Frank Alvarez shared second. Rookie Joe Miano played third. Dock Connors, who spent the previous season with the Kansas City Monarchs of the Negro League, covered shortstop. Frank Renko, another rookie, subbed as a utility infielder. Frank Pecci, another Blackwell player from 1954, Ray Samples, who joined Gainesville midway through the past season, and Bill Guice, with experience in the West Texas-New Mexico League, formed the outfield. Manager Carnett, a lefty who could pitch, backed up the outfielders. The moundsmen, all right handers, were Jim Speer in his third year, Bob Millard with Gainesville in 1954, Bob Moore who got his start in Organized Baseball with Gainesville late in 1954, Rick Marrs, returning from military service, Tom Rea, with two years' experience in Class C, and rookie Mike Morrison.

Chicago shuffled things in July as Ponca City fell to seventh then last place. Plyler had won the catching spot from Migalolo then was replaced by rookie James Huber; he finished the seasons playing some third base and outfield. A first baseman, third sacker and outfielder were sent down from

Lafayette (LA): Charles LaCoste ousted McCorkle, Bob Picciano retired Miano, and Dick Wright joined the outfield that had been depleted when Bob Boyd, who had played thirty-nine games for Lawton, after seventeen contests for the Poncans was dealt to Seminole for the rest of the season, and Ray Samples became the property of the Orioles at their Paris (TX) farm. Renko had taken Connors' placed at shortstop then was himself replaced by Ken Phillps just back from the military who found himself yielding playing time to rookie Buzzie Keller. After Morrison had lost four of five decisions in eight games, he was released and rookie Ernie Proud came in to fill the gap. Such became the ways of player development when the parent owned and called the shots about all the players.

Ken Phillips was a rookie with Independence in the K-O-M in 1952 and made a brief appearance with Gainesville in 1953 before a detour in the Army. 1955 was his last professional season. (Pc-46)

They opened at Ponca City as the Jets on May 22, with a 4-3 loss to the McAlester Rockets, the Yankees' Class D operation. A little more than a week after moving to Ponca City, the temporarily-named Jets, who had not had much success winning with pitching and batting, won a game because of a tornado. Long after the 360 fans had gone home to their storm shelters on May 27, managers Carnett and Lawton's Travis Jackson were arguing with plate umpire Jim Kenne-

Ray Samples was a rookie at Gainesville in 1954. The Cubs traded him to the Orioles' affiliate at Paris, Texas in the Sooner State League late in 1955. (Pc-47)

dy whether the game should be deemed completed or suspended. In the sixth inning, Lawton had just scored the tying run when the tornado sirens sounded at 9:35 p.m. Kennedy called President Clanton who ruled that the game would revert to where it had been at the bottom of the fifth with Ponca City leading 1-0 and would be treated as a complete game. Between June 11 and 18, the Jets dropped eight consecutive games by a single run. Boyd during his brief tenure saved the Jets from two no-hitters getting two hits against Lawton on June 10 then another two-hit performance against Shawnee on June 14. On June 28, the Poncans were charged with ten errors resulting in a ten inning 9-8 loss to Paris. At some point after July 1, the Jets became the Cubs. The name change and new flannels did not improve the play. On July 5, Carnett smacked a bases-loaded home run only to see Frank Pecci pass another Cub on the base path for an out. Ernie Proud, with six straight losses, was the hard luck pitcher and it showed again when he lost to Muskogee in twelve innings 2-1 on July 20 de-

spite allowing only four hits and striking out twenty-two Giants. An SOS went out that the little Cubs were in distress because they needed $8,000 to finish the season. The parent Cubs turned down their plea for help. Paring back expenses to $6,000, on July 21, the Association announced that in a twenty-four hour fund drive fans and local businessmen had given $4,000 toward insuring continued operation through the end of the season. On July 26, there was free admission. The hat was passed and $1,235 was raised from the crowd. The one bright spot of the season came that evening when Bob Millard threw a gem at McAlester whipping the Rockets 6-0. The Cubs would finish the season.

The Cubs were on a roll at home having won twelve of thirteen following an August 9 10-4 rout of Shawnee on sixteen Hawks' walks. On August 16,

Bob Millard spent his career as a Cubs' property. He reached Class B in 1956. (Pc-48)

1955 Ponca City Cubs.

even fourteen hits could not help the Cubs prevent Ardmore's Charlie Purtle from collecting his twentieth win of the season. The Paris Orioles ruined Dock Connors' night after receiving the fans' designation as MVP on September 4. The Cubs would go out with a whimper as Paris progressed to the playoffs while the Cubs suffered their eighty-third defeat.

By August 25, Ponca City had sole possession of eighth place. In the last two weeks of the season, the Cubs won six and lost seven while the Seminole Oilers won only five of fourteen. The two teams ended at 56-83 in a double occupancy cellar. With 21,477 admissions plus 7,692 from Gainesville the club was seventh in attendance. The batters were seventh overall with an anemic .231 average. They were a distant last in RBI production, struck out the most times, and were last in number of hits. The top batter who played the full season was Dock Conners hitting .256 with nine home runs and forty-three RBIs. Catcher Frank Pecci, on option from Des Moines, didn't hit for average (.227) but led with sixteen home runs and fifty-nine RBIs.

The pitchers collectively performed well finishing with a 3.90 ERA. They had sixty-nine complete games, allowed 771 runs only 522 of which were earned, yielded 677 walks but struck out 1,044 batters. The Cubs' hurlers led the league with ninety-five wild pitches and nine balks. Jim Speer led the team in wins with fourteen against fifteen losses for the best record and percentage. Bob Moore and Ernie Proud both had ERAs below 3.00. Bob Millard was 9-10 and 3.08. There was no All Star team in 1955 but even had there been, it would have made no difference for Ponca City. It was enough to make Ed Carnett swear off managing in baseball. He traded in his spikes for running a county club then managing sales. On May 26, 2012 he threw out the first pitch for the American League game between Seattle and Los Angeles. At this writing is living in Ringling, Oklahoma with his wife and family.

1956

Bill Platt served baseball in Ponca City as a sportscaster, business manager and, when Mo Mack was suspended, third baseman. (Pc-50)

Automobile dealer David Sutton stepped up when Ted Parkinson stepped down in early 1956. A new non-profit to which the franchise was transferred was formed under the name Ponca City Baseball Club. Joining Sutton as officers were first vice-president Howard Blauvelt, Melbourn Leche second vice-president and Julius Marks secretary-treasurer. This entity would hold the club for the remainder of the league's existence. The second division jinx that had followed the franchise since it left Chickasha continued. Jack Costello, age twenty-three who played and was student manager at Seton Hall and ran teams in the Navy, was hired as business manager from Florida Southern University's baseball administration program. He quit on May 24, and sportswriter Bill Platt again figuratively stepped up to the plate. Pitcher John Zafarana was hired the next day to relieve Platt and do double duty. He was released as a player on August 6, with a 3-4 record and 6.53 ERA,

The Cubs entrusted their 1956 and 1957 rookies to a five year product of their farm system, catcher Don Biebel. This was Biebel's first shot at the helm. He was familiar with Ponca City, however, from trips there during the two seasons he spent with Carthage, Missouri, of the K-O-M League. Return-

Don Biebel had risen to Class A Des Moines in the Western League when the Cubs tapped him to manage Ponca City for its final two seasons. He served as a Cubs coach from 1980-1982, 1986-1987, and 1992-2000. (Pc-51)

Lou Johnson lost part of an ear in a car wreck driving to a 1956 game in Muskogee. He reached Wrigley Field in 1960 but came into his own with the Los Angeles Dodgers where he was a regular for three seasons. (Pc-52)

ing from spring drills in Lafayette, Louisiana, the season began on April 24, with Chicago weather: cold, wet, windy. Three hundred hardcore fans at Ponca City watched Paris win 7-1. Rookie Dave Hall's first twenty-three and two-third innings in pro ball failed to yield an earned run; the only run scored on him was by a passed ball on May 5. Hall appeared in forty-eight games finishing 15-11 with 3.95 ERA. Mike Morrison, a carryover from 1955, was three hits away from three gems. On May 6, he beat Seminole 2-0 on one hit. Then on May 21 he threw a one-hitter in a game at McAlester winning 8-1. He one-hit Lawton on June 8, for a 2-1 victory, his seventh of the season and fourth straight complete game. The Cubs stole nine bases against Muskogee for 9-5 win on May 22. The famous back to back triple plays were turned on May 28, in a game with Greenville that the Cubs won 11-1.

Weather plagued the league the first month of 1956 and Ponca City was not immune. With Ponca City ahead of Paris 6-3 on May 30, the umpires called the game called after a tornado warning was issued. Ignoring the precedent set by Uke Clanton, League President George

Sammy Drake was up and down from AAA to the Cubs several times, finishing baseball in 1965. He and his brother Solly were the first African-American brothers to play in the Majors. (Pc-53)

Barr said the game had to be completed; on August 6, Paris came from behind to win the delayed game 10-9. The following day driving to Muskogee, a car load of Cubs flipped after a blowout. Outfielder Lou Johnson was seriously injured, losing much of an ear. Mike Morrison was treated and released. The rest caught a ride to the game. One month into season, Ponca City was in sixth place winning as many as they lost: 21-21. Outfielders Greenwood and Gragg were hitting .344 and .321 and Morrison (6-1) and Hall (5-2) were among the top ten pitchers.

On June 26, Ponca City made league history when it fielded the first completely African-American outfield: Lou Greenwood, Sammy Drake, and Billy Williams against Seminole. Two days later, the Cubs were 28-38 in last place. Greenwood and Gragg were still hitting and Morrison was still in the top ten at 7-4 and leading the league with ninety-eight strikeouts. Second baseman Dennis Loudenback set a record by hitting home runs in three consecutive at bats, one against McAlester on July 12, and two at Seminole on the thirteenth.

Clubhouse facilities were rough and not particularly secure. There was no money to pay for a club house attendant. On July 18, a thief stole $549 from player wallets there. Sammy Drake lost $118, close to a month's salary, Gragg and Owens $80 each. The Ponca City fans passed the proverbial hat to raise $286.19 and a civic group added $25. Manager Beibel divided it pro rata.

The 1956 season was the most balanced in league history. The winning percentage of the first place Ardmore club was .597. Fifth place Ponca City was .500, thirteen games out of first. Team batting was .254. Russell Gragg led the league with 183 hits and a .352 average. Fielding was sound at .9398. The weak spot was on the mound. The Cubs led the league in free passes with 896 and were second with 106 wild pitches. Team ERA was 4.94 while average run production was 6.18. The previous season,

Rookie Ed Donnelly did well enough with the 1956 Ponca City club to wind up with the parent Cubs for two months in 1959. Most of his career was in AAA. (Pc-54)

Ponca City would have finished a strong fourth with the same numbers. In terms of successful alumni, the 1956 Cubs were the best team in league history. Sammy Drake, Lou Johnson, Billy Williams, and pitchers Jim Brewer and Ed Donnelly all played at least one season in the Majors. Two of the 1956 Cubs, Dennis Loudenback and Al Owens, were traded to the Orioles' organization and played for the last small town Oklahoma minor league team, the Ardmore Rosebuds, in 1961.

The 1956 team played .500 ball at 70-70 before 20,674 to finish only two and one-half games behind fourth place Paris. A young African-American outfielder from Mobile, Alabama, joined the club in June, 1956. His bonus was a free bus ticket to Ponca City and a cigar for his father. He played infrequently hitting only .235 with no home runs and four RBIs. The parent Cubs assigned Billy Williams back to Ponca City for 1957. That year in a 126 game season he was an All Star hitting .310 with ninety-five RBIs and seventeen home runs, giving the 21,203 who came out to Conoco Park a preview of the kind of fielding and power hitting that would put Billy Williams into the Baseball Hall of Fame.

With a brief detour to Salt Lake City, Jim Brewer spent 1962-1976 in the Majors with the Cubs, Dodgers, and Angels. He won a World Series ring in 1965 and was a National League All Star in 1973. He coached Oral Roberts University from 1978 through 1986. (Pc-55)

1957

The Ponca City Baseball Club launched an "All Out Drive" March 1 to raise $10,000 in advance sales to assure the season. The team had $2,000 in the bank and debts of $4,000. Bill Edwards, heading the drive, is quoted in *The Sporting News*: "[u]nless we get that amount, there won't be a team here this year." If the drive were successful, the $4,000 deficit from 1956 would be retired and there would be operating funds of $8,000 for the coming season. In a cost saving effort, the Cubs would forego hiring a business manager and the directors would handle the front office chores as volunteers.

For 1957, the league had adopted a 126 game season beginning May 1 to avoid weather cancellations in the spring. The little Cubs trained with the parent team and all the other prospects at Chicago's new spring base in Mesa, Arizona. The Cubs' opener at Muskogee was postponed

Billy Williams spent 1956 and 1957 with Ponca City. He moved steadily through the Cubs' ranks, landing at AAA Houston in 1960 before becoming the 1961 National League Rookie of the Year and 1987 induction to the Hall of Fame. (Pc-56)

but not for weather. The Sugar Ray Robinson versus Gene Fulmer fight for the middleweight championship was televised that evening and Giants management speculated fans would stay home. As it turned out, the game could have been called on account of the weather. All of the season openers were rained out. On May 13, Jack Curtis, who would spend 1961-1963 in the Majors, struck out sixteen and with the bat of manager Biebel, who tripled and scored on a wild pitch, gained a win 4-3 over the Seminole Athletics. On May 30, Muskogee and the Cubs traded 7-0 shutouts. At June 4, the Cubs were in last place at 9-20. Biebel was the only player hitting above .300.

Billy Williams, who played every game in 1957, gave hard luck pitcher Paul Dean, Jr. of the Lawton Braves his fourth consecutive loss by hitting a walk off homer with a man on to top Lawton 3-1. Gus Niklas ruined Lawton right hander Bill Holmes' bid for a perfect game when he stroked a single with two out in the ninth as the Braves beat the Cubs 5-0. On June 17, seventeen year old rookie Jack Tashie set the league high for 1957 with seventeen strikeouts for one of his six wins, this time over Seminole 5-2. On July 4, Ponca City had climbed to seventh at 21-34 and never left that spot. Carl Reynolds, Tex Gholson, and Don Biebel smashed consecutive home runs at Conoco Park in the third inning of the July 11, game with Paris. The contest was won 12-11 in extra innings on Reynold's RBI single. Carl Sorenson stroked his first home run with the bases loaded to provide the July 22, win over hapless Seminole. Gholson's grand slam was not enough as the Athletics took revenge 9-7 the next meeting.

The excitement in August didn't come from the Cubs but was from the shooting of Ardmore manager J.C. Dunn on August 8. For the third time that season, Jack Curtis pitched both ends of a double header, taking wins from Lawton 4-1 and 6-0 on August 23. Billy Williams led the Cubs in average (.310),

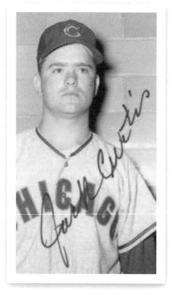

Jack Curtis won eighteen of the 1957 Cubs' fifty-two games, earning a spot on the All Star team with Billy Williams. He came up to the parent Cubs in 1961 and pitched three more seasons for the Braves and Indians. (Pc-57)

home runs (17) and RBIs (95) and was named to the last Sooner State League All Star team.

The other All Star was Jack Curtis whose fifteen wins led the league as did his 219 strike outs. He was also tops in complete games and innings pitched. The Cubs had a winning percentage of .413 with him and .366 without him. His record and ERA of 3.71 was better than All Stars Steve Barber of Paris (9-9, 4.56) and Seminole's Crash Corrigan (9-14, 3.78). As a team, the Cubs had the worst gloves in the league with a .935 average and Sooner State League high of 299 errors. They were also last in batting with a .235 percentage topping the league only in stranding 1,035 runners but second with ninety-five home runs. They also finished last in the pitching department with a team ERA of 4.97 leading with eight balks.

In three seasons, the little Cubs had produced six Major Leaguers. Jim Brewer of 1956 and 1957 won a World Series ring with the Dodgers in 1965. Ed Donnelly of the 1956 squad made it to Wrigley Field in 1959. Another two season Ponca City alumnus, Sammy Drake saw duty with the Cubs in 1960 and the 1962 New York Mets. Lou Johnson, who lost part of his right ear in the 1956 car accident, was a regular outfielder for three seasons with the Los Angeles Dodgers. Jack Curtis had a cup of coffee with Cleveland in 1963. Billy Williams, of course, played for the Cubs and the Oakland A's between 1959 and 1976. He was Rookie of the Year in 1961, and held the National League record with 1,117 consecutive games played.

By February it was apparent the Sooner State League had breathed its last. With the demise of the last Class D league west of the Mississippi, down came the Ponca City Baseball Club. Conoco Park followed shortly. It was demolished for a parking lot later that spring.

SEMINOLE OILERS
1947-1950
MCDUFF'S SEMINOLE IRONMEN
1951
SEMINOLE OILERS
1954-1956
SEMINOLE ATHLETICS
1957
SOONER STATE LEAGUE

The citizens of Seminole voted a bond issue to build a new ball park. (Se-1)

SEASON	ATTENDANCE	RECORD	FINISH	AFFILIATION	PLAYOFF FIRST ROUND	PLAYOFF FINALS
1947	30,003	48-98	Fifth	Tulsa (Texas League AA)		
1948	40,053	75-62	Third	Chicago AL	Beat Lawton 3-2	Beat McAlester 4-2
1949	33,258	54-84	Eighth	Chicago AL		
1950	21,366	55-83	Sixth			
1951	16,915	37-103	Eighth			
1954	16,840	61-79	Seventh			
1955	26,775	56-83	Eighth	Kansas City		
1956	31,249	74-56	Third	Kansas City	Beat Lawton 3-1	Beat Ardmore 4-3
1957	17,379	46-79	Eighth	Kansas City		

1947

The charter Sooner State League franchise for Seminole was awarded to Hugh P. "Red" Alexander. After accepting a position as scout with the Cleveland Indians, and with Ardmore being an Indians' farm club, he had to sell the franchise. In February, 1947, *The Sporting News* reported that he was selling to the Texas League Tulsa Oilers who would operate it as a farm club for their and Chicago Cubs signees. As things turned out, Cy Fenolio, whose bid for a team in his native Okmulgee was stillborn at the hands of voters who turned down a bond issue to construct a stadium, became the owner on March 4, 1947, with a partial working agreement with Tulsa.

The Seminole City Council scheduled a bond issue election for erection for a $17,000 grandstand for March 16, 1947. It passed 352 to 171. Blair Construction was engaged to build it but the quickest it could finish the project was May 20, assuming good weather. Fenolio went forward, signing unemployed veteran players, college boys, and the best of the tryout performers. After playing a May 3-6 series as a home team on the road, temporary bleachers were put up so the local fans could see their brand new Oilers. The concrete and steel grandstand was finished before May was over. Like Jeff-Lee Athletic Park in McAlester, there were twelve rows of grandstand seats.

By April 6, three weeks before the season was to begin, the club had twelve players under contract. Owner Cy Fenolio cobbled together a homeless ballclub from tryout camps, semi-pros, K-O-M League castaways, and Cubs farmhands sent down from Tulsa. The initial roster included manager John Tabor, on assignment from Tulsa, four rookies sent down from Tulsa: pitchers Nolan Scoggins, Elmer "Jimmy" Jeter, Jack Doyle, and outfielder Skip Bednar from Bethany, Oklahoma's Putnam City; and two semi-pros from Okmulgee: outfielders Gene Creekmore of the 1949 Elk City Elks and Jack Case. Others were third baseman Frisco Roberts, a 1938 Okemah team mate of Dwight "Rip" Collins, first baseman Whalen Glover from Ada's East Central State College, and three from tryout camp, outfielder Paul Perrin and second baseman Sparky Adams, both of Henryetta, and pitcher Don Reno of Morris.

In addition to being generally acknowledged as the sartorially shabbiest team in the league, the little Oilers were unable to play a home game until nearly a month into the season because their ball park was not finished. In

Cleveland scout Hugh Alexander won the original Seminole franchise but had to relinquish it after Ardmore signed a working agreement with the Indians. Alexander had a promising baseball career until he lost a hand in a farming accident. (Se-12)

John Tabor played professionally in 1919 and 1920 then scouted and coached sandlot. Two of his finds were Pepper Martin and Hank Iba. He was hired in 1945 to refurbish the dilapidated Tulsa County Texas League Park, making it one of the top fields in the country. Tulsa loaned Tabor to Seminole to launch the team. (Se-3)

a six-team circuit, the inaugural edition of the Oilers won forty-eight while losing ninety escaping the cellar only because of the hapless Duncan Cementers' 39-99 finish. While only eight pitchers saw duty, including manager Hugh Willingham, the positions were a revolving door. Of the twenty-three catchers, infielders and outfielders, only three, catcher George Sojka and outfielders Jerry Creekmore and Bob Bednar, played the same position in over one hundred games. Two played at first, five played at second, five at third, and four at shortstop. They fielded at .923 with 418 errors. Sojka caught 113 games committing thirty-eight errors with twenty-three passed balls. As a team, the Oilers batted .256. Jack Baumer (.349), Bob Bednar (.303), Norm Jones (.314), Max Reese (.357) and manager Hugh Willingham (.303) all hit over .300. Rookie Elmer "Jimmy" Jeter from Mt. Airy, Iowa appeared in forty-one games winning eighteen of the forty-eight Seminole victories. With a 3.17 ERA he was named to both the 1947 All Star teams. Despite his success, life in the minors did not agree with Jeter and after toiling in 1948 at Tyler, he returned to the farm in Iowa. Frisco Roberts was the son of a Major Leaguer and a Seminole Indian from Okemah, who had played at Johnson City, Tennessee in the Class D Appalachian League before the War and semi-pro after. He was named to the shortstop position on the All Star team selected by the managers that played mid-summer against pacesetter Lawton. For 1948, Baumer moved up to Tulsa and Roberts jumped to Otto Utt's Duncan club.

In the six team 1947 league, 30,003 came out to see the ragtag Oilers finish fifth with a 48-98 record under three managers: John Tabor who returned to tending the grounds at Tulsa's Texas League Park, Cy Fenolio in the interim, and Hugh Willingham who would stay at the helm through 1949 and play a role in baseball in Seminole through 1956.

1948

A limited working agreement with the Chicago White Sox was in place for 1948 providing another source of players for returning manager Hugh Willingham. The Oilers signed outfielders Bednar and Creekmore, catcher Sojka, and pitchers Everette Neal, and Jim Wesley from the 1947 team. The season opened with Mayor Ed Whitbeck and Miss Aleen Martin, daughter of Pepper Martin, working as the battery for the first pitch before the opener with McAlester. The Oilers sported new uniforms, wearing white jerseys with a large maroon block "S" on the left front and white caps with a maroon block "S" and brims of the same color; the road outfits were the same except being gray and "Seminole" appearing in script rather than the "S".

With his team on top, June of 1948 was an excellent time to sell and that is what Fenolio did. A group led by oilman W.F. Rumse, volunteer business manager Ray Davis, and banker Raymond Harber formed Seminole Oilers Baseball Corporation, Inc. to acquire the franchise and its property. Other investors were Elee Cutsinger, Earl Martin, Don Davisson, John Grew, Loyal Bowman, and Frank Brown.

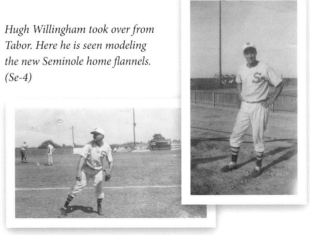

Hugh Willingham took over from Tabor. Here he is seen modeling the new Seminole home flannels. (Se-4)

Willingham pitched a "blooper" ball launching it in an arc that fell over the plate. (Se-5)

Wedding bells rang on June 25, before the game with Duncan, when second baseman Tony Donofrio wed fiancée Inez Campbell at home plate. Manager Willingham gave away the bride as shortstop Joe Polinski sang "Because."

Seminole rode good pitching from rookies Ken Skidmore, an All Star at 20-9 with a 2.86 ERA and Don Wescott, 14-8 and 2.57, and manager Hugh Willingham with his blooper ball at 10-6 and 2.74. As a team, the Oilers hit only .247 with a weak .328 slugging percentage and the lowest number of home runs, twenty-one, in the League. Playing in 105 games, manager Willingham led the team in batting with a .341 average. Creekmore, an All Star, was the only other .300 hitter at .302. Willingham led the second edition to a 75-62 third place finish. In the playoffs they first knocked off second place Lawton and then regular season winner McAlester on September 18, with a 6-5 win for the first league championship in an eight team circuit. More than 10,000 additional fans came through the gate at 1,700-seat Oiler Park.

1949

Forty-nine new field boxes were installed before the 1949 season. The stands lacked a roof. With bleachers, Oilers Park could accommodate 2,500 fans. The playing field was symmetrical with the fence 318 feet away down the lines and 400 feet to center.

In the second year of the alliance with the White Sox, the top three pitchers from 1948 returned but only Creekmore and pitcher/first baseman Harry Olmstead were back as position players. The White Sox failed to send adequate prospects. The Oilers did, however, ride to game sites in the comfort of a new, customized twenty passenger bus. Chicago traded to the Browns' team at Ada two outfielders, Billy Milligan and Steve Molinari, who

Seminoles 1949 pitchers. (Se-6)

would combine for seventy-six home runs in 1950. Rookie Gerald Brezen led the team in batting with a .286 average. Only Wescott at 11-9 had a winning record on the mound and at 2.70 an ERA under 3.00. That was the high point of the season. The 1949 Oilers completed the season in the cellar at 54-84 before 33,258 under Paul Schoendienst, scout for the parent team. The shareholders of Seminole Oilers Baseball Corporation who had purchased the Oilers from Fenolio were beginning to have doubts about the wisdom of their investment after Chicago terminated the working agreement. Nonetheless, the owners firmly denied rumors that Seminole baseball was in financial jeopardy.

1950

The 1950 season saw Seminole operating as an independent. F. Ray Davis, still business manager, had only three players as 1950 began: infielder John Miller, outfielder Don Krueger and pitcher Harry Olmstead. For all practical purposes new manager Kelly Wingo had to put together a completely new team. Working from scratch he combined one veteran, Floyd Geiger, several limited service players, and lots of rookies to make a team that managed to finished sixth ahead of the Duncan-Shawnee club and Lawton's worst team ever. The high point of the season was when Johnny Francis, recently obtained from Class C Muskogee, no-hit Lawton 4-0 on August 12. In seven innings he walked three, struck out three, and didn't let a ball out of the infield.

Harber, a well-respected banker, denied springtime rumors that the Oilers were in financial *extremis*. The team's performance did not attract fans. Pat Murphy, local radio personality, moonlighted as the club's publicity director with the sole mission to boost attendance. He labored mightily but with little success. The fans stayed away after that with attendance averaging 287 for the remaining home dates after the season opener. Manager Kelly Wingo broke his leg sliding to a base on June 4, the thirty-seventh game and became a bench manager, a luxury the team could not long afford. By the end of July, the franchise was on the precipice of forfeiture for failure to pay league dues. Wingo was released.

At the end of July when it was apparent the Oilers couldn't make payroll and were in arrears on most bills including league dues, business manager F. Ray Davis, who had been part of the original investor group, resigned in late July shortly before Kelly Wingo was fired. The team was in disarray. On August 2, president Jack Mealey threatened to revoke the franchise unless it became current in payment of league dues. As a banker, Harber was well aware of the "greater fool" rule: there is always a greater fool waiting to buy your bad deal. The Oilers' owners, feeling foolish for having lost so much money on a last place team, looked for and found their greater fool in the person of the flamboyant self-proclaimed

Banker and baseball booster Ray Harber. (Se-8)

Harry Olmstead pitched and played first base for Seminole in 1948, 1949, and 1950, his last season. He managed part of 1951. (Se-7)

Kelly Wingo broke his leg on June 4, becoming a bench manager. He was released at the end of July as the ball club drifted toward insolvency. (Se-9)

Shawnee's Fred McDuff, the 'Ironman," saved baseball when he bailed out Seminole in August, 1950. (Se-10)

king of oil field equipment dealers, Shawnee's Fred McDuff, the "Ironman."

At this juncture, Fred McDuff intervened with a cash infusion and a new name, "McDuff's Seminole Ironmen." McDuff paid $11,000 for a bus, the lease on Oilers Park, balls and bats, equipment, the privilege of renaming a team from Oiler's to McDuff's Seminole Ironmen, and the contracts of the 1950 team. The Ironmen won nine of their first ten games for McDuff including a no-hitter by newcomer John Francis. Floyd Geiger, a twenty-four year old infielder, and hurler Harry Olmstead, were named co-managers until McDuff settled on Geiger. When Geiger's Army unit was called up for Korea in August, the reins were turned over to Dennis Rackley, who had been accused of lack of hustle as a member of the 1948 Ada Herefords and who was cut from the 1950 Ada squad during spring training. The Ironmen finished a surprising sixth at 55-83. There was optimism for 1951.

1951

There were only two players under contract, pitcher Harry Olmstead, 10-12 in 1950, and Don Krueger, a .259 hitter obtained from Duncan, when spring arrived in 1951. McDuff acting as his own business manager and Harry Olmstead held tryout camps in Hugo, Okemah, and Seminole from which three rookies were signed. McDuff hired a former Oklahoma City Indian to lead the Ironmen and assemble a team. Dwight "Rip" Collins, not to be confused with James "Ripper" Collins of Gas House Gang fame, had been in the semi-pro ranks since the end of the 1947 season. He accepted the challenge of taking over. He had guided the semi-pro Elk City, Oklahoma, Elks to runner up in the 1950 National Baseball Congress tournament in Wichita.

Third baseman Dennis Rackley and pitcher Johnny Francis joined Omstead and Krueger

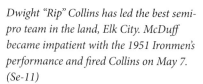

Dwight "Rip" Collins has led the best semi-pro team in the land, Elk City. McDuff became impatient with the 1951 Ironmen's performance and fired Collins on May 7. (Se-11)

K-O-M veteran Bill Stumborg had joined Collins from Elk City, and took the Seminole helm for two weeks until Dutch Prather relieved him. (Se-12)

Len Gilmore won fifteen of Seminole's thirty-seven 1951 victories. He pitched Pittsburgh's final game of the 1944 season. (Se-13)

in welcoming Collins. Of the several dozen who appeared in McDuff flannels, twenty-seven played in fewer than ten games. Among those were twenty pitchers including Jimmy Cobb, notorious for his two and two-thirds balk-filled innings with Pauls Valley in 1948; he lasted one game.

McDuff hired one-legged former Chicago pitcher Monty Stratton to throw out the first ball in the Ironmen's first home appearance; Ada won 17-8 before a full house of 1,784 in the stands, more than ten percent of season attendance as things turned out. That was an indication of the play to come. With the Ironmen at 5-13 (.277), Collins was involuntarily returned to his Okemah home on May 8. A team mate with Collins on the Elk City semi-pros and refugee from the K-OM, weak fielding flychaser (.833 fielding average) Bill Stumborg took over, winning three and losing twelve until released and replaced by unemployed Dutch Prather who was hired on May 25, to complete the season. The Dutchman took over an unruly bunch. To celebrate the new field general succeeding Collins, McDuff released Francis, winner of last season's no-hitter, both catchers, and another pitcher.

Prather contributed his .414 bat to the cause but he was unable to make chicken salad out of chicken feathers. The revolving door of seventy-four players was more confusing than in 1947. Rookie catcher Gene Green was the only Ironman to play eighty games at a position. Four played first base, four at second, five at third, seven at shortstop, nine in the outfield. The players were slack and undisciplined. In July, with Fred McDuff's "Just keep letting them have it" blessing, Prather fined twelve of his fifteen players at one time for violating curfew. The July 17, edition of the *Seminole Producer* had a headline: "Compared with Oilers, Ironmen are in a Sad State of Affairs." The accompanying article pointed out that at the same point in time the 1950 Oilers were 29-43 while the Ironmen were 18-61. The

only bright spot on the team was former Major Leaguer Len Gilmore who actually posted a winning percentage with fifteen wins against fourteen losses. He won forty-one percent of the Ironmen's games. When he wasn't pitching, Seminole had a .198 winning percentage. The Ironmen did not win a doubleheader although they came close on the last day. Gilmore pitched both ends of a twin bill against Shawnee winning the first 7-0 and barely dropping the nightcap 9-8. The last Ironmen performed at a 29-78 (.271) level after May 25. This included a league record twelve consecutive road losses. McDuff had to keep pumping money into the venture because only 15,131 came to watch the team after the opener.

McDuff was quoted in the June 27, 1951, issue of *The Sporting News* that the team was for sale. "It is just too expensive" he said but "I've bowed my neck and we will go through the season." After splitting a doubleheader with Shawnee on the last day of the season, McDuff remarked "We bowed out in a blaze of glory, and I hope Seminole has a team next year."

On December 27, a sale of the franchise, nine players, and options on equipment and a bus to Hayden Bryce, manager of the local Mistletoe Express office, was front page news in Seminole. Bryce's business plan was to set up a non-profit, assemble an executive committee, and solicit donations. McDuff told the *Producer,* "I hope that [Bryce] profits by my experience with the team —take account of what I've done and stay away from that." McDuff promptly withdrew his guaranty deposit from the National Association. Bryce couldn't come up with the financial wherewithal to swing the purchase. Hugh Willingham with the local American Legion scrambled to raise $10,000 to keep the team and even lined up a working agreement with Detroit. Despite these efforts and after a ten day extension from a previous January 14, deadline, the Seminole franchise reverted to the league. Duncan, Gainesville and Paris, Texas, as well as Ardmore—two weeks after Art Willingham packed up his ball club for a two year sojourn in Sherman-Denison, Texas—vied for the open place. Ardmore won the competition for the Seminole franchise. There would be no baseball in Seminole in 1952 or 1953.

1954

That charter city of the Sooner State League had been without baseball since Ardmore Baseball Association took the Oilers after its Indians had moved to Sherman in 1952. In August, 1953, Art Willingham offered the franchise for sale for $5,000. In September, he said he would operate a team in Sherman either in the Sooner State League or a revived East Texas League *if* 1,000 season ticket books at $30 each had been sold by December 1, 1953.

When no buyers for the franchise or tickets came forward, and with Seminole fans led by A.S. Wells dangling dues money for 1954 before him, he moved the Sherman-Denison team to Seminole the following February. It was the only independent team in Class D west of the Mississippi.

Willingham renamed the club "Tri-City" to appeal to Holdenville and Wewoka where he planned to play some games. Had civic boosters not sold 350 season tickets at $50 each, the Oilers might have played all their game in those two cities. The city of Seminole, which owned Oilers Park, would not make repairs or bring it up to league standards until he had done so. Only eighty-three season passes had been sold by March 12. With Art Willingham posting a $4,000 guaranty, the repair work began in late March.

After sitting vacant for two seasons, Oilers Park needed significant work to be made ready for the Tri-City club that had relocated from Sherman in early 1954. The dugouts were re-roofed, a new press

box built, clubhouses were erected, the boxes were repaired, the lighting upgraded and the scoreboard upgraded. The City hired 1947-1949 Oilers' manager Hugh Willingham as park superintendent. He immediately spread forty loads of top soil. Willingham used convict labor to place the neglected playing surface into professional shape. One of the nicest facilities in the league, the biggest problem with Oilers Park was the sparse crowds.

Art Willingham was confronted with having to build a team from scratch since the 1953 Twins collapsed completely at season end. At March 4, he had only four players under contract including local players Shed Hearn of Earlsboro and Gerald Kristler of Seminole who failed to make the cut. Operating with no working agreement, Willingham

Tommy Warren appeared on parole in 1954. Before departing to take over the Borger, Texas club on June 20, Warren had won ten of eleven decisions for the Oilers. (Se-14)

Don Phillips was one of five player under contract to Willingham who were carryover from the 1953 Sherman-Denison Twins. (Se-15)

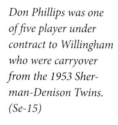

George Brunet pitched in every season between 1953 and 1985. He held the all-time minor league record with 3,175 strike outs. He threw for the Athletics, Astros, Angels, and Pilots before embarking on eleven seasons in the Mexican League. He was inducted into the Mexican Salon de Fama in 1999. (Se-15)

hired Tulsa deputy sheriff, 1944 Brooklyn Dodgers pitcher, and newly paroled ex-convict Tommy Warren to assemble and lead a team. They spent the spring trying to assemble a team from the old Twins, Oklahoma City, Shreveport, and Pampa cast offs, local boys and his Cuban connection. With no clubhouses, the team slept and suited up at the Grisso Hotel. Thirty-four position players and twenty-four pitchers appeared for the Oilers during 1954. In a "name the team" contest, Sasakwa School Superintendent O. E. Hatcher was the first to submit "Oilers," winning a season pass. The independent Tri-City Oilers began their struggle of 1954.

Five of the 1953 Twins, Dan Goeken, Don Phillips, Ken Post, and pitchers Bob York and Gerald Kistler were back. A left handed rookie who would become a much traveled legend was optioned to Seminole by the Philadelphia Athletics, the team that signed him as a free agent: George Brunet. A starter for the 1953 Gainesville Owls, George Cockrell, was inked as was Stan Papciak who threw for Shawnee the prior year. The rest of the club was a collection of rookies and sophomores released from other teams.

Mayor Ray Harber threw the first pitch to Wewoka city attorney Buck Cartwright. Before 2,200 fans, Stan Papciak doubled home the winning runs for a 5-2 victory over Shawnee. A 13-11 win over Gainesville put the Oilers in first place on May 3. Two weeks later, six Oilers were on the disabled list and their star was fading. On Memorial Day, Willingham published an open letter in the *Producer* imploring the fans to purchase tickets to the holiday game against Pauls Valley for $1.00 because bad weather earlier had severely depressed attendance. The team needed to raise $1,200; it didn't. Having lost eight of thirteen, the Oilers slid to fourth on June 3. By mid-June 1954, with six players on the disabled list and the Oilers slumping from first to sixth, attendance plummeted.

Marlys Davis took over the 1954 Seminole and was the only woman to run the business operation of an Oklahoma club until Patty Cox Hampton was recognized as the outstanding minor league baseball executive in 1979. (Se-17)

Long time Willingham protégé Fred Davis jumped ship to take a job with an Oklahoma City television station. Willingham was the front office until Marlys Davis, former assistant with the Hutchinson, Kansas, club and graduate of the baseball administration program at Florida Southern University, was named business manager.

Willingham had had his fill of baseball. Paris, Texas, interests were trying to lure the team away and seemed to have the financial wherewithal as did a group of Seminole business people trying to hold on to the team. His price was $6,000 to cover current accounts payable and $1,160 National Association deposit reduced by current receivables of $3,000, and, for an additional $1,000, the buyer could have the uniforms, team equipment, concessions equipment, the bus, and four player contracts. On June 18, a public meeting was held in Seminole where Willingham aired the club's financial woes to about seventy-five people. The players hadn't been paid on June 15, nor had the electric bill. The players were staying only until June 27; after then they would become free agents. His ultimatum was that he would sell to Paris unless some group quickly came forward or if neither Seminole nor Paris took the team off his hands, he would return the franchise and sell the player contracts. Art Willingham ended his baseball ownership when he turned back the franchise he had owned since 1950. His last act was to release Tommy Warren so he could take the job as manager of the Borger, Texas, team in the West Texas-New Mexico League. Sooner State League president Ucal Clanton on one hand had said he would give Seminole every chance to save their Oilers but on the other he had obtained owner approval for a move to Paris. By June 22, Seminole had $3,000 in hand and Paris had pledges for $4,000. President Clanton quickly approved the Seminole Community Baseball Club, a non-profit, to take over the franchise. The June 22, game was not played because the transfer didn't occur before the 6 p.m. deadline for an 8:15 game. The June 23, game was not played because the electricity had been shut off. Following the sale of the club to Seminole Community Baseball Club, the name "Tri-City" was scrapped. Don Goeken took over the team until a manager from the Gonzalez chain, Ray Taylor who had hit .365 while leading Chickasha's 1952 Chiefs, was hired on June 26.

The seventh place finish was twenty games ahead of the Cleveland affiliate at Pauls Valley but that was

Ray Taylor began 1954 managing Bryan, Texas but after a 1-9 start resigned. He took the Seminole job when it opened in June. (Se-18)

about the best that could be said for the season. The Oilers batted .262, were third in the league in fielding at .939, and the pitchers, eighteen of whom had under forty-five innings, were sixth with a collective 5.49 ERA. Herman Charles and manager Taylor led the team with .326 averages; Goeken was the other .300 hitter. The Oilers were 26-32 under manager Tommy Warren when he left the team on June 21 for "urgent personal business." With a remarkable 10-1 record, he would be the club's only winning pitcher. The next best was Papciak at 12-12. None of the sixteen others had a

winning percentage. Eight position players didn't make ten games. Attendance was an anemic 16,840, an average of 240 per game. There were no All Stars among the 1954 Oilers. The 1954 Oilers were the last Sooner State League team to operate without a Major League working agreement.

1955

Seminole Community Baseball, Inc. was a non-profit with strong civic leadership. It followed the Shawnee model for community ownership. Its board included banker R.T. Harber, oilman Jimmy Austin, C.P. Ellis, Jim Brewer, Bill Best, Ivan Glasser, and Roy Beckwith. They had raised $6,500 immediately to buy out Willingham and then contributed $1,000-$1,250 each month during the remainder of the 1954 season   Hugh Willingham (not related to Art), the new business manager hired after the 1954 campaign, negotiated the working agreement with the newly located Kansas City Athletics that would keep the Seminole franchise afloat for the Oilers' last three seasons. Browns veteran farm hand and 1948 All Star for Ada, Charles Hopkins, was given a chance to manage a team that allowed only one veteran and required at least seven rookies. The only holdovers from the 1954

A Browns' farm hand who was at Ada in 1948, Charlie Hopkins made his managerial debut with Seminole in 1955. The parent Athletics soured on him and gave him his walking papers on June 5. (Se-19)

Al Evans, a catcher for a dozen seasons with the Red Sox and Senators, picked up where Hopkins left off. His Oilers finished last at 56-83. (Se-20)

1956

For 1956, the A's brought in a new roster under the eye of eighteen-year minor leaguer Burl Storie. It looked as though new manager Storie's 1956 Oilers were going to repeat as sole occupant of the basement. The opener was rained out. Six weeks into the season, the club was in last place at 13-25. By July 5, they had scrambled up to seventh place at 29-39

Burl Storie took the 1956 Oilers from last place to the play-off championship and Seminole's second pennant. (Se-21)

The financial situation became grave when July 15, 1956, was to be last game before the last place Oilers folded. League president George Barr called a special meeting to drop Seminole and finish the season with seven teams. With the Oilers in seventh place, Seminole Community Baseball president T. J. Plummer announced that local businessmen

T. J. Plummer led the community effort to save the 1956 Oilers from insolvency. (Se-22)

independent team were pitchers George Cockrell, who ended his short career in 1955, and George Brunet, who was to pitch for thirty more seasons until 1985. Hopkins caught thirty games and was hitting .298 on June 6, with the Oilers in last place. Disappointed in the team's performance, the parent A's fired Hopkins, and brought in veteran Senators catcher Al Evans as a rarely playing manager. On a team that won only fifty-six games, the Brunet and Cockrell tandem accounted for nineteen of those. Cockrell's 3.12 ERA was best on a team that was last in the league with a 4.63 cumulative ERA. Team hitting was .246 while slugging percentage was an unimpressive .338. Playing in every game, outfielder Charles Secrest handled plays better than the team average (.946 vs. .929) and was second on the squad in hitting with a .307 average as he batted in eighty-eight runs. The top batter on the team also led the league. Harold "Flash" Gordon tagged Sooner State pitching for 213 total bases for a .448 slugging percentage and .345 batting average. Without those two .300+ hitters, the rest of the Oilers batted a weak .225. Evans had no magic to pull the club out of the cellar. The 1955 Seminole nine made their host city the first in the league to have three eighth place finishes. Attendance was up nearly 10,000 to 26,775, a remarkable feat considering the Oilers finished in last place.

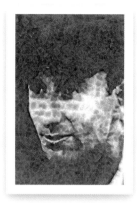

Don "Dino" Williams earned a promotion to Class AA Little Rock following his 1956 performance at Seminole. He joined Minnesota briefly in August, 1963. (Se-23)

had raised $2,025 at that July 15 game to keep the club operating. To meet budget and complete the season that money plus direct financial and player assistance from the parent Athletics under the working agreement put them over the top.

Gordon and Secrest were back and would add their .344 and .330 bats to the 1956 campaign. They were not, however, the two Oilers who were to make the Show. Rookie outfielder Hal Jones and pitcher Don "Dino" Williams would spend time with the Indians and Twins. The pitching staff was new with ten rookies passing through.

In the biggest turn around in league history, Storie's Oilers charged from the cellar on July 29, to go 45-27 the remainder of the season and capture

third place and the Oilers' first trip to the playoffs since 1948. Things went their way. For example, they found the long ball. On July 29, Gordon, Secrest and Buddy Plaster tattooed Muskogee pitching for three back-to-back home runs. The staff was second in the League on the mound allowing only 4.23 earned runs. Mike Mazzamorra at 14-4 had the lowest ERA in the league at 2.28. Outfielder David Gorrie hit .278.

At bat, the A's farmhands were a second division club with a .248 average. That notwithstanding, the Oilers were not to be denied. After getting past second place Lawton in four games in the first round, Seminole took on pennant winner Ardmore with whom they had split the regular season series ten games each. Tied at three wins apiece, the two teams came together on September 16, at Ardmore. In new Cardinal Park, the Oilers smothered the Cardinals 16-5 for the championship. Surprisingly, only catcher Tony Cannizzo was named to the All Star team. The Seminole fans responded. Attendance was 31,249, nearly double 1954's number.

1956 Seminole Oilers. Kansas City policy, like the Dodgers and Giants, was to dress lower minor league farm clubs in hand-me-downs regardless of the local club's name. Here they wear 1953 Philadelphia Athletics uniforms. Manager Burl Storie is on the far left of the top row. Hal Jones who later played in twelve games for Cleveland and Don "Dino" Williams, who appeared in one game for the Twins are, respectively, fifth and sixth from the left on the Top row. (Se-24)

230

1957

Carl Jenkins succeeded Plummer as president of Seminole Community Baseball. The financially-strapped club again ran into trouble before season end. The last president of the club, Jack Clarkson, disclosed that financial aid from parent Kansas City and private funding from local businessmen assured that Seminole would finish the season. Only 17,379 saw Seminole's last team stumble to a 46-79 last place finish.

The Oilers became the "Athletics" in 1957 as part of the terms of the working agreement with Kansas City. Many of the 1956 Oilers moved up in the A's organization to Class C Pocatello of the Pioneer League and Abilene of the Class B Big State. Flash Gordon was the only position player to return. After appearing in eleven games at Pocatello, 1956 Oiler Jerry McKinnis was sent down. After three appearances for Seminole, he quit baseball; one season in Class D had been enough. Journeyman in the high minors since 1946, Omer Lee Anthony was tapped to lead the final edition of the Seminole club. Despite his 1.42 ERA in twenty-five games, and Flash Gordon's repeat of his .344 performance the prior year, the parent A's simply didn't provide much talent. The Athletics took over eighth place in the first week of the season beginning 1-5

and remained there until the end. The high point of the campaign was on August 22, when Vince DiGiulio collaborated with Gene Cochran to no-hit Greenville 3-2. DiGiulio relieved Cochran with one out in the third inning. The Majors scored two in the fifth on three walks, a hit batsman, and an error. Earl Hamper saved the win when he singled in the tying and winning runs in the bottom of the seventh inning.

The pitchers' collective ERA was 4.85 while the team batting average was .241, not the league's worst in either category. The Athletics' opponents simply scored more runs. While the little A's crossed the plate 572 times, the opponents did it 683. No Seminole player was named to the fan-selected All Stars because the team sent in no ballots. Only Will "Crash' Corrigan, 9-14 and 3.78, was named to the season-end All Star team. Only ten of the thirty-three players who appeared for Seminole were playing professional baseball in 1958.

In a strange irony, the franchise that began in Seminole finished in Ardmore while the one that began in Ardmore ended in Seminole. No city in the Sooner State League experienced more last place finishes: four. Yet, both times the Seminole Oilers managed to finish in the first division they won the playoffs.

Oiler Field is regularly used today. (Se-25)

SHAWNEE HAWKS 1950-1957
SOONER STATE LEAGUE

SEASON	ATTENDANCE	RECORD	FINISH	AFFILIATION	PLAYOFF FIRST ROUND	PLAYOFF FINALS
1951	44,428	96-44	Second	Dallas (Tex Lg.)	Lost to McAlester 0-3	
1952	44,680	73-67	Fourth		Lost to McAlester 1-3	
1953	39,441	86-53	Second	Brooklyn	Lost to Ada 1-3	
1954	42,189	92-48	First	Brooklyn	Lost to Ardmore 2-3	
1955	37,817	77-61	Second	Brooklyn	Lost to Muskogee 2-3	
1956	24,872	56-84	Eighth	Brooklyn		
1957	22,301	64-62	Fourth	Brooklyn	Lost to Paris 1-3	

Memorial Park shortly after completion in 1949. (Sh-1)

Lack of a playing facility had kept Shawnee out of the Sooner State League in 1947 and 1948. The Shawnee School Board would not lease Jim Thorpe Field to a ball club that, like McAlester, would have to tear up the football field to play there.

Another two box level, twelve-tier, roofless Blair Construction product, the ball park at 700 W. Burns in Memorial Park was erected in 1949 as a tribute to the past and present members of the armed services. Its capacity was 2,000. The outfield was symmetrical with the center field fence measuring 385 feet from home plate and 325 feet down the lines. It was on the then far west side of Shawnee just south of U.S. Highway 270 (now the Kickapoo Spur) when it was built. Today it is on the campus of Shawnee High School and home of the baseball Wolves. The Shawnee Memorial Commission declined Otto Utt's overtures to relocate in 1949 mainly because lighting was not up to professional standards and the outfield was bounded by a five feet high cyclone fence.

The franchise that withered in Duncan found good soil in Shawnee. The Hawks finished in the first division six of seven years, losing in the first round of the playoffs each time. Two strong years as an independent were followed by five as a Brooklyn farm team.

1950

Attendance in Duncan had been about 6,600 in thirty-five dates. On August 8, Utt announced that five Duncan home games against Seminole and McAlester between August 13 and 17, had been moved to Shawnee's Memorial Park.

When 1950 was at mid-season and Memorial Park had been upgraded, Shawnee was ready for a team in the Sooner State League. With clubhouses, dugouts, and a paved road, Memorial Park was a big improvement over the Duncan Bowl. The

Hawks *neé* Uttmen occupied the Shawnee ball park for the next seven seasons.

Pitcher Bill Heerdt married Virginia Darity of Duncan before the August 13 game. The Uttmen celebrated with a 13-8 win over McAlester. After losing to Seminole the next night, Utt announced the team was not returning to Duncan. Heerdt beat Seminole on six hits 11-5 on the fifteenth. When the Uttmen beat McAlester on August 17, Utt made application to formally move the franchise to Shawnee. Cy Stewart of Lawton wanted the team to remain in Duncan because of the proximity. As the vote to move had to be unanimous, he finally relented that afternoon. The move was effective the next day.

Relocating the Uttmen was not greeted with unalloyed enthusiasm. McAlester favored the switch since games at Shawnee would be a one day turn around rather than overnight stays as was the case with playing at Duncan. Lawton estimated that with Shawnee in the league it would incur additional expenses of about $700 over a season. Lew Johnson, the sports editor of the *Lawton Constitution* didn't mince words:

> Just how much longer are league officials going to allow Otto Utt to bully his way around the circuit? The rotund baseball 'executive' has soured what used to be one of the top baseball cities in the state on the national pastime, and is now starting on No. 2 — with the unanimous blessing of presidents around the league. I imagine Duncan fans are relieved . . . . They should be. . . .Otto has given them everything but a baseball team since the league was formed in 1947.

Shawnee's last professional team, the 1930 entry in the Western Association, had been called the Robins and that is what the transplanted Uttmen were called by sports editor Roy Angel of the *Shawnee News-Star* until the team was re-named the next February. Pauls Valley ruined the Robins' debut with a 20-1 plucking.

Local baseball celebrity Kelly Wingo took over after Otto Utt moved his Duncan team to Shawnee. (Sh-1)

Dutch Prather resigned on August 21 after receiving a fine. Utt substituted at the helm on August 22. He hired his second baseman, local Shawnee product and veteran minor leaguer Kelly Wingo to finish the season. Wingo's first game as a manager was ruined when Pauls Valley edged the Shawnee nine 5-4.

1951

Shortly before Christmas, 1950, Chet Fowler, fifteen year Texas League umpire, purchased the team from Utt. The Shawnee Athletic Association, Inc., a non-profit through which Fowler operated, held a contest to name the team. A bird more aggressive than the Robin was suggested by M. B. Case. The team would be called the Hawks.

Under the leadership of Lou Fitzgerald and operating without a Major League working agreement, the 1951 Hawks finished second in the regular season race only to be eliminated by McAlester in the first round of the playoffs. After three years playing for Texarkana of the Big State League, Lou Fitzgerald took Shawnee to its best winning percentage ever in 1951. He compiled a 169-111 record, a .603 percentage, in his first two seasons as a manager. In 1951 he played in every game, 127 at third base and thirteen at second, leading the league with a .379 batting average. He kept the number of rookies close to the minimum four throughout the season. Four of the five starters won twenty games while the fifth with a 10-4 record, local rookie Perry Haddock fresh out of Oklahoma Baptist University, led the team with a 3.07 ERA.

Of the four, Cuban Lindy Chappoten (20-6), Mel Burgess (20-11), and Bill Lenihan (21-10) were limited service players while Lowell "Tuck" Rhodes (20-11) was a rookie. As a Dallas Eagles affiliate, there was some movement among their farm clubs—Shawnee and Class C

Lou Fitzgerald had risen to the Texas League as a player. He took the Hawks to a second place finish before dropping the first playoff round to McAlester. He managed in the minors through 1969 and scouted into the 2000s. (Sh-4)

Texas League umpire Chet Fowler bought the transplanted Uttmen and renamed them "Hawks" in view of affiliation with the parent Dallas Eagles of the Texas League. (Sh-3)

1951 Shawnee Hawks. (Sh-5)

A pair of Hawks in 1951. (Sh-6)

Gladewater and Class B Gainesville—but for the most part the club that was on the field when the season began finished. The regulars hit impressively. First baseman Art Garrett contributed a .285 bat, second sacker Jim Jolly was a .284 hitter, shortstop Claudio Barcelo posted a .303 average, outfielders Bob Saulsberry, a Shawnee native, slugged .358 with twenty-three home runs, Gerald Cowen had .349 with thirteen home runs, and Wes Gibson came in at .353 with thirteen homers. Catcher Pat Roach was behind the plate in 134 games and while he hit only .226 he fielded at a .980 level and handled the pitchers with skill. Garrett, Gibson and Saulsberry had spent 1950 with Chickasha which had a hook-up with Dallas that season.

Under Fowler's ownership, 44,428 passed through the gates of Memorial Park. The prospects for baseball in Shawnee were bright.

1952

Local attorney Irwin Owen, a successful criminal defense lawyer and prolific writer, saw the success of the 1951 Hawks and sought to profit from it. He organized Group Investors, Inc. to purchase the team from Fowler who had left town to become business manager of the Vernon, Texas, club in the Longhorn League. For the 1952 season, the team would again operate as an independent with Fitzgerald at the helm. Owen served as president and business manager. The honeymoon didn't last long. By June, Owen was quoted as saying "The town [Shawnee] here isn't educated to what it takes to have a Class D club." He set a deadline and would move the team to Gainesville, Texas, on June 20. The community raised $6,500 to finance the team for the remainder of the season and keep the Hawks in Shawnee. Nonetheless, the franchise was for sale.

Under personal contract to Dallas, the Eagles moved Fitzgerald to the helm of their floundering Longview, Texas, team in the Big State League on June 26, and promoted Jim Jolly to his first and only managerial position. Rolando Olmo, Dave Rolette, Billy Ray Jones, Gil Waldrip, and Lloyd McPherson all had Sooner State League experience while Jolly, Burgess and Haddock were back from 1951. The pitching on the 1952 team did not equal that of the previous year. There were no twenty game winners and only one member of the staff, Oklahoma City fireman Len Gilmore who only appeared in games played in Shawnee, had an ERA below 4.00. For example, rookie and Ardmore native Jim Kenaga,

Perry Haddock joined the Hawks from the local Oklahoma Baptist University campus. (Sh-7)

235

Hal Long caught Hawks' hurler in 1951 and 1952. (Sh-8)

who would go on to become a physician, appeared in twenty-one games, starting eleven, finishing three. Credited with the league's only tie in a game against Ada, his ERA was 5.18 explaining in part his 1-8 record. He followed Fitzgerald to Longview and, after eleven games, was drafted for two years military service. The team managed to finish fourth at 73-67-1 with a .271 batting average and a league-leading 937 walks received before McAlester swept the Hawks in the first round of the playoffs.

1953

Led by William Clem and Fred Davis, a baseball operator, Shawnee Baseball Club, Inc. was formed in October, 1952, to purchase the Hawks from Owen but there was a detour. When the Pittsburg, Kansas, franchise in the K-O-M League was placed on the block, Shawnee Baseball bought that club planning to move it to Enid. The Clem group's K-O-M franchise couldn't find a home; Enid, Oklahoma, and Arkansas City, Kansas, both turned down offers to move there. The K-O-M folded before the 1953 season began. Shawnee Baseball Club, Inc. had been all for naught and was left holding a worthless franchise in a failed

Jack Mealey briefly got his wish of running a ball club in Shawnee.

league. Davis was to reappear in 1954 briefly with the Hawks and then with Art Willingham at Seminole before departing for Oklahoma City and the new television industry.

The Shawnee Hawks team was sold, instead, to Shawnee Hawks, Inc. headed by Dr. Jack Baxter and operated by former League President Jack Mealey. Irwin Owen had an interest in the new for- profit entity. A working agreement that was to remain in effect

Boyd Bartley came with the 1953 Brooklyn working agreement after the K-O-M disbanded. (Sh-10)

through the rest of the team's life was inked with the Brooklyn Dodgers. The Dodgers' farmhands finished second, first, and second in 1953, 1954, and 1955 respectively, with attendance never falling below 37,000. Under the full working agreement, after 1953 the Hawks wore hand-me-down Dodgers uniforms, occasionally with a hawk emblem on the sleeve.

Brooklyn had enjoyed a long, successful relationship with Ponca City in the Class D K-O-M League finishing first in 1948, 1950, and 1951. The 1952 Ponca City Dodgers under the leadership of former Brooklyn shortstop Boyd Bartley finished in a tie for second at 68-58. When that league failed, the Dodgers were looking for a new Class D home. They found it in Shawnee.

For the first time, the Shawnee club was dominated by rookies. The league had changed its rule for 1953 and now only two veterans and at least seven rookies had to be on the roster. The Hawks made good use of one veteran slot by signing Pueblo, Colorado's Frank Golob, recently discharged from the Army, who had pitched for three seasons at Duncan and was to do the same for the Hawks through early 1955. With Bartley taking the other, veteran Lindy Chappoten was traded to Texarkana for twenty sets of flannels.

Although spring training with the Dodger farm hands at Vero Beach, Florida, began with nineteen 1952 Ponca City Dodgers on his roster, only pitchers Jim Peterson and John Roth followed Bartley to Shawnee. With one of the best teachers in baseball in the dugout, the Hawks finished second. The team made it on pitching. The three regulars, Frank Golob (10-5), Don Huffman (20-8), and Jim Peterson (19-5) were supported by Derald

Oklahoma City's Don Demeter was sent to Shawnee for his 1953 rookie season. He joined the parent Dodgers in mid-July 1958 and remained in the Majors through 1967. (Sh-11)

Wooten (7-2) and Jerry Wright (8-2) who were only around for part of the season. The Hawks led the league in pitching with a 3.74 ERA for the twenty-two hurlers who passed through Shawnee in 1953. That compensated for the team's seventh place finish in batting, a weak .241.

Jack Banta guided the Hawks in 1954, 1955, and 1956. He had appeared with the Dodgers in 1946, 1947, and 1948. He began managing after developing a sore arm. (Sh-12)

1954

Garbed in old Dodgers' flannels, the 1954 Hawks completely dominated the League winning the pennant by ten and one-half games and leading in all categories: batting (.302), fielding (.949) and pitching (3.80 ERA). Bartley moved on to Thomasville, Georgia, for the 1954 season and was replaced by retired pitcher Jack Banta who inherited Bill Davidson, Jim Davis, Charles Rogers, Frank Golob and Derald Wooten from the 1953 Hawks as well as Tuck Rhodes who won twenty games for the Shawnee club in 1951.

1954 Shawnee alumnus Stan Williams had a 109-94 record with a 3.48 ERA in fourteen Major League seasons. He was a National League All Star in 1960 and had a World Series win over the White Sox in 1959. (Sh-13)

Banta wasted no time in battling with the umpires. He was booted and fined $10 in the opener. Stan Williams who was to throw for eleven seasons for the Dodgers, Mets, Indians, Red Sox, and Twins, joined the team late in the season and finished with a lackluster 3-5 record and 4.57 ERA in fifteen games and sixty-one innings. Don LeJohn, who was to have a cup of coffee with the 1965 Dodgers and earned a World Series ring as part of that adventure, hit .359 at second base and shortstop. While there were no twenty game winners, the Hawks were consistent on the mound with Frank Golob winning nineteen, George Green and Don Kenway seventeen apiece, and Marv Roberson sixteen plus a league best 2.52 ERA. Besides LeJohn, the infield all hit over .300: first bagger Fred Harrison (.323), keystone Bill Davidson (.311), and hot corner Ray Mitchell (.371). The outfield equaled the infielders' feat. Conrad Devlin hit .302, Willard Fox .329, and Jim Humbert .307. While the two catchers, Charles Rogers and Willie Morse, had subpar years at the plate, behind it they were among the League's best with fielding averages of .981 and .980 respectively. Davidson, Mitchell, LeJohn and Roberson were named All Stars.

Don LeJohn hit .359 as a 1954 rookie for the Hawks. He toiled in the Dodgers' farm system the next ten years. He made it to Dodger Stadium in June, 1965 and appeared in the World Series against the Twins. After 1966 in AAA, he began an eighteen year managerial career for the Dodgers. (Sh-14)

As an indication of how the 1954 season would develop, Robertson no-hit Pauls Valley 9-1 on May 26. Dearld Wooten won his May 31, game in relief with four perfect innings plus hitting a grand slam home run to drive in the tying and winning runs for an 8-5 victory over Lawton. Frank Golob had beaten every team in the league by July 14. Fox set the team records for triples, runs scored, and stolen bases on August 21. There were a couple of setbacks, though. When Shawnee dropped a pair to Lawton on July 23, it was the first time an opposing team had swept the Hawks since September 1, 1952. The umpire called a balk on Tuck Rhodes when rookie catcher Jim McGee stepped out of the catcher's box to catch a throw for an intentional walk in a contest against Gainesville on August 10. The Hawks came within a hairsbreadth of moving on to the playoff finals before dropping the fifth game of the semis to fourth place Ardmore, a team they had dominated the Hawks in the regular season.

1955

The franchise changed hands before the 1955 season when a non-profit organization, Shawnee Athletic Association, Inc., took over as a community-owned ball club. The club had pledges of $6,400. Irwin Owen served as titular president but turned the reigns over to David Mayne toward the end of the 1955 season.

Banta was back in 1955 with Harrison, Humbert, Morse, and Golob plus Tom Sleeper and Harry "Gene" Wallace, both of the 1953 Hawks, after their detours in the Army, and second sacker John Ethridge from 1952. The ninth Sooner State League season was fated to belong to one of the best team to appear in the circuit, the 1955 Lawton Braves. The second place Hawks finished only slightly behind the Lawton nine in hitting (.264 vs. .261) and fielding (.950 vs .946). The mound staff posted a respectable

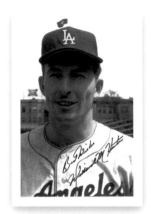

With a 16-10 record and 2.77 ERA in his 1955 rookie season with Shawnee, Willard Hunter made it to Los Angeles in 1961 then was traded to the expansion New York Mets where he compiled a 1-6 record at the old Polo Grounds. He returned to New York for part of 1964. (Sh-15)

4.03 collective ERA but could not compare with Lawton's hurlers' league record 2.49. Rookie Willard Hunter, who would go on to pitch for the Angels, Yankees and Mets, was 16-5. The team had the services of the rookie Minton twins, pitcher Frank (17-7, 2.61 ERA) and outfielder Fred (.274), who combined to beat Paris 7-6 on June 2. Frank got the win and Fred's two run single put the Hawks ahead to stay. They performed the same magic on June 12, with Frank two-hitting Paris and Fred batting in the only run. On May 5, Tommy Sleeper went on a tear against Muskogee with two triples, two doubles and a single batting in seven of the Hawks' runs for a 14-3 win. Ten days later Sleeper hit a walk off home run with two on in the sixteenth inning to defeat McAlester in a three hour forty-one minute affair. Al Jarvis, who was with Boyd Bartley's 1952 Ponca City club, was the sole Hawk to hit above .300. Minton, who won both his playoff starts, was the staff ace with his low ERA. Hunter was not far behind at 2.71. Once again, the Hawks dropped a semi-final by

one game to Muskogee, a team they had dominated during the regular season in sixteen of twenty-five contests.

Al Jarvis had played for Boyd Bartley at Ponca City and was the only .300 hitter on the 1956 Hawks. He later drowned in a fishing accident. (Sh-16)

Bill Kunkel was the only member of the 1956 squad to make it to the Show. He had his debut with Kansas City in 1961. He was with the Yankees in 1963. He turned to umpiring in 1966. He called balls and strikes in the American League from 1968 through 1984. (Sh-17)

1956

The 1956 version of the Hawks had the worst record and finish of any team Shawnee fielded. Hawks hurlers set a dubious mark when they walked the first seven Muskogee batters who appeared in the sixth inning of the June 16 game. In Banta's third and final season at the helm, his charges exploded to a 5.44 team ERA, last in the league, and fielded with iron gloves for a .934 average with 350 errors. Matt Perry (8-7, 5.97 ERA in 181 innings) had the only winning record. Bill Kunkel, who went on to spend 1961-1963 with the Athletics and Yankees, finished with a 3.85 ERA and 9-13 record. Eldon Wheeler was 7-7 with 181 strike outs in 135 innings and posted the top ERA at 3.27. Sleeper in his last professional season led the club in hitting with a .333 average. First basemen Tony Lembo (.320) and outfielders Bill Dunman (.315) and Glen Plaster (.304) passed the .300 threshold. Lembo was the only Hawk named to the All Star squad.

Attendance plummeted in 1956, as a last place team was seen by only 24,872 paying fans. The Dodgers had to inject $2,500 for the Hawks just to finish the season.

Switch-hitting Bill Dunman played two seasons of professional baseball with parts of both at Shawnee. He hit .315 for 1956. (Sh-18)

1957 Hawks scorecard. (Sh-19)

Ed Serrano was a Mexican League veteran. For 1957 he was able to bracket the short Sooner State League season with appearances for Durango-Laguna and Monterrey. (Sh-20)

1957

Mayne stepped aside in December, 1956, with the club $4,000 in the red. Jim Jolly, field manager of the 1952 team the last half of the season, took over front office duties and continued through 1957. O.N. "Gunner" Smith became president of Shawnee Athletic Association but was unable to retire the debt. In January, 1957, the Association tendered the franchise back to the league at the same time McAlester was throwing in the towel. A group of baseball boosters, Shawnee Hawks Fan Club, headed by businessman Vernon Chapman was able to raise $4,000 to satisfy the operating deficit. Jim Jolly was kept on to operate the club during its last season.

Promoted for 1957, to Class C Great Falls, Montana, of the Pioneer League, Jack Banta was to take   another Dodger farm club to a last place finish. He was succeeded at Shawnee by Mexican League veteran Ed Serrano who was taking his first shot at managing. Enid High School star catcher Wade Arnold, shortstop Don Williams and outfielder Bill Dunman were back from 1956's cellar dwellers. With several sophomores from the Dodger's Thomasville, Georgia, club, the mainly rookie 1957 team hit, fielded and pitched in the middle of the League pack to finish fourth at 64-62, a game and a half in front of Greenville. Because Ardmore was in first place on July 4, Shawnee dominated the fan-selected All Star team that beat the Cardinals 4-3 on July 10. Serrano managed the Stars and held down second base. Shortstop Don Williams, outfielders Bill Dunman and Bob Burnell, catcher Wade Arnold, and left handed pitcher Willie

Wayne Arnold was a blue chip prospect from Enid, Oklahoma. He came as close as two appearances in AAA. He was out of baseball by 1963. (Sh-21)

Williams joined their boss on the squad. Arnold was the only Hawk to be named to the post-season dream team. Serrano led the Hawks with a .318 average followed by Arnold's .302. Walt Merrigan had the low ERA at 3.30 and led the team in wins with thirteen. After winning game one of the semi-final series, the Hawks ended both their season and history at home dropping the third straight game to the Paris Orioles.

Seminole, Lawton, Greenville, and Muskogee withdrew from the League following the 1957 season. The Shawnee club folded in February, 1958, when only the birds (Hawks, Orioles, and Cardinals) had working agreements, and it was deemed impractical to play the coming season as a four team league.

John Kimbrel had his best of four professional seasons with the 1957 Hawks. After 1959 and 1960 in the Army, he had lost his pitching skill, earned a Ph.D., and retired to academia. (Sh-22)

Memorial Park in 2008. (Sh-23)

PHOTO AND ILLUSTRATION CREDITS

Lg-1 Oklahoma Heritage Association ("OHA") from *The Oklahoman*
Lg-2 John G. Hall ("Hall")
Lg-3 Hall
Lg-4 ©Peter G. Pierce ("Pierce")
Lg-5 mcalesterphotos.com
Lg-6 Bobby King ("King")
Lg-7 ©Pierce
Lg-8 sportsartifacts.com
Lg-9 Author's collection
Lg-10 *The Ardmoreite*
Lg-11 ©Pierce
Lg-12 Derril McGuire ("McGuire")
Lg-13 OHA from *The Oklahoman*

ADA

Ada-1 © Brace Photos by permission
Ada-2 Author's collection
Ada-3 © Pierce
Ada-4 Sam Zygner from *The Forgotten Marlins* (2013)
Ada-5 Andrewsfield.blogspot.com *from* Ft. Smith Museum of History
Ada-6 Charles Hopkins
Ada-7 through Ada-12 King
Ada-13 Oklahoma Historical Society microfilm collection *Ada Evening News*
Ada-14 35th Infantry Regiment Association
Ada-15 Mobile (Alabama) Sports Hall of Fame
Ada-16 Bill Thrash ("Thrash")
Ada-17 Cape Cod Baseball Hall of Fame capecodbaseball.org
Ada-18 National Baseball Hall of Fame Library from OHA *Indians, Cardinals and Rosebuds*
Ada-19 through Ada-26 Thrash
Ada-27 *The Paris Times*
Ada-28 Thrash
Ada-29 Fern Smathers

ARDMORE

Ar-1 Sylvia Moore
Ar-2 Author's collection
Ar-3 and Ar-4 McGuire
Ar-5 OHA from *The Oklahoman*
Ar-6 © Pierce
Ar-7 Brent Horton's Tyler, Texas Minor League History
Ar-8 McGuire
Ar-9 Historical Society of Pottawatomie County and Santa Fe Museum ("Pott. County")
Ar-10 Anna Sollars
Ar-11 Ernesto Klein Wallerstein ("Klein")
Ar-12 *The Ardmoreite*, Ardmore, OK
Ar-13 through Ar-16 Klein
Ar-17 © Brace Photos by permission
Ar-18 Galliard Collection, Ardmore (OK) Public Library
Ar-19 through Ar-23 McGuire
Ar-24 Betty Anderson
Ar-25 Barbara Sessions ("Sessions")
Ar-26 McGuire
Ar-27 Sessions
Ar-28 Anson Shuman and *The Ardmoreite*

Ar-29 through Ar-31 *The Ardmoreite*
Ar-32 Texas League of Professional Baseball Clubs
Ar-33 through Ar-35 *The Ardmoreite*
Ar-36 and Ar-37 Author's collection

BARTLESVILLE

Bv-1 © digitalballparks.com by permission
Bv-2 © digitalballparks.com by permission
Bv-3 and Bv-4 Hall
Bv-5 Author's collection
Bv-6 gambo-t-Wil1 (a sharing blogspot housed under ootdevelopment.com) ("Gambo")
Bv-7 Hall
Bv-8 Gambo
Bv-9 and Bv-10 Hall
Bv-11 bochertfield.com
Bv-12 Hall
Bv-13 Gambo
Bv-14 Hall
Bv-15 veooz.com
Bv-16 Hall
Bv-17 baseballprospectus.com
Bv-18 Hall
Bv-19 Gambo
Bv-20 Hall
Bv-21 boblemke.blogspot
Bv-21 Hall

BLACKWELL

Bl-1 through Bl-6 Hall
Bl-7 boblemke.blogspot
Bl-8 through Bl-10 Hall
Bl-10 boblemke.blogspot
Bv-11 National Archives and Record Administration

CHICKASHA

Ch-1 Newspaper morgue Grady County Historical Society, Chickasha, OK ("GCHS")
Ch-2 © Pierce
Ch-3 through Ch-5 GCHS
Ch-6 Carta Vieja, Panama from 1955 Official Baseball Guide
Ch-7 GCHS
Ch-8 Author's collection
Ch-9 GCHS
Ch-10 OHA
Ch-11 and Ch-12 GCHS
Ch-13 Gambo
Ch-14 *Pauls Valley Democrat*
Ch-15 GCHS
Ch-16 cubanbeisbol.com
Ch-17 and Ch-18 GCHS
Ch-19 *Sherman (TX) Herald-Democrat*
Ch-20 and Ch-21 GCHS
Ch-22 *Sherman (TX) Herald-Democrat*
Ch-23 Morton Museum of the Cooke County Heritage Society, Gainesville, TX ("Morton")
Ch-24 © Pierce

DUNCAN

Dn-1 pitchblackbaseball.com
Dn-2 OHA
Dn-3 Stephens County Historical Museum, Duncan, OK ("SCHM")

Dn-4 pitchblackbaseball.com
Dn-5 SCHM
Dn-6 © Pierce
Dn-7 ©Pee Wee Cary
Dn-8 SCHM
Dn-9 Pott. County
Dn-10 Author's collection
Dn-11 and Dn-12 Pott. County
Dn-13 © Pierce
Dn-14 Irving Kimberg ("Kimberg")
Dn-15 ztopics.com

ENID

Ed-1 through Ed-3 OHA
Ed-4 OHA from Royce Parr
Ed-5 and Ed-6 Andrewsfield.blogspot.com *from* Ft. Smith Museum of History
Ed-7 Author's collection
Ed-8 OHA
Ed-9 and Ed-10 © digitalballparks.com by permission
Ed-11 McGuire
Ed-112 Microfilm collection Clovis-Carver Public Library, Clovis, NM

LAWTON

La-1 Author's collection
La-2 Monday and Lucille Bohl from Gale McCray ("Bohl")
La-3 find-a-grave.com
La-4 Gambo
La-5 footballcardgallery.com
La-6 Bohl
La-7 giantsfarmphotos.tumblr.com
La-8 Author's collection
La-9 and La-11 Oklahoma Historical Society microfilm collection *Lawton Constitution*
La-12 Bohl
La-13 Oklahoma Historical Society microfilm collection *Lawton Constitution*
La-14 Morton
La-15 tradingcarddatatbase.com
La-17 Bohl
La-17 and La-18 through La-22 Oklahoma Historical Society microfilm collection *Lawton Constitution*

McALESTER

MA-1 through MA-7 mcalesterphotos.com
MA-8 Oklahoma Historical Society microfilm collection *McAlester Capital-Democrat*
MA-9 Author's collection
MA-10 OHA from *The Oklahoman*
MA-11 Bobby Tuminello ("Tuminello")
MA-12 Barbara Benson
MA-13 and MA-14 Tuminello
MA-15 OHA
MA-16 OHA from *The Oklahoman*
MA-17 Tuminello
MA-18 OHA from *The Oklahoman*
MA-19 and MA-20 Hall
MA-21 baseball-birthdays.com
MA-22 mcalesterphotos.com
MA-23 Barbara Benson
MA-24 collectorsweeky.com
MA-25 mcalesterphotos.com

MIAMI

Mi-1 through Mi-5 Hall
Mi-6 Andrewsfield.blogspot.com *from* Ft. Smith Museum of History
Mi-7 through Mi-13 Hall
Mi-14 wikipedia commons
Mi-15 Hall
Mi-16 and Mi-17 Gambo
Mi-18 © digitalballparks.com by permission
Mi-19 Hall
Mi-20 baseballprospectus.com
Mi-21 through Mi-27 Hall

MUSKOGEE

Mu-1 and MU-2 Three Rivers Museum , Muskogee, OK ("Three Rivers")
MU-3 Andrewsfield.blogspot.com *from* Ft. Smith Museum of History
MU-4 Gambo
MU-5 Stubblefield Family from *McCook (NB) Gazette 1949*
MU-6 OHA
MU-7 Gambo
MU-8 King
MU-9 Gambo
MU-10 Thrash
MU-11 Author's collection
MU-12 and MU-13 Gambo
MU-14 Three Rivers
MU-15 Gambo
MU-16 Three Rivers
MU-17 Wayne McCombs
MU-18 Kimberg
MU-19 Gambo
MU-20 Hall
MU-21 Gambo
MU-22 Author's collection
MU-23 *Pauls Valley Democrat*
MU-24 Gambo
Mu-25 Three Rivers
MU-26 Gambo
MU-27 helmenthut.com
MU-28 Gambo
MU-29 Author's collection
MU-30 thompsonian.info/colts62
MU-31 Three Rivers

PAULS VALLEY

Pv-1 Spalding Official Baseball Guide 1931
PV-2 and PV-3 *Pauls Valley Democrat*
PV-4 Gambo
PV-5 © Pierce
PV-6 *Pauls Valley Democrat*
PV-7 © Pierce
PV-8 Gambo
PV-9 through PV-12 *Pauls Valley Democrat*
PV-13 giantsfarmphotos.tumblr.com
PV-14 and PV-15 *Pauls Valley Democrat*
PV-16 through PV-18 Kimberg
PV-19 *Pauls Valley Democrat*
PV-20 and PV-21 Santa Fe Depot Museum, Pauls Valley from Adrienne Grimmett
PV-22 Morton
PV-23 and PV-24 Gambo

INDEX

Boldface indicates page where photo of the subject appears.